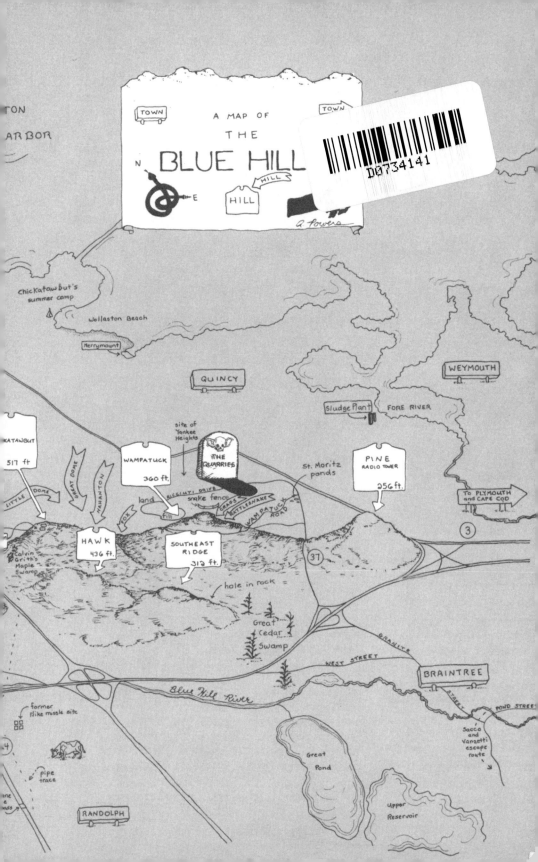

# LANDSCAPE WITH REPTILE

Books by Thomas Palmer

*The Transfer*
*Dream Science*

# LANDSCAPE
# WITH REPTILE

*Rattlesnakes in an Urban World*

## THOMAS PALMER

THE LYONS PRESS
GUILFORD, CONNECTICUT
AN IMPRINT OF THE GLOBE PEQUOT PRESS

For Harold L. Babcock, M.D.
*Be ye therefore wise as serpents, and harmless as doves*

The Lyons Press is an imprint of The Globe Pequot Press

10  9  8  7  6  5  4  3  2  1

Printed in the United States of America

ISBN 1-59228-000-5

Library of Congress Cataloging-in-Publication Data is available on file.

# Acknowledgments

Many people helped me write this book, and I needed all of them. Most especially:

Carolyn Kirdahy, Ken Pauley, and Edward Pearce of the Boston Museum of Science

Ralph H. Lutts of the Virginia Museum of Natural History (formerly of the Trailside Museum, Milton, Massachusetts)

Norman Smith of the Trailside Museum, Milton

Gus Ben David and Tom Tyning of the Massachusetts Audubon Society

Joe Martinez, José Rosado, and Van Wallach of the Museum of Comparative Zoology, Cambridge

Jay Copeland and Thomas French of the Natural Heritage Program, Massachusetts Department of Fisheries, Wildlife, and Environmental Law Enforcement

Larry Master of the eastern regional office of the Nature Conservancy

Captain Al Swanson of the Metropolitan District Commission archives

David Hodgdon of the Friends of the Blue Hills

Hobart Holly of the Quincy Historical Society

Ed Bolster of the Canton Historical Society

author David Quammen

Tom Johnson and Katrina Kenison of Cambridge

Bob Abrams of Milton

Charles Hess of Norwood

Michael McWade of Weymouth

Robert Fritsch of the Wethersfield, Connecticut, Police Department

Dr. Meg Hawley of Brigham and Women's Hospital, Boston

William R. Boles of the *Boston Globe*

Terry Ryan and Eric Sorensen of the Quincy *Patriot Ledger*

and the weekend staff of the research division of the Boston Public Library

The endpaper map is based on a 3-D computer image provided by Richard Gelpke of the University of Massachusetts at Boston, using the SURFER program published by Golden Software, of Golden, Colorado.

I am particularly indebted to my illustrator, Ann Powers, who contributed much more to this project than I had any right to expect. May I be so lucky again!

# Contents

# Introduction

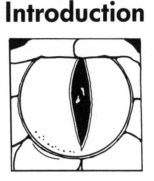

This is a love story. It's about a creature few people have seen, perhaps even fewer admire. Once widely feared, he has retreated into the same junk heap of rumor and indifference that protected him four hundred years ago, when the only people who knew him were as distant and fabulous as himself. Now they are gone and so is he, almost.

We will call him *Crotalus.* From the Greek *krotalon,* rattle. Short for *Crotalus horridus,* or even *Crotalus horridus horridus* if you believe, as some do, that the swamps of Carolina and Texas shelter a not quite identical twin.

Here in Massachusetts he favors the high, stony places. Where the bare bluffs break out of the woods, where the sun beats hardest and the buzzards ride. Places where it takes considerable vanity to find him and kill him.

He lacks friends. His sins are notorious. He grows too big, too alien — somehow the mere fact of his presence is a reproach. Because if we made the world, we would have left him out.

Sometime in the last twenty thousand years or so a person of whom we know nothing except that he must have existed had walked far enough south from Alaska to encounter a rattlesnake and was bitten and died. He had no way of knowing he was the first. Maybe his companions scooped out a grave, maybe he left his name on a sunny canyon or hillside. What can be said with some confidence is that the connection wasn't lost between the event and its result — rattlesnakes are conspicuous, and a bad bite worsens rapidly.

Since then a trend has become evident — more people, fewer snakes. It shows no signs of moderating. Here in the Northeast *Crotalus* has already abandoned Canada, Maine, and perhaps Rhode Island. In this state it is estimated that for every one million people there are twenty rattlesnakes. That's scarce — if this is a war, we have won it.

But the slaughter isn't quite complete. Just south of Boston, within view of the statehouse, a range of low, rugged hills interrupts the suburbs. They're only a few miles long. A superhighway cinches them tight against the city. Every five minutes another Logan-bound jet fills them with noise. But if you look for *Crotalus* here, you might find him. If you don't, you'll have to drive seventy or a hundred miles west before you get another chance — to the edge of the Berkshires, in fact. All the snakes in between are history.

These eight or ten rocky knuckles are known as the Blue Hills. I live in a town of twenty-five thousand at their northern base. I can leave; the snakes can't. But for the purposes of this story we're not going to leave; we're going to keep at least one foot firmly planted inside their narrow limits. That's my only promise — that and a half-grudging pledge to stick to the facts. Half-grudging because I wish they were otherwise. But who couldn't improve on the facts, any facts? That's why stories exist — to cut the raw taste of the facts.

But it is the construction of stories at the expense of the facts that is at the root of the situation *Crotalus* faces today, and is the cause of my lover's complaint.

But enough of preliminaries. Let's begin.

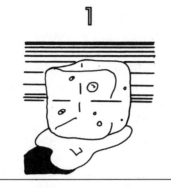

# Yankee from Atlantis

It is an interesting but not quite historical fact that *Crotalus* was here and gone long before we arrived. When I say "we" I mean humankind in general — the two of us and some five billion others currently in possession, not to mention the even greater eruption of breeze sniffers and doctors of philosophy going back to whichever African we choose to honor as our first representative — and when I say "here" I mean the Blue Hills: two miles by seven, mostly hard rock, and more or less cemented in place since the Triassic.

But to resume: *Crotalus* was probably here in the Blue Hills long before us. And yet when we finally arrived, he was gone. We had to wait many generations for him to appear again.

There's no mystery why he left. He was driven out by a mile-deep ocean of ice. This ocean advanced like a mountain and actually forced the earth's crust down underneath it. He could stand a cold winter or two; he couldn't stand ten thousand winters stacked up and marching.

Where did he go, then? South. To a band or pocket of warmth probably in the neighborhood of the Gulf of Mexico, which was as much as one hundred feet shallower at the time, so much of the world's water being locked up in ice. In those days boreal forests typical of Alaska covered much of the Appalachians and the Midwest — dense, boggy woods full of fogs and mosquitoes. To their south a zone of maples and birches made parts of Georgia look like Quebec. These are among the few American landscapes that rattlesnakes have never invaded. If the continent had lain a little more to the north — if there had been no Florida, no Louisiana, no Gulf coastal plain — *Crotalus* might have had nowhere to go. We would know him today as a handful of bones.

The ice didn't last forever. Several times, for reasons still unclear, the great blankets slowed to a halt and rotted in place, entombing themselves under their burden of loot. New England's sandy outworks — Long Island, Cape Cod, Martha's Vineyard, and Nantucket — mark the peaks of their latest efforts. A little warmth got into them; they vanished.

They left a bare, steaming wasteland. The dark earth soaked up the sun, and the chilly lakes shrank. Here was a bonanza: half a continent plowed up and empty. So another invasion — not frozen and crushing but subtle, tenacious, and protean — first the tundra heaths, trampled by mammoths, then the clumps of willow and spruce, the flocks of seed-dropping birds, the deepening soils — a sort of ten-thousand-year springtime announced blossom by blossom.

*Crotalus* took advantage. A man or woman can walk from Georgia to Maine in three months; an adult timber rattlesnake is almost never found more than two or three miles from its birthplace. So we can assume he traveled at leisure, perhaps not appearing in a place until centuries after it was ready to support him, maybe dawdling at a Hudson or a Potomac for fifty generations — but he did get here, bit by bit.

By then we were already a factor. Weak, almost hairless, famished, and haunted by that most human of landscapes, the invisible world, we had nonetheless learned how to kill big, woolly beasts. So we trailed them along the edge of the ice, chanting and scheming — rhinos, bears, bison, horses, lions, mammoths, all suitably meaty and filling, their rank hides good to cover our own, their proud hearts softened by our prayers. We may in fact have wiped most of them out.

The first signs of our presence in the Blue Hills date from about ten thousand years ago. In the Middle East, at Jericho, we were already sowing grains and building cities; here we were still hunting in packs. But the land wasn't so fat as before. Forests had sprung up in the wake of the Ice Age herds, the seas were flooding the lowlands, and the last mammoths had walked away with our magic. So we had no use anymore for our heavy weapons, our elegant six-inch stone points. We turned to flinging arrows at birds and digging up cattail roots. We became fish eaters, crab pickers; we piled up clamshells and harvested berries. Once again the trees closed over our heads.

It was about this time that *Crotalus* found his way back to Massachusetts. He hadn't changed his habits. He didn't know what we were; he didn't ask. It was the rocks that interested him — the old mountain stumps full of cracks, the rocks and the small, furry creatures that scampered over them.

We're both still here. We're both invaders, both warmth-loving southerners playing tag with the ice. We're the clowns, you could say, chasing each other across the footlights while the next catastrophe prepares backstage. But we know nothing about that. To tell the truth, I really don't care whether or not the ice comes again — it won't come tomorrow. I like living things better. I like their fortitude, their ancestral cunning. This isn't a story about ice — there may be no such thing, I suspect, as a story about ice. Ice is one of the difficulties that make stories possible.

**2**

# A Prospect

My dear blue Hills, you are the most sublime object in my Imagination.

— John Adams, in a letter from Amsterdam to his wife, Abigail, in Braintree, Massachusetts (1782)

The Blue Hills are elusive. They are not the Alps, the Tetons, or even the Palisades. Countless boosters have pointed out that nothing stands higher at the water's edge between the Maine border and Mexico, but you can sail into Boston Harbor on a clear day and not even notice them. They slope gently on that side; they barely lap at the sky.

If you come up from New Bedford on 24, or from the Cape on Route 3, you stand a better chance of seeing something. At three or four miles you spot a broad height of land up ahead; it seems a little too high for the road. There's nothing on top but trees and patches of rock. That's not Boston, you think — there's no Boston in sight. Instead of climbing to meet it you start to descend. Large green signs begin to fly past in bunches. The road can't continue, the road is splitting; you have to choose.

Don't expect to get a good look at the Hills from Route 128, the beltway these approaches feed into. Although it skirts their steepest southern slopes, its curve dictated by their own, you have too much else to do — traffic is heavy, and you're in someone's way.

Take a plane, then. The Hills are conspicuous from above. Not by themselves, but in contrast — a dark mass at night, a bank of greenery in June. Aerial photographs show a blunt-ended wedge tapering eastward, a solid color in a vast web of confetti. A couple of roads cross them. A couple of ponds crater their edges. Nothing else on the map shows a comparable vacancy.

But if you're still curious you'll have to proceed on foot. Drive to any of the trailheads, leave your car, and climb.

The lower slopes are rougher. This is a dry oak woods full of broken rock and matted leaves. The rock is angular and dark, faintly green in the vicinity of pines and hemlocks. In ten minutes or so, just as you start to get warm, the light brightens up ahead. The trail mounts a couple of ledges and burrows out of the woods. Here is the rooftop — a broad, open clearing floored with huckleberry and bedrock. A few gouges in the stone hold pockets of rainwater. Somehow you have been thrust into the sky.

Now everything becomes clear. There are eight or ten hills. They lie in a loose swarm, like turtles hauled up on a beach. All of them have broad, brushy summits bared to rock where they fall away, summits invisible from below. Though you can see lower slopes on the others, you can't see those on your own. None are more than a few hundred feet up, but that's higher than anything for thirty miles. In between lie swampy valleys covered in trees.

It's louder up here — 128, visible through gaps to the south, rumbles like a bowling alley. A sinking jet screams overhead; your skull hums. But a certain silence persists nonetheless, a factor of distance. You can hear voices far down in the woods. A brown leaf rustles on a knee-high scrub oak. No one knows where you are except you.

Now you're glad you've come. You stroll around on the rock, noticing things: a gum wrapper, a gull floating aloft, a contrail. That headland way off to the north, near the limit of vision — what is it? Gloucester? New Hampshire? In the far-spreading harbor eight or ten scattered islands match your eight or ten hills. Boston's cluster of towers looks like a summer house at the bottom of a garden.

This is all the Blue Hills offer in the way of sublimity. Maybe it's nothing remarkable that the face of the planet extends as far as you can see. No doubt there's hardly a city in the world that doesn't have a hill outside it, a perfectly ordinary hill made attractive by the largeness of vision it pretends to lay at one's feet. It's a mystery to me, however, why more people don't visit these. With the exception of Great Blue, which has a road going up and a stone donjon on top, chances are you'll have the summit to yourself. As if there's no particular need, out there, to see where one lives.

I admit that once one has gone up a hill there's not much to do except turn around and come down. And it would be hard to argue that doing so every now and then makes one any more knowledgeable, aware, virtuous, well balanced, or whatever than if one had stayed home. But I promise you that if you take the time to scale one of these hills, on a day when the air is clear and the wind not too cutting, you'll be in no hurry to give up the spot. You'll sense something here not available elsewhere. Because every landscape has its secrets. This is one of them.

# 3

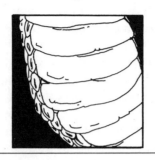

# Snake Heaven

An awful wretch to look upon, with murder written all over
him in horrid hieroglyphics.

— Oliver Wendell Holmes
*Elsie Venner* (1861)

Let's say I'm a rodent. I've got four legs, a tail, and a warm little
pelt. I'm always gnawing on something. If I don't my front teeth
will grow right back into my brain.

Say I'm a chipmunk. I don't ask for the moon. Give me acorns,
hickory nuts, stone walls, and $O_2$. I'm nervous — whatever it is, I
screech and dive for my hole. Hell, I only weigh three ounces.

I sneak out at night. I stuff my face. I keep watch with my glossy
little eyes.

If I'm unlucky I don't see him. He's already there, coiled up.
Where the dead snag fell over, the shallow pit under the roots.

I approach cautiously, tail high. I want to get my nose in some
beechnuts. I'll dig if I have to.

There's a noise, a hard rustle. I jump away. Too late — something hit me. High on the rump, a sharp stab.

I'm running for the hole. My ass is on fire. One leg seizes and I
roll in midair. I crack my head on a rock; I jump up and go.

Now I'm back in my nest. It's quiet, I'm shivering. I've got three
ways to go out. Forget beechnuts; I'm scared.

My other leg starts to kick. Something's wrong, I'm not right. I'm clawing up all my fluff. I'm a wild man.

Now I'm flopped on my side. I can't seem to move. My breath is coming too fast. There's a little light by the entrance — I'm staring at it.

A few minutes later *Crotalus* sticks his head down the hole. I am dead but still warm. His tongue slithers in and out, quivering; he nudges me with his snout; he looks up and gapes, stretching his jaws.

He swallows me headfirst. I squeeze down his throat, arms and legs at my sides. My tail vanishes last. For several days he stays in my hole; I'm a lump in his midsection. Then he's hungry again.

This is the script. It's performed over and over. Ambush, venom, death — if it didn't work it wouldn't happen. Rattlesnakes are a kind of sausage periodically stuffed at one end. They have the appearance of design; they're remarkably well equipped.

It's widely assumed, in biology, that every part has its purpose — that if a structure exists, then it contributes somehow to an organism's ability to survive and reproduce, or is at least a remnant of something that once did so, or a genetic by-product of something else that has or had such a function. In *Crotalus*'s case the kit includes night vision, camouflage coloration, a pair of heat-sensitive pits below the eyes, teeth hollowed out like hypodermics, and modified salivary glands wrapped in muscle in such a way that during a bite the deadly proteins inside can be forced through the teeth and into the prey. And as structure implies function, so rattlesnakes imply chipmunks, and chipmunks imply acorns, and acorns imply hillsides — every player being a sort of map-in-pictures of the kind of world he expects to live in. Therefore no one is surprised when sea gulls are not found in caves, nor oysters on mountaintops.

From the rodent point of view, *Crotalus*'s lie-in-wait artistry is just one more sinister tribute to the rodent way of life, along with a hawk's miss-nothing eyes, a weasel's razorish teeth, and the ICI Corporation's best-selling rat nemesis, Talon G. Rodents are by far the most successful of mammalian groups. The oceans aside, they are found more or less anywhere there is anything to eat. One of the less bragged-about accomplishments of the human species is the transformation of vast areas into prime rodent playgrounds.

They are not usually obvious except in cities. Once, in broad daylight, I saw a mob of twenty or thirty rats scatter down an embankment at the Watertown Arsenal, just west of Boston. Squirrels fat with birdseed infest my back yard. Technically they are wildlife but they don't need protectors. They have solved us; we live in between them.

It's different in the Blue Hills. A Blue Hills squirrel notices you. If he's on the ground he'll go off like a shot and race up a tree. If you pursue he'll go higher, using the trunk as a dummy. He doesn't expect handouts. He doesn't trust you, in fact. Not too long ago, in Stoughton (an adjoining town to the south) you could turn in squirrel heads for money. The selectmen would mark them and give you a receipt for the town treasurer. In 1741, 535 heads were presented and paid for. That same year you could get a full English pound for a wolf's head, but apparently nobody had one.

Squirrels and chipmunks aside, it's rare to see any kind of rodent in the Hills, although almost every other rock conceals a moldy cache of old nuts. The best way to get an idea of the number of small, gnawing creatures that actually inhabit them is to come in early winter on a still day at least twelve hours after a dry dusting of snow. Preferably that snow will have fallen on fresh ice covering all the seeps, pools, trickles, and puddles that border the wet places. They'll be easy to recognize — perfect expanses of white wandering under and around the brush and pockets of grass.

Get up close. Squat down on your heels. That snow which looked so virgin is scribbled all over with delicate histories. Last night while you were asleep, or maybe this morning, dozens of tiny feet ran around here. You can count their toes — the impressions are perfect. Through routes are rare; it looks more as though the sprites were going nowhere in particular, fussing around from one tussock to the next, dashing out and back in hurried little loops, restless as fleas but afraid to leave home. Look around. There are no untracked areas. Maybe you're no expert, but it seems as though it would take more than a mouse or two to leave a record like this — it was busy around here. So where are they now? The light is good, the twigs are bare — you ought to be able to see them. If someone offered you ten thousand dollars, could you produce one? Probably not.

Most of the time there is no ice and no quarter centimeter of dry snow, and visitors can't set themselves riddles. Most of the time, in fact, it seems as though nothing lives in the Hills. On any summer day you can spend the entire morning walking the paths and see nothing except a jay or two and the thin cloud of gnats circling your head. In that case, go home. You are sweaty, you are tired. You can come back next week.

The experts believe adult timber rattlers rarely suffer for lack of rodents to eat. In colonial times areas like this supported snakes in much greater numbers. Out west, where human pressures are less, some species actually become common.

Whatever the case, it's clear that rodents are vigorous enough to withstand a wide range of horrors. In the Blue Hills these include hawks, owls, foxes, weasels, house cats gone wild, blacksnakes, milk snakes, copperheads, and perhaps coyotes. Most of them take other things as well, but it's doubtful they could get by without rodents. Since they all compete for the same finite resources, it's not surprising that they are each expert in their way.

Take a milk snake, for instance. A milk snake is a brightly patterned, nonvenomous, and muscular snake about three feet long, closely related to the king snakes. It got its name from its habit of prowling around barns, where it was thought to milk cows. In fact it's attracted by rodents, which are attracted by good shelter and stored grain.

A milk snake's teeth won't do a rat much damage. It doesn't have the *Crotalus* option of biting once and tracking down a dead victim. And yet they're similar in other ways. Both have keen senses of smell, neither can travel very fast, and both are narrow enough to get into tight places.

A milk snake kills by seizing its prey and throwing a couple of loops around its body. Every time the prey exhales the snake squeezes a little tighter. Eventually the animal can't draw in enough air and suffocates. If you let a milk snake wrap around your arm, sometimes it'll do the same thing — it squeezes surprisingly hard. Boas and pythons kill the same way. Twice in the last decade, eight- or ten-foot pet pythons, supposedly harmless, have gotten into cribs and suffocated infants.

A blacksnake, on the other hand, is built for speed. Big, slender, and nervous, it scouts around in daylight, watching for movement, ready to seize whatever looks likely — frogs, toads, other snakes, mice, sparrows. A battle between a blacksnake and a large frog is a clumsy, bruising, drawn-out affair. The snake lunges; the frog leaps; the frog kicks and scrambles, the snake's teeth in its leg; the snake lets go, strikes again, misses, and pursues. If the snake is big enough, and if the frog can't lose him, the duel usually ends with both parties exhausted and the frog in the snake's mouth, held by double rows of hooked teeth.

The snake can't kill the frog. The frog has to be swallowed. That takes time also; if the frog is caught by the legs it will have to watch while a sort of sleeve is drawn up over its head. Supposedly the frog suffocates inside the snake. The snake, its throat blocked, breathes by extruding a long two-channeled tube, the glottis. Eventually snake and frog move off to a preferred hiding place. All that's left is a little flattened grass.

Three snakes, three methods. You might think that *Crotalus,* with his one-bite attack, his fast-acting juices, and his enhanced defensive abilities would so outclass the milk snakes and blacksnakes that they would at length disappear — in fact, the only way to establish such assets, in Darwinian terms, is by outperforming those kin groups which possess them to a lesser degree — but all three snakes and methods prosper in the Blue Hills. Theory says that this is because the available prey, and their approaches to it, are sufficiently varied to prevent one hunting machine from crowding out the others. This seems reasonable enough, but I would take it a little further. I would say that if you have a tract of woods, you want it to contain as many different kinds of rodents and rodent hunters as possible. You want it to show what time and circumstance can do when they get seriously entangled. And if there are to be snakes, you want snakes with a vengeance — snakes in the water, snakes in the rocks, snakes underground, even snakes in the trees. Each should be curiously marked, each expert in his own particular manner of being. Why should you want all of this? I don't know, it's hard to say. But you do. That's snake heaven.

# 4

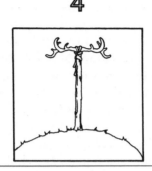

# An Exemplary Victim

And I am in the wilderness alone.

— William Cullen Bryant
"The Prairies" (1832)

The first white man in the Blue Hills was probably a sportsman,
Latinist, and law graduate by the name of Thomas Morton, formerly of Clifford's Inn, London. He got here a year or so after the
*Mayflower* unloaded at Plymouth, and had been thrown out twice
by the time the Puritans settled at Boston. Each time he was set in
a boat and dispatched to England; each time he contrived to get
back. He had no family here, no position, and no property. It
seems that he simply liked the place.

He wasn't afraid to go out in the woods. Unlike his neighbors, so
many of whom heard Satan's own voice in the dusk at the edge of
their clearings, he took a scandalous pleasure in quitting the coast
with only his hawk and his fowling piece, somehow confident that
he would return not only whole, but unspotted.

Did he actually climb the Hills? He lived at Wessagusset (Weymouth), then at Passonagisset (Quincy), the latter only three miles
or so from their easternmost heights — it would have been hard to
avoid them. At Quincy he camped with a handful of indentured
servants contracted to one Captain Wollaston, who planned to sell

them in Virginia. Morton convinced them to stay and be their own masters. "If this land be not rich," he said, "then is the whole world poor."

It was rich. The country Henry Adams would describe several hundred years later as "the stoniest glacial and tidal drift known in any Puritan land" was at the time fat enough to keep even marooned Englishmen alive, as the *Mayflower* settlers discovered when their biscuit ran out. The marshes were full of quahaugs; the spring months brought the cod close inshore; in his only book, *The New English Canaan,* published in Amsterdam in 1637, Morton bragged about shooting turkeys from his front door and carrying them ten steps to the cookroom. He feasted on bears, ducks, pigeons, lobsters, deer, and whatever corn, squash, and beans he could talk out of the Indians. He drank as well, though he had to ship in his brandy. He denied that the natives lived miserably: "If our beggars of England should, with so much ease as they, furnish themselves with food at all seasons, there would not be so many starved in the streets, neither would so many gaols be stuffed, or gallows furnished with poor wretches, as I have seen them." The Indians were long-lost Trojans, he believed, descendants of Aeneas, and spoke Greek and Latin, though not so well as their fathers.

But Morton hadn't always been so comfortable. His introduction to paradise, six hard months at a similar outpost at Weymouth just down the harbor, had started out hungry and ended in disaster when Myles Standish arrived in a boat from Plymouth with eight swordsmen and suddenly and inexplicably began cutting down Indians. He killed three, hanged a fourth, and murdered a fifth not far off. This made it impossible for a small group of whites to live anywhere nearby. Three were ambushed in the woods shortly thereafter; the rest scattered. That Morton was able to begin over again in Quincy three years later suggests that he wasn't held personally responsible.

Morton had a gift for getting along with Americans. These were the Massachuset, a much-reduced tribe of several hundred or so concentrated on the south side of Boston Harbor. They hadn't always been scarce — only twenty years earlier they had chased Samuel de Champlain into deep water by mobbing him with fleets of dugout canoes. Eight years later a different French captain went aground on Peddock's Island; they burned his ship and slaughtered him and his men. But in the winter of 1616 a mysterious Eurasian infection swept them away — some estimates put their losses as high as 90 percent. The ten who lived didn't always have strength to bury the ninety who died, and Morton found their bones scattered all over their abandoned towns. By then the Massachuset needed allies. Their old enemies in the interior hadn't been touched and were raiding their remnants.

Morton gave them muskets, bullets, knives, metal implements, and a minor degree of protection. In return he got food, valuable furs, and company. He didn't want their land, their signatures, or their souls, and so he was readily preferred to his less accommodating neighbors at Plymouth, who wouldn't trade firearms or brandy and didn't like dancing much either.

This is not to say that Morton was any kind of humanitarian or epitome of tolerance, but he wasn't trying to please God as well as himself, and he didn't imagine that if his experiment failed all of New England would be thrown into darkness. The Pilgrims didn't have that luxury. They meant to take root; they saw a world choked with evil. Therefore they considered it their desperate privilege to battle for righteousness, and they knew that Morton wasn't righteous. They also knew that his fur business was spoiling their own.

Once again Myles Standish set off up the coast to do justice. This time the Indians stayed home and he merely arrested Morton and led him back to Plymouth. At his hearing Morton embarrassed the magistrates by pointing out that he'd done nothing illegal. They shipped him off just the same on the next boat home.

He was back in less than a year. In fact he arrived in the company of Isaac Allerton, the colony's agent in London, whom he had assisted with some legal work. Allerton scandalized Plymouth further by letting Morton stay in his house. Before long Morton was reinstalled in his old outpost at Quincy, attracting all the riffraff and malcontents for miles.

Apparently Governor Bradford and Standish decided he was more trouble than he was worth, since they left him alone for some months. By then there were dozens of other settlers scattered around Boston Harbor and its islands, some of them raising corn on the Massachuset's deserted plantations. Technically these lands already belonged to the Massachusetts Bay Company, whose main fleet arrived in June 1630 — eleven ships, seven hundred men and women, countless cattle, goats, and hogs, and a governor, officers, and charter. They immediately took up where Plymouth had left off.

There had been warnings. John Endecott, a sort of advance man for the Company, had visited Morton's base while Morton was away and chopped down his Maypole, a tall cedar topped with deer antlers set up as an altar to Bacchus. While there Endecott declared that he was changing the outpost's name from Merrymount, Morton's choice, to Mount Dagon, after the Philistine sea god whose temple Samson had ruined. After Morton's return Endecott summoned all the harbor-area planters to Salem and demanded their submission to a set of articles instituting God's word as the law of the land. All subscribed except Morton. He wanted a proviso inserted that such laws would have effect only insofar as they weren't repugnant to the laws of England — a reasonable request, considering that the exact same language happened to appear in the Company's charter. But Endecott wouldn't hear it.

So the stage was set. It was evident that Morton liked his freedom and intended to live as he pleased no matter who moved in alongside him, reckoning that his rights as an Englishman would preserve him from Englishmen. In so doing he threatened to show others that the Massachusetts Bay Company couldn't rule on earth with an authority indistinguishable from God's.

On September 7, 1630, three months after the fleet put in, the hammer came down: Morton was ordered rearrested and banished from the colony, the costs of deportation to be met by the sale of his goods. On the day he shipped out aboard the *Handmaid,* Merrymount was burned in his sight. At its next session the Bay Company's governing body, the Massachusetts General Court, voted to prohibit all use of firearms by Indians.

And so Morton's sportsman's paradise became the land of the people Israel. In the years following, the Bay Colony discovered a genius for getting rid of individuals who disputed its not always self-evident mission — Anne Hutchinson, John Wheelwright, and Roger Williams, not to mention various Anglicans, Quakers, Wampanoags, adulterers, and witches. It's no exaggeration to say that the rest of New England was settled by this rich crop of exiles. Generations of historians, from Cotton Mather to John Palfrey to Samuel Eliot Morison and beyond, have tried to show that a lengthy regimen of purges, however unbeautiful, was necessary to cement a sense of common identity and purpose in the vast solitudes of the New World. The question they generally avoid is what this tradition might have amounted to if it hadn't met a contrary current beginning with Morton and culminating in Jefferson and Paine. At any rate, it's not irrelevant to ask how much this Scripture-fed animus against aliens and outsiders contributed to the war against *Crotalus* about to begin.

But to Morton again: sixteen years later, in 1644, he reappeared in Plymouth. Times had changed. His friends the Massachuset had been further thinned by smallpox; the fur trade was ruined; Merrymount had been cut up into farms. He had no money and no friends. Myles Standish threatened to shoot him for hunting ducks on his property. Thanks to his activities in England — the anti-Puritan satire of *The New English Canaan* and his attempts to void the Bay Company charter — it's hard to see why he came back at all; he could expect nothing but abuse. "As for my part," wrote former governor Winslow of Plymouth to Governor Winthrop of Massachusetts, "I would not have this serpent stay amongst us."

Morton became a quasi-fugitive, moving from Plymouth to Gloucester to Maine and south again to Rhode Island. But he was apparently watched closely, and when passing through Massachusetts on a second trip north he was caught and jailed in Boston.

Not wanting to arouse any allies he might have in England, or give him a chance to use his formidable tongue, the authorities delayed trial and kept him in irons for a year. Morton was reduced to begging for pardon. At last, when it became apparent how helpless he was, they fined him £150 and let him go. It's not known whether he ever returned to the Blue Hills. Two years later, "old and crazy," he died at Agamenticus, Maine.

Was he merely unlucky? Would it have been wiser to attend church, refrain from oaths, and drink only with white men? As his book demonstrates, he could laugh at what was laughable, and the Puritans struck him as very ridiculous — maybe he couldn't believe that anyone so humorless could actually destroy him.

But *The New English Canaan* isn't all wit and venom. Nearly half is made up of one of the few accounts of Massachusetts as it was before any efforts to reform it, as if it were this that kept drawing him back (interestingly enough, none of these descriptions are by Puritans). It shows that he paid considerable attention to what he saw in the woods, and to what the Indians told him. And he doesn't leave out that Blue Hills native to which his enemies so often compared him:

> There is one creeping beast, or longe creeple (as the name is in Devonshire) that hath a rattle at his tayle, that discovers his age; for so many years as he hath lived, so many joints are in that rattle, which soundeth (when it is in motion) like pease in a bladder, & this beast is called a rattlesnake.

# 5

# Habeas Corpus

These hills don't look like hills; they are too blue.
— Robert Lowell, *The Old Glory* (1965)

Maybe it's time to actually put this creature on paper.

Most people know what a snake looks like: a sort of eel or worm covered in scales. A lot of people don't want to know any more. If they see a snake, a reaction takes over, and though they continue to stare they're doing their best *not* to look, focusing on only a small piece at a time, or squinting a little off to one side, all the while squirming and grimacing like dessert guests presented with tarantula pie. And so the snake disappears into a sort of limbo set off by fear and disgust. It's at once perfectly obvious and impossible to see.

But even without this disability a snake often fails to become visible. Several years ago I was at a large reptile park, or serpentarium, outside Rapid City, South Dakota, and came across what looked like the largest rattlesnake that ever lived. It was coiled near the front of a display case about a yard wide. The only light came from above and behind me — a dusky and anemic daylight seeping down through the high dome of smoked glass roofing the exhibit.

This was a formidable beast. It was about the size and shape of an old nylon tire — round, dull black, and motionless. It had the heavy, sagging look of a big snake, as if it had kept growing long past the point of utility and could barely drag itself across the cage to swallow its biweekly rabbit or chicken. If it had had any markings, they had all faded out.

I bent down. A snake at rest can usually be observed breathing. Every fifteen or twenty seconds a strip of skin along either side of its spine stretches slightly as it inhales. I couldn't see any motion. There was no evidence, either, that it had noticed me — no tongue action, no impalpable tension.

My face was flush with the glass. Only that and a few inches separated our eyes. His looked like polished beads, the crescent pupils hair-thin.

Then I saw it: he was dusty! And not ground-in dust either, but the pale, wispy stuff that gathers on woodwork and light bulbs. This was a fake snake! An ersatz behemoth, molded in plaster and expertly painted.

I moved back, smiling. This seemed to me very clever. If you need a big snake, and they happen to be scarce, make one yourself!

I watched several mother-with-kid parties drift past the display. The dummy aroused no suspicion. Perfect, I thought.

Just down the way stood one of the attendants, a pretty high school girl in a pastel uniform, clearly bored stiff from having to stand around all summer in the half-lit steam exhaled by crocodiles and philodendrons. I joined her and nodded at the display. "That's not a real snake."

"Yes it is."

"I don't think so. It's dusty."

She shrugged and moved off. I hadn't penetrated her reverie. Maybe she didn't know, maybe she didn't care.

I went back to the glass. The snake hadn't moved. I wasn't so sure anymore — yes it was dusty, but so what? Big snakes are famously sluggish.

I still don't know what exactly I was looking at, though I examined it for another five minutes. If it was a fake, it was a remarkable one. If not, I never found out. And it struck me as amazing that any live animal could prevent me from distinguishing it from a copy of itself, no matter how artful — a live mouse, for instance, would never look at home in a row of stuffed ones. But a snake, as they say, is the most subtle of beasts.

Several days later I was climbing Bear Butte, a forested pile of red rock that rises out of the prairie some miles east of the Black Hills. This butte is sacred to the Dakota, and some of them had pitched tents in the parking lot. I saw a few of their prayer bundles fastened to the pines up above. About halfway up, as I was crossing a bunchgrass slope beneath some talus along a well-beaten trail, I heard a rustle and saw a rough, brick-colored length of reptile slither uphill about a yard from my feet and vanish the next instant. It had nowhere to go; the grass wasn't thick and the ground was packed dirt. But it was gone just the same. A few pokes with a stick revealed nothing. That, I am not at all certain, was a rattlesnake. I didn't see another for two years.

All this is merely to emphasize that one can look at a snake and in fact see very little. It often seems as though the emptiness it leaves when it vanishes is more vivid and characteristic than the animal itself.

There is no lack of pictures of rattlesnakes. As early as 1628, when Morton was sailing back under guard to England, a good engraving appeared in a Latin edition of Francisco Hernández's *Quatro Libros de la Naturaleza,* first published in Mexico City in 1615. It shows a coiled, cross-banded snake with a swollen head and a rattle on its tail. There are rattlesnakes in Mexico; there are rattlesnakes nearly everywhere from Massachusetts to Argentina, though hardly anywhere else. But since the Aztecs and Mayans avoided realistic portraiture, this is probably the earliest extant image of the creature in a natural aspect.

Is it adequate? Yes, in the sense that it equips someone who's never seen him to pick him out in a crowd. In fact, this picture is closer to the best modern photographs than it is to the state of affairs the day before it was made. But suppose rattlesnakes had never existed — would this picture exist? Definitely not. It's secondary; it takes a real living thing and reduces it to an artifact. So in some ways it's worse than nothing. It gives the impression you've seen something that you have not seen. It offers itself in place of that other.

I'm not arguing against representation. All I mean to suggest is that pictures generally say as much about their makers as about their ostensible subjects. There's a gap between us and *Crotalus,* a significant gap.

Hernández had many successors. In April 1989, the Quincy *Patriot Ledger,* the largest daily newspaper south of Boston, published several photos of *Crotalus.* They show a stout, rough-scaled snake with a light-colored head and a dark tail lying coiled on a bed of wood shavings. It's hard to tell how big he is. The rattle doesn't show clearly. But once again an image has been substituted for a genuine presence — there are no more rattlesnakes than before, but there are tens of thousands of readers with a dubiously improved claim to acquaintance.

These grainy likenesses are courtesy of a genuine Blue Hills *Crotalus* living at the Trailside Museum at Milton, Massachusetts. You may visit him there; he shares a glass-fronted case with a slightly smaller cellmate, a copperhead. He's the color of dead leaves, not the muddy browns of the dominant oaks but the bold, stricken yellows of hickories and chestnuts in October.

You probably won't see him move. You definitely won't hear him rattle. He's used to your kind.

There's something, I admit, quietly malevolent about his expression, like a face painted on a razor. In an adjacent case, under glass, is a skull of a rattlesnake; in it you can see the long fangs he so artfully conceals. They're folded back inside his cheeks; when he strikes his mouth gapes like a hinge and flies at the target. This happens so fast that no one knew what it looked like until modern high-speed shutters froze the action.

Look at him — is he thinking about death? Unlike many snakes, he has a distinct neck, a thin shaft running into the typical arrowhead knob of a viper, the cheeks swelled out to each side with long bubbles of venom. On top, instead of the eight or ten neat plates of a harmless garter or water snake he has a whole swarm of tiny scales jammed in every which way.

You can look at him, can't you? He's perfectly ordinary — for a rattlesnake. Thanks to the glass front, you can study him close up — his catlike pupils, his armored head, his uncanny motionlessness. His rattle looks like a string of beads made of old waxed paper.

He's kept here, I'm told, for educational purposes. So that people will know him on sight — so that other, nonpoisonous species won't be killed in his name. But he's not at his best indoors. He's a showpiece, a sort of denatured advertisement for himself.

Granted, he gives the impression that he'd just as soon bite you as not, but it's a notorious fact that you can make anyone look criminal if you lock him up.

On his right stands an immense, glass-fronted closet containing a fearsome yellow-eyed owl twice the size of your head. On his left a short flight of stairs leads down to a fish tank full of algae and minnows. None of these creatures seems the least bit aware that anything odd has happened to him. Outside you can watch otters splash around in a high-walled concrete pool, or toss alfalfa pellets into a flurry of mallards, or simply bask in the sun like a snake. But you might feel that things have been made too easy. You might, if you're anything like me, feel that this little Eden, with its charming walkways, its well-kept inhabitants, and its interpretive signboards, is just another of those similitudes or facsimiles with which, in our passion for symbols, we have infested the world — and you might wonder a little impatiently why you just don't hike up the slope and past the fence and into the actual, unannotated, and rock-strewn woods, where there are other purposes at work and the welcome isn't nearly so warm. Because that, after all, is where *Crotalus* lives.

Only he's not easy to find there either. About a hundred years ago Charles Breck, Milton town treasurer, wrote, "In all my tramping over the Hills in the summer season I never saw but one, and that a very small one." Breck, a surveyor, was regarded as the most thorough outdoorsman in town. There are plenty of people who have made a project of looking for *Crotalus,* with no better success. The last bounties on rattlers in this area were paid before the Civil War, though they were still being collected in Vermont as late as 1971.

Does he exist at all? Since 1894 the Blue Hills have been administered as the largest park in the Boston metropolitan system and have had tens of thousands of visitors annually; in that time no one, so far as is known, has been poisoned by a rattlesnake.

Of course it will never be possible to prove that he is *not* present. Unlike bald eagles, grizzly bears, or Arctic wolves, *Crotalus* doesn't need an entire Alaska to hide in. Precisely where he can and cannot be found is still a controversial matter in Massachusetts. In Palmer, an industrial town in the half-rural Worcester hills, a hay cutter was bitten in 1900 even though no snakes had been seen there for fifty years. Better yet, in May 1955 Captain Pieter Hinkamp, U.S. Navy, attacked a rattler with a shovel in Jamestown, Rhode Island, the first and last ever reported in the town's three-hundred-year history.

I like it that way. I like the idea, however dubious, that *Crotalus* can go about his business for decade upon decade in the midst of his enemies without showing his face. I like to think that when he is finally declared extinct in this state it may be just another instance of his discretion. We know he can be wiped out — the evidence is overwhelming — but why should he make it easy?

However, we're not going to get a good look at him if we already think we know what he is — last of his kind, embattled remnant of the wild, etc. That's only the latest of his disguises. What we want is an image not already familiar as argument. What we want is the beast himself.

There's a lot of rock in the Blue Hills. Of course New England is famously stony, but I mean the kind of rock old mountains are made of, the extra-hard, brutal stuff that's left over after other rocks have broken up and worn away. Dirt, which is used-up rock mixed with humus and which remains the basis of our national wealth, doesn't accumulate readily in the Hills. What little develops tends to get burned up or washed away. Whenever a big pine or oak blows down you can see how little the roots had to cling to — often they come up in a pitifully thin mat studded with stones and revealing, underneath, a sheet of bedrock as fresh and unweathered as a newly cut curb. This is granite porphyry, a dark gray stuff even harder than granite. It's the reason no Yankee plowman ever bothered with the Hills. Even the sheep farmers never took their stone walls above the two-hundred-foot contour.

But for *Crotalus* this rock is life. It keeps his enemies at a certain distance. It gives him deep cracks and crypts for the winter. It opens gaps in the trees where he can warm his fishy blood in sunshine. And there's enough of it — enough hills, enough slopes, enough steep acres of rubble — to hide a few survivors when his main haunts are emptied. Down on the plain there are just too many snake killers and too few retreats.

So he's still here if you can find him. The experts say come in early May or late September, when the nights are cold and the snakes lie out in daylight near their communal rock chambers, soaking up heat. Come on a clear, windless day when the rock is warm to the touch. Don't come without ankle boots and don't come to think about other things. The snakes know where they are; you don't.

If you do this all day you can examine maybe 2 percent of the rock in the Hills. That probably won't be enough to find *Crotalus*. But if you do it again, and keep doing it — choosing your days, mapping your efforts, and seeking out rock not visible from the trails — then sooner or later you're going to meet him.

He'll be coiled, most likely, in a spot where you were about to step. He may rattle or not; maybe he'll slide back out of sight. If you've been moving with care he may not even see you. Whatever his size, he'll look bigger than he is.

Up until this moment you have probably not quite believed in him. Or maybe you did, but you thought only other people could find him — after all, you've looked into thousands of leaf-filled crevices like this one. But there's something there, you'll admit. You're staring at it, aren't you?

So the question — what next? With luck you are at least eighteen inches away. You can back off deliberately. You can look around for other snakes. You can keep quiet and watch him indefinitely.

But there's another choice, of course. Rattlesnakes are easy to kill. Any stout stick or rock will do it. One blow breaks his back.

However, if you've come this far, if you've looked this hard, and you still think you're not finished till you've seen him thrashing and dying on either side of the kink you've put in his spine, then I say go to it quickly and take full satisfaction. Because in a moment it's just going to be you and a dead snake. You can't kill it twice. There's simply one less left to smash.

But I had promised to put *Crotalus* on paper. I can see that this doesn't do it. Let's go on.

# 6

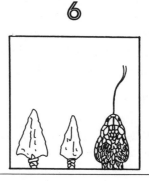

# Black Arts

An old Swede once walked with an Indian, and they encountered a red-spotted snake in the road: The old man therefore went to seek a stick in order to kill it, but the Indian begged him not to touch it, because it was sacred to him. Perhaps the Swede would not have killed it, but on hearing that it was the Indian's deity, he took a stick and killed it, in the presence of the Indian, saying: "Because thou believst in it, I think myself obliged to kill it."

— Peter Kalm, *Travels into North America* (1771)

You wouldn't think anyone would have trouble distinguishing between a human being and a rattlesnake. And as a matter of fact it's never been a problem, for obvious reasons. And yet people have never stopped trying to blur the difference.

This is a function of language, a sort of irresistible shorthand: if you call someone a snake, for instance, you don't mean that he is legless and scaly but that he is low, vile, and treacherous. Like a sorcerer, you transfer the supposed qualities of one to the other, and the resulting picture is so vivid that it almost succeeds without evidence.

Writers have never been embarrassed to go in for this kind of monkeying. But times change, and sometimes it seems as though the magic wears thin. Let me give you a few examples (italics added):

> Their bold yet crafty features, their cheeks besmeared with ochre and vermilion, white lead and soot, their keen, deep-set eyes gleaming in their sockets, *like those of rattlesnakes,* gave them an aspect grim, uncouth, and horrible.    (Parkman)

> Silently out of the room then glided the glistening savage,
> Bearing the serpent's skin, *and seeming himself like a serpent*
> Winding his sinuous way in the dark to the depths of the
>      forest.    (Longfellow)

> When certain that he was undiscovered, the Dahcotah raised his person again, and bending forward, he moved his dark visage above the face of the sleeper, *in that sort of wanton and subtle manner which with the reptile is seen to play about its victim before it strikes.*    (Cooper)

> It was easy enough after a time to drive away the savages; for "a screeching Indian Divell," as our fathers called him, *could not crawl into a crack of a rock to escape his pursuers.*    (Holmes)

Here we have four of our classic authors comparing snakes to men and men to snakes, all in specifically American settings. What's interesting is that the men in question are all American Indians. I could multiply examples — it's clear, however, that when these nineteenth-century literary toilers wanted to fix in metaphor what was most Indianlike about their Indians, they brought out a snake.

Now even if we knew nothing of our own history we could find a clue or two here, considering the usual outcomes of encounters between people and snakes. If you hear, as you can, modern suburbanites referring to inner-city youths as "maggots" or "vermin," then you've stumbled on a similar process.

The reason I say the device fails is that the late twentieth century has different ideas about what Indians are and what snakes are, and when we find the two so frequently linked it strikes us less as a fertile poetic discovery than as a dried-up and fossilized reflex with ugly overtones.

But what I want to look at is a parallel tradition somewhat less easy to unearth: if transplanted Europeans used snakes to libel Americans, what did Americans use them for?

The Massachuset didn't survive long enough for anyone to compile examples of their rhetoric. Within a century of invasion they had been reduced to a few dozen indigents trying to fend off starvation in the swamps around Indian Lane in Canton. Interestingly enough, those New England tribes which did weather the shock and make it down to the present with something of their original folkways and numbers intact — the Wampanoags at Mashpee and Gay Head, and the Micmac and Passamaquoddy in eastern Maine — all lived in marginal areas that were too sandy or too cold for either Puritans or rattlesnakes.

But a few stories have come down from elsewhere in the forested East, and they suggest that Indian attitudes toward *Crotalus* were consistent through much of the region.

In 1764 Alexander Henry, a British fur trader, was canoeing from Sault Ste. Marie to Fort Niagara with a band of Ojibwa, woodland Indians from the western Great Lakes. As they were setting up camp one evening at Point aux Grondines on Lake Huron, he spotted a rattlesnake and, predictably, ran to the canoe for his gun. One of the Indians asked what was the matter. When he heard, he not only begged Henry to stop but alerted the others, and they all gathered their pipes and approached the animal.

It was coiled but not rattling. The Indians surrounded it, lit their pipes, and began blowing smoke in its face. They talked to it also, calling it Grandfather. It seemed to Henry that the snake enjoyed the attention.

After a half hour of this the snake moved off slowly and the Indians followed, asking it to protect their families at home and to grant them a full cargo of rum at Niagara. They begged it also to disregard Henry's hostility, and made clear that they had nothing to do with it.

When the snake was gone the Indians wanted to turn back, contending that it had come to warn them against going on. Henry persuaded them to continue. The next morning they set off across a broad arm of the lake and put up a sail. Before long the wind started to rise. Troubled, the Indians called on the rattlesnake for help. The storm increased. The Indians took a dog, tied its forelegs together, and threw it overboard. When this brought no improvement they gave up another dog and some tobacco, asking *Crotalus* to accept these and spare them — in particular, to remember that it was Henry and not they who had insulted him. By then the waves were breaking into the canoe.

The Indian beside Henry remarked that it would make more sense to surrender the white man, since he was to blame. Fortunately the squall blew out and there were no further offerings.

At about the same time, the Quaker naturalist William Bartram got into similar difficulties while visiting a Seminole village in the St. John's region of Florida. One morning when he was sketching botanical specimens in his hut, he heard a commotion outside and learned from his interpreter that a rattlesnake had invaded the camp. Since no one would want to risk offense the interpreter predicted that he, Bartram, would be asked to get rid of it.

Bartram, cannier than Henry, guessed what might follow from this and told the man to inform everyone that he was deep in delicate work and would not be going out.

In a few minutes three warriors appeared at the door. They confessed that they lacked courage to deal with the monster and that, since they knew Bartram collected all sorts of animals, they were pleased to make him a gift of this one.

George Orwell once found himself in an analogous bind with respect to an elephant. Like him, Bartram shouldered his duty. He found the snake roaming from hearth to hearth through the camp, with a crowd of women and children watching in terror. He picked up a pine knot and approached the animal. When it coiled up and faced him he beaned it, killing it. Then he cut off its head, brought it back to his hut, removed the fangs, and deposited them in his collections.

Soon he heard another disturbance outside. His interpreter reappeared and informed him that some Indians were coming to "scratch" him for killing a rattlesnake in the camp. Bartram thought of escape, but before he could exit three more warriors appeared, two of them brandishing knives and declaring that he was entirely too "heroic and violent," and that they were going to improve his manners with a little bloodletting. They grabbed him; he struggled.

Suddenly the third Indian, who happened to be Bartram's patron in the camp, intervened and declared that Bartram was his friend and a courageous and stalwart character whom he had sworn to protect and therefore could not tolerate to be insulted. The other two abruptly and heartily agreed. Then all three of them went off shouting his praises.

Clearly this "ludicrous farce," as Bartram called it, accomplished two things at once: it removed the rattlesnake and deflected its wrath. Henry's Ojibwas also thought the animal capable of great harm, though their respect seemed more sincere. Snakes are more scarce in the North; maybe the Florida Indians saw too many of them not to forgo a few economies in veneration.

There's evidence that other tribes held like attitudes. Among the Penobscot of Maine, for instance, stories about *Crotalus* were told only in winter, so that no snake would hear and take offense. And when such tales were permitted, a euphemism such as Grandfather, or, among the Cherokee, Bright Old Inhabitant, had to be substituted for the more exact term. When coming upon a snake the Pomo of California tried to forestall any resentment by making a formal apology on the spot.

This isn't to say that Indians never killed rattlesnakes. In Virginia Captain John Smith, champion of Jamestown, saw warriors with rattles tied in their hair. But as with all animals considered spiritually powerful, a precise protocol shielded the hunter. When the Potawatomi of Ohio disposed of a snake carcass they sprinkled tobacco and repeated a ritual prayer. Perhaps the only tribe genuinely willing to insult rattlers were the Apache, who on meeting one would say, "Go into your hole, you evil creature, and take the evil world with you." But then they were famous outlaws.

So it seems that Americans were as eager to give manlike qualities to snakes as the Europeans were to give snakelike qualities to them, the Americans. *Crotalus* wasn't merely a dangerously venomous set of teeth in the woods — not at all, he was a proud and jealous independent power, sensitive to insult but not beyond manipulation. When a bite occurred it was seen not as an accident but as a form of retribution, the victim having invited it through some criminal oversight.

The Puritans denounced this kind of thinking as the vilest superstition. But they were far from free of it themselves. In 1675 when the Wampanoags rose up and burned and slaughtered their way clear across New England, the colonial preachers saw it not as a natural response to forty years of abuse but instead as a supernatural judgment — God was angry at his people and had sent the Indians, his bloody angels, to let them know it.

In fact, it seems that what Indian and Puritan feared most wasn't powerful and vindictive forces coming from the invisible and intervening decisively and even tragically in human affairs, but instead a world where such events would *not* take place — a world uncoupled from the human, a world *not* made coherent through a structure of symbolic and moral relations. Because although they rarely said so, both Indian and Puritan imposed a duty on nature: they required it to surrender meanings.

And surrender them it did, though they changed over time. The Americans, seeing so many whites kill snakes with impunity, began to do it themselves. The Puritans, now several generations removed from their original fervor, began to wonder if every goat or pig stuck with arrows might have a more proximate cause than divine displeasure. A new world was emerging, a world of farms, roads, and woodlots, a world of cash wages and not-so-wild beasts. *Crotalus* was no longer a god; he was not even a devil. He became a sort of weed.

As I said before, we don't know what relations existed between the Massachuset and *Crotalus*. Once the Puritans arrived, the contest in and around the Blue Hills wasn't over how to look at a rattlesnake, but over who would live and who would die, and the Indians died. So did all the other large, potent creatures they might have honored as brothers in spirit — wolves, bears, eagles, lions. Even today, when we have learned to be sentimental, these last wouldn't be welcome in our landscape. But they were here. The people here knew them. Before we called their names.

# 7

# Tree House

Turning from the ocean's surface, next survey
The fir-clad mountains, which behind you lay.
There the GREAT BLUE HILL rears its cloud-capped head,
And knotted oaks their verdant foliage spread.

— Henry Maurice Lisle, Milton attorney (1803)

Sometime around 1885 the Reverend Albert K. Teele, longtime pastor of Milton's First Evangelical Church, proposed erecting a bronze statue of an Indian on a rock shelf forty feet up on the southwest side of Great Blue Hill. It never happened. Today the same backdrop, an immense, unwrinkled brow of stone looming over the flats with the whole weight of the range behind it, is used as a message board by enterprising adolescents who ascend after dark with brushes and buckets and block out their initials in white paint ten feet high. After a while equally daring family men follow in daylight and paint over the letters in rock-colored gray. This desultory combat is played out in front of tens of thousands of commuters who sit in traffic twice a day on Route 128 just below. It's been going on forever; few notice.

Great Blue forced 128 to slither under its nose. A part circle, or beltway, drawn around Boston had to either ride across its rear or gather it up whole; at a quarter mile wide and fifty stories high its summit discouraged violation. Since the inner route would have sliced through dozens of opulent suburban estates, the engineers favored a cut-rate track to the south, which crossed a five-mile stretch of marsh and forest already reserved as parkland and conveniently undeveloped.

This was in the late 1940s, the first brash dawn of the age of the expressway. Having swallowed Great Blue, 128 likewise gathered in all the lesser hills to the east. On a map they form a rocky sediment lying in the bottom of its curve. Around Boston anything inside 128 is considered solidly metropolitan.

Great Blue anchors the entire range to windward. Not so much a mountain as a huge blister of rock, it's the highest and most barren of all and looks southwest across the swampy plain of the Neponset River toward Canton, Norwood, and Walpole, with Rhode Island like a rumor in the distance. The horizon is low and unmarked; it ends in a distinct line about twenty miles away. Route 128 skims across the flats underneath, where a cloverleaf draws off traffic to the north.

Once the beltway went in, it was soon noticed that a good piece of these once-remote flats now lay between a major interchange and the most dramatic natural object for miles. Therefore no one was surprised when that old tempter, modernity, finally sidled up in the late seventies in the form of the Codex Corporation, a high-tech manufacturer, and proposed to build a multimillion-dollar headquarters on a scenic and venerable trotting-horse farm between the freeway and the hill.

It wasn't 1949 anymore. People had learned that what developers give with one hand they take away with the other. And so by the time the dust settled, former Celtics basketball star Dave Cowens, Robert Redford, and Governor Michael Dukakis had all loudly lamented our foolish romance with bulldozers, though the votes that mattered belonged to the Canton town fathers, who had been thoroughly dazzled at the outset by heaps of tax dollars and refused to let go the bait. Today, several economic downturns later, the Codex building has been let go at half price and the man who built it relieved of further duties. Perhaps if we had offered him a chance to erect a bronze statue of himself, or even paint his name in letters no one would paint over, he would have taken that as his monument and put his brick palace elsewhere.

Let's face it, the world dares us to leave our mark. The more we can do, the more reason to do it. No doubt the Acropolis lost some rugged charm when the Athenians capped it with marble. If we could rearrange the stars so that every July Fourth they traced out a portrait of George Washington, do you think we would hesitate?

For our corporate Alexanders here in eastern Massachusetts, there is nothing so attractive as a wooded hilltop. For some reason the same spot they might have chosen to camp out at as boys is now equipped in their dreams with six hundred parking slots and a prizewinning postindustrial fortress. Drive along Route 20 toward Worcester, or along 495 where it crosses the Massachusetts Turnpike, and you will see dozens of these strip-windowed megaliths dropped onto the heights like so many Gibraltars.

They are not particularly inviting. No one approaches on foot; visitors drive up a long, suave ramp through the woods and emerge onto a terraced plateau banked with wood chips and polka-dot matrices of knee-high yew bushes. The views are immense on all sides. Rafts of late-model cars carpet the asphalt. People are curiously absent.

The building watches you from the summit. You can't see through its mirrorlike glass. It carries no identifying logo, no hint as to what goes on inside. You get the feeling that if you get any closer you'd better have a good story.

I don't mean to be facetious. But it's clear that these hilltop piles are not just workplaces, they are shrines and retreats. So we ask, like Herodotus: What gods live inside? The buildings don't say, but one senses that whoever they are, they are gleaming, bloodless, and would at least like to become awesome.

When the Blue Hills were set aside no one imagined that anyone would chisel off their tops and crown them with air-conditioned colossi. People rode to work on streetcars, roads were chopped out with pickaxes, and teams of horses burst out of firehouses. The Hills were empty because no one could make money building streets and houses on elevated rock. But as it happened the planners left out Pine Hill, the summit at the end opposite Great Blue, and today it has its own moonbase—office park canted high over the freeway.

Why do these triumphs annoy me? Why, when I want to go for a walk, do I prefer empty woods to full parking lots? In 1891 Charles Eliot Jr., the man most responsible for the Blue Hills Reservation, told the Advance Club of Providence that natural scenery provides an "antidote to the poisonous struggling and excitement of city life." But what is the city the antidote for?

Maybe I'm brainwashed. Maybe I've swallowed the now-hoary notion that the world is somehow richer and deeper in the heart of the woods than it is on the sidewalk in front of one's home. But why is a twenty-foot garden hose any less remarkable than a three-foot rattlesnake?

I won't get into that now. Suffice it to say that as a matter of temperament I prefer sycamores to mailboxes, huckleberries to gladioluses, and damp sphagnum to electric garage door openers. Yes, it's true, if the Blue Hills are subdivided, I won't go there anymore.

Mr. Eliot meant no favor to *Crotalus* when he arranged a bond issue to buy up the Hills. There's no sign in his published works that he had even heard of him. A landscape architect, he belonged to Frederick Law Olmstead's famous Brookline firm and was a son of the president of Harvard; he saw a chance to give Boston something large and he took it. Thanks to his efforts Olmstead's in-town parks were matched by a bigger, wilder array on the rocky rim of the city: the Middlesex Fells, Beaver Brook, Stony Brook, and the Blue Hills.

But as much as I stand in his debt, I have to say that he doesn't attract me. He saw his parks as cheap medicine for those less fortunate than himself. He prescribed a ride on the streetcar, a rented buckboard at the park boundary, and a drive through the woods on the carriage roads he laid out, with frequent stops to admire the scenic views he prepared by cutting the brush along the shoulder and on the distant cliff or valley at the center of his composition.

This seems to me to miss the whole point. It was precisely the absence of roads that made the Hills worth preserving. And who was he to tell us what ailed us?

But it's still his park today. If his streetcars are gone, if his nerve-racked urbanites now live in the suburbs and drink bottled water, his work survives in the actual form of the woods, which are entirely different thanks to his efforts.

In 1890 there was, strictly speaking, almost no forest in the Hills.

It had all been cut down, over and over. That was about all they were good for, before mere emptiness became a value — too high for sewers and streetcars, too stony for crops or livestock. Even the rock itself was inferior to Quincy's granite.

The Hills still produced firewood, kindling, and a poor brand of charcoal. Two hundred years of continuous cropping and burns had resulted in a sort of dried-out chaparral of oak and chestnut sucker growth littered with ashes and bristling with gray-white, fire-killed skeletons waiting to fall down. Every fifteen or twenty years the cutters came in and chopped the suckers from the stumps. They left the trimmings where they fell; the sun baked them dry; the next burn charred them black. Fires occurred every year — ground fires in the spring, maybe some hot ones in the fall. A few cart tracks wandered through this interminable thicket of bleached sticks and brown, clinging leaves. There was no shade in it, no depth, no relief. It was nearly impassable. A few patches remain today — if you try to force your way through one you will look, when you emerge, as if you've been attacked by octopi armed with charcoal crayons.

Eliot knew that a mature New England forest is rarely threatened by fire. The canopy shuts out the sun and keeps the soil damp. If the duff burns before leafout or late in the fall, few grown trees will suffer. It takes an eight-week drought at the least, and maybe a moth attack, hot winds, or skilled arsonists, before anything like a holocaust becomes possible.

Eliot wanted this kind of forest for the Hills — the cool, dim-ceilinged kind, green as an apple inside and high enough to catch gold light at daybreak. He believed he knew how to get it. Here's his program:

- Late in the year, after the first snow, send gangs of men to all parts of the Reservation. Have them cut all dead wood, cart away that which is salable, and burn the rest in heaps.
- From February through April, when the danger of ground fires is greatest, divide the Reservation into hundred-acre parcels and assign one man to each. Equip him with water cans and a Johnson pump. Put out all fires.
- In late summer, send men with hatchets throughout the Reserva-

tion to chop sprouts and suckers from all fire- and ax-killed stumps. Do not harm seedling trees.

• After several years, when all the stumps have stopped sprouting and seedling trees are established, thin the seedlings. Continue to burn dead wood and suppress fires.

Today, a century later, Eliot's work is visible in the young and ever-deepening tent of greenery covering most of the Hills. He never planted a tree — he merely discouraged tree killing. Something like 60 percent of southern New England is now shaded by these youthful, second-chance woods, and they probably don't look that much different from the ones the English colonists spent two hundred years trying to uproot. We are tree-positive now; we hope to dissuade land-hungry Third Worlders from aping our ferocious example. But are we ready to return even a fraction of Ohio and Indiana to their original timber?

What you get, you keep. What you keep becomes yours. Then you can decide what lives and what dies. This is how we look at the world.

Eliot never saw his forests grow up. He died at thirty-seven of spinal meningitis; his father wrote his biography. A massive stone bridge across a tiny gully at the top of Great Blue memorializes him, expressly contravening his wish that all stonework and ditching in the Hills be as simple and modest as possible. But it reminds us that almost every three-acre scrap of catbirds and grapevines in this part of the world is now identified as "The Somebody P. Someone Nature Preserve" or "The I-Died-Rich Woodland Sanctuary," as if the least atom of what lies at our feet is ever ours to give or receive.

Power of life and death. Dominion, aegis, mastery. Though the Hills look pretty wild, they are not; if anything, they show how much doctoring a large park can absorb. Because the return to nature wasn't trusted to occur naturally.

This attitude is most obvious in the response to the gypsy moth. The moth, a tree eater particularly partial to oaks, was accidentally introduced into Massachusetts from France in 1869 and appeared in the Hills in 1904. It's a terrible thing to see an entire forest burst into leaf only to be chewed bare again in a matter of weeks. The

Metropolitan Park Commission answered by sending dozens of men into the Hills to paint moth egg cases with creosote. It appeared to work: four years later the campaign was called off, there being hardly enough eggs to bother with.

But the moth was back the next year, and then again in 1914. It seemed that every decade or so it made serious inroads despite all control measures. Then, in 1924, the commission began spraying with lead arsenate. It worked, but not well enough. The next year more was applied. Once again the result seemed just short of ideal. And so by 1938, several escalations later, thirty thousand pounds of this poison were being mixed with fish oil and spritzed over the Hills.

Lead arsenate isn't seen much today. Around the time of World War II it was finally recognized that the chemical not only decreased in effectiveness with use, but accumulated in soils and reappeared in produce, often at levels so high that crops for export were turned back overseas. Many thousands of acres of orchards in Oregon and Washington became so toxic that nothing would grow in them. Stymied, the Blue Hills managers turned to a new and supposedly much less hazardous moth cocktail, so light it could be spewed out of airplanes — DDT.

It hardly seems credible today that anyone could imagine the Blue Hills would benefit from repeated drenchings with poison. But in 1947 we had just finished off the Nazis and weren't intimidated by caterpillars. And we still regard ourselves, with reason, as the most formidable enemy any would-be superbug is likely to encounter. We haven't abandoned that cherished bit of nonsense called "the balance of nature" — upset it, we say, and we'll make you regret it. As if we weren't ourselves the biggest troublemakers around.

In 1981 Massachusetts suffered its worst moth outbreak yet. Something like 2.5 million acres of hardwoods were gnawed to rags. I was living in New Haven that spring and can report that the wooded slopes west of town were opened to the sky and chewed to the nub, their only vital sign an all-day drizzle of moth turd.

But there was no spraying that year. Late in June, when the worms ran out of salad, they starved by the billion. A virus known as nucleo-polyhedrosis wiped out the remnants. Within weeks ten counties and three states had greened up again. Nary a caterpillar remained. The next year they weren't half as bad, and the year after that they were forgotten. They've hardly been seen since.

And so one has to ask what might have happened to the Hills if they hadn't been soaked, year after year, with the latest in synthetic toxins — if someone had noticed, for instance, that a Mr. Tate of Randolph or a Mr. Shorer of Braintree hadn't sprayed his woods and hadn't lost any trees. Maybe someone did notice. But he was before his time; we were taking no chances.

The fact is that the Blue Hills are kept on a sort of permanent probation. Their task, in a landscape where space is expensive and nearly every square yard must produce, is to represent Nature. We believe that Nature is beautiful, hence we won't allow them to become ugly. Treelessness, for instance, is a serious offense. Therefore if something threatens to produce it, whether it be an army of grubs or two developers and a politician, we want to know.

This history of intervention, this urge to make nature more natural, is the modern story of the Hills. It begins with Eliot and continues today. We shouldn't be surprised if it becomes ironic; it is riddled with ironies.

Take the Great White Pine Fiasco. Here, as in the war with the moth, an enormous effort was made toward a result that would probably have occurred regardless.

White pines are without doubt the most magnificent giants in New England — long-armed hilltoppers clothed with masses of soft, feathery needles that are blue-green in life and rich rust-orange in death, when they form deep, glowing carpets upon which countless small-town trysters have lain down to ruin. A white pine appears on one of the first coins struck in Massachusetts. Battles were fought over them in Maine, where the king claimed them for his fleet. Thoreau framed his cabin with joists cut from white pines.

They flourish in poor or marginal soils — rocky hillsides, sand flats, dry ravines, old pastures, boulder swamps — places where their greatest weakness, an inability to grow in deep shade, is less likely to exclude them.

Of course once they reach a certain size they can leave any curtaining beeches or hemlocks behind. At that point they may have another hundred years left to grow — a second, solitary life high in the upper regions with sunsets and thunderbolts. Stand on any Blue Hills summit and you can see dozens of these ancients rearing up out of the woods like weeds the mower has missed. They include the largest trees on the Reservation, many of which were already the largest when Eliot admired them a century ago. At that time they were confined to a few hard-to-reach ledges and private holdings where no cutting occurred.

Today there are white pines everywhere in the Hills: bushy little seedlings that spring back underfoot; doomed, spindly saplings dropping needles in deep shade; rugged, fire-blackened relics clinging to the treelines; and pure same-age stands now so thick that the first snows barely penetrate. What is curious is that they are no more common here than in any patch of woods in the surrounding towns. Curious because a half century ago they were the object of the most ambitious restoration project ever undertaken in the Hills — one that, had it succeeded, might have turned the park into the sort of biological desert typified by those high-tech farms on which a single strain of wheat is planted from horizon to horizon.

Between 1904 and 1938 more than two million white pine seedlings were set out in the Hills. That works out to 285 per acre, or about one every three steps. Although thousands of other trees were started in the same period — mostly hemlock, red pine, and spruce — their numbers were negligible in comparison.

The records don't say why this massive intervention was considered necessary, though it may have been accelerated by the chestnut blight, another terror from overseas that wiped out large portions of Eliot's still-youthful woods during World War I. Maybe white pines were the cheapest tree going. Maybe they were considered the most "natural" alternative, since at that time many students believed that most of New England had once been blanketed with them, having mistaken the thick stands that sprang up after the Civil War on nearly every abandoned farm for exact replicas of the primeval forest (today these stands are known as "old field white pine" and are fast giving way to mixed hardwoods). But whatever the rationale, an enormous labor resulted. In one year alone, 1913, three hundred thousand trees were set out.

So where are these pilgrims now? They would be anywhere from fifty to ninety years old, or just approaching magnificence. Can they be identified? Is it possible to point to any pine in the Hills and say, "Out of those two million, this is one"?

No.

All right then, maybe individuals resist labels. But given the number of right-size examples, given the number we know to have been set out, couldn't we select a dozen likely-looking stands and say, "Out of these, at least *some* were planted by hand between 1904 and 1938"?

No.

The problem is that here in Massachusetts, at the heart of their range, white pines don't need help to make forests. All they require is a little light, a fertile parent nearby, and a stiff wind or a couple of squirrels to scatter seed. A truly daunting task would be to locate an acre of woods within forty miles of Boston where you could *not* find white pines. And since the Park Commission foresters wisely neglected to plant in neat rows, it's impossible today to tell which if any of their innumerable darlings survive. Their work remains in plain sight but has vanished completely. It's as though they had gone to the North Pole to make ice.

Maybe this kind of foolishness is inevitable in a place like the Hills, where no effort has been spared to create the *appearance* of wildness — where Nature, once considered the most formidable of opponents, has somehow become a hothouse flower requiring expert care. And if we define Nature sentimentally, if we say Nature stops where the blacktop begins, then yes, there certainly is less of it than there used to be, and it makes perfect sense to quarantine those scraps which remain near our cities and nurse them into showroom condition.

But let's be serious. Is Boston or New York really any less natural than a shellfish bed or a greenbrier thicket? Did we drop out of the sky? Don't we belong here as well? How is it that Nature can produce a billion mosquitoes but not a single toothbrush?

We are in the process, I think, of mistaking our own singularity for a sort of blanket exemption — as if Nature, rather than everything we are and have been and can be, were instead a childhood playmate we have lately outmuscled. We think it lives on our charity; we like to scold each other on its behalf. If it falters — if we addle it with poisons or choke it with sewage or carve it to bits and eat them piecemeal — we say, "Look what we've done, we've killed it." But it is always murdering itself. It manures itself with extinction.

No, I would say that what we discovered about a hundred years ago, when Eliot set aside the Blue Hills, wasn't so much regret for our carnage and a newfound humility, but an even greater ambition. Now that we had shown we could cut down, chew up, and plow over the greater part of a continent, a continent we had first succeeded in crossing only a century earlier, we meant to capture Nature itself and set it up in style in a few choice locations so that we might admire it forever, in much the same way that the pharaohs planned to conquer eternity by embalming their grandfathers.

And so we made ourselves responsible for and anxious about a landscape that was valuable chiefly because it had *not* been cared for — a place that two hundred years of neglect and inattention had somehow made eligible for sanctity. And we wanted it to become even more overgrown and aboriginal, more wild and "untouched," even if that meant two million white pines and an all-out chemical war.

Did we succeed? Remarkably enough, yes.

Today the Blue Hills don't have the ragged, tramped-down look of typical megapolitan woodlots like Concord's Walden Pond or Prospect Hill in Waltham. Not every old beech is ringed with ancient, scabby initials; if you walk off the trails you do not immediately scuff up old beer bottles and rotten plastic. Though the park includes a golf course, a ski slope, a pond popular with swimmers, and portions of three federally funded interstates, these do not quite dominate. Wherever you are, there is always a hinterland nearby, a less frequented upland or swamp where the boulders lie exactly as the ice dropped them and a gang of crows or jays will protest your intrusion.

And what woods! Pine, hemlock, aspen, hickory, oak, sprout chestnut, and red maple nearly everywhere, with a richer mix of elm, yellow birch, ash, black willow, and sycamore in the fertile bottoms, a scattered understory of dogwood, witch hazel, hornbeam, spicebush, and sassafras, with cherries and red cedars on the hilltops, black alder and tupelo on the swamp edges, Atlantic white cedar in several aromatic and impenetrable stands, apples and tamaracks run wild, and maybe even a few half-mythical walnuts, basswoods, and American yews.

Nobody mapped out this forest in advance. Once the cutting stopped, it grew up in spite of our ham-handed solicitude. And yet I defy anyone to show how it might be improved in terms of variety, depth, color, vigor, and sheer overall bosky exuberance. All we have provided are its limits.

Today the Blue Hills function as an outdoor schoolroom, nature show, fitness center, love nest, berry pantry, bird collector, riding academy, hermitage, drinking spot, and leafy backdrop for several millions of people around greater Boston. Eliot's genius was to recognize that the time had arrived in this part of the world when trees were more valuable simply to look at than for anything else. We don't need the firewood; we can get charcoal elsewhere. "Nature," however, is in short supply. It's becoming almost as scarce as rattlesnakes.

In recent years the Reservation managers have been less quick to intervene in the regrowth of the Hills. They let the gypsy moth do its worst. They don't burn fallen timber. When the hilltops catch fire they don't always put them out. And they have stopped planting as well. Here and there, deep in the woods, you can find a few young and forlorn-looking spruces and red pines, offspring of the thousands introduced long ago, but they're not native here and they don't compete well — their prospects are dim.

Eliot probably wouldn't have approved of these policies. Despite his laissez-faire attitude toward reseeding, he was a landscape architect, not a naturalist, and saw no particular wisdom in a hands-off approach. In fact, he argued strenuously against it, recommending that the old fields still extant among the skirts of the Hills be kept open by regular mowing and pasturing: "If the reservations are left to Nature, monotony will follow." Though he lived in a time when forests had not yet reclaimed most of small-farm New England, he still echoed the dismay his Puritan ancestors felt at the green walls surrounding their clearings: "Nature, indeed, is constantly striving to abolish even the meager existing variety." Fifty years had gone by since Emerson's and Thoreau's joint announcement that wildness is sacred; he didn't agree.

But I don't think Eliot would be disappointed to see what's become of the Hills. They are still open to the public. Thousands invade them on summer weekends. And even his less obvious legacy, his sense that Nature can't be trusted to become natural on its own, is reflected in the militant environmentalism of the Reservation's current guardians, the state Department of Environmental Protection and the Massachusetts Audubon Society. In their view Nature is not merely a sort of garden in the rough, ready to be trimmed and trained into a delectable series of all-weather pictures, but instead a living, breathing goddess lying in a ditch and smudged all over with dirty fingerprints — common decency, if nothing else, demands intervention.

Is this reasonable? If the Blue Hills achieved perfection before we arrived, are we likely to improve them? Words like "pristine," "unspoiled," and "virgin" — the eroticism of the preservationists — are coming more and more to refer to places that are as heavily monitored, managed, graded, inventoried, and amortized as any oil field or chemical plant. The "wildest" of animals — the great cats, the great apes, whales, crocodiles, and grizzly bears — have been so reduced and restricted that their remaining populations, dependent on game wardens and international law, are about as splendid and savage as a Vermont dairy herd. Clearly, then, when we put aside a piece of land and disallow certain uses we are not doing any different than we did before. No, we are merely casting our net wider, asserting our control in even stronger terms, declaring ourselves essential to that very "Nature" we once defined by our absence. But we would laugh at any artist who tried to paint himself out of his pictures.

There are now approximately five times as many people living around the Blue Hills as in Eliot's day. The old farm-woodlot patchwork has vanished under a glossier mosaic of subdivisions, office parks, and greenspace. The towns along 128 are what the growth planners call saturated, meaning that they no longer have enough loose pieces of open land to support further development on the prevailing mammoth, car-happy scale. If you want to build a shopping mall, a planned community, or just an oversize parking lot you have to retreat another ten miles to Route 495, the next beltway out, which rumbles all the way from Cape Cod to New Hampshire. Many American cities are now encircled by two or more of these eight-lane notochords; they've been compared to the growth rings on a tree.

But if you don't want to build anything, if you just want to get a close look at what already happens to exist, you don't have to drive anywhere. You can go to the Blue Hills.

It's late summer. In the deep woods three months have passed since any direct sun reached the ground. Silence, moist heat, and a million-stemmed blizzard of greenery; lime-colored algae on damp tree trunks and big, spongy mushrooms pushing up through dead leaves. Maybe a catbird stops by to look you over, a fat spider in its beak. Flies crawl knowledgeably over a fresh heap of horse turd. *Crotalus* is here — somewhere, anywhere.

This is "Nature," correct? The old Mother, the Redeemer, all the things that keep happening when nobody's looking. You are asked to walk softly here — no fires, no feces, no beds made of pine boughs, no lolling naked in the brooks. You are asked, in fact, to pretend that you barely exist — that this is a sort of church that threw you out long ago. But is that what it is?

Several mosquitoes bumble out of the shin-high sarsaparilla. A thread-waisted wasp scurries here and there on the trail, its rear end bobbing obscenely. Why did you stop? Why are you listening?

The trees stand like a crowd of silent, tireless dreamers. They shut out the sky; they clutch buried rock.

No, it's not them you came to see — they are merely the setting, the means, the strangeness that promises clarity — it's yourself that fascinates you, the suspense that looks out of your eyes. You are here also — that's the remarkable thing.

Up the slope a cascade of rough, dark-colored boulders shows through the lush, rainy green.

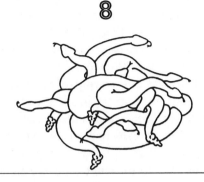

# Primitive War

I have never been happier, more exhilarated, at peace, rested, inspired, and aware of the grandeur of the universe and the greatness of God than when I find myself in a natural setting not much changed from the way He made it.

All of a sudden, behind me, Rosalynn began screaming in obvious terror.

— Jimmy Carter, *An Outdoor Journal* (1988)

True or false:

    A. Everybody likes wildlife.

    B. Rattlesnakes are wildlife.

    C. Everybody likes rattlesnakes.

False, obviously. Try this, then:

    A. God made the world, and saw that it was good.

    B. The world includes rattlesnakes.

    C. God made rattlesnakes, and saw that they were good.

You could get an argument about that, too. One more:

    A. All needless suffering is evil.

    B. Rattlesnakes cause needless suffering.

    C. Rattlesnakes are evil.

Here, at last, common sense, logic, and prejudice agree.

Once upon a time there were plenty of rattlesnakes around Boston. There was plenty of everything: all the early reports emphasized streams stuffed with fish, woods bursting with game, and skies black with fowl. This was the New World, the land of fantastic wealth and endless horizons. Even William Bradford, the first governor of Plymouth Colony and perhaps the most circumspect and unenthused Yankee of all, had to admit that the *Mayflower* party had planted themselves, not in a vacuum, but in a "hideous and desolate wilderness full of wild beasts and wild men." *Full of*, he says. And why not?

The Plymouth farmers immediately set about beating back the excess. Their job isn't finished today. Snake murder, for instance, is one of the most time-honored methods of carrying on the great work. In the words of the Texas folklorist J. Frank Dobie: "I grew up understanding that a man even halfway decent would always shut any gate he had opened to go through and would always kill any rattlesnake he got a chance at."

Who kills snakes? More accurately, who doesn't? If we limit ourselves to our public men (not our betters, as we know, but our quintessence), we have, besides President Carter:

Ben Franklin: "In some of the uninhabited Parts of these Provinces, there are Numbers of these venomous Reptiles we call RATTLESNAKES; Felons-convict from the Beginning of the World: These, whenever we meet them, we put to Death."

Thomas Jefferson: "There is in man as well as brutes an antipathy to the snake, which renders it a disgusting object wherever it is presented." (Not an outright confession, but suspicious.)

Teddy Roosevelt: "We killed several of the gray, flat-headed, venomous things; as we slept on the ground, we were glad to kill as many as possible."

And, in our own back yard, Henry Adams: "To me the whole show has a weird effect of not knowing what to make of itself, as though it were one of those harmless snakes that we used to kill by striking with a stick in the back."

Instances are equally abundant among writers. John Burroughs, gentlest of naturalists, once saw a black racer swallow a catbird nestling. He slaughtered the snake. In *Esquire* magazine, the poet James Dickey admitted to a fondness for spitting diamondbacks through the head with a blowgun. And in perhaps the most perfect writerly exploit of all, Marjorie Kinnan Rawlings once smashed a cottonmouth dead in her bathroom with a copy of her best seller, *The Yearling*.

But this is a long way from the Blue Hills. I don't mean to suggest that there are no circumstances in which it isn't proper and even obligatory to kill a snake. But what are they exactly?

It's been quite a while since this question had a chance to become important around Boston. By the time of the Revolution *Crotalus* was already in full retreat. Thoreau gives no evidence that he ever saw one in Concord; he probably had a better opportunity in Canton, directly under Great Blue, where he taught school for a summer, but mentions none there either. Charles Henry Dana, author of *Two Years Before the Mast*, was born in Cambridge in 1815 but had to sail around Cape Horn before he saw his first *Crotalus*, probably *C. ruber* or *C. viridis;* while living on the beach at San Diego he dispatched them by the dozen and collected their rattles as trophies. He described their warning buzz in detail, comparing it to the sound made by the "letting off of steam from the small pipe of a steamboat," as if his readers at home had no occasion to know it. A few years later, when Oliver Wendell Holmes, holder of the chair of anatomy at Harvard Medical School, became interested in rattlesnakes, he sent all the way to the Berkshires for one.

So it appears that if *Crotalus* was ever widespread in this area, he was no longer so by 1800, or about two centuries after the snake killers debarked. Did he melt away like the Massachuset? Was he provoked to war and then crushed? Exactly how much work was required to eject him?

In 1674 John Josselyn — like Thomas Morton, an English adventurer with royalist sympathies — reported a surprise meeting with *Crotalus* in his *Two Voyages to New-England*. It occurred at the back door of Long's tavern in Charlestown, just over the river from Boston. He and one Captain Jackson watched a four-and-a-half-foot snake "as thick in the middle as the small of a man's leg" swallow a live chicken. This monster might be more convincing if it wasn't "spotted with black, russet, yellow, and green, placed like scales" — a formula lifted verbatim from an account published by William Wood forty years earlier, in 1634. But Josselyn spent most of his time in the Scarborough region of Maine and so probably didn't get much opportunity to see warmth-loving rattlesnakes. And as he meant to become the chief authority on the natural marvels of New England, he undoubtedly felt obliged to describe *Crotalus,* who was already a legend in old England and rumored to "flye upon [a man] and sting him so mortally that he will dye within a quarter of an houre." Josselyn claimed that these vipers attacked with their tails, scorpion-fashion, and that their venom stung "worse than a satyr's whip." He also reported that porcupines lay eggs, an observation never since verified.

But this chicken-eating Charlestown rattler, perhaps a native of Bunker Hill, may have had a basis in fact, Josselyn's literary crimes notwithstanding. Charlestown, originally called Mishawum, was the first home of the infant Massachusetts Bay Company on this side of the Atlantic. The Company held several sessions of its Court of Assistants there in the summer of 1630. It wasn't until October that Governor Winthrop and his advisors ferried the government and charter a mile or so across to the knobby Shawmut peninsula, which they named Boston. The histories attribute this move to the lack of good water in Charlestown — there was only one spring, and the tides covered it twice a day; several deaths had already been charged to it. But Shawmut had other merits. According to the aforementioned William Wood, who had reason to know, it was free of "the three great annoyances of wolves, rattlesnakes, and mosquitoes." It's a fact that Winthrop worried about *Crotalus.* In the summer months, as he confessed to his journal (modestly titled *History of New England*) in 1631, he always carried some snakeweed in his pocket — a common herb, species unknown, that was reputed to be the only help for a bite. Is it possible that he found Charlestown a little too snakey? Was *Crotalus* the straw that tipped him against it? If so, then we should take down the sacred cod at the statehouse and put up a rattler, since it's thanks to *Crotalus* that Boston is Boston, and not Charlestown.

No doubt I am inflating my hero. But I think the evidence will show that there was a time when nearly every Bostonian concerned himself with *Crotalus,* if only to destroy him on sight.

In the first several years of its existence the Bay Colony absorbed about two thousand immigrants, most of them necessarily farmers.

There wasn't room for them all in Boston; though they gathered there to hear services on the Sabbath, they needed more land for themselves and their animals than the peninsula's few hundred acres could offer. And so settlements sprang up almost overnight at nearby Roxbury, Dorchester, Mattapan, Cambridge, and Watertown. The much smaller and weaker colony at Plymouth, although ten years older, proved much less dynamic.

The good farmland occurred mostly in pockets. Boston sits atop an old and partly drowned volcanic basin characterized by a variety of ancient rock types partly blanketed by glacial debris. This debris — mostly clay, grit, and boulders — blocked up the old drainage, creating numerous swamps, and buried whatever soils the ice didn't scrape out. As a result, there weren't many spots where an ox team could pull a plow more than ten yards in a line. Most had already been cleared by the Massachuset. This situation so annoyed the new tenants that hundreds decamped as soon as possible, trekking through the wilderness to the rich alluvial bottoms of the Connecticut River valley.

But the same conditions that pinched English farmers put *Crotalus* at ease. He didn't mind if the ice had scraped the high ground to bedrock, leaving it naked at a thousand outcrops and ledges; that meant easy access to the kind of subsurface cracks he required to escape freezing. Today he survives nowhere north of New Jersey without the help of exposed rock. In the swampy tidewater of Virginia and southward he can weather the cold months in old stumps and muskrat holes, alligator-style; there he doesn't have to reckon with New England winters.

Boston proper was built on and around three drumlins — whaleback hills made of clay, sand, and gravel. There's no rock in these ice-molded dunes, and it's probably no accident that there were no rattlesnakes either. But there's plenty of harder stuff in the immediate vicinity, much of it right at the surface: the puddingstones of Newton and Roxbury, the quartzites and volcanics of Dorchester and Mattapan, and the marine slates of Somerville and Chelsea. It stands to reason that if these exposed rocks were not eminently suitable as rattlesnake havens, then the Bay Company Puritans would not have gotten to know *Crotalus* as soon as they did.

How long did it take? We have noted that the governor regularly carried snakeweed eighteen months after his arrival. Unfortunately he neglects to say where, if anywhere, he encountered snakes. William Wood, Josselyn's source, is more specific; he lists those places where *Crotalus* was *not* met with, as if that were the exception: Shawmut Neck, Plymouth, Newtown (Cambridge), Agawam (Ipswich), and Nahant. The last is a rocky islet; all the others are low lying and covered with glacial drift and outwash — good for sand pits, bad for rattlesnakes. Wood was aware of the link between *Crotalus* and bare ledges, and was the first to notice it in print: "These creatures in the winter time creep into clefts of rocks or into holes underground where they live close until May or June."

His findings appeared in *New England's Prospect,* an account of Massachusetts published in London in 1634, when the colony was not yet five years old. Little is known about its author. Apparently Wood landed at Salem in 1629 with Endecott's advance party and stayed until 1633, the year smallpox all but annihilated the remaining Massachuset Indians. Maybe he didn't like Puritan discipline; maybe he wanted to see Virginia and the Barbadoes. But he is by far the best early writer on *Crotalus* and much else, less slapdash than Morton and not so excitable as Josselyn.

Wood doesn't say how many rattlesnakes he ran into. He does mention a Rattlesnake Hill "westward from the plantations" — unfortunately one of the few features not included on the map published with his book. There's a Rattlesnake Hill outside Boston (there are several around the state) but it's in the eastern Blue Hills, due south of town. Since Watertown, on the Charles River, was the westernmost settlement at the time, he may have meant Prospect Hill in Waltham, where, he reports, there was "great store" of rattlers. None live there today.

But if he didn't count snakes, he did count snakebites: in four years, he says, *Crotalus* poisoned five or six men, several cows, and a mare. That may not seem like much, but it's a lot. Today, when there are a thousand times as many people around Boston, there are a thousand times fewer bites. The total for the last two hundred years, in fact, doesn't match that for the first four.

So either the Puritan fathers were remarkably unlucky or there were many more chances for accidents back then — in other words, many more snakes.

*Crotalus* haters might argue that the reptiles had to be exterminated to make the area habitable — that they *were* removed is beyond dispute — but the truth is that large numbers of people and rattlesnakes coexisted here for generations before the new order arrived. Current estimates suggest that as many as ten thousand Massachuset Indians lived around Boston Harbor in 1600, on the eve of the plagues. Despite large families and repeated waves of immigrants, it took the Puritans years to recover that number. Maybe the Massachuset understood that lots of snakes meant fewer rats and mice to eat up their corn, beans, and pumpkins. At any rate, it's obvious that if they had wanted to wipe out *Crotalus,* they had the means. Instead, it was they who were wiped out.

No rattlesnakes lived in the southern English counties, where most of the colonists came from. Neither were there any bears, lynxes, lions, or eagles. The last English wolf died around 1500; it seems that Englishmen, in contrast with the Massachuset, didn't believe that small farms and large wild animals went together. Maybe this was because they depended heavily on domestic stock — easy prey for skilled predators. The Massachuset had only dogs.

Whatever the reason, as soon as the colonists got ashore they put into action a sort of eleventh commandment aimed at wildlife: Kill everything. In almost no time the natural bounty the first reports had celebrated, and which the Massachuset had somehow enjoyed beyond memory, ebbed back over the horizon.

Beaver and mink, mainstays of the fur trade, vanished in an instant. The great auk, a kind of penguin, and the sea mink, perhaps a clam eater, exited in tandem; they are now extinct. Turkeys were rare by 1670. In 1727 Nantucketers complained that they saw no more whales off their shores. That same year settlers on the upper Neponset, which arcs around Great Blue, sought legal action against mill owners downstream; the dams had cut off the alewives, once an annual bonanza. It seemed that the region's legendary abundance was indeed becoming a legend.

There was no conspiracy here, no mapped-out plan of attack, but merely a habit of mind wherein each pioneer imagined that the world was his oyster. And it was glorious, no doubt, to make something rise out of nothing — to see the forest give way to light, to nail a wolf hide to a doorpost, to drive a herd into a new meadow.

In such circumstances a peculiarly native set of attitudes had their origin.

But for *Crotalus* it was the worst moment since the glaciers. Because for the next two hundred years, or until New Englanders finally and reluctantly gave up the land — the land that brought so few of them wealth — nearly every square inch of his turf in eastern Massachusetts was going to belong to someone, someone who most likely lived on the spot, worked outdoors, and had little choice but to squeeze whatever sustenance he could from his stony allotment. In other words, this land was going to be occupied, most of it occupied more heavily and conscientiously and stubbornly than it ever would be again. And during that time there would be no Metropolitan Park System, no patchwork of state forests, no parcels set aside for large reptiles to hide in. No, it would just be him, *Crotalus*, and his hard-pressed landlords, each of whom would have the power of God.

# 9

# Joe Blow and Jake the Snake

In severest winters, after deep snows, the crow ventures near
the abodes of man.

— Reverend Albert K. Teele, *The History of
Milton, Mass., 1640–1887* (1888)

Everyone needs enemies. It's easier to get along without friends
than to give up the ill-wishers and their cunning disguises. Life
isn't perfect; they are to blame.

What makes a good enemy? First of all, he should hate you. He
should be swollen with resentment — he should shiver outside in
the cold while you sit down to eat. If you smile, he winces; if you
laugh, he chokes. There's something about you. He can't stand it.

Preferably he'll be not much like you and your loved ones. This
is necessary to avoid confusion. But he's not a stranger; he cares.
It's vital to him that he succeeds against you. And if you don't
smoke him out, he will.

Who is the enemy? In my lifetime we have had corporate execu-
tives, ghetto hoods, secret communists, Asian peasants, Kremlin
masterminds, homosexuals, turbaned mullahs, and various kooks,
microbes, and tropical drugs. The enemy is nothing if not protean.

How do you deal with an enemy? What a question! You don't
turn your back — you stand up and hack him. If there was any

doubt before, it vanishes. If you're beating him bloody, what else could he be?

Of course it's always possible to delude oneself, to make an enemy where there was none before. Better that, however, than to do without. Let the world know what it means to annoy you. Sometimes one enemy hides under cover of another; sometimes it's useful to pretend as much.

Above all, make sure all those you attack are defeated. Who they are isn't so important.

I only go into this because it seems to me that the campaign against *Crotalus* was pursued far beyond victory. It's as though once it got started it became an end in itself.

Rattlesnakes have relatives overseas, some of them dangerously venomous, and so it was *Crotalus*'s misfortune that the Puritan cultural tradition happened to include an ancient anathema exemplified in the Genesis story: snakes are eternally damned to war with mankind. If you think that the Massachusetts Bay Company's leaders, many of them university graduates, were too sophisticated for this kind of thinking, listen to Governor Winthrop (from his journal for July 5, 1632):

> At Watertown there was (in the view of divers witnesses) a great combat between a mouse and a snake; and, after a long fight, the mouse prevailed and killed the snake. The pastor of Boston, Mr. Wilson, a very sincere, holy man, hearing of it, gave this interpretation: That the snake was the devil; the mouse was a poor, contemptible people, which God had brought hither, which should overcome Satan here, and dispossess him of his kingdom.

If a cat had been observed battling a rat, would the cat have been recruited into the struggle between God and Satan, and identified with the latter? I doubt it. I suspect he might have remained merely a cat.

In 1987, 250 years later, *Crotalus* was still being credited with underworld connections by people you might expect to know better. In January *The New York Times Magazine* published a piece by Warren Sloat, author of *1929: America Before the Crash*, recounting his epoch-making struggle with a demon rattler at his grandfather's farm in Forkston, Pennsylvania.

Here are the facts: Sloat, then fifteen, encountered a small rattlesnake in the woods near the house. He found a stick, crouched down, and beat the snake to death. Nothing to brag about, you might think, and yet Sloat turns the incident into a triumphal rite of manhood and claims that as a result of his steely performance he lost his baby fat, became a formidable athlete, and found success with the ladies: "Never before had I known so sweet an hour."

Of course any heroic combat requires a worthy antagonist, and so the snake's eyes are made to glitter with "emerging hatred" and a "ruthless sense of revenge" — years later, the author says, the animal "still yawns and licks his pungent teeth in the grasses of my undying memory." Here we have the classic Stalinist tactic of transforming one's victim into an impossible monster so that his murder can be passed off as simple justice.

I'm not suggesting that there's anything criminal about killing rattlesnakes. But is snake bludgeoning really a moral imperative? Is that what gives it its kick?

At any rate, there's evidence that Pastor Wilson's affirmation of the snake-Satan link didn't go unheeded by his parishioners. As early as 1713 Thomas Walduck, a colonial official and correspondent of England's first association of scientists, the Royal Society, was able to report that "a man may live there [New England] 20 Years now & not see one [*Crotalus*]." Apparently a crusade was in progress, a crusade already far advanced. Walduck noted that rattlers disappeared wherever the English settled, and proposed the curious theory that they were wiped out by their own poisons. There was a root, it seems, that the snakes had to swallow after every meal, an antidote to the venom they introduced into their prey, and since English farming practices destroyed this root, *Crotalus* was helpless against his own juices — fit end for a villain!

One wonders why Walduck overlooked the obvious explanation, that snakes became scarce because they were sought out and killed.

A year earlier the Royal Society had received another letter from New England, this one by that celebrated Puritan witch-hunter and dervish Cotton Mather, and it contained a much more likely clue to *Crotalus*'s malaise:

> The Rattle-snakes have their Winter-habitations on our Hills, in hideous Caves, and the Clefts of Inaccessible Rocks. In the Spring they come forth, and ly a Sunning themselves, but still in pretty

feeble circumstances. Our Trained Bands in some of our Countrey towns, take this time, to carry on a *War* with the *Snakes,* and make the killing of them, a part of their Discipline.

Here we have the first mention of that practice which is still the most effective means of ridding northerly climates of rattlesnakes: slaughter at the dens. Walduck gives no impression that he ever actually saw a rattler; this is probably why.

Recent tagging studies in New York and elsewhere have demonstrated what has long been suspected, that *Crotalus* returns to the same stony retreats year after year. He doesn't find them by accident; it's believed that he follows scent trails laid down weeks and even months earlier, when he and his denmates dispersed out into the countryside. Newborn rattlers will follow these trails, making it likely that they'll enter the same dens as their relatives. It is thought that if a snake can't locate these invisible threads in the fall, he becomes helpless; he will wander erratically until he freezes, or at best takes shelter in an unmarked crevice that may or may not offer the right wintering conditions. In this way every snake becomes attached to a specific den site, the best ones concentrating the bulk of any given population.

The Puritan farmers soon discovered, as Reverend Mather makes clear, that the most effective way to keep rattlers out of the hayfields in July was to go to the dens in May and kill as many as possible. During that time they are aggregated, conspicuous, and vulnerable. Thanks to *Crotalus*'s low reproductive potential a series of annual raids on a site stands a good chance of wiping out all but the stragglers, or even emptying it completely. It is a remarkable fact that wherever in Massachusetts you find a named feature such as Rattlesnake Hill, Rock, or Ledge, you will find no rattlesnakes. Apparently wherever they were obvious enough to become eponymous, they were too obvious to survive.

This strategy doesn't work well against snakes in Florida, Texas, and the Southwest, where winters are warm enough to allow rattlers to hole up in a variety of locations. There they have to be massacred piecemeal, and are more likely to persist in undeveloped areas.

But here in the North they are vulnerable — even in the mountains there are not that many south-facing ledges that are both clear of trees and fractured correctly — and so long-term pressure often ends in extermination. Most of the snakes that remain have been isolated for generations in a few favorable spots.

By about 1700, then, *Crotalus*'s two-legged enemies had discovered his weak points and mobilized to destroy him. Mather's "Trained Bands" — later famous as the minutemen — were probably the least of the story; all anyone needed to become hell on snakes was a stout stick, a little righteous enthusiasm, and a free afternoon. There were no professional hunters, at least to begin with — *Crotalus* grease, father to the expression "snake oil," although widely used as a liniment, was neither so scarce nor so precious that it could support full-time collectors. It's more likely that snake bashing was a strictly local and amateur pastime, pursued fitfully by men and boys in small groups and decreasing in popularity as the snakes themselves vanished.

And so this legendary monster fades from view in a hundred long-ago springtimes — warm, balmy days when the colonial farmers, their hired men, and their boys left the fields and paddocks and tramped up to the rock faces for a few hours of mayhem. Perhaps a favorite dog had died mysteriously the previous year; maybe a neighbor had shown off a particularly lengthy string of rattles; all we know for certain is that there were more than enough snake killers for the available snakes, and that where the fathers found dozens, the sons found ones and twos, and the grandsons none at all. Where *Crotalus* survived, the war continued; where he did not, he was forgotten. Satanic or not, he claimed few victims of his own.

By 1800 *Crotalus* was more or less forgotten throughout New England. Its remaining wilderness, northern Maine, was too cold for him; everywhere else he had been driven out of sight. With independence a new attitude toward the American landscape had emerged, a combination of pride, rationalism, and high hopes exemplified by Jefferson's *Notes on the State of Virginia* (1785). In books of this type written by Yankees — Ira Allen's *Natural and Political History of the State of Vermont* (1798) and Timothy Dwight's (1821) *Travels in New England and New York* (both men, like Jefferson, founders or presidents of universities) — *Crotalus* is mentioned only to be dismissed as a relic, absent from settled areas and of no particular concern to anyone. In low-lying eastern Massachusetts, cleared and occupied for over a century, it would be easy to assume he was gone.

But if we ignore the accounts of eminent men and look into the humble, anonymous records of the various backwater towns, we find that *Crotalus* was still hanging on here and there. Many of these communities, apparently irritated by his persistence, offered bounties on his life. The awards, though fairly high, made nobody rich. It seems the town officials were confident that no one would show up with eleven thousand pounds of snakes, the amount turned in at the 1988 annual rattlesnake roundup at Sweetwater, Texas.

These bounty records provide a rough guide to the places around Boston where rattlesnakes could still be found in the eighteenth and early nineteenth centuries. Allowances must be made for changed boundaries — Dorchester, for instance, once stretched all the way to Rhode Island, and Stoughton included the modern towns of Sharon and Canton, and thus a slice of Great Blue — but for the most part it's not difficult to identify the sensitive areas. Can we assume that towns offering bounties still had snakes in them? I think so. In many cases tallies were made of rattles brought in for payment (the rattle and about an inch of tail were considered equivalent to a whole snake).

The 1700s were the golden age of bounties in Massachusetts. Nearly every town was a farm town, dependent on its own corn, sheep, and chickens, and dozens of them offered rewards for animal raiders, ranging from a few pence for blackbirds and woodchucks to a pound or more for wolves and bobcats. The larger entity, the commonwealth, didn't bother with these robbers, but it did offer a much more generous prize, a prize often left out of its histories: £100 for the scalp of an adult male Maine Indian, £50 for the same hair and skin from a woman or child. Bounties still exist; recently the local CBS affiliate reported that street gangs in the Franklin Hill projects have offered $1,000 for any Boston police officer killed on their turf.

*Crotalus* never earned any such premium. The most ever paid for him, as far as I can determine, was one shilling sixpence, or about the price of a quart of rum, offered by Dorchester in 1785. Dorchester has since been swallowed by Boston; at the time, however, it included Hyde Park and Readville, places where rattlers were seen as late as the early 1900s, only a mile or two from the Blue Hills — it was probably a Blue Hills population that this bounty was aimed at.

At the other end of the scale, the lowest award on record was offered by Stoughton in 1834, fifty cents, down from a dollar in 1808. Since prices in general declined by about the same proportion during the interval, I suspect that the change is a simple adjustment rather than an economy measure; 1834 is the last year a bounty is recorded anywhere around Boston. By then snakes were probably too scarce to stir up town meetings.

Although the earliest bounties came from a variety of locations — Worcester, North Brookfield, Dedham, Medfield, and Westborough — by 1750 they have all vanished except in communities adjacent to the Blue Hills: Stoughton, Canton, Milton, and Dorchester. Here they continue for another seventy-five years or so, suggesting that the Blue Hills snakes were more elusive and troublesome than most. In 1771 William Shaller of Stoughton brought in sixty-four rattles; at a shilling apiece they were worth more than £3, or the retail equivalent of fifteen gallons of rum — a haul like this made snake hunting worth its while. Three years earlier, in 1768, Joseph Billings of Canton killed fifty-eight; he celebrated by drinking his lunch at May's tavern. Despite this carnage, in 1793 the Stoughton town meeting found it necessary to pass a motion directing the selectmen to write to the neighboring towns containing snake dens "to see what action might be taken to destroy them." Whether or not any action was taken, in 1808 a woman named Polly Billings was bitten in the Randolph Woods a few miles away.

Clearly the strategies pursued elsewhere — slaughter at the dens by local farmers, militia companies, and bounty hunters — were not as immediately effective in and around the Blue Hills, though not for lack of effort. The reason, perhaps, is that the Hills, seven miles long and oriented east-west, offer a greater continuous rampart of sunny, south-facing ledges than can be found anywhere east of the Connecticut River valley. To get at these potential den sites, snake killers had to either climb over the range from the north or wade in through the swamps along the Blue Hill River — a small stream that skirts the Hills' southern foot and now stitches back and forth through culverts under 128 — minor difficulties, but perhaps significant. At any rate, it's a fact that the area where *Crotalus* proved toughest to evict in colonial times is the only one where he survives today.

Why did the bounties dry up? Around the Blue Hills they peaked in the period immediately following the Revolution, and after 1800 they disappeared quickly. It would be tempting to blame the decline in the farm economy and the abandonment of the land resulting from the building of railroads, the opening of the West, and the local shift toward manufacturing — bounties, in this sense, could be seen as relics from New England's still-luminous pastoral age — but these towns, barely twenty miles from Beacon Hill, never suffered the wholesale outmigrations typical of the more remote uplands. Milton, for instance, more than doubled in population between 1800 and 1900, with similar increases in Quincy and Stoughton. And bounties survived modernity elsewhere: West Haven, Vermont, paid them well after World War II, and Tioga County, Pennsylvania, spent about $1,200 annually between 1960 and 1975 for *Crotalus* rattles at a dollar apiece (the latter ordinance was instituted in 1949 with the argument that fewer snakes would make Tioga more attractive to tourists and home buyers).

No, it's much more reasonable to suppose that bounties disappeared around the Blue Hills for the same reasons as elsewhere — because rattlesnakes either were wiped out completely or became so scarce that no one bothered to worry about them. In other words, the awards succeeded.

And so ends the heyday of *Crotalus* in eastern Massachusetts. What a narrow thread he hangs by! Two hundred years of persecution, an entire cultural tradition of outrageous libels, enemies multiplying like rabbits, and he has not yet had to face pesticides, herpetologists, superhighways, and park rangers armed with six-guns.

But we will leave him here for the moment, at about 1825 — obscure, defeated, and cut off from his kin. Another century must pass before anyone will think of mourning him. In the meantime we'll step aside and look at some of the other victims of life who chose, and still choose, to hide out in the Hills.

## 10

# Why Calvin Grith Doesn't Live in the Woods

It is very unhappy, but too late to be helped, the discovery we have made that we exist.

— Ralph Waldo Emerson, "Experience" (1844)

From about noon until sundown in good weather, the solitary walker in certain parts of the Hills is startled to find a stranger staring at him. This stranger customarily stands by the side of the trail, or a little distance off into the woods, or, if above treeline, atop a knob or slab of bare rock. He is male. He wears street clothes. He is usually under forty. And though he stands with his arms crossed or akimbo, he looks anything but relaxed. He is frozen, rooted in place, as if facing terrible penalties for the slightest carelessness.

His only freedom is his eyes. These stare nakedly into the walker's as he approaches. They never relent. They collect and concentrate everything that is forbidden expression. If the walker, unsettled by their intensity, attempts to distract them with a nod or a greeting, he gets no response. He feels, in fact, as if he has broken a taboo — as if his small gesture, so ordinary elsewhere, is here expressly prohibited. Sometimes the stranger's eyes flicker slightly. Sometimes, in rare instances, he will actually nod back, but the nod has a forced, involuntary quality, like the grunt following a blow to the gut.

Once the walker has encountered one of these strangers, he usually sees others. They are scattered through the woods near the road, standing at turns in the paths or loitering in hollows between boulders. The road itself is lined with parked cars, many of them expensive and masculine: slate-gray BMWs and Mazdas, freshly washed and vacuumed Camaros and Blazers. Some of them contain a single occupant sitting low behind the wheel.

If the walker crosses the road and climbs up through the woods to one of the bare, rocky summits he will find another dozen or so men scattered across it, sometimes in a space no larger than a living room. Here again the regime is utter silence and searching, impenetrable glances. All that breaks the quiet is the occasional scratch of a lighter and, if the day is warm, the soft, greasy mutter of suntan oil on bare skin.

Maybe the walker resents having a favorite hilltop invaded by these grim and tongue-tied flirts. Maybe he thinks the dance of desire goes better with smiles and banter than with endless silences and stony stares. And maybe he'd prefer it if the woods down below weren't littered with candy-red Trojan wrappers and wads of old bathroom tissue. But the walker is mistaken if he thinks these strangers could care less whether he finds them annoying. They want him to leave; they're on serious business. They don't intend to smile, to make jokes, to exchange names. That's not what they're here for.

The Bay Colony Puritans put people to death for this kind of risk taking. They saw little alternative; they were commanded by God. A German, Johann Gutenberg, had thrown the holy ordinances into their laps — how could they not take them up? It was merciful, they thought, to kill the body for the hope of the soul.

Since then we have retired the hangmen but not the attitudes, and sin is as popular as ever. Hence the need for spots like the Hills. There's an emptiness here where people can make space for themselves, a little breathing room for those who need to operate on the sly: lunch-hour cocksmen, trash dumpers, firebugs, freelance woodcutters, illegal duck hunters, dope growers, and so forth. This isn't to say the Hills aren't policed; they are. But they include six thousand acres and no permanent residents.

Just under the southeast slope of Chickatawbut Hill, near where Route 28 crosses the Reservation between Milton and Randolph, there's a red maple swamp of about fifty acres. It's not remote or inaccessible. You can walk through it along a low dike that protects a natural-gas pipeline parallel to the road. It is, however, wet most of the year, and has a dense understory of sweet pepperbush, so that even in winter it's hard to see into.

Maple swamps are notoriously awkward to negotiate on foot. The trees stand a yard or so apart on mossy knobs made of their raised roots. The shrub layer also grows out of these knobs, so that stepping from one to the next, the most practicable course, means spending most of one's time clinging to bushes. In between the knobs, where the going is clearest, the surface drops another eighteen inches into a series of buckets that form the floor of the swamp. Though not particularly miry, these buckets contain water. The ice that forms in them isn't trustworthy. It's possible to slog from one bucket to the next, stepping over the roots and bulling through the greenbrier, but why bother? The swamps aren't large and are easy to skirt. Entering one usually means becoming almost exclusively concerned with getting out.

On a Sunday morning in August two years ago I was walking along the path over the pipeline when I noticed something odd in the swamp alongside: three or four soggy, half-rotted tree limbs lying flat in the mud and bridging the gap from the dike edge to the nearest tangle of roots. Farther in, another half-sunk fascicle connected these roots to the next clump beyond it. It seemed unlikely that this pattern was accidental. Someone had been making improvements.

I stepped down onto the bridge. Once away from the dike, the work became obvious — a fragmented but continuous chain of decayed limbs dragged together like toothpicks and set down over the soft spots. They made a rude, winding causeway into the thicket.

After a while, past a few more turns, the ground rose a little and the buckets filled in. The dead limbs gave way to a well-trodden path beaten into the moss. This was a surprise — a dry island in the middle of the swamp. The lush, glossy-leaved pepperbush grew densely here, too. I couldn't see more than a few yards in any direction.

I went on. It was clear that whoever built the trail had been using it recently; where it left the dike it was too inconspicuous to draw casual traffic. Apparently I had strayed into someone's private retreat. I made a point of being as quiet as possible.

The first sign of occupation was a knee-high mound of soggy newspaper beside the path. It looked as though someone had dumped several platefuls of dark, brownish oatmeal on top. It wasn't until I leaned down and sniffed that I realized the oatmeal was in fact shit and this was a privy.

About a yard past the newspapers, on the same side of the trail, was a heap of ballpoint and felt-tip pens nearly as high. There were hundreds of every variety. They had been rained on, many were capless, and some had leaked. I tried a few and found none that worked.

I don't know why I went on. It's a bad idea to creep up on anyone in the woods. I had seen no one, however.

One more turn and the path opened out into a large roomlike space walled in by pepperbush. Six or eight split-trunked maples grew up through it. It looked like a dump; dozens of soaking-wet blankets, sheets of plastic, heaps of clothes, and bloated garbage bags were scattered all over. Several buckets and pots half full of rainwater and drowned bugs hung from nails on the trees. Everything was open to the sky. Near the middle, in a sort of saddle between a pair of maples, lay the collapsed remains of a tent, now flush with the ground.

I began to breathe a little easier. Clearly this was the former tenant's center of operations. He had left behind an incredible mess.

I saw nothing I wanted. I poked around a little, stepping over debris. A collection of rain-heavy quilts and blankets sagged low on a web of clotheslines — it had poured the night before.

The tent was little more than a piece of rope strung between trees with a half-dozen plastic tarps draped over it. They were much shorter on one side; it looked as though the owner had slept with his head under the rope and his body stretched out under their lengths. The rope barely cleared the ground and the tarps looked like the covers of an unmade bed, with puddles of wet in the creases.

I went around to the front end. The whole outfit seemed to me more than a little pathetic. If you wanted to live like this I could see why you might need a good hiding place. Whoever camped here had brought in truckloads of junk but still hadn't kept out the rain.

Looking down, I saw a small hole or opening under the front of the tarps. The ground fell away there and left a little pocket of earth with a scrap of sun shining in it. In that pocket lay a book. The book was open on its spine and its pages were dry. While I watched, a stubby, reddish hand emerged from under the tarps, turned a page, and withdrew.

I took two quick steps back and started crashing through the bushes to the other side of the campsite. I didn't mind all the noise — I wanted to make noise, to make clear that I was leaving in a hurry. I didn't stop until I was all the way back at the dike.

From there I walked to the car and drove a couple of miles to the Metropolitan Police headquarters on Hillside Street, an old farm-house-style building with stables in back and a paddock across the street. Inside were three or four cops drinking coffee around the counter. I explained that there was a bum living in the swamp off Route 28 under Chickatawbut Hill and that he had filled it with garbage. It wasn't clear whether they knew about him or not. I left and went home. I'd had enough for the day.

I didn't call to ask about the result. I had heard that the police occasionally rousted squatters from out-of-the-way spots in the Hills, and I didn't envy them the task of dealing with this one. But whether they moved him or not, I felt less than comfortable with my own role in the business. The man had done me no harm. He wasn't camped on my front lawn. Granted, he was none too fastid-ious, but he had invested considerable time and effort in making a home for himself, a semipermanent hideout where he could enjoy the same freedom and solitude that attracted me to the Hills. And though he had turned it into a pigsty, I knew that that wasn't the reason I had gone to the cops. I had gone because he had scared me. I had allowed him to scare me — I had made it almost inevita-ble, creeping into his lair.

So it wasn't until the following November that I felt relaxed enough to reenter the swamp and see what, if anything, had be-come of his kingdom.

It was all gone. Though the causeway, the island, and the open space were intact, every scrap of cloth, paper, and plastic had vanished. Soft dead leaves matted the former floor of his living room. Dozens of tiny mushrooms speckled his empty middens. The only sign of his tenancy was in the saddle between the maples, where the earth was still smooth and compacted from the weight of his body.

I doubted he had made such a clean getaway on his own. Apparently the cops had dug both him and his mess out of the muck. I was glad they had done it. I was glad they had returned this place to its delicate, dark-watered self. But they hadn't quite gotten all of him. Something remained, something weightless and sad, like the ache that lingers in a hospital room on the morning after a death: the bed smooth and fresh-sheeted, the night table bare, the curtains open to the sky.

About a year later, in the course of research for this book, I was looking through a clipping file on the Blue Hills in a local library when I came across a front-page story about myself from the Quincy *Patriot Ledger,* though I received no mention in it.

## HERMIT CALLED BLUE HILLS SWAMP HIS HOME

### By Eric Sorensen

QUINCY, Sept. 3 — It's not much, this swamp.

But for 2½ years, Calvin Grith called it home.

Hard by Route 28 just south of the Milton line, in a brushy world where footprints quickly fill with water, Grith built a maze of paths covered with crude boardwalks of sticks and logs, say Blue Hills Reservation officials.

He slept beneath a well-camouflaged blanket-and-tarp structure strung from trees. He dug small holes in the ground for his drinking water, which he praised for its purity.

"He swore by it," said Reservation Interpreter Richard Kimball. "He said it was fine."

Kimball and Ross Tomlin, regional reservation supervisor, said the 56-year-old Grith, who was evicted last week by Metropolitan Police, was the second hermit found in the 6000-acre reservation in the past year. Tomlin said a third hermit may still be living in a remote section of the Metropolitan District Commission park.

Discovered last month, Grith initially told reservation workers that he had lived there for only a few weeks, said Tomlin.

"He said how cool autumn was and we said, 'You must mean last autumn,'" said Tomlin. "So when all was said and done, he had been there 2½ years."

Kimball, a former social worker who spoke extensively with him, said Grith would reveal little about his past while adamantly asserting his right to live in the woods.

"It's almost like he's withdrawn from society because he's so against the way we're running things," Kimball said.

Judging by the condition of his site, he said, Grith had lived in the area for years. Tree bark had begun to grow around the ropes he used to string up his shelter, he said, while piles of debris in the area — license plates, old tires and rims, toys, crude cooking materials — appeared to come from years of collecting.

Kimball said Grith went undiscovered all that time because the swamp off the Braintree Pass trail is so wet — his sleeping area was only inches above the water line — and because he caused no trouble. He apparently did not drink liquor and seemed to spend his time writing, observing the local wildlife, and collecting scores of items.

But last month, park rangers began noticing piles of debris and wondered where it could be coming from, Kimball said.

Police and reservation officials told Grith he had to leave because no camping is allowed in the park. They gave him time to cart away much of his belongings.

Last week, with much of his stuff still hidden in the swamp, Grith was led away in handcuffs. He was charged with trespassing and littering.

"We had no choice," said Metropolitan Police Patrolman Robert Daly. "Enough is enough."

Grith pleaded not guilty to the charges yesterday. He was released and a pretrial conference was scheduled for November.

Tomlin said Grith had told him he had nowhere to go but back to the park.

But police said Grith gave as an address the Boston Health and Hospitals shelter, run out of Boston City Hospital, when arrested last week by Patrolmen Paul Halpin and John Herbert.

And a shelter official this week said Grith frequently stayed at the shelter last winter, often for medical treatment for swollen legs.

Grith, located Tuesday near the hospital, declined to discuss for the record his stay in the park.

"I don't have much faith in human nature," the clean-shaven, balding Grith said as he collected cans and bottles in front of Blanchards Liquors on Northampton Street in Boston's South End. "The less said about anything, the better."

He declined to say where he is from, nor would he confirm having told Tomlin he lived in the Blue Hills for 2½ years.

Tomlin said MDC officials are concerned about people staying overnight in the park because of the legal ramifications of people living on the state-owned land.

"Of course we have a morbid fear that we'll have another Bill Britt," said Tomlin, referring to the self-styled hermit who spent eight years on MDC property in Chestnut Hill. State officials tore down Britt's "wigwam" and removed his belongings from the site in July.

Tomlin said park dwellers might also pose a threat to visitors and to the sensitive ecosystems in the area.

The reason I say the story is about myself is that I concluded, after checking my notes, that I had set it in motion. I discovered Grith on August 9; the story appeared September 3; it said that the police had first visited him several weeks earlier. And so, despite the claim that roadside debris had alerted them to his presence, it seemed more than coincidental that they'd unearthed him only days after my report, when they'd already had at least two years to do so. I hadn't seen any roadside debris; Grith had gone to considerable lengths to conceal himself. Maybe the police preferred not to confess that it had taken an amateur to clue them in. Maybe they already knew about Grith but had let him alone, thinking no one would notice. At any rate, I hadn't given my name, so it was equally possible that my contribution had been simply overlooked or forgotten.

I thought about taking advantage of the reporter's legwork and going down to City Hospital to see if I could locate Grith. I'd tell him who I was, ask if he remembered our encounter, and explain why I'd gone to the cops — though I didn't intend to apologize. I wanted him to know that I was by no means unsympathetic to his love for the woods, and to say that if he chose to set up elsewhere in the Hills and I happened across him, maybe the result would be different, particularly if he wasn't surrounded by ten tons of trash. I also wanted to know what he had seen and heard in his months in the swamp, and what sort of things he liked to read.

But I didn't go. The more I thought about it, the more lame seemed to me any approach I could make. Hadn't I brought him enough trouble? Judging from his remarks in the story, he wouldn't be happy to see me. I imagined catching up with him at a downtown soup kitchen or by the hot-air vents in back of the library, and having to stand and listen while he coughed out curses and a dozen other all-weather types looked at me with new interest. No, I wasn't that curious.

It's difficult, no doubt, to find a place around Boston where one can live in the open, heap up one's junk, pay no rent, and be left alone. Grith had found such a spot — he liked it so much that he was willing to get rained and snowed on for weeks on end, at the risk of his health, for the pleasure of keeping it. Why? What drove him out there? What did he find?

Bill Britt, the other hermit mentioned in the story, froze to death in his shelter at the Chestnut Hill Reservoir. He wasn't so secretive as Grith; he was expert, however, at creating sympathy for himself, and though arrested many times he always managed to get out and get home. The summer after his death I was issued a summons for trespassing at the same reservoir, having taken my two-year-old daughter over the low fence to the water's edge, and at my court date the officer who nabbed me told me that Britt, although famous around town, had always lived much to himself, and had been dead for nearly a week before he was discovered, giving the local rats time to get at him.

We were at the courthouse all morning — I and two others, both Boston University students, paid $50 in court costs apiece — and while there I also learned that the four of us would probably never have met if a wealthy woman living in a Newton mansion overlooking the water hadn't spotted us that afternoon and called the police. Apparently our presence offended her, even though she would have needed a telescope to make out our faces.

Informants, policemen, courtrooms, boundaries, newspapers — just a few of the pitfalls that organize our landscape. It's a bad sign when anyone attempts to escape them — not so much for what it says about our system and its failures, but because those who are driven off don't prosper. It was a bad sign for *Crotalus* when he drew back to the Hills. It was a bad sign for Bill Britt when he decided to sleep out all winter. And it was a bad sign for Calvin Grith when he moved into the swamp. Anyone could evict him.

Even so, the outcast's resources — economy, fortitude, and invisibility — have a long history in the Hills. Forty years before the Civil War a small hut stood on the north side of Nahanton Hill, just up the slope from where Eliot's road now passes. It was occupied by a pair of undesirables known only as "the Frenchman and his wife." They lived without money, fishing in the brooks, gathering berries, and now and again stealing down to the then-common farms to grab chickens and whatever else came to hand. This went on for some years, thanks to their talent for stealth, but it ended abruptly. One day a party of men from Braintree trekked up past the ledges, located their hideout, and torched it.

In the 1960s the next hill over, Chickatawbut, was also recognized as prime bandit habitat, only in this instance the bad actors were to be brought in on purpose and marooned at the summit in something called the Center for Juvenile Offenders — a handful of cinderblock barracks formerly belonging to the Air Force's 3rd Missile Battalion. But word got out, and local opposition killed the scheme. Here the castoffs were ejected even before their arrival.

Clearly there is something about a sizable and close-at-hand patch of woods that convinces room seekers of every kind that they need look no farther. Countless expulsions haven't damaged this appeal. What was Grith's maple swamp if not a larger, freer version of the world he had left? In it all the property was his property, all the rules were his rules, and the sun itself rose just to shine on him. Maybe he didn't approve of the sort of people he ran into at the shelters downtown, but unlike the eagle-eyed lady in Newton, he couldn't order the police to get the riffraff out of his sight; he *was* the riffraff. And so he built his palace where money and policemen didn't go.

Are the Blue Hills really up for grabs? Can one go there, in Thoreau's phrase, to "live deep, and suck out all the marrow of life"? Yes, at least temporarily. Though it's illegal to spend even one unauthorized night on the Reservation, there's evidence throughout of more lengthy stays. On the exposed south-facing bluffs of Wolcott Hill, for instance, there's a sort of natural cellar-hole between two rock buttresses. At its bottom are some bed-clothes and firewood left by the last tenant. In the deep woods on the back side of Southeast Ridge there's a burrow or dugout tunneled into the slope and still cocooned in several layers of cloudy plastic, though it obviously hasn't been occupied for a while. Week-end campers typically produce a charred spot on the ground and a little brand-name debris. Most settlers probably don't stay for more than a week or two, and then only in good weather.

But the most considerable establishment I ever saw belonged to a tall, gaunt, and slightly crazed-looking individual who lived on the southwest slope of No Name Hill.

He chose his site carefully. It lies about a half mile from the nearest road, which is as out of the way as you can get in the Hills. It's well drained, tree-shaded, and within a hundred yards of a perennial brook. Most important, it's well hidden; it occupies a shelf or pocket of level ground partway up the slope of the hill. No sign of this pocket is visible from the trail that passes quite close underneath. Anyone walking by would think the slope continues upward until it breaks out in bare rock, as it does along the rest of the hill. And so even the off-path walker would be unlikely to discover it, since bushwhacking through the treelines usually means fighting through a zone of waist-high scrub oak as dense as steel wool and as stiff as upholstery springs — it saves trouble to cross the scrub only on trails, which are numerous enough.

I would never have learned of this pocket if I hadn't seen it on a topographical map. On my next visit to the area I took the map and a compass. This was in October; I was hunting for *Crotalus.* Just above the pocket were some steep ledges that looked promising.

I entered it from below. Before I was ten steps in, something a little distance ahead brought me up short: a narrow, gray-green Army-style tarp stretched taut over a roof cord and sheeted out at a gentle angle on either side, so that its peak was only a yard off the ground and it was open all around. The space underneath was packed with gear under plastic. All the leaf litter in front had been scuffed away. The oaks here were tall and well spaced and there was no underbrush.

This was after my encounter with Grith, and I had learned better manners, so I called out several times, even though I didn't think there was anyone home.

Suddenly a lean figure scrambled out from under the front of the tarp and stood up. He was over six feet tall and wore clean outdoor clothes. He was short-haired, stubbly-faced, and bareheaded. He stood with his arms at his sides and looked straight back at me, like a recruit called to order.

I didn't like this very much but it seemed too late to retreat. So I came up within talking distance and said something like, "Nice spot you got here" or "I wondered if there was anyone home." I tried to be very relaxed and low-key because it was obvious he was extremely tense — just looking at me seemed to tax him severely.

He held his head back slightly and stared, his eyes wide and straining, as if he couldn't quite get me in focus. He had too much on his mind to handle small talk. Every word he said emerged with difficulty. But somehow I got the idea that I had nothing to fear — all he wanted was to hold himself together until I left. Just the same, I didn't look around much or ask about his arrangements.

Before I left, I nodded up the slope and said that there might be snakes in the rocks and that I was looking for them, this being the right time of year. Then I asked if he'd seen any. He came down very definitely in the negative, so definitely that I wondered if what he really meant was, "You have absolutely no reason to be here." I said that I'd have a look anyway, smiled at him, and went on. As I was climbing the slope I glanced back and saw him standing in the same place, watching me. At last, just before the leaves filtered him out, he began moving around.

I didn't find any snakes on the ledges. I went out via the hilltop. Poor bastard, I thought, now he's wondering when the cops will arrive. But it would have been awkward to say I wasn't going to do anything.

A year later, again in October, I entered the pocket at the same place. I was curious to see what had become of his campsite. I also wanted to check out the ledges again.

He was still there. So was his spartan tarp shelter. I saw him standing in front by his woodpile.

We had almost the same conversation as before. I did all the talking, and the talk was only about snakes. He seemed even less comfortable than last time. I wanted to ask if he recognized me — I couldn't tell if he did — but he looked so bottled-up and spooky that I was afraid to be even the least bit familiar. Clearly he wasn't used to visitors. It was easy to imagine that he hadn't said a word since I saw him last. But he seemed to be in good shape otherwise. As I walked away, another crop of leaves loud under my feet, I thought, This is getting interesting.

I went again during a thaw early in March, five months later. It was a quiet, overcast day, the trees brown and bare, wet snow on the ground. It had occurred to me that I had seen him only in good weather.

This time I approached from another direction, across the slope. I was about fifty yards away when I saw his tarp, stopped, and called out. When he moved I saw him also. He had been standing out front.

He immediately began striding toward me. When he had covered about half the distance he stopped, his hands in the pockets of his large, worn-looking jacket.

"How's it going?" I called out.

He didn't answer. He looked like a big dog watching a mailman.

Something told me that it might be unwise to get any closer, so I skirted around him upslope, bypassing the pocket. He took a similar course, always staying between me and his camp. When I was under the ledges I turned and climbed straight up, not stopping until I was out of the trees and on top of the rocks. He pursued until he reached my tracks in the snow, then advanced a little farther. Now he was standing at the base of the ledge and peering up at me through the treetops, his face upturned and his eyes cold and aware. His gaze was peculiarly intent.

Come one step closer, I thought, and I'm out of here.

But he didn't move, and so I sat down on a dry rock and lit a cigarette. I was a little bit peeved, and as I happened to be getting over a head cold, I took out my handkerchief and gave him a couple of long, sonorous, foghorn-style blats that could have been heard all over the valley.

They seemed to break his concentration. He looked away and walked around a little, as if unsure what to do next. The wet snow clung to his boots; his ski cap hid his face. After a minute or two he turned and went back down toward his camp. I couldn't see that far; it was hidden under the trees. Apparently the meeting was over. I finished my smoke, blew a few parting blasts on my nose, and left.

Thinking about it later, I was able to find reasons why he might not want visitors. There was snow on the ground, there were hikers on the trails, and my tracks could give him away. Just the same, I felt as though I'd been run off by an expert. He seemed to know I could be counted on not to report him; he'd also apparently sensed I could be spooked. Therefore he saw no need to suffer through any more talk about snakes — the less said, the better.

I have no idea whether he actually did any thinking along these lines. What was clear, however, was that I had assumed that my knowledge of him, along with my willingness to keep it under wraps, gave me leave to drop in on him anytime. He'd shown me I had no such liberty.

I waited seven months until my next visit. Once again I came in *Crotalus* time, early October. It was two years since our first encounter.

He was gone. I stopped some distance away, incredulous — though I saw no sign of his tarp, I had gotten so used to meeting him there that I expected him to pop up out of nowhere. The space was empty, though — just a patch of level ground, a scattering of oaks, and a carpet of brown leaves.

At least, I thought, I can get a close look at it now.

He'd left the place in excellent condition. His hearth, a deep pit a yard square, had been filled in with dug-up rocks, the yellow earth still caked on them. His latrine, another pit, had been plugged with dirt. He hadn't burned all his firewood; it was piled up by the former entrance to his shelter. He had used dead snags only, cutting them with a chain saw at their base and dragging them back whole. There were plenty still standing by the campsite, apparently reserved for emergencies. A small, almost unnoticeable mound with a couple of old garbage bags showing through suggested a trash dump, but I would have needed a shovel to find out. A chopping block with a big notch in it stood by the woodpile. Otherwise the place was immaculate. In the latrine a few beans or lentils had sprouted.

I also found a narrow foot-trail slanting down from the pocket to the bridle path underneath. Where it met the path a fallen log and a patch of huckleberry concealed it from view.

I followed it back to the pocket and walked around the camp a little more. I was reluctant to leave. Here, I thought, is the way it ought to be done. You find a high, sheltered spot where people don't go. You cut wood after dark when the trails are empty. You bring in food and gasoline on your back. You burn only dry fuel. You hide your fire in a pit. You keep your gear covered. And when you've had enough, you go. You don't leave your crap for the next guy.

Though I have no way of knowing, my guess is that this man lasted out two or more winters in the Hills. Maybe he would say he was comfortable. Maybe, thanks to his skills and preparation, he didn't mind a bit when one Arctic front after another roared by overhead and the sun's pale, icy ball barely broke the horizon between one iron midnight and the next. But the fact is that I know almost nothing about him.

Why would anyone do this? Why, when life is cold enough, reject even the animal heat of one's neighbors? Why not just disappear altogether?

Maybe this is the wrong question — I know I can't answer it. But it's clear that there is something in the Hills that attracts not only real estate men and editorial writers but also some of the most private, resolute, and desperate characters to be found around Boston — people for whom this patch of woods represents not just a weekend playground or an heirloom under siege but a rare chance to live in something like freedom and dignity despite the best efforts of mosquitoes, blizzards, and nosy intruders like myself.

I would say that this, if nothing else, makes the Hills precious — that people for whom our landscape provides nothing but barriers and riddles think they can glimpse relief here. There ought to be more outside our cities than the usual stiff collar of suburbs. There ought to be places where the rules, at least in imagination, are still fluid, and can be tested in comparative safety. Even if it's a bad sign when someone like Grith moves into the Hills, it might be a worse one if it was never attempted. That would suggest that even their emptiness had lost its power of hope, and that there was no longer any useful difference between a day in a doorway and a night alone in the woods.

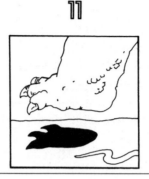

# 11

# Family Matters

I have little to say about Snakes.

— Charles Darwin, *The Descent of Man* (1871)

## The Journey into the Underworld

In the last chapter I may have given the impression that *Crotalus* made a conscious decision to retreat to the Hills. Anyone who has seen a rattlesnake's brain — a squashed string of neural beads no bigger than a grain of rice — might have trouble with that idea. And yet all over the world, in nearly every culture from which we have evidence, snakes are traditionally ranked among the shrewdest and most crafty of beasts. Why is that?

Charles Darwin, no mean cogitator himself, once remarked on the human predilection for discovering something like our own wits at work in nature. Thus when we see bees building a comb or beavers making a dam, we suppose that they approach the job much as we would, with an agreed-upon definition of the problem and a solution chosen from several likely alternatives.

In his usual diffident way, Darwin wondered whether such analogies might be presumptuous. It was not, he suggested, that the finished results didn't display remarkable architectural skills. But he wondered whether they were arrived at by our methods; just because something is cunningly made, he asked, does that mean it was constructed by experts? What if this kind of genius is a simple function of ancestry? What if animal engineers have no idea what they're building, but merely act out inherited scripts?

Since then neither beavers nor bees have been observed making anything except what they are so proficient at making.* Stupidity — in the form of unworkable projects, pointless speculation, and endless disputes over trivia — is seen more and more as an almost exclusively human trait. Most animals can't afford to be stupid. They may not know much, but they know what their parents knew.

Darwin sniffed out the mechanism by which certain forms of knowledge could be created and passed on without help from a directing intelligence. He claimed that, given enough time, the normal course of events could transform microscopic specks of marine plankton into creatures as subtle and marvelous as rattlesnakes and human beings. And not only was such a process possible, he argued, but it had happened; we were among its products. Therefore what connected us to things like toadstools, houseflies, and hummingbirds was not the mystic hand of a Creator, but actual chains of inheritance.

If human beings are notably stupid, this is one of the most boneheaded and numbskulled propositions ever advanced. It forced thousands of already touchy traditionalists to take up zoology and paleontology and devise contrary accounts of the evidence. But why should any sane person want to argue about trilobites and orangutans? Do they argue about us?

It's ironic that Darwin was attacked so heavily for degrading humanity when he so clearly personifies the real distance between us and our relatives. It probably makes no difference to *Crotalus*, for instance, whether he was created by the God of Genesis or the God of Watson and Crick; it matters only to us. It's amazing how much it matters.

When I first heard about evolution, in about 1962, I thought it

---

*If a recording of running water is played inside a beaver enclosure, the beavers will plaster the loudspeaker with mud and sticks.

was a terrific idea. I liked to imagine that I was a large, bulky dinosaur — a *Brontosaurus,* say, or a *Diplodocus* — and that as I shuffled along an ancient beach I looked out at the water and thought, Wouldn't it be great to be an ichthyosaur? Suddenly, magically, my arms contracted into sharklike fins, my legs fused into a powerful tail, and I humped into the surf and shot away like a bullet. Later, if I felt like it, I leaped from the water, grew huge, leathery wings, and flapped off like a pterodactyl, or waded onto the sand, sprouted daggerish teeth, and grinned horribly over the treetops like *Allosaurus.* All this without leaving my bed at nap time.

Clearly I mistook the extraordinary plasticity of dinosaur form for a sort of feast of personal possibilities, and supposed that evolution was a means by which long-dead reptiles changed shape at will. In this I echoed Darwin's distinguished precursor, Jean Baptiste de Lamarck, who imagined that snakes acquired their lengthy bodies by repeated efforts to squeeze through tight places. I don't remember when I learned that even dinosaurs were stuck with the bodies they were born with — I think it was after I stopped taking naps.

Darwin's theory pushed aside all the attempts to explain evolution by positing innate tendencies, predetermined plans of improvement, and progress toward ideal forms. In his view variation, or the difference between parents and offspring, was more or less inevitable and fortuitous; it was only when these variations gave some advantage in life that they were likely to be preserved, in the form of greater proportions of surviving descendants. In this manner the smallest improvements tended to spread throughout interbreeding populations — not because they were fated, but because they worked. Over time this engine of change, which he called natural selection, produced the almost infinite tangle of endlessly ramifying lineages that make our planet such a remarkable object.

With this in mind, it's almost pointless to ask "Why *Crotalus?*" The only answer is "Why not?" But let's proceed.

About twenty years ago a French embryologist named Raynaud took fertile eggs out of a reticulated python at various intervals and examined them closely. He was interested in that most snakey of qualities, limblessness. One of the things he discovered was that his unborn pythons weren't naked below the waist throughout their development. At one point tiny mounds of tissue known as limb buds appeared on either side of their cloacal regions, much like the ones that in most higher vertebrates eventually become legs. But his snakes were not freaks; almost immediately the epithelial cells covering these buds began to die. The buds stopped swelling, their growth more or less halted. It was as if a message had been received: *Upon thy belly thou shalt go.*

Leglessness isn't a common condition among land animals. For us, certainly, it would be a disadvantage. And yet according to Darwin, no such characteristic can develop unless it somehow favors survival. Raynaud's pythons suggest that some long-distant snake ancestor did indeed possess legs, just as the gill slits on a human embryo recall our fabulous aquatic origins. Then why were they abandoned?

Most of the students who have looked at this problem agree that leglessness, although essential to our notion of snakes, is in fact a "secondary" condition. They argue that the crucial step in the making of snakes wasn't the loss of limbs, which could only produce helplessness in a lizardlike ancestor, but instead the progressive elongation of the body. Once this hypothetical progenitor had stretched out enough for "undulant motion" — the typical snake method of getting around — to become reasonably efficient, the legs were no longer necessary and probably became a hindrance. Therefore they shrank and shrank and eventually disappeared.

This argument takes strength from the example of several lizard families that appear to be undergoing a similar transformation. In Florida, for instance, in almost every vacant lot in every half-built subdivision lives a diminutive lizard, a skink, known to experts as *Lygosoma laterale*. No bigger than an earthworm, it lives in the dark spaces under dead leaves and old trash, and seems to like them just fine despite having to share them with centipedes, scorpions, and black widow spiders often larger than itself. This skink, though equipped with four perfectly serviceable legs, each ending in five scaly, threadlike claws, has a narrow, cylindrical body perhaps twenty times as long as it is wide. If you surprise one of these lizards by lifting off its cover, it may dash off, but as often as not it will squiggle away like a miniature snake. Once it does either, it is usually impossible to find.

There are skinks with squat bodies and powerful legs. There are also lengthy skinks with no legs at all. What makes them all skinks, and thus members of the far-scattered family Scincidae, which includes something like 90 genera and 1,300 species worldwide, is that they all have, among other things, bony plates in their skin and a distinctive notch in their tongues. *Crotalus* belongs to the family Viperidae; we ourselves belong to the family Hominidae, of which we are the sole surviving representatives. A family, taxonomically speaking, is no more than an educated guess about blood relationships based on features in common. All skinks, for example, are assumed to be more closely akin to each other than to species from any other family. Since skinks run the gamut from heavy-limbed types to perfectly naked torpedoes, and since the original skink was a basic lizard and almost certainly had good legs of its own, it's assumed that the loss of limbs is a recent development among skinks, and that those species which have done so haven't diverged sufficiently to constitute a family of their own — in fact, some students believe that the phenomenon occurred independently in several lines of descent. There is, however, one other characteristic that all the leg-dropping skinks have in common besides lengthiness: they live on the ground and like to burrow through its top layer, whether it be dead leaves, soft sand, or dry earth.

Here's a clue to the origin of snakes, if we choose to believe it.

The fossil record is notoriously poor in snakes and snake ancestors. Snake bones, especially those from the head and jaws, tend to be light and fragile, and thus poor candidates for preservation in nonmarine sediments. Fossil vertebrae are more common, but it takes a lot of imagination to reconstruct an entire extinct beast from a few vertebral segments. And so although primitive snakes appear with some frequency in the late Cretaceous, the third and last act of the astonishing Age of Reptiles, no prior forms have been unearthed that are clearly intermediate between them and the then already extant lizards from which they presumably derived.

This lack of connecting forms is not an uncommon problem for bone diggers. Often numerous remains of closely similar species will be found in adjacent strata, suggesting that one was clearly ancestral to the other, but if evolution proceeds as claimed, then there ought to be at least a few in-between types bridging the gap. Almost always there are not; Darwin was so sensitive on this point that he devoted a whole chapter of *The Origin of Species* to an argument for the partial and fragmentary nature of the fossil evidence, and declared that "he who rejects this view of the imperfection of the geological record, will rightly reject my whole theory."

When you consider how much work has gone into tracing our own ancestors, who barely yesterday separated themselves from the apes, and how many riddles remain despite the finds of the Leakeys and others, it's easy to see why the bones of a small, snakelike lizard who allegedly lived one hundred million years ago might prove elusive.

But there is more to a snake than a lizard without legs. Unlike lizards, snakes lack eyelids and cannot blink; they have a hard scale, or spectacle, over the eye. They also lack external ear openings and can't hear airborne vibrations. A lizard, like most animals, has two lungs; most snakes have only one. And while most lizards' jaws are anchored firmly to the skull, giving them a powerful if inflexible bite, in snakes this connection is remarkably tenuous, and the jawbones themselves can stretch apart at chin and snout, so that what snakes lose in biting strength they make up in an ability to gape the mouth several times the width of the head — very important for an animal that eats large prey and cannot chew.

Thus it seems that the genius of snakes, evolutionarily speaking, has been their dedication to the idea that less is more — fewer legs, fewer ears, fewer eyelids, a single lung, a sketchy jaw, and so forth. This is often referred to as a "degraded" or "degenerate" condition, meaning that structures previously evolved have been abandoned or lost, and perhaps accounts for some of the uneasiness people feel about snakes — it's as though they gave up higher things for the wriggly pleasures of wormdom.

But to return to our problem, now slightly revised: if we are going to argue, in the absence of fossil evidence, that the original snake was a legless lizard, then why aren't they more like the stretched-out lizards that exist today? Where did they get all these additional features?

Unless new bones come to light, this question will never be answered. Snakes crawl into earth history fully formed, like Superman emerging from a phone booth. We know that snakes are reptiles; we know that their skulls are more like those of ancient lizards than those of the other possible candidates for paternity (crocodiles, dinosaurs, turtles, rhynchocephalians, et cetera); we know that various lizard groups are susceptible to elongation and limb loss. What we don't know is where, when, and how the first snakes arrived, other than that it must have happened a long time ago. Darwin believed that the best theory is that which satisfactorily accounts for the greatest number of facts. There is such a theory about snake origins, a persuasive one, but it is fifty years old and there are still plenty of bone-men willing to profess themselves doubters. And in science, doubters are sacred.

This theory, the work of several people, is an evolutionary scenario based on a few ancient bones and comparative anatomy. Long ago, it presumes, a line of small, ground-dwelling lizards followed a skinklike route into elongation and leglessness. Elongation allowed these lizards to increase size and strength without gaining diameter; therefore they could continue to pursue their prey through the rooty interstices of the soil's top layers, and perhaps get at more of them than their relatives could. Other adaptations followed: the loss of the now-useless legs, the fusing of the eyelids into a hard, transparent, and dirt-resistant scale, a sharpening of the olfactory sense, and a de-emphasis on vision and hearing. Eventually a new sort of beast was created, an "endless hook" (Thoreau's phrase) almost exclusively subterranean or cryptozoic, a predatory worm with jaws and teeth that could move efficiently through its narrow, darkened world of termite tunnels and burrowing grubs.

This isn't an entirely hypothetical animal. Of eleven living families of snakes, all but two include members that are at least partial burrowers, and five of them contain nothing else. Of these latter, the most completely benighted are the thread snakes and blind snakes — small, rarely seen tropical forms that spend their lives underground and whose eyes, like a mole's, have retreated under the skin. They also lack the enlarged, bandlike belly scales of typical snakes and are nearly toothless as well; it's believed that they eat mostly ant and termite larvae and eggs.

When the thread and blind snakes were first closely examined, it was discovered that in spite of their apparently specialized character they have several primitive or lizardlike traits. Like the boas and pythons, for instance, which are among the first snakes to appear as fossils, they retain remnants of hind limbs and a pelvic girdle; in addition, their skulls and jaws are more solid and tightly knit than those of any other snakes. Hence most investigators placed them near the root of the snake family tree, arguing that they were directly descended from an ancient, burrowing, and lizardlike type from which all other snakes derived.

Skeptics popped up immediately. If these were the original snakes, they asked, why didn't they appear as fossils until fifty million years after several nonburrowing forms? They also suggested that the supposedly primitive skull characteristics represented a secondary adaptation to a mode of life that favored hard-headedness over jaw-stretching ability. As for the vestigial hind limbs, the skeptics pointed out that in certain boas and pythons they served as sexual stimulators in mating behavior, and therefore were not as useless as they looked — whales, for instance, were sometimes born with similar appendages, and if genes for hind limbs were so persistent, who was to say that the internal remnants in these snakes weren't simply left over from an "advanced" boalike ancestor?

These were powerful objections. Though it was answered that tiny snakes don't fossilize well, and that the skulls were genuinely lizardlike and the hind limbs genuinely primitive, some critics maintained that the first snakes could just as easily have been terrestrial or aquatic, as in fact the earliest remains suggested. In this view the thread and blind snakes evolved later, from small, surface-dwelling forms, just as certain lizards appear to be moving underground today. A third school argued that these creatures weren't snakes at all, but had evolved independently from the lizards, and therefore might with as much justice be called chameleons or iguanas.

Scientists seem to relish controversies like this, and many aren't reluctant to imply that those with views contrary to their own are muleheaded idiots. Darwin himself remarked that they rarely change their minds, and that the success or failure of his theory would depend on its fortunes among the next generation of naturalists, who were not already committed. The theory of the burrowing origin of snakes might still be just one proposition among many if not for the work of a comparative anatomist named G. L. Walls, who shortly before World War II took a close look at the structure of the serpentine eye.

He discovered a very bizarre instrument. In most higher vertebrates, for instance, the lens is elastic, and tiny muscles attached to its rim can stretch it in order to focus an image on the retina. In older people some of this elasticity is often lost, and so we need glasses to read. In snakes, however, these muscles don't exist, and the lens can't be deformed; instead another set of muscles has taken over the job. These muscles are contained exclusively in the iris, the colored portion of the eye; in humans and most other animals they serve only to control the width of the pupil. In snakes, however, they can raise the pressure inside the eyeball itself, forcing the lens outward and expanding the focal length of the eye as a whole. This novel method of adjustment is unique to snakes.

There are other peculiarities. I've mentioned the fusion of the eyelids into a hard, transparent scale. Snakes also lack a fovea, the spot on the retina where the color-sensitive cones are most concentrated. In addition, their optic nerve fibers are bundled like no other animal's. Taken together, these and other anomalies amount to a reworking of the visual organ so complete that in an anatomical sense the eyes of a lizard and a man are more alike than either's are like the eyes of a snake.

In Walls's opinion this could have only one explanation: at some point in snake history the eyes were no longer necessary and shrank to mere sacs of pigment, tiny light-sensitive specks, and when good vision became adaptively important again — in other words, when snakes reemerged on the surface — their eyes were rebuilt on lines totally unprecedented in vertebrate phylogeny. This experimentation is continuing; Walls went so far as to say that there was more variety to be found in the serpentine eye than in the entire spectrum of higher animals from sharks to mankind.

These findings pushed opponents of the burrowing-origin theory to lonely spots on the sidelines, where they remain today. They claim that the theory must remain doubtful in the absence of good fossil evidence. Few will challenge them there, but they've produced no competing hypothesis half so convincing. And so those who make it their business to know are generally agreed that sometime early in the Mesozoic, when the dinosaurs were still preparing to conquer the world, a small, lizardlike creature grew long and narrow, dropped his legs, and swam into the earth, where he stayed just short of forever. When he finally reemerged, perhaps fifty million generations later, he was something new to the world — a snake. He had profited in exile; though he looked like a worm, he had powers worms never dreamt of. When the dinosaurs died, he lived; when the cold crept down from the poles, threatening paralysis, he hid from it in his old birthplace underground. He would never grow legs again; he would never speak beyond a hiss or even hear his own voice. He would be a model for a certain kind of life, a watchful, slithering, predatory kind, and as long as circumstances favored that model, he would prosper.

There are other animal lineages that have left one element only to return to it with talents acquired elsewhere. Air-breathing lungfish crawled out of the ocean and plunged back as dolphins; dinosaurs sprouted feathers, rode the winds, and abandoned them to run across the plains on ostrich legs. We ourselves owe our binocular vision and our grasping paws to a stint in the treetops. Snakes took a darker route; they crept into the earth and let its shadows mold them.

In mythology the earth is always regarded as the home of the dead and the mother of life. Heroes — Odysseus, Jesus Christ, Dante, Milton's Satan — must always descend into it before they can unlock their power. Our premier storytellers, the Greeks and the Jews, recognized that snakes had been underground and had learned secrets there; the Furies, all-seeing guarantors of Greek vengeance, were hags with snakey locks who could not be satiated until Athena escorted them back into the depths. In the Garden a snake lay at the root of the Tree of Knowledge; he knew more than he said.

Nowadays it is not generally admitted that snakes know anything we don't, or that there might be more under our feet than rock and more rock. The world, the living world, has become a sort of vast, pumping membrane too mindless to grasp its own secrets; it remains for us, the tiny reasoners, to squirrel them out. And so the mystic truths snakes learned underground, once celebrated as myth, are now even more mythical — "knowledge" belongs only to large-brained types like ourselves. But are large brains the essence of wisdom? Don't ask a snake.

## Eating One's Betters

The tree of life swarms with cannibals. If we believe, as is more or less obligatory for those susceptible to argument, that all living things are descended from a few experiments in protein synthesis carried out in the primordial oceans, then we must also admit that life is impossible without devouring one's relatives. Even the green plants, which nourish themselves on sunshine and water, need carbon from the air — carbon that has been burned out of other living things, which in turn inherited it from others, and so forth. And so we arrive at the much-remarked-upon fact that life and death are so necessary to each other that they are practically indistinguishable, at least as compared with nonlife.

Since prehistoric times moralists have recognized that there is something regrettable, if not tragic, about this compulsion to sacrifice kindred existences in order to preserve our own, and innumerable systems grew up to ensure a blameless approach to dinner — oftentimes it was pretended that the animal or food crop in question willingly surrendered itself in return for honors received in song and prayer. Only the threat of starvation could excuse killing and eating the wrong things in the wrong times and places. And yet there is probably no bird, beast, or vegetable anywhere in the world that human beings haven't tried to make a meal of at one time or another.

Here we have the age-old tension between tradition and experiment that was largely a function of genetics until *Homo sapiens* came along. It's no accident, for instance, that the teeth which push through a kitten's gums are excellent tools for biting and killing; cat ancestors lived in a world containing enough small, catchable animals to make meat eating a workable variation on fruit eating or bug eating. And since prey animals came in all sizes, the cats themselves split up into forms ranging from household tabbies to saber-toothed tigers, each genetically adapted to a particular diet.

Given this tendency for life to concoct hungry mouths to fit available foods, you might think that wherever you find a fat, juicy animal in abundance you will find another animal to eat it. Not so — evolution takes time, lots of time, to seize opportunities. Like so many other features of the theory, this is particularly evident on oceanic islands.

In July 1609 a ship en route from Plymouth, England, to Jamestown, Virginia, was caught in a storm and wrecked on the then-uninhabited island of Bermuda. Given up for lost, the survivors built two more ships out of the wreckage of the first and reappeared in the Chesapeake ten months later. One of the factors in their survival was a colony of web-footed birds they called sea owls (probably *Pterodroma cahow,* the now all-but-extinct Bermuda petrel). These birds were so unused to being eaten that they not only would decline to fly away when approached, but would come when called and permit themselves to be hefted, as if to prove they were fat enough for the stewpot. Thanks to them, no one went hungry.

In the past few hundred years many such isolated simpletons have vanished from history, usually as a result of being eaten too often: dodoes, moas, various giant tortoises, and others. The reason they didn't disappear earlier wasn't that they weren't vulnerable, but that none of the land-based predators which might have exploited them had managed to reach their antipodean retreats. Bats, for instance, were probably the only land mammals to colonize Bermuda before human beings, but no bat had evolved that could subdue and eat petrels. That would have required a series of stepwise adaptations perhaps impossible in so limited an environment.

All this is merely to highlight the Darwinian dictum that no creature can evolve until a place already exists for it, and even then there's no guarantee. It's hard to argue, for instance, that a brainy, tool-using biped like ourselves couldn't have prospered in the Age of Reptiles, and yet none came along, despite 120 million years' worth of tinkering. Is it reasonable, then, to suppose we are not only the greatest masterpieces of evolution, but that all the action beforehand consisted of lame warm-up attempts?

Fossils show that snakes did find time to take the stage in the Mesozoic, beating us out by some 150 million years. These snakes were most likely the small, purblind, burrowing types discussed earlier. What made them snakes and not lizards were certain features common to all modern animals of the same name, their descendants: a reduced style of eye, an ear buried in jaw muscle, certain spinal characteristics, and so forth. But it's a long way from these modest, retiring, and somewhat specialized forerunners to world-famous productions like cobras, pythons, and rattlesnakes. What came in between? What brought the snakes out of their purgatory and gave them power, speed, and venom?

The earliest fossil snakes come from Spain, North Africa, and Argentina. They weren't burrowers; one, *Simoliophis,* lived in salt water and probably ate fish. Remains don't become common until the Eocene, the opening act of the Age of Mammals, and then they are mostly primitive boas. Boas are much larger and bulkier than any worm snakes now extant, and though some may have been at least partial burrowers, like the modern sand boas or the rainbow boa of California, there were others that approached python size and could not have survived on the small eats available underground. This suggests that they had gotten their eyes back and were already surface hunters.

And so, as often happens in this story, it's necessary to invent candidates to fill in the gaps — here we need stepstones between small, subterranean ancestors suggested by the serpentine eye and larger, sighted forms found in a variety of habitats.

One thing that would have proved valuable, even indispensable, to an underground predator is a keen sense of smell. A good nose could have led such a creature to its prey through a dark, cramped environment where eyes and ears would have been useless. Odors can spread through damp earth; many burrowing animals and insects use them to communicate and order their lives. Most snakes have and use two noses: the traditional one open at the nostrils and a second, more highly developed one known as the Jacobsen's organ, a pair of holes in the roof of the mouth into which the forked ends of the tongue are inserted after it has flickered out and back, testing the air. Receptor cells in these holes connect directly to the brain's olfactory lobes, informing them what the tongue has picked up.

The ancient burrowing snakes may or may not have been tongue-flickers, but it's likely that they sniffed out their meals, pushing through the soft earth and breaking into the retreats of various worms, slugs, grubs, lizards, spiders, and centipedes. Often, however, the snakes must have encountered prey too large to swallow, and since they had given up their forelimbs, they had no way to rip it apart.

Here was a chance for selection to operate — in other words, for natural variation to initiate a change in form.

Suppose that a population of worm snakes lived in an area rich in a type of prey that only extra-large adults could handle. These individuals would get more to eat and reproduce more successfully, raising the average size of the population. Suppose also that getting at this prey required squeezing through tight crevices between rocks. That would put a ceiling on optimum size and, once it was reached, favor those individuals who could stretch their jaws wider than their same-size relatives. Thus genes for limber jaws would tend to spread through the group.

Suppose that this population was isolated by a lava flow or a saltwater intrusion, reinforcing its divergent character. Suppose that when contact with other snakes was reestablished, the hybrids were unsuccessful — too small to handle the large prey, too large to do well on the smaller prey the unchanged group favored. This would tend to keep the groups reproductively separate and favor individuals who bred only within them, even if the two groups spread into each other's territories. Eventually crosses would cease. And two same-area populations that do not normally interbreed are, by definition, separate species.

This is strictly speculation, of course. But it shows how change *might* occur — how pressures for increased size and swallowing ability might, without eliminating the small, wormlike burrowers, produce larger versions, which could in turn produce larger, and so forth. It is perhaps significant that the period in which boas first become abundant, the Eocene, is also the time when rodents first enter the record and proliferate.

Now we are past speculation — we're just short of fantasy. But considering that many kinds of rodents burrow and raise their young underground, and that these young tend to be small, numerous, and abundant, is it unreasonable to suppose that certain sightless, diminutive snakes began to stumble on them in their travels, gulp them down in quantity, and develop such a taste for them that they eventually pursued both them and their parents back into the light, becoming larger and better-sighted on the way? We know that snakes had already moved aboveground in the Cretaceous, but apparently without much success, and the few examples so far discovered were probably evolutionary dead ends. With the boas, however, we have a group that blanketed the world in no time, geologically speaking, and is still quite successful today, as if conditions were suddenly ripe for narrow, stealthy hunters with a nose for tight places — conditions that have remained in force ever since, thanks to the ubiquitous rodents.

I won't chase this butterfly any further. But let me just add that there exist today two poorly known and somewhat mysterious semiburrowing snakes, the sunbeam snake of Thailand and Mexico's *Loxocemus*, that have given taxonomists fits because they combine "primitive" features — paired lungs, rigid skulls, and small and unimpressive eyes — with the size, scalation, and eating habits of typical modern snakes. Could they be living signposts on a serpentine path leading out of the dark? Do they point to *Crotalus* in the way that certain proto-monkeys point to us? The tree of life is full of bottlenecks — in the long run most species will have no descendants, while a few others will remake the world. Maybe these two represent the latter.

At any rate, once snakes reached the surface to stay, they became a success story. Along with the lizards, which can muster approximately 3,000 living species to their 2,700, they prove that reptilian creativity wasn't used up with the dinosaurs. Granted, birds and mammals have been even more prolific and dominate the colder regions, but their main claims to advancement — warm-bloodedness, flight, the placenta, extended care of the young, and sociability — haven't prevented reptiles from acquiring comparable innovations and using them to spread into nearly every existing habitat. There are snakes that live in oceans, deserts, rain forests, mountains, mangrove swamps, coral reefs, and major cities. Some weigh three hundred pounds; some congregate by the thousand. Many are so rude as to prey on their betters, and will eat anything they can swallow, including large dogs and small boys; many are so dangerous that they have almost no natural enemies. But with all that, they are still irredeemably voiceless, secret, and earthbound — low, the phrase goes, as a snake.

Some historians have suggested that the birds and mammals, with their hot-running engines and elevated energy requirements, could never have become dominant if not for the concentrated foods made available by the spread of the flowering plants. If this is so, then one might say that flowers brought forth the snakes, since many snakes live almost exclusively on warm-blooded prey. Would we like them better if they ate only cold crawling things like themselves? But we are all the same substance — men, snakes, rodents, birds, flowers. We can't live by chewing rocks. Feeding each other is what we do best.

## Becoming an American

There are few truly native North Americans. We ourselves are all Africans, whether we walked in from Siberia before icemelt filled the Bering Sea or arrived a thousand generations later in the wake of Columbus. To qualify as aborigines we would have had to appear here first and be able to show continuous residency. A few creatures can do so, but not many. *Crotalus* is one of them.

It has been evident for some time that the chief laboratories of creation are in the tropics. The majority of living species are found there; most of this majority are found nowhere else. Nearly all temperate-zone species have close relatives in the tropics; only a tiny minority of tropical species have relations near the poles. And since most of this diversity is concentrated in the rain forests of Africa, southern Asia, and the Amazon, burning these forests is a cheap way to castrate the world.

*Crotalus* is a viper. This is a technical term meaning that he has lost all the teeth in his upper jaw except the two frontmost, which have grown long and wicked and can be folded back when not in use. Each of these teeth is hollowed out and has a hole at each end, making a channel for venom.

About a third of the world's venomous snakes are vipers. The remainder — cobras and their relatives, and the rear-fanged colu· brids — have, in many cases, evolved venoms more toxic than any viper's, but none have the full hypodermic apparatus; in the cobras, for instance, the venom flows down an incompletely sealed groove in the front of the fang, and the jaw retains several non-grooved teeth. This looks like a halfway version of a viper's dentition, and has contributed to the opinion that vipers are the most advanced snakes in the world. Interestingly enough, the most successful family of all, the colubrids, is largely nonvenomous, and some of its members prey on vipers.

Hardly anyone thinks the vipers originated in North America. The most popular choice is Southeast Asia. This is an inference based not so much on fossil evidence, which is typically sketchy, but on current patterns of distribution. Australia, another choice, has few backers, because there are no vipers in Australia — one would have to assume that they evolved there, moved away, and left no descendants, in spite of considerable success elsewhere — possible, but unlikely.

Before evolution was generally accepted, it was assumed that all species had been separately created in the spots where they occur. Many believed that God wouldn't consent to extinction and that before long, living examples of the stupendous beasts the first paleontologists had begun to dig up would be found roaming little-known parts of the world, where human beings had not yet killed them off — Thomas Jefferson hoped to surprise mastodons at the headwaters of the Missouri.

On his voyage around the world aboard the *Beagle,* Darwin noticed several peculiarities of animal distribution that seemed to him difficult to explain on the basis of the "no evolution/no extinction" scenario. Island dwellers, for example, tended to be much less like other islanders than like creatures from the nearest land mass. In addition, there were parts of the Andes that were more like parts of the Alps than like the jungles below, and yet the Creator had perversely excluded his Alpine specialties and instead put in cold-adapted versions of his Amazon fauna. Patterns like these fascinated Darwin, and some thirty-odd years later he stated that if he had to gamble he would pick Africa as the birthplace of man, for the simple reason that the most manlike apes, chimpanzees and gorillas, lived nowhere else. A half century elapsed before fossil evidence began to prove him correct.

Origins, then, are a guessing game, a puzzle for evolutionary detectives. Similar species may be scattered all over the world like bits of chrome and glass on a highway; the job for the investigator is to map them in sequence and follow them back through time in imagination, hoping to home in on the spot where their most recent common ancestor first appeared. The game remains not much more than a pastime, an occasion for ponderous jousting in the professional journals, unless someone goes to the spot, digs, and turns up some old bones. Then the books are revised.

The vipers still inhabit this early, speculative phase. They are a group of about 180 broad-headed, tube-fanged snakes found on all continents except Australia and Antarctica. Their eyes all have vertical, catlike pupils, probably an adaptation for night hunting. They tend to be squat, slow-moving, almost lethargic snakes, although the bite motion itself, or strike, is lightning quick. Many hunt by lying motionless and waiting for prey to pass by, and many have bold, blotchy patterns that help to break up their outlines and aid concealment. From a rodent's point of view, a viper is a sort of demonic mousetrap, easily avoided once noticed but with a horrible talent for remaining invisible. Like most snakes, vipers are cold-blooded and cannot warm their bodies except by absorbing heat from outside. This excludes them, for the most part, from areas more than 45 degrees distant from the equator — Siberia, Quebec, Patagonia, and so forth. Europe, pumped full of heat by the Gulf Stream, is an exception; here the common adder, a small and not particularly dangerous viper, has been found across the Arctic Circle in Scandinavia, which makes it the most northerly snake in the world.

All vipers, by definition, belong to the family Viperidae, one of thousands of artificial groups constructed by taxonomists in order to reduce the natural world to a semblance of order. It in turn belongs to the Serpentes, a subdivision of the Squamata, which is included in the Reptilia, a class of the Vertebrata, which is the largest branch of the Chordata. The man who first outlined this pyramid of nesting boxes, Swedish botanist Carl von Linné, hoped thereby to trace out the divine hierarchy of creation and show how all living things are based on an inspired canon of blueprints. Since Darwin, however, it has been conceded that heredity, rather than immanent form, must be the basis of classification, and that no group is legitimate unless all its members can be assumed to have derived from a single, vanished progenitor, a progenitor ancestral to members of no other group. In our case, then, we are looking for a lone Adam of a snake, a big-daddy viper responsible for the entire assemblage.

The vipers are a diverse clan. They include the rattlesnakes and copperheads of North America and the bushmaster and fer-de-lance of the New World tropics. In Africa they are represented by the aptly named genus *Bitis,* best known for the puff adder and the gaudy and monstrous gaboon viper. From India comes the Russell's viper, the irascible man-killer that Sherlock Holmes beat to death with a cane in "The Speckled Band." In contrast, some of the bamboo vipers of Malaysia are so docile that bushels of them are strewn about certain shrines in the way Easter lilies are heaped up in Boston churches. Europe has a variety of small, inconspicuous adders.

A large, varied, and cosmopolitan family presents difficulties to the genealogist. He has arrived too late; the local, formative period is long past, buried somewhere under a worldwide blanket of descendants. Australia is some consolation; its lack of vipers means, most probably, that they evolved after Australia split away from the other continents, which would make these snakes younger than the boas and perhaps the cobralike elapids, which are both common there. On the other hand, viperid diversity in both the Old and New worlds indicates a lengthy presence in both hemispheres, suggesting that they must have crossed the Bering land bridge in one of its earlier incarnations, before the planet cooled and Siberia and Alaska became more or less unlivable for reptiles of all kinds.

So where did they start from? Usually in such cases the first choice is the region where the group is currently represented by the greatest number of species, on the theory that most descendants evolve close to home — this is the reasoning that led Darwin to assign us to Africa. In the vipers' case, however, there are several centers of diversity: Africa, southern Asia, and the New World. And although the New World dominates the species count, all three areas contain vipers variously adapted for life in the trees, on the ground, and in the loose soils of arid regions. Therefore none is obviously primary.

Another approach is to examine the range of variation within the group, throw out those types which appear most highly adapted and specialized, and attempt to imagine a basic, generalized ancestor from which all the others could have derived. Then the living form that most resembles this creature can be assumed to be primitive, and the place where it lives can be nominated as the most probable birthplace.

There is such a beast among the vipers: the Fea's viper, a small, poorly known species native to the craggy montane forests of Burma, China, and Tibet, which was first brought alive to the West in 1985. Unlike most vipers, it has smooth scales, an oval rather than triangular head, and enlarged head plates — all characteristic of the more basic colubrids, from which the vipers are presumed to have descended. It does, however, have a set of legitimate viper fangs. Enough, we might say — here's our grandaddy snake, still living in the Asian jungles from which all vipers emerged.

The problem with this solution is that when primitive types like Fea's viper do manage to survive despite hordes of improved descendants, they tend to do so in remote, little-changed locations where the competition is less fierce, not in their places of origin — Australia, last stronghold of the marsupials, is a prime example. And so an experienced spoiler would argue that snakes like Fea's viper could just as easily have evolved in Brazil, spread throughout the warm regions, and later have been displaced everywhere with the exception of these lonely mountainsides, where a single example survives as a relic.

But we haven't exhausted our resources. All vipers are not alike; it so happens that they fall into two neat groups, Fea's viper excluded: the Crotalinae and the Viperinae. These groups aren't randomly scattered across the globe. The crotalines are confined to Asia and the Americas, whereas the viperines live only in Asia, Africa, and Europe. What separates them, morphologically speaking, is a pair of heat-sensitive pits between eye and nostril — the crotalines have them, the viperines do not.

These pits function as rudimentary eyes attuned to infrared radiation, enabling their possessors to locate warm-blooded prey in the dark. A nerve-impulse study published in *Science* in 1952 showed that the pits could register the heat of a human hand held twelve inches away. An earlier study found that blindfolded crotalines, or pit vipers, could strike accurately at a still-warm light bulb wrapped in cloth at about the same distance. This ability vanished, however, if the pits were plugged.

These pits are useful for our purposes because they constitute what taxonomists call a specialization. A specialization is a feature possessed by an animal not because it is left over from a direct ancestor — like the human appendix, for example — or because a genetic accident just happened to produce it — like your uncle's green eyes — but because it is an adaptation to a certain mode of life and equips the creature to pursue that mode more effectively. Specializations are not easily erased within a lineage. If they are no longer useful, they tend to leave traces — many of us, for instance, still possess lower-back muscles that have no other function than to twitch a now-vanished tail. Therefore we can assume that vipers with pits cannot be ancestral to vipers without, because if they were, the latter would show signs of once having had them. (It's hard to see, besides, what kind of viper wouldn't benefit from pit organs.)

And so we can cross the Americas from our list of likely viper homelands. All American vipers have pits; the first vipers did not. If the first vipers evolved here, how is it that there are none left, when so many vipers in Europe and Africa show that doing without pits is no great handicap? Should we assume that a pitless viper appeared here, crossed to the Old World, gave rise to lineages both with pits and without, and that only the former managed to cross back, where it flourished thanks to its ancestors' mysterious demise? That's a lot to assume — too much, really, unless we are forced to it.

Asia is the only continent that can boast both types of vipers. In Indochina, for instance, each group has representatives: the Russell's viper for the viperines, and several types of arboreal pit viper for the crotalines. What if both groups emerged there, one spreading west toward Europe and Africa (the viperines) and the other spreading east into the New World (the crotalines)? This is the simplest explanation for the existing pattern, and the one most favored today. Its only real competition comes from students who argue that the vipers could have originated in Europe or Africa, produced the pit vipers in Asia, and then the pit vipers alone moved on to America, their retreat blocked by the already successful viperines.

And here is where the question will doubtless rest — a fragile tissue of probabilities — unless someone happens to unearth some old bones. These bones would ideally include a series of snakes running from an ancestral Fea's-type viper to more typical modern forms, with one branch showing an increasingly large cavity on the maxillary bone as the pit organ developed. The most logical place to look for such relics is Southeast Asia. Unfortunately, most of Southeast Asia has been tropical rain forest since the age of the dinosaurs (much of it now disappearing), and rain forest is perhaps the most difficult environment on earth for fossil formation. Constant heat and humidity, ideal for microbes, tend to ensure that even the largest bones and teeth decay to nothing long before they can be buried out of reach. And so it is probably no accident that the first viper fossils yet discovered come not from Asia but from Europe and North America, where they appear almost simultaneously in strata about twenty million years old. These bones are too modern in form to have come from an original-stem viper. The snakes who left them, however, were among the first vipers to prosper in areas destined to be both rich in deposits and heavily prospected by bone-men.

There is one additional bit of evidence that tends to weight the scales in favor of the Asian-origin hypothesis. Vipers as a group display a variety of reproductive strategies — some lay eggs, some bear their young alive. Among the egg-layers, some deposit the clutch shortly after fertilization and some hold the eggs for a time. A few live-bearers surround the embryo in a tough, whitish, shell-like envelope from which the young emerge at birth; in others this envelope is reduced to a delicate membrane. It has been observed that vipers living in cold climates are generally live-bearers, pre-sumably because the mother is better equipped to give her embryos the heat they need by warming herself in the sun than by secreting them as eggs in a dark, out-of-the-way spot. Apparently this advan-tage outweighs the mother's additional risk in decreased mobility.

This pattern of temperate live-bearers and tropical egg-layers doesn't quite hold in the New World. Here nearly all the vipers are live-bearers, even those from hot climates. And in the only genus with representatives on both sides of the Pacific, *Agkistrodon* (cop-perheads and cottonmouths), the Asians include egg-layers, while the Americans are all live-bearers. If, as is suggested, live-bearing is an adaptation to cold weather, then it looks as though the ances-tral American vipers passed through some chilly times, chilly enough to suppress an innate capacity for egg-laying long after. We know that the Bering Strait region, the most likely pathway between the hemispheres, began to pass from a tropical to a tem-perate climate about thirty million years ago, when the vipers were presumably expanding. And so if we had to guess whether they crossed from Siberia to Alaska or vice versa, we'd have to choose the former, since only the American vipers show signs of a cold-adapted past. Once again, an Asian origin is indicated.

Tracking down fossil snakes has never been a particularly hot pursuit in paleontology. Remains are scarce; the search lacks the glamour of the hunt for thunder lizards or ape men, and the wealth of materials for analysis available in sequences of marine invertebrates is likewise absent. And so the story is still shadowy throughout, full of gaps and inferences, filled out more by analogy than by actual evidence. But it improves somewhat toward the end. Once the road to *Crotalus* curves into North America, it becomes somewhat broader and plainer, thanks to an increase in fossil sign-posts. One can no longer speculate so freely. The bones begin to mirror our times. We can almost see our hero emerging.

## The Belled Viper

John Adams, writing home from Philadelphia, in 1777, to his wife
Abigail, listed several American products that, in his opinion, any
envoy of the young republic ought to carry to Europe in order to
make friends and amuse the ladies. A few of his choices can still be
found in the Blue Hills, just across town from his birthplace: red-
winged blackbirds, cranberries, and rattlesnakes.

A rattlesnake is a very distinct ornament of the tree of life. Most
snakes lack rattles; no rattlesnakes do. The sole exception is *Crotalus catalinensis,* a Mexican species restricted to a sun-baked island
about the size of Nantucket in the Gulf of California. This snake,
although technically a rattler, never develops more than a single
shelly button on its tail.

Names for rattlesnakes appeared in several exotic languages as
word of *Crotalus* filtered abroad: the Spanish *cascabel,* the German
*klapperschlange,* the French *serpent à sonnettes* or *crotale.* In contrast
to slippery appellations like moccasin or hoopsnake, there was
never any confusion about what sort of beast was intended; rattlesnakes belong to one of those rare animal taxons whose popular
names define them exactly. There are two genera and thirty-one
species distributed from southern Canada to Argentina, with the
majority concentrated in the southwestern United States and
northern Mexico.

If rattlesnakes were known only from a few preserved specimens, like mammoths or Tasmanian wolves, there would undoubtedly be considerable controversy over the function of the peculiar
jointed organ at the end of their tail. Some would say it was in-

volved in mating rituals; others would argue that it wafted scent into the air; a handful might even claim that it was the chief reason the animal became extinct. Those who asserted that it was primarily a noisemaker would be reminded that snakes are deaf. Perhaps a few world-renowned specialists would have been permitted to lift a pickled *Crotalus* from its bath of preservative, hold up its rattle, and shake it gently. Others might have copied the device in dry materials and mounted it on a stick; some of these might have produced results audible clear across a lecture hall. But a few opponents of the noisemaker theory would probably have held out indefinitely, confident that no living snake would show them up.

As it is, however, we know what the rattle does: it rattles. It rattles when its owner is disturbed, menaced, or intruded upon. Often the snake coils up as well and faces the danger, its head drawn back and lifted. Prudent investigators will back off at this point, because the next response is a bite.

The rattle is a chain of hollow, papery, and interlocking shells of which only the lowest and most recent is firmly attached to the snake. Every time a rattler sheds its skin it adds another shell to the string. The shells break off fairly easily, and few adult snakes retain the original button present on newborns, although most will have at least a half dozen of its successors.

Many snakes, if disturbed, will coil up and vibrate their tails furiously, sometimes hissing as well; black racers are a prime local example. If the snake happens to be lying in dead leaves, a considerable noise results. It can't compare, however, with the angry buzz of a full-grown rattler, which is one of the premier attention-getters in the natural world.

Most students agree that the rattle functions primarily as a defense, warning larger animals and would-be predators that the creature possessing it is perhaps as formidable and dangerous as it seems. Of the seventeen species of pit viper found in the United States, fifteen (the rattlesnakes) have rattles and two (the copperheads and cottonmouths) do not, and since there is not much difference between the groups otherwise, it looks as though the rattle is a very successful device in evolutionary terms — snakes with rattles producing many more species than snakes without.

But the utility of any given feature doesn't guarantee its appearance; otherwise many more snakes would have rattles. A snake that could use one is the saw-scaled viper, a small and highly venomous species native to Old World deserts. In the absence of a rattle it has evolved a skin so rough and burred that it can, when threatened, produce a loud, evil-sounding rasp simply by rubbing its coils against each other. No rattlesnake has developed any such behavior, presumably because the rattle provides all that is needed in the noise department.

Many dangerous snakes, in contrast to their nonvenomous relatives, sport features that appear to have no function other than to draw attention to themselves. These include the cobra's spreading hood, the coral snake's striking colors, and the bold white lining of the cottonmouth's gullet, which is flashed like a badge at passersby. And so it looks as though deadly force, in the form of powerful toxins, is often more effective in defense when accompanied by loud warnings. Some harmless snakes mimic the color and behavior of venomous species found in their neighborhood, often with astonishing fidelity, as if their family trees had been pruned for millennia by predators expert in detecting fakes.

Only rattlesnakes, however, come equipped with rattles. This suggests that rattles — unlike wings, say, or poison glands — will never become a common theme in evolution. They are too specialized, too narrowly devoted to a function easily performed by other means — there are a thousand ways, for instance, to look and sound fearsome. All rattlesnakes, moreover, appear to be closely related on the basis of other characteristics, so it seems that the rattle evolved only once in their lineage, and that all existing species should be referred to that event.

What can be said about this original rattler? Perhaps his parents were vigorous tail-beaters but lacked rattles. Perhaps a chromosomal accident, or mutation, ensured that when he shed his skin, a hard little bit remained attached to his tail, a bit duplicated with each subsequent shedding, so that when he vibrated it, he produced an altogether more chilling and strident result. If he had died young, this innovation might have died with him. But he did not die young — whatever its virtues, his invention survived in his progeny and eventually developed into the loud, reliable, and unmistakable buzzer shared by all rattlers today.

Where and when did he live? It's unlikely that he made his home on the Asian side of the Pacific, because if he did, we might expect to find rattlers there today. It's more probable that he was an American, and appeared after the great Cenozoic cooling had begun, so that his descendants couldn't spread back into Siberia, though they occupied nearly all the dry land between Quebec and Patagonia.

There is, however, one large and successful clan of American pit vipers that does without rattles. This is the genus *Bothrops,* from the Greek *bothro* and *ops,* "pit" and "eye," referring to the pit organ. Though not well known in the United States, the group numbers almost fifty species, half again as many as the rattlesnakes, and includes such widely feared *sudamericanos* as the fer-de-lance, the jaracara, and the barba amarilla, or yellowbeard. A recent book on conservation in Belize, Alan Rabinowitz's *Jaguar,* includes a vivid eyewitness account of a lethal bite delivered by the latter.

*Bothrops* is mostly confined to tropical forests between the Yucatán and Brazil, even though not all of its members are tree dwellers. In those areas within its range where the shade gives way to more open country, as in the savannas of Venezuela, it tends to be replaced by tropical varieties of *Crotalus.* Rattlesnakes, on the other hand, are rarely found in the dense, steamy habitats favored by *Bothrops.*

Is there a message here? Have these two groups more or less divided up the New World, with *Bothrops* taking the rain forests centered on the equator, and *Crotalus* the more arid subtropical zones? Though the pattern is far from perfect, in North America it becomes blatant: Arizona, for instance, has seventeen species of *Crotalus* and not one *Bothrops.*

It's easy to hide in a rain forest. Many naturalists have remarked on how rare it is to come across a snake there, even when a wide variety of species are known to be present. In these circumstances a snake that rattled with any frequency might needlessly draw attention to itself. A snake that relied, in contrast, on camouflage and cryptic coloration might meet with less trouble. It would not have to expose itself to get warm, temperatures being uniformly high. It could hole up underground or in a tree cavity, emerging only when hungry. If attacked, it could bite, but too many bright colors might warn off its prey. And so a rain forest viper would do well to be silent, inconspicuous, and responsive only to the most obvious threats — the *Bothrops* strategy exactly.

It's different on the plains. Hiding places are fewer; if a snake comes out to hunt, even at night, it's more likely to be seen. Cold weather can be a problem, requiring some basking in the open. And chances are there will be a number of large, heavy-footed grazers around, grazers that might inadvertently trample snakes that lie still, but which might learn to stay away from loud rattling ones. And so a prairie or desert snake, especially one equipped with strong venom, might do well to put less emphasis on concealment and more on noisy bluff. Something like a rattle could come in handy.

Prairies and deserts have become increasingly widespread in North America over the last thirty or forty million years. The rise of the Rockies and the Sierras cut off rain-bearing winds from the Pacific; cooling climates forced tropical forests back toward the equator. Hordes of rudimentary camels, horses, and bison learned to gallop across the fresh vistas, their molars newly flattened and thickened to grind tough, siliceous grasses. Tree squirrels moved east, or upslope; ground squirrels replaced them. Here was a situation ripe not for *Bothrops* but for a more bumptious, open-air kind of viper, a swaggering kind with a chip on its shoulder. It wouldn't abandon discretion but it wouldn't confine itself to the underbrush either. It would move out into the bare, empty spaces and stand its ground against all comers — a squat, scaly worm with "Don't touch" on one end and "That's why" on the other.

I don't mean to prophesy after the fact. There is such a viper; it is *Crotalus*. Rattlesnakes, sunshine, and aridity are linked; even here in the forested East, rattlers are concentrated in those areas baked hardest by the sun, as if still nostalgic for treeless horizons.

So we are ready to construct a scenario at last. We begin forty to fifty million years ago, in the rowdy youth of the new Age of Mammals, with a primitive Asian pit viper, or crotaline, that somehow found its way across the Bering Strait region and into the Americas. This pilgrim was probably much like our modern-day copperheads, which are less specialized than other pit vipers and which are the only ones now present on both sides of the Pacific. The immigrant later gave rise to two daughter-groups, *Bothrops* and *Crotalus,* each wildly successful and each broadly adapted to a major climatic zone. He himself was not nearly so enterprising, never adapting to either wet forests or dry highlands, and is today largely confined to the eastern United States, where he is represented by two little-changed descendants, the copperhead and the cottonmouth.

Mr. B. H. Brattstrom, perhaps the premier student of these matters, doubts that *Bothrops* is derived from a transplanted copperhead. *Bothrops* is so similar, in his opinion, to the East Asian genus of rain forest crotalines, *Trimeresurus*, that it makes more sense to suppose that two pit vipers crossed into Alaska, a copperhead and a *Trimeresurus*, and that while the former gave rise to *Crotalus*, *Bothrops* is derived from the latter. He suggests that the Bering region was so warm at the time that this pioneering *Trimeresurus* never had to venture out of the tropical forests on its way, and that if the two genera — *Bothrops* and *Trimeresurus* — didn't happen to live on opposite sides of an ocean, they would never have been separated by name, since they are barely distinguishable otherwise.

I'm not equipped to second either view on this point, and Brattstrom himself admits that his position rests on scant evidence. What remains beyond doubt, however, is that the pit vipers, like so many other invaders, made hay in the New World. There were no resident vipers to contend with — perhaps no venomous snakes at all, but only a collection of boas left over from the Mesozoic. In their absence the crotalines evolved forms adapted to nearly every ice-free patch of earth on either side of the equator, so that with time there was hardly a rat or mouse anywhere in the hemisphere that could retreat to its nest with the confidence that no wedge-faced reptile would follow him in.

At some point in this multimillion-year efflorescence a snake with a rattle appeared. This was the first *Crotalus*. It's reasonable to suppose he hailed from the North American Southwest, since this is where the great majority of living species are found. There was something about him that made him especially suited to dry places, so that even in the tropics, which were more or less preempted by *Bothrops*, he found room to expand. By the time *Homo sapiens* came along and began to inquire into his ancestry, this snake had become the dominant pit viper of North America and had given rise to a number of outrider forms that had invaded the eastern forests, the southern swamps, and several other habitats notably different from his high, arid birthplace.

Up to this point we have pretended that *Crotalus* was somehow present, albeit dimly, in all of his forebears: the long-ago lizard who dropped his legs and dived underground, the burrowing snake who crawled back into the light, the Old World rat poisoner who traded most of his teeth for a pair of long, hollow fangs, and the cat-eyed viper who arrived in America with a set of heat-sensing pits. While it's true that *Crotalus* could not have existed without these ancestors, no genuine Darwinist would admit that they made him in any sense necessary or inevitable; every living species, in this view, is the latest in a series of happy accidents. And so there is something unavoidably fraudulent in a step-by-step journey down a family tree; it can't help but resemble a story, and every story needs a hero. But there are no heroes in evolution, only products of change. It is only when one looks back and sees all the twists and turns any lineage had to negotiate that *Crotalus*'s emergence in the present begins to look like a triumph. That's why the notion of a handful of man-apes messing around with pebble tools strikes us as charged with futurity, because we know the consequences. But what events of today will prove pivotal for the history of life a mere two million years hence?

But to resume: once the vipers reach North America we begin to have a check on our story, a few isolated facts in the form of fossil bones. If our narrative can't accommodate them, so much for our narrative. It's safe to say that if the origins of *Crotalus* ever come to light, they'll lead the way.

Up until quite recently the earliest rattlesnake known was represented by two fangs and a handful of eroded vertebrae labeled "1637" and "1638" in the collections of the American Museum of Natural History, on Central Park West in New York City. They were sifted out of ancient sandbanks at a place called Driftwood Creek, in Hitchcock County, Nebraska. Stratigraphy, the science that investigates old sediments and arranges them in order of deposition, assigned these bones a date in the Lower Pliocene, or about four million years ago. They are indistinguishable from modern ones belonging to *Crotalus viridis*, the western rattlesnake, a widespread species still living in the area. Plenty of other *Crotalus* fossils had been found, some from species now extinct, but none dated back further than the Pleistocene, which began 1.8 million years ago. Since it was known that snakes in general were as much as 100 million years old, and that climatic constraints required the pit vipers to arrive here from Asia not much less than 40 million years ago, it looked as though these finds didn't amount to more than the final page of the story.

Then, in the mid-1960s Bob Slaughter of Texas's Southern Methodist University found some ancient snake bones at a site near the town of Coldspring on the Trinity River north of Houston. Since he was primarily interested in mammals, he sent them on to J. Alan Holman, an expert on Cenozoic reptiles then at Illinois State. In 1966 Holman announced that the bones included a single viperid vertebra — it had the typical spiky form that only the vipers developed, though the spikes themselves had broken off. Since the deposit dated from the late Miocene, or about ten million years ago, it pushed back the viperid presence in North America by a considerable margin.

Because of the vertebra's poor condition, it wasn't possible to assign it to any existing species. If Holman wanted to stretch the facts, he could have used the vertebra to establish a new, extinct form. But he recognized that it was simply too worn and decrepit to define any such category — a modesty rare among paleontologists — and in labeling it "Viperidae, species indeterminate" he admitted that it could have belonged to a copperhead, a *Crotalus*, a *Bothrops*, or even, wonder of wonders, a pitless Old World viper. So although he confirmed what Brattstrom and others had long suspected, that the vipers didn't arrive yesterday in the New World, he brought us no closer to the original rattlesnake.

Things got more interesting about ten years later when George Corner of the University of Nebraska State Museum looked through some green and black Miocene silts on a farm near the town of Red Cloud in Webster County, Nebraska, and discovered nearly four thousand snake bones. They were much better preserved than fossils taken from sand or gravel, and they included three fangs and fourteen vertebrae that Holman, after close examination, found to be remarkably similar to those belonging to the all-rattler genus *Crotalus*. If he had been willing to place them there, they would have taken honors as the oldest rattlesnake ever discovered. Unfortunately, the characteristics that distinguish *Crotalus* vertebrae from those belonging to copperheads and other pit vipers are subtle and difficult to confirm from only a handful of examples, and so it was with a powerful sense of disappointment, I suspect, that he wrote: "Nevertheless, I believe it is best to withhold generic identification until skull elements associated with vertebrae are found." *Crotalus* had slipped away again.

Clearly there were crotalines of one kind or another at large in the American West during Miocene times, along with three-toed horses, hornless rhinos, and countless other now-vanished beasts. Some of the larger mammals are so abundant as fossils that every badlands cloudburst exposes them by the thousand. The climate at the time has been characterized as warm temperate, and it was moist enough to support rich grasslands much like parts of Texas and Oklahoma today, where there is no shortage of rattlers. If *Crotalus* had enough in the way of hard parts to document himself with any frequency, we would doubtless understand his origins better. As it is, however, nearly all his relics come from much younger sites where conditions were peculiarly favorable to preservation: California's tar pits, Ice Age limestone sinks in Florida, and caves in the Ozarks, the Appalachians, and Nevada.

A few years after Holman just missed *Crotalus* at the Red Cloud site, he helped excavate another about two hundred miles to the north and west, in Cherry County, Nebraska. It dated from the early Miocene, making it about twice as old as the other two, and it yielded a single spiky vertebra about the size of a spitball. Now in the Michigan State Museum, it is labeled "Viperid, genus and species indeterminate" — once again Holman's scruples won out, although he did admit that the bone looked more like a rattler's than anything else. At twenty million years old, this telltale crumb of prairie grit is as near as anyone has come to *Crotalus*'s long-gone beginnings.

And so the net gain of nearly a half century of fossil-based research on rattlesnake origins can be summed up in a sentence: Vipers are at least twenty million years old in North America, and nothing has emerged to contradict Brattstrom's theory of an early Cenozoic migration from Asia and subsequent diversification. This may not seem like much, but it is no small achievement when an evolutionary hypothesis survives for forty years without qualification or revision. If, for instance, a snake midway between the vipers and boas had been found on this continent, or some old bones had turned up showing that other snakes besides vipers possessed the peculiar vertebral spines, we would be looking at a much different picture. As it is, the efforts of Holman and others documented a sudden irruption of advanced snake families into North America in Miocene times, seconding the view that the major modern developments in snake evolution occurred in the Old World, and that subsequent dispersals via Alaska revolutionized the local scene, crowding the natives and making way for a purely American phenomenon like *Crotalus*.

In an ideal bone digger's world, thousands of ancient rattlesnakes and rattlesnake forebears, sensing our needs, would have headed for the nearest marsh, swum out to its center, and buried themselves deep in anaerobic muds so that their skeletons might have been preserved intact for the rockhammer. In that case we might see just when the pit organ began to leave a hollow in the maxillary bone, separating the crotalines from the viperines, and we might also notice when a small hump began to grow out near the top of that hollow, dividing the rattlesnakes from the copperheads. The first snake to display the least sign of this hump might, by current definitions, be named *Crotalus pater-* or *materfamilias,* and we would have our original rattler.

But as it is, bone hunters and snake historians may have to get used to a certain paucity of evidence, just as New Englanders have learned to do without *Crotalus*. And even if Holman and his successors beat the odds and discover an entire series of missing links — skulls and associated vertebrae covering all the stages between an ancient copperhead and a modern rattlesnake — we may still be no closer to identifying the first rattler. Rattles leave no marks on the skeleton, and it may be impossible to tell which animal in the series was the first to carry one.

Insoluble problems litter the paths of most inquiries. This grandaddy *Crotalus* is no phantom, no imaginary monster; every rattler alive carries his genes. And yet he conceals himself perfectly; twenty million years cover his bones.

Sometime in the last century Charles Darwin visited the London Zoo carrying a paper bag with a stuffed snake inside. He proceeded to the monkey house, where a keeper let him into one of the larger cages. He then took the snake out of the bag, placed it on the ground, and went out. "After a time," he writes, "all the monkeys collected around it in a large circle, and staring intently, produced a most ludicrous appearance."

This seems to me the most reasonable response to a snake. No anger, no fear, no comic-book heroics, but instead a tacit admission of ignorance and a willingness to appear laughable. Maybe there is something ridiculous about treating a reptile as some sort of equal, as a possessor of secrets worth keeping. But snakes aren't bound by our prejudices. They took shape without us. It's hard to believe they came here so that we could despise them.

# 12

# A Change of Heart

## Incognito

> The devil, that old serpent, shall now be dragged up out of
> hell.
>
> — Jonathan Edwards, in a sermon to his parish at
> Northampton, Massachusetts (1739)

If Darwin showed the way to a new understanding of the natural
world, one that emphasized kinship and continuity rather than
exile and domination, it came too late for *Crotalus*. Even today
there is no shortage of New Englanders who consider it more or
less obligatory to kill any suspicious-looking snake they encounter.
"One less accident waiting to happen," they might say.

In 1834, while Darwin was still on board the *Beagle*, Stoughton
became the last Boston-area town to concern itself officially with
*Crotalus*, offering fifty cents apiece for all rattles turned in to the
selectmen. At about the same time a state-appointed guardian sold
off the last scrap of land belonging to the Massachuset, originally
part of a six-thousand-acre reservation on the southern edge of the
Blue Hills. The original Bostonians no longer needed any land of
their own, it was argued, since they had become "practically extinct."

The early decades of the nineteenth century form a watershed in New England history — much more so than, say, the Revolution, which only confirmed a state of semiautonomy that the colonists had preserved since their arrival. Before these years New Englanders were farmers, sailors, fishermen, Indian fighters, schoolmasters, draymen, and Bible legalists, with farmers predominating; afterward they were bankers, manufacturers, pieceworkers, factory hands, professors, urbanites, and policemen. A maritime economy based on agriculture, shipping, and fisheries gave way to an investment economy driven by machine power, railroads, and cheap consumer goods — a familiar pattern on both sides of the Atlantic, but here the transition had the additional effect of finally breaking the Puritan hold on the popular imagination. For generations the church fathers, with considerable help from the state, had struggled to maintain the founders' vision of the world as a sort of floating way-station where souls were tried on their road to eternity, and this effort nearly blocked the arrival of Enlightenment ideas; a Thomas Jefferson, for instance, could never have emerged from Boston, and Ben Franklin chose not to go back. After the divide, however, this ancient and homegrown compound of spiritual anxiety, moral fervor, and social intolerance flew apart, one of its embers lighting the fire that led to Mrs. Stowe, Harper's Ferry, and Appomattox.

In its absence the world looked like a different place. Landscapes were no longer viewed as shadowy doubles of more permanent locales, a practice still apparent in some of the place names around the Blue Hills: several Purgatory Brooks, a Satan's Kingdom (a not particularly diabolical outcrop), Hell Swamp, Devil's Brook. European travelers complained less often about the hearthside conversation at New England inns, which seemed to them drearily obsessed with obscure heresies and the means of discovering whether one had or had not been redeemed. Boston presses began to print works by local men who were not primarily divines. Jonathan Edwards's fame was eclipsed by Henry Wadsworth Longfellow's. No more red-skinned demons carrying fire out of Canada; no more stern-faced judges reading out the law of God; no more endless tree chopping and stone digging for everyone not otherwise employed.

Events on this side of the divide are recognizable even if distant:

Daniel Webster leading a Sunday fishing party to Ponkapoag Pond; Thoreau retiring in disgust from a teaching career after a summer trying to keep Canton's young men in order; two young immigrants, Sacco and Vanzetti, arrested for the shooting of a payroll clerk in Braintree. On the far side, however, events have a fabulous, hardly credible quality: Thomas Swift, a prominent citizen of Milton, is buried in Dorchester and large rocks are dragged over his grave to keep out wolves; the Plymouth magistrates hear a startling confession from a farm boy and put him to death, then throw in a pit and burn the ewe and she-goats he identified as his sex partners; a governor of Massachusetts loses his way at night in the woods near his house, crawls into a bark hut, and holds the door shut next morning when a woman in deerskins tries to shove it aside, muttering.

They were people like us, no doubt. But the world they inhabited is no longer visible, and so they go about their business with the remarkable aplomb of fantasists — climbing transparent staircases, skirting celestial minefields, rowing boats across cow pastures, and pursuing sea monsters through kitchen gardens. To say that they lived and died here, within sight of the Blue Hills, doesn't bring them any closer.

A few dates will help locate the divide:

*1814*    The Roman Catholic Church certifies its first members in the town of Canton, five recent immigrants from Ireland.

*1819*    The town and parish of Canton legally separate, so that taxpayers will no longer be required to support the Congregational minister.

*1826*    The Granite Railway opens in Quincy, one of the first rail lines in the United States, built to carry quarried slabs from the eastern end of the Blue Hills down to tidewater on the Neponset. Blue Hills granite is used to construct the Bunker Hill Monument and the federal customhouses in Boston, New Orleans, and San Francisco.

*1830*    Harvard College erects a twenty-foot tower atop Great Blue Hill in order to establish a meridian from its Cambridge observatory.

*1831*    Boston engineers examine Ponkapoag Pond as a possible municipal water source.

Events like these finally acknowledged that the founders' vision had been outrun by time, and that the Holy Commonwealth at the head of the bay had been transformed, in the space of two centuries, into something entirely different: a New World metropolis.

And so the moral and spiritual energies that had been devoted for so long to purging and purifying a communion of saints had to find work elsewhere, and the locus of authority once divided between the magistrate's bench and the meetinghouse pulpit migrated even further toward the ballot box and the bankbook. The next generation of preachers — Emerson, Thoreau, and the abolitionists — steered clear of the churches, and for the farmers' sons and daughters still sitting inside, the weight of eternity perhaps seemed less burdensome than the challenge of scratching a living out of an exhausted landscape.

Oddly enough, this landscape of old pastures, dirt tracks, patchy woods, and scattered villages — the product of ten generations of human and animal labor — began to seem attractive, even precious, as it edged toward decay. It had once represented little more than a foothold, a space from which everything unpleasing to God might be eliminated. Now that it had surrendered its terrors, yielded up its fertility, and speckled itself with venerable graves, it began to become a place in its own right — not just a proving ground for the elect, but a piece of the world, of God's world, and perhaps as rich in possibilities as any heaven or hell.

This discovery worked a revolution in local attitudes. For two centuries it had seemed as though the Bay Colony Puritans lived in a world not worth describing. Though they were furious writers, they wrote mostly outlines of church doctrine, recipes for salvation, analyses of biblical law, and endless digests and rehashes of each other's opinions. To be educated at all meant preparing to add one's own voice to this chorus of scarecrows. Very little of this work is worth reading today. Only in their histories does any hint of the Puritans' actual circumstances emerge, and even here events are often obscured by the need to frame everything in cosmic terms.

Now, however, it was as though a cloud had lifted and the world stood revealed, not the old world of portents, providences, and traps laid for the unwary, but a new one of rain, sunshine, salt water, fresh air, and granite rock. We know from travelers' accounts that it had existed before. Ben Franklin, Cotton Mather, and a few others had gone so far as to become interested in it. But for the first time the material world was seen not as a shifting curtain barely masking the divine countenance, but as an independent entity, a presence-in-depth possessing secrets of its own.

Boston was a century or more behind Europe in this respect, and decades behind Philadelphia and Virginia. The revolutions effected by Newton, Linnaeus, and Voltaire had raised barely a ripple in Massachusetts. And even after the dam broke, after it was admitted that the real world might become a worthy object of inquiry, a feeling lingered that science ought to remain a branch of theology, and that the laws of nature should be regarded as the ordinances of God. The theory of natural selection, for instance, with its vision of a continuous and not necessarily conscious process of creation, was distinctly unpopular. Many of its converts were unwelcome at Harvard, and the leading Boston publisher, Ticknor & Fields, lost ground to competitors in New York by declining to publish Darwin, Huxley, and others.

But the change did come, and a world hitherto ignored came under fresh scrutiny. Here is how an original member of the Boston Society of Natural History (later to become the Museum of Science) described the situation:

At the time of the establishment of the Society [1830], there was not, I believe, in New England, an institution devoted to the study of Natural History. There was not a college in New England, excepting Yale, where philosophical geology of the modern school was taught. There was not a work extant by a New England author which presumed to group the geological structure of any portion of our territory of greater extent than a county. There was not in existence a bare catalogue, to say nothing of a general history, of the animals of Massachusetts, of any class. There was not within our borders a single museum of Natural History founded according to the requirements and based on the system of modern science, nor a single journal advocating exclusively its interests.

We were dependent chiefly upon books and authors foreign to New England for our knowledge of our own Zoology. There was no one among us who had anything like a general knowledge of the birds which fly about us, of the fishes which fill our waters, or of the lower tribes of animals that swarm both in air and sea.

Some few individuals there were, distinguished by high attainments in particular branches and who formed honorable exceptions to the indifference which prevailed, but there was no concentration of opinion or knowledge, and no means of knowing how much or how little was known. The Laborers in Natural History worked alone without aid or encouragement from others engaged in the same pursuits, and without the appreciation of the public mind, which regarded them as busy triflers.

This sounds much like the Eisenhower-era critiques prompted by the launching of *Sputnik.*

At any rate, the second quarter of the nineteenth century in New England brought in an unprecedented vogue for birdwatching, botanizing, stargazing, and rock collecting. Thousands flocked to hear a Swiss naturalist, Louis Agassiz, lecture on matters as abstruse as Ice Age geology and the anatomy of the lower animals. New Englanders had long been famous for their ability to absorb interminable learned disquisitions from the pulpit; now a new sort of gospel had been unearthed, the gigantic history of God's beneficence as revealed in creation, and crowds of amateur exegetes poured out into the countryside with bug nets, flower presses, and hand lenses, searching the landscape as minutely as their ancestors had searched their own souls. Thoreau, writing in 1842, complained that "you cannot go into any field or wood, but it will seem as if every stone had been turned, and the bark on every tree ripped up."

Agassiz was perhaps the most popular man in Boston in the mid-nineteenth century. An expert on fossil fishes, with a leonine profile, an endearing accent, and immense charm, he arrived here on a lecture tour in 1846 and received such a welcome from the new Brahmin aristocracy created by the railroads and cotton mills that he decided to stay, and accepted a professorship at the Lawrence Scientific School, a newly minted branch of Harvard intended to vault the college into modernity. Agassiz had made his reputation through the study of preserved specimens in European zoological collections. He now proposed to create a similar collection in Cambridge, one that would take full advantage of the new worlds coming to light in the American West and make Massachusetts an international center of research and education in natural history.

Thanks to his remarkable fund-raising abilities, a massive brick-and-granite edifice opened its doors on Divinity Avenue in November 1860, the Museum of Comparative Zoology. Its public galleries illustrated Agassiz's version of the divine plan of creation as evidenced by the forms of animal life. In its basement, however, his acquisitive instincts reached their fullest expression: in 1859 alone, 435 barrels and 98 cans of pickled specimens were delivered, and in the following year he welcomed 91,000 additional items representing 11,000 species. Here was a true latter-day Noah determined to reassemble the world in miniature, only instead of floating his prizes above the Universal Deluge, Agassiz meant to drown each of them separately in a bottle of alcohol, and he obtained a special exemption from liquor taxes for that purpose.

The museum staff was quickly overwhelmed by the flood of cadavers pouring in from all points, and many items dispatched to the basement vanished inside and weren't relocated until years later. By then Agassiz's son Alexander had replaced him as director and instituted a more workable admissions policy. In the meantime, the mania for collecting and preserving had had consequences in the Blue Hills.

In 1868 J. A. Allen published a "Catalogue of the Reptiles and Batrachians of Springfield, Massachusetts" in the *Proceedings of the Boston Society of Natural History*. In it he listed a snake hitherto undocumented in the Massachusetts portion of the Connecticut River valley, *Agkistrodon contortrix*, otherwise known as the copperhead. Allen stated that a well-known den of these vipers existed on Mount Tom, a steep basalt ridge dominating the valley, and that several were killed there annually.

Rumors of a venomous companion to *Crotalus* weren't unheard-of north of the Connecticut line. John E. Holbrook, a professor at the South Carolina Medical College and the grand old man of American herpetology, had told New York naturalist James DeKay that he had found copperheads in the Northampton area under Mount Tom and had received others from Vermont. The species wasn't listed, however, in the two previous catalogues of reptiles native to Massachusetts, those of Smith (1835) and Storer (1839).

Aware that he was breaking new ground, Allen canvassed a number of naturalists for news of copperheads in the Bay State. Here is what Addison Verrill, professor of natural history at Yale, wrote him: "There is, or was, a specimen of *Agkistrodon contortrix* in the Museum of Comparative Zoology collected at the Blue Hills,

Milton, Massachusetts, where it is said they are not uncommon."
Allen printed Verrill's remark without comment.

The copperhead had long been a familiar character in Connecticut and southward. First described by Linnaeus as *Boa contortrix,* it
was also known as the chunkhead, the red adder, and the rattlesnake pilot. Its name had passed into slang, first as a Yankee term
for the Dutch inhabitants of New York, then as a derisive epithet
for northerners who sympathized with the South during the Civil
War. Though not so formidable as *Crotalus,* copperheads have the
paired fangs and venom glands of a viper and their bite is unmis-
takably toxic. How, then, had Dr. Storer been able to declare (in his
1839 survey) that "many groundless fears will be removed from the
minds of anxious parents by a knowledge that only a single venomous snake is known to exist in Massachusetts"? And where did
Joel Allen, a professor at the Museum of Comparative Zoology and
an authority on local wildlife, find the confidence to report, in
Winsor's *Memorial History of Boston* (1880), that *Crotalus* was "the
only dangerous species in the area"?

Clearly the Bay State copperheads, if in fact they existed, had
found a way to remain shadowy and obscure long after most other
native snakes had been described and identified — no mean
achievement for a sizable reptile with a sickening bite. *Crotalus,* for
instance, had been known and noticed since the first settlement of
Boston, and Josselyn (1672) hadn't overlooked species as small and
unprepossessing as the green snake and the milk snake. Why then
did the copperheads take so long to emerge?

Professor Verrill, the man who alerted Allen to the pickled Blue
Hills specimen in Cambridge, had been a student of Agassiz's at
the museum before he moved to New Haven. Like many of the
great man's assistants, he had been alienated by Agassiz's dictato-
rial manner and his penchant for appropriating subordinates' research. Perhaps Verrill was the first local naturalist to become
aware that there were copperheads in eastern Massachusetts,
thanks to the specimen at the museum; he cannot, however, receive
credit for the discovery. That belongs to the person listed as "Collector" for item number 660 in the museum's *Catalogue of Reptiles,*
dated 1862 and found at Milton, Massachusetts — William Forbes.

Forbes is an interesting character. Born into a Scots family resident in Milton since the Revolution, he was the son of one of the

greatest drug lords in New England history, John Murray Forbes, who made a fortune selling opium in China and later compounded it in midwestern railroads. This wealth came in handy in 1860 when the younger Forbes, then a junior at Harvard, accidentally beaned a watchman in a midnight Bible-napping incident in the college chapel and nearly killed him. Forbes was expelled; in the resulting settlement the guard, a Mr. Hilton, received funds sufficient to enable him to buy up nearly an entire city block facing Harvard Yard.

Forbes later redeemed himself by becoming a cavalry commander in the Civil War. On July 6, 1864, at Aldie, Virginia, he had his horse shot from under him by the legendary Confederate raider John S. Mosby and went south as a prisoner. After his release he married a daughter of Ralph Waldo Emerson. In 1879 he became the first president of AT&T.

But Forbes didn't escape the rage for nature study that overtook Boston's elite following the ascension of Agassiz. As a sophomore at Harvard he had been elected vice president of the undergraduate Natural History Society, founded twenty years earlier by members of Thoreau's class. His father happened to own a large piece of the Blue Hills. Perhaps the young Forbes was wandering their summits on a warm morning after his disgrace when he came upon a reddish, thick-bodied snake, killed it, and brought it to the museum. It was the first northern copperhead placed in the collection. The very next addition, number 661, was another snake of the same species personally entered by Louis Agassiz; it came from Cumberland Gap, Kentucky.

Copperheads have probably inhabited the Blue Hills since prehistoric times. Today they are believed to be approximately twice as numerous as rattlesnakes there. None, however, have been found any nearer to Maine, which makes the Hills the extreme limit of their range in the Northeast. The precise extent of their domain is the subject of a thirty-year-old deposition pasted inside the back cover of the appropriate volume of the museum's *Catalogue of Reptiles:*

2/28/59

This is to certify that I, Charles A. Clark, now residing at the Karlson Rest Home, 73 Baker St., Lynn, Massachusetts, being of sound mind and body, wish to make known the fact that I have never collected, or have seen, *Agkistrodon contortrix* in Essex County, Lynn Woods, Lynn, in the many years I have been collecting there.

Signed:     Charles A. Clark

3/15/59

Witness: Edward L. Leiblein
Witness: Kinsman Lyon

This curious document originated in 1914, when the then-youthful Clark collected several copperheads for the museum and they were listed as having come from the Lynn Woods, an area of rugged granite bluffs on the north rim of the Boston basin. Forty-five years later someone must have looked at the entry, noticed that it was the sole record of copperheads north of Boston, and wondered if it was an error. A timely visit to Clark at the Karlson Rest Home confirmed the suspicion, enabling the anonymous detective to go back to the entry, cross out "Lynn Woods," and write in "Blue Hills," thereby shrinking *Agkistrodon*'s northeasterly salient by some twenty miles.

A trivial matter, you might think, but not for *Agkistrodon*. Here in Massachusetts he lives on the ragged edge of his range, barely penetrating the state from the south and thriving nowhere except in a handful of particularly favorable sites: the Blue Hills, Mount Tom, and perhaps a few other stations in the Connecticut River valley. This must account for the long lag before his official discovery by Forbes. Hundreds of copperheads were probably killed in and around the Hills by eighteenth-century bounty hunters looking for *Crotalus;* they left no trace in the records, however.

Elsewhere *Agkistrodon* has had similar difficulties spreading much north of the old high-tide marks of the glaciers. In the Mississippi River valley, for instance, his northern limit is the southeast corner of Iowa, and he nowhere reaches the southern shores of the Great Lakes, much less Canada. *Crotalus,* in contrast, was once common in the gorge below Niagara Falls, and can still be found in Minnesota and central Vermont. So it appears that there is something about cold climates that is even harder on copperheads than on *Crotalus.* In Connecticut, where they intermingle, it has been noticed that *Crotalus* prefers to bask on the highest, sunniest ledges, whereas copperheads are more often found in shadier pockets farther downslope. Perhaps it is this apparent reluctance to take full advantage of available sunlight that has kept *Agkistrodon* out of the northern tier of states. His more secretive habits, however, have enabled him to survive and prosper in many suburban areas from which *Crotalus* has long since been evicted.

Is it possible that there is a third viper in Massachusetts, one so clandestine and retiring that not a single example has yet found its way into a bottle of ethanol? Probably not. Since Agassiz's time hundreds of sharp-eyed snake enthusiasts have tramped over nearly every square inch of the commonwealth. New species are still arriving at the museum, but they are tiny frogs from the cloud forests of Peru or rare burrowing snakes from Laos. Most of the local types are already fully represented, and no further specimens are invited — in fact, *Crotalus* and *Agkistrodon* have become so scarce in the state that killing them is prohibited under any circumstances.

The first Puritans in Massachusetts had no trouble seeing through *Crotalus*. He was, they believed, a sort of worm from hell, a particularly noxious representative of the original American darkness, and they dealt with him accordingly. And yet when the Puritan program finally collapsed in the early nineteenth century — when even the fieriest preachers had to admit that the Holy Commonwealth wasn't likely to emerge from the materials at hand — it appeared that *Crotalus* had not only survived but had acquired a cousin. What kind of victory was this?

One could almost argue that *Agkistrodon* had arrived from Europe, because it was from Europe that the new America was coming. This was the America of mass immigration, of cities springing up like weeds — Cincinnati, Chicago, St. Louis, and San Francisco. This America was as drunk on nationhood as Napoleon's France and as obsessed with busyness as Victoria's Britain. Feverish, polyglot, muscular, and chaotic, it would rush to the Pacific, break in half, and plunge into war in the time it took the Puritans to penetrate forty miles inland. For generations New England had been a half-forgotten outpost of empire, trading with the world but turning it back at the shoreline, often most concerned with preserving an ideal of religious and moral conformity long since abandoned at its source. In 1774 New England went to war in order to safeguard this backwardness; in that war it joined itself to a nation. That nation, it soon discovered, was not going to submit to New England. If New England meant to have a future, it would have to be within the covenant that created the nation. And in accepting that covenant, New England lost the basis of its special identity, which would flare up for the last time in the generation of Emerson and Hawthorne. In contrast, the South went on to reject the amalgam, and remained a place apart for much longer.

But this isn't our story. What matters to us is the route *Crotalus* took through the new world on this side of the divide, a world in which New Englanders lifted themselves free of the landscape and showered it with railroads, banks, newspapers, mill towns, summer homes, coal furnaces, sewer lines, and learned societies. *Crotalus* wouldn't change; he was too much the homebody. But he was bound to look different in different surroundings.

## Transmutation

The power of fascination attributed to this genus is too absurd to require our serious consideration.

— D. Humphreys Storer, M.D., in *Reports on the Fishes, Reptiles, and Birds of Massachusetts* (1839)

*Crotalus* is sometimes described as a snake of the "forested East," despite his predilection for bare, ledgy places. And any summertime walker standing atop one of the Blue Hills today would have to agree that the East is indeed forested, since the carpet of tree-tops beginning just downslope extends to the horizon in all directions, blue water excepted. Thanks to the effects of foreshortening, Boston itself looks like no more than an old, all-but-healed gash in the greenery; closer at hand, Dorchester, Dedham, and Milton barely peep out of the undergrowth. If it weren't for the bald, sprawling landfills in Quincy and Randolph, and a half-dozen expressways carved out here and there, one might imagine oneself in Arcadia.

It wasn't always like this. A hundred fifty years ago, when no one in Massachusetts could cook a meal, heat a building, stoke a foundry, or power a locomotive without turning wood into ashes, any full-grown tree was a remarkable object. By then Boston was getting nearly all of its lumber and much of its fuel wood from as far away as Maine, having eaten up everything nearer. Most of the countryside around the Blue Hills, still largely rural, supported crops and pasture; the remainder, mostly swamps and waste ground, had been cut over and burned so many times that the soil itself was evaporating. In 1853 Thoreau learned, to his dismay, that a machine had been invented for chopping knee-high huckleberry brush into a flammable bran. "At this rate," he wrote, "we shall all be obliged to let our beards grow at least, if only to hide the nakedness of the land and make a sylvan appearance."

This was the situation Charles Eliot faced forty years later when he proposed to create a forest in the Blue Hills. It is still visible in some of his photographs: a stark sepia landscape as leafless in summer as winter, where every sapling or fencepost left standing has the forlorn look of an orphan left over from a hurricane. Trees large enough to give shade survived only in the village centers, where elms sheltered the greens, or in ancient rows on the roadsides, or deep in swamps, or on rich men's estates. In between lay mile after mile of gnawed scrub and bare, bouldery earth.

But this was no wasteland. If trees were scarce, wood was not; railroads and coasters brought it in by the ton. And if the old rural economy had withered, the one whose meager surplus consisted mostly of butter, wool, salted meat, and restless farm boys, by about 1830 or so a more robust organism had grown up in its place, one that poured out shoes, glass, paper, cotton cloth, and gunpowder. From the Blue Hills it would have been visible as the new quarrymen's settlements along Willard Street in Quincy, or in the warty growth of red brick over the Neponset at Lower Mills, or even as the turnpike laid out to cross them at Randolph. Paul Revere's old workshop in Canton now included several rolling mills that turned out miles of copper sheathing used to protect oceangoing vessels from shipworms; high pastures that commanded fine views, such as those along Adams Street or Canton Avenue in Milton, were sprouting clusters of elegant twelve-room country seats. In certain weathers Boston exhaled a yellow cloud of woodsmoke several miles wide.

And so for the first time since the Puritans put the ax to this landscape it was changing again. No longer dependent on local hay, cider, and corn, it had learned how to subsist on machine sheds and ingenuity. The old fears — fear of outsiders, fear of innovation, fear of hellfire, fear of tomorrow — were losing much of their grip. Tomorrow had arrived.

In 1830 a group of Boston men began meeting regularly, first in each other's homes, then in a rented hall over the Savings Bank on Tremont Street, then in a building they purchased one block east on Mason Street. They wrote a charter, elected officers, and assigned one another duties. They agreed to assemble a library and present papers detailing their personal researches in geology, meteorology, botany, zoology, and related topics. These papers, along with minutes of their meetings, would be published in a bulletin available to out-of-town members. They called themselves the Boston Society of Natural History.

This was by no means a new idea. England's Royal Society, for instance, dated back to the seventeenth century, and Ben Franklin had organized a similar group in Philadelphia before the Revolution. But it would be years before Harvard College stirred itself to offer adequate instruction in these sciences, and those interested were necessarily amateurs.

One of the tasks the members set themselves was to clear away some of the lies and misinformation that had collected around various aspects of the natural world. At a meeting in 1851, a letter was read from a Dr. J. B. Johnston of Sherbrooke, Canada, reporting the case of a girl afflicted with a bad cough and stomach pains who had vomited a newt on her doorstep and was apparently cured. Dr. Johnston had kept the animal, identified as *Salamandra sylvatica,* alive in water for a week. When it died he pickled it and sent it to Boston along with his account.

Jeffries Wyman, M.D., later to become the society's president, stood up to address the matter. The facts, he declared, were open to doubt, and he doubted them. There may have been a newt on the doorstep, quite possibly the same now in their possession, but he couldn't believe it had spent any length of time in a girl's stomach. He cited a case in his experience involving an insane man who had swallowed a toad: the toad "was ejected, dead, within a half hour." In another instance a Reading, Massachusetts, man had reported himself freed of an abdominal complaint when he coughed up a snake. Dr. Wyman had obtained the animal, examined it, and found that its stomach contained no human food but only another snake. These and other considerations led him to believe, in respect to the newt, that no such animal could "exist in the human stomach alive for any length of time." These creatures were common enough, however, and it was easy to see how a belief in their power to cause illness might be reinforced if one happened to turn up at the right time and place.

Dr. Wyman spoke in the best empirical tradition of the society, which held that popular wisdom deserved the same respect as any other account of the facts, at least until close inquiry found it wanting. In 1848 he had been appointed the first professor of zoology at Harvard, where he performed some notable experiments on the still widely accepted doctrine of spontaneous generation. He later became the first man to scientifically describe a new species from Africa, the gorilla.

This idea of noxious reptiles working harm from within wasn't recent in Massachusetts. In 1638, when Anne Hutchinson, then four months pregnant, was brought before the Boston church to be excommunicated for heresy, her son and son-in-law tried to question the length of the ten-hour proceedings. John Cotton, teacher of the congregation, replied that "instead of loving and natural children, you have proved vipers, to eat through the very bowels of your mother." His counterpart across the Charles in Cambridge, Thomas Hooker, had written: "Every natural man and woman is born full of sin, as full as a toad of poison." The notion later reemerged in Hawthorne's short story "The Bosom Serpent," in which a young man mysteriously sickens and mopes around town, muttering, "It gnaws me! It gnaws me!" Thoreau gleefully turned the tradition on its head when, in his journal for July 7, 1851, he boasted of stopping for a drink at Nut Meadow Brook: "I do not drink in vain. I mark that brook as if I had swallowed a water snake that would live in my stomach. I have swallowed something worth the while. . . . The man must not drink of the running streams, the living waters, who is not prepared to have all nature reborn in him — to suckle monsters."

Thoreau had been elected to the Society of Natural History six months earlier; perhaps he had just read Dr. Wyman's account in the *Proceedings*. At his death in 1862 he bequeathed all his collections to it: his pressed plants, his bird's eggs and nests, and his Concord Indian artifacts, all identified by himself.

Like Agassiz, the society welcomed specimens. By 1854 its Herpetology Department had catalogued 480 items, including 227 pickled snakes. Some of these were Blue Hills rattlers, the most recent a Milton example donated by Dr. C. C. Holmes of that town.

Physicians dominated the society. In 1854 thirteen of its nineteen officers had medical degrees. The mounting prestige of science had given them a new social eminence. Perhaps they foresaw the day when some of the decayed authority of the Puritan soul-doctors would be revived in them. They were respectable figures; D. Humphreys Storer, the man who overlooked *Agkistrodon* in the 1839 state-financed *Reports on the Fishes, Reptiles, and Birds of Massachusetts,* later became New England's foremost teacher of obstetrics and in 1866 was elected president of the American Medical Association. He had weaknesses as a taxonomist, however — in these same *Reports* he reprinted an account of a curious snake from Gloucester whose spine had developed a series of vertical undulations much like those traditionally attributed to sea serpents. The animal's head had been smashed during capture, complicating identification; even so, it apparently didn't occur to Dr. Storer that this supposedly unique specimen of a new, seagoing species might be nothing more than a young blacksnake with a congenital deformity.

A significant oversight, one might think. But when these men were at school they had never been invited to take a hard look at the world under their feet — to peer through a microscope, dissect a flower, or crumble dirt in their hands. For over a century Harvard College had clung to a quasi-medieval curriculum based on philosophy, ancient languages, and mathematics; these were regarded as the complete equipment of an informed mind. It was only in the recently organized medical colleges that a more open, experimental approach was emphasized, an approach that matched book learning against the new and previously overlooked testament written into the stuff of the living world. Those who had been through such a course must have realized what large portions of Massachusetts had gone unexamined, and that they were better positioned than anyone to begin the work.

In an age of specialists it is perhaps difficult to imagine how a group of amateurs meeting casually could represent the most advanced local stage of an entire realm of knowledge. But until Agassiz arrived and assembled his staff, this was indeed how matters stood, and it accounts for the Athenian atmosphere of the society's early meetings. Natural history, as defined by Linnaeus, traditionally included all of geology, botany, and zoology, along with as much chemistry and physiology as was applicable. Since these sciences were virtually unknown in Massachusetts, the society's members immediately began filling the gaps with lists of mollusks dredged from the Charles, collections of rocks picked up on the beaches, and swarms of beetles pinned under glass and identified with Latin binomens. Some of the members became so absorbed in this work that they abandoned their medical practices and became full-time naturalists, often at considerable sacrifice; the lucky ones later received academic appointments. In Europe, New England — unlike California, say, or Japan — was no longer regarded as a rewarding spot to send collectors, since most of its native plants and animals had long since found their way into the major museums. But there were no museums in Boston, and students had to go to London or Geneva merely to find out what inhabited their own back yards. This was the situation the Society of Natural History meant to remedy.

In its heyday, from its founding in 1830 until the Civil War, the society's membership included nearly everyone who mattered in American natural history, and its meetings were considerable events. No new theory or doctrine could establish itself without winning this audience, and many lively debates centered on matters such as the evidence of Ice Ages, the significance of the huge, birdlike tracks found in the rocks of the Connecticut River valley, and the history behind present patterns of animal and plant distribution. Agassiz, perhaps recognizing the role the society had played in his welcome, often came over from Cambridge to lead discussions; William Barton Rogers, the geologist who later founded MIT, was another frequent participant. In the meantime the collections accumulated: rattlesnakes from the Blue Hills, pickled crabs from Mexico, whale parts from Hawaii, volcanic glass from Sicily.

*Crotalus* advocates might argue that snake bashing is snake bashing, regardless of whether the victims are stockpiled in alcohol or tossed, tailless, into the bushes. But sciences that concern themselves with living populations of wild animals, such as ecology and ethology, had barely been thought of, and classification, or taxonomy, still dominated natural history — even minerals were sometimes given Linnaean names. In this view a pickled snake was not merely a pickled snake but a natural fact, an irreducible datum in the splendid patchwork of creation, and there was tremendous interest in learning how the picture was organized. A snake, for instance, could be compared with snakes of other kinds, and snakes in general with other reptile groups; with luck certain patterns might emerge. Nobody supposed that these patterns were fortuitous. They revealed the working methods of the Almighty in designing the world. Now that the literal truth of the Bible was in question, now that the divine will was no longer so visible in everyday life, there was a hunger to ferret God out of his last hiding places, and scientific men commonly introduced Him into their writings, awarding Him entire credit for the ingenious arrangements and consistencies they had uncovered, as if the natural world were a wonderland He had built to advertise His magnificence. And so a pickled rattlesnake became a valuable and necessary object, perhaps no more and no less valuable than anything else God had seen fit to produce.

This wasn't the *Crotalus* the Puritans knew. For them nature was fallen, and all its inhabitants reeked of the original crime — none more so than the serpent. Now he was losing his evil glamour; now, if he claimed he was as sharp-toothed as ever, he would encounter

Emerson's lofty dictum: "We like to see everything do its office after its kind, whether it be a milch cow or a rattlesnake." Clearly a new spirit was at large — confident, unburdened, frankly progressive. Even Hawthorne, perhaps more haunted than anyone by the old New England darkness — the naked demons butchered in the woods, the infants blasted by witches, the vipers coiled underneath the meetinghouse floor — chose to work out the poison, not in prayer but in novels — novels! — as if he'd forgotten what piety was.

Is it possible that all the tree chopping and snake killing had finally had their effect? Is it possible that this landscape simply no longer contained enough shadows to masquerade as an ordeal?

At any rate, for Storer, Agassiz, Wyman, and company there was never any question of deviltry or malice associated with *Crotalus*. Dr. Wyman addressed the society on the subject of his rattle, having dissected several for that purpose. Reading through the *Proceedings* — the endless lists of books and specimens acquired, the new subscribers announced from Illinois, Tennessee, and Texas, the visits by eminent scholars from abroad, the remarkable erudition displayed in monographs on lichens, fossil shells, and rock crystals — one might suppose that the society was well on its way to becoming a great research institution.

That wasn't in the cards. Over the years the members, perhaps wisely, steered the society away from original work and toward education. It was a victim of its success; by the 1860s most of the Yankee colleges had hired instructors in natural history, and Agassiz and his museum, along with Professors Wyman in zoology and Asa Gray in botany, had shifted the center of action across the Charles, to Harvard. Perhaps the last time the vanguard of American science occupied the society's meeting rooms was in the first months of 1860, when a series of informal debates was held concerning a remarkable new hypothesis from England.

One of the drawbacks to the Linnaean approach to nature was its static, purely descriptive quality. It assumed a Creator; it assumed a unit of creation, the species. All species were distinct, and all living things belonged to one or another. Any species necessarily bore a greater or lesser degree of resemblance to any other. If these similarities were abstracted and made the basis of groups, then the jumble of life could be organized as a set of hierarchical categories and any newly described creatures inserted at their proper position.

Linnaeus admitted that his groups were arbitrary, and that other schemes of division might serve just as well. Even so, as his system was elaborated by his numerous acolytes, and more and more animals and plants were worked into its mesh, the suspicion grew that many of these groups were *not* arbitrary, and represented more than a naturalist's whim. To say, for instance, that any animal that had a backbone, breathed air, and fed its young milk, whether it flew like a bat or swam like a dolphin, must be classified as a mammal and entered in the Mammalia seemed like a generalization of a different order than the claim that daffodils, bananas, and canaries all belonged to the group comprising Things That Are Yellow. It was hard to avoid feeling that the Creator had worked systematically also, and that it was no accident that there were no fish with hair, nor birds with teeth. And thus many naturalists concluded that in defining these groups they were not merely sorting beans into boxes, but were burrowing into the mind of God and unearthing His blueprints for creation.

Several generations later this idea reached its apogee in the work of Baron Cuvier, a French bone collector and intellectual colossus who was the spiritual father of Agassiz. His study of the fossils of the Paris basin, which included relics of enormous fishlike reptiles and numerous other cryptic behemoths unknown to history, led him to conclude that there had not been one creation but many, each terminated by a universal catastrophe akin to the Flood, and that after each of these slate-cleanings the Creator had reseeded the planet with myriad new, improved species — all of them, however, modeled on a few basic body plans that He had adhered to from the beginning: the Vertebrata, the Articulata, the Radiata, and so forth. Hence the Linnaean system was enabled to migrate back into time — not the biblical time of its inventor, but the unimaginable gulfs of rock-making time recently unveiled by the geologists.

Here was the spectacle Boston's elite found so exciting. The God of their fathers had been, above all, awesome: here was a God who flattened mountains, emptied seas, and called entire worlds out of nothing, over and over, only to hurl them to ruin. Agassiz didn't claim to know why the deity had seen fit to redo His work so often, but he did point out that certain species in one era hinted at what would appear in the next; the ungainly wings of flying reptiles, for instance, prophesied the much more sophisticated ones that would be seen in birds. And so he was able to argue that each new creation brought improvements on the old patterns, and that these experiments were forecast in advance, each being essential to the divine master plan for life on earth. The most recent and glorious product of this plan was, of course, the human race. In short, Agassiz saw the living world as no more than the outermost crust of the mind of God, and species — or individuals, for that matter — had no existence except insofar as they manifested certain stages in the divine train of thought.

If this sounds like what Emerson might have said if he had been trained as a taxonomist, it is no accident. Both he and Agassiz had drawn much of their inspiration from German idealism, Emerson via Coleridge and Agassiz via Schelling and Dolliger. During the 1840s and 1850s the two men jointly dominated New England intellectual life, and toasted each other regularly at the Saturday Club, a monthly gathering of literati that included Longfellow, Parkman, and Holmes. Given their Puritan background, New Englanders would probably have been uncomfortable with any naturalist who did not place God at the center of creation. Unlike Emerson, however, Agassiz presented himself as a scientist, not a mystic, and thus left himself vulnerable to arguments from the evidence.

Agassiz's account of the history of life, sometimes called catastrophism, rested on two assumptions: first, that species, like all ideal or Platonic entities, were immutable; second, that no lines of descent extended across breaks in the geological record. If, for instance, remains of an animal still living were found in rocks underneath the Ice Age deposits, Agassiz would deny any genetic connection, since the glaciers had destroyed all life on earth. He would argue, instead, that the remains represented a distinct and separately created type, and would be sure to find some minute characteristic in the fossil that proved it could not belong to the same species as the living animal.

In 1858 the first copies of *The Origin of Species* began to find their way across the Atlantic to Boston. Their effect on Agassizean idealism was immediately toxic. Darwin suggested that species were not facts in the mind of God, but merely collections of attributes invented for the convenience of taxonomists. He pointed out how much these purportedly immutable types varied in nature; in certain genera no two experts agreed on how to define them. But these were familiar complaints. What made the *Origin* so powerful was the alternate explanation it proposed for the diversity of plant and animal life: descent with modification, sometimes known as evolution, a process guided not by any preconceived plan but by a tension between ordinary increase and environment called natural selection.

To anyone accustomed to looking at nature through Agassiz's eyes, this was equivalent to arguing that the Parthenon had been constructed by termites. Once again God had been booted out of His role as the all-seeing, all-ordaining Mind Behind Matter and replaced with a principle that could as easily have been called Business as Usual. It was no use to answer that natural selection was itself the device by which the Almighty steered the world toward His ends (though many would take that tack later); too many claims had already been made for special creation. And so Agassiz, the scientist, would have to shore up his old argument that all species had been brought into being by supernatural fiat against a theory that substituted a perfectly ordinary and natural process, a process no more mysterious than water running downhill.

He began in classic style by pretending that Darwin didn't exist. Someone gave him a copy of the *Origin;* he couldn't find time to read it. Some of his students did, however, as did thousands of others when an American edition appeared. People insisted on talking about it. Finally he was goaded into dismissing it as "an ingenious and fanciful theory." Unlike Emerson, however, who was similarly unimpressed, Agassiz couldn't escape a more formal response. In a series of debates with colleagues willing to present Darwin's side — first with botanist Asa Gray at the American Academy of Arts and Sciences, then with geologist William B. Rogers at the Society of Natural History — he tried to beat back the plague.

He failed miserably. He was pedantic, obtuse, distracted; he got tangled in minutiae; he couldn't seem to grasp the main issues. It was as if he knew he was vulnerable but hoped to avoid a decision. The debates bombed as theater. Neither Gray nor Rogers chose to press his advantage, and many in the audiences were unaware that anything unusual had happened. But it was the end of Agassiz's preeminence among American naturalists. The younger generation no longer took him seriously as a theorist. Though he later promised to refute Darwin in print, he never attempted it. He wasn't the same man as before — somehow, at the height of his glory, he had become an anachronism.

Boston's elite remained loyal to its hero. He had taken their money and built a famous museum. He had educated their children and married one of their daughters. He had battled, albeit without much success, against a foreign idea they considered vulgar and dangerous. They rewarded him by pretending for years afterward that there was nothing particularly original or compelling in Darwin's work. In this the Brahmin aristocrats showed a few hints of their besetting vices: insularity and fatuous self-regard.

Agassiz likewise remained loyal to his old theme of special creation. He went to Brazil and found evidence that glaciers had recently filled the Amazon basin — proving, he thought, that the entire planet had been covered and all advanced life exterminated (he did find signs of ice, but they were a quarter billion years old, not a few hundred thousand). His son Alexander, after making a fortune in Great Lakes copper, built a research yacht and sailed around the world; one of his aims was to disprove Darwin's famous theory of atoll formation. Although he wrote at length on the subject, he couldn't seem to decide on an alternative; his work is forgotten today.

But it would be a mistake to suppose that Agassiz's run-ins with one of the greatest figures in the history of science in any way diminish his real achievements. In fossil history, in glacial geology, in embryology and systematics he was a genuine leader. In the latter, American half of his career, when he worked mostly as a teacher and fund raiser, his efforts were equally seminal. If he looks like a dinosaur now, it is only because he suffered the usual fate of scientists willing to champion contemporary views, views that cannot qualify as science unless they are provisional and open to attack from all quarters. He took one path, posterity galloped by on another.

Darwin freed anatomists of creation from the need to ponder the rationale behind *Crotalus,* much less the mysterious purposes behind truly fearsome enigmas like the AIDS virus and the malaria parasite. Species arise from other species; they are accumulations of circumstance. The riddle of a benign, Emersonian deity who nonetheless called such monsters into being was left to theologians. In its place lay a world that, once seeded with life, could bring forth any number of fantastic changelings, with or without supernatural assistance.

Agassiz remained a member of the Society of Natural History until his death in 1873 at sixty-four. His many eulogists in Boston and Cambridge carefully avoided any mention of Darwin. The excitement provoked by the *Origin* had quickly given way to the much greater excitement of secession and war. By 1865 the society had opened an elegant new building on Berkeley Street, but its meetings had lost much of their wide-open, groundbreaking quality. Natural history, which had begun as a gentlemanly hobby for physicians and clergymen, was now in the care of professional geologists, botanists, and zoologists, and no amateur could hope to keep up with all the latest developments. By 1870 only six of the society's twenty-seven officers had medical degrees, and some sections — the entomologists, for instance — had begun to meet separately. The collections inaugurated forty years earlier by Dr. Storer, who donated a pickled iguana, two whale vertebrae, and "a piece of skin from the breast of a male penguin," had expanded hugely. Unfortunately hundreds of specimens had been destroyed by insects and spoilage, and the cost of proper maintenance was so high that there was talk of giving away large portions and limiting further acquisitions to items of New England provenance. No figure comparable to Agassiz arrived to fascinate Boston with additional wonders of creation. The next two or three generations of Brahmins, many of them fabulously rich, would be more likely to collect French impressionists or Japanese ivory than pressed weeds or pickled snakes.

But *Crotalus* necessarily wore a different face in the wake of the naturalists. Over the years he had done duty as a New World basilisk, an agent of darkness, a dangerous pest, a source of valuable medicines, and, in the revolutionary years, as a sort of American mascot, a model of republican virtues. Emerson had granted him a spark of divinity; for Agassiz he was a marcher in the procession of life, and exhibited the Parade Master's infinitely painstaking wisdom. Darwin divorced him from his Creator, but made him no less extraordinary for that. Like every other living thing, he was the fruit of a billion anonymous couplings stretching back to the deepest root-ends of organic time.

These weren't all the roles *Crotalus* would play. No one had yet discovered that he was an example of "wildlife," or entered him as evidence in an indictment of modernity. He was still bludgeoned to death more or less wherever he appeared. One of his current uses, as a stick to beat back office parks and condominiums, would have been inconceivable. But he had demonstrated a certain ability to outlast all the guises he was obliged to wear — to twist and turn ceaselessly and yet somehow remain the same. Before long the very fact of his survival would begin to draw attention. It would look as if he had unaccountably missed his own funeral.

## Elegy

It has been well stated that rattlesnakes have no place in a settled country.

— Laurence M. Klauber, California herpetologist, in Bucherl
and Buckley, *Venomous Animals and Their Venoms* (1968)

When Route 128 wrapped its eight lanes around the southern edge of the Blue Hills in the early 1960s, it sliced off approximately 1,500 acres of the Reservation in Canton, Randolph, and Braintree. Shortly thereafter Route 24's six lanes slithered up from the south and split this amputated parcel in two. And so the once-coherent 7,000-acre park fell into three separate pieces: a large one inside 128 including all the hilltops, a much smaller fragment west of 24 centered on Ponkapoag Pond and its fringing cedar bog, and a diminutive scrap of about 200 acres east of 24 and south of 128, usually known as the Randolph section.

The Randolph section is probably the least-visited part of the park, even though it is bounded on the east by a populous residential area. Numerous fires have prevented most of it from developing beyond a stunted, knotty oak thicket dense enough to repel even determined bushwhackers and reminiscent of the worst features of flypaper and Velcro. At the height of the Cold War the Air Force bulldozed a tract in its center and installed a group of Nike missiles intended to preserve Boston from nuclear attack; they came out just as quickly when a new treaty banned them, and the rotting concrete of the launching pads is now decorated with redolent brown heaps of stable sweepings courtesy of the MDC's Mounted Patrol. Perhaps the highway planners thought that in carving this parcel from the rest of the park they would render it vulnerable to developers; I can think of no other reason why they built a full-size, two-lane bridge-overpass across Route 24 connecting it to the Ponkapoag section. No roads were ever linked to this bridge, and today it is merely a wide place in a path through the woods.

The same pipeline trace that passes through Calvin Grith's maple swamp on the other side of 128 also crosses the Randolph section on a north-south axis. The gas company keeps the trace clear of brush in order to service the buried pipe, and the rough road alongside provides a convenient path through the undergrowth.

A few summers ago I was walking north along this trace on a hot, dull afternoon when some deer tracks in a clayey stretch underfoot caught my eye. At least I thought they were deer. Deer have been scarce in the Hills since the expressways went in, and are now limited to the occasional straggler drifting down the marshy valley of the Neponset from Sharon or Walpole — in the early sixties the completion of 128 walled a herd of about twenty inside the park, but they disappeared shortly thereafter, most of them probably killed on the highways.

But here were deer in plenty. It looked as though at least several dozen had walked through the soft spots, all headed north like myself. What's more, their paired-comma prints were monstrously large and splayed out, as if their cloven hooves had doubled in size and lost most of their stiffness. So far as I knew, nothing larger than a snapping turtle inhabited the park, although very occasionally a stray moose wandered down from New Hampshire — in 1989 one took up residence in the wooded median of 128 in Dedham and had to be shot.

Bison?, I thought. Elk? Caribou? This was my first visit to the Randolph section. Somehow it seemed to have become annexed to Wyoming.

I went on, watching the ground. The peculiar tracks followed the trace across a series of low rises, hemmed in tight on either side by dwarfish oaks knee-deep in huckleberry. From the top of each rise I could see across the shallow dip to the next, but no farther. I knew that the trace butted against 128 less than a mile ahead. All the evidence seemed to indicate that before too long I could expect to meet many massive quadrupeds as mysterious as Sasquatch or the Himalayan yeti.

I had just topped another rise and was looking off toward the next when a big bovine head loomed over its crest. It was followed by the rest of the animal, a huge cinnamon-colored beast with knobby knees. It stopped and looked at me, motionless. Of course, I thought, suddenly yanked back to earth — cows.

More cinnamon shapes ambled over the crest. Some turned aside to browse along the edge of the trace. A couple were accompanied by calves. There were at least a dozen in sight, with more coming up all the time. The ones that noticed me stopped and stared, and the others slowed down — they began to bunch up on top of the rise.

I am a child of the suburbs, and have had little experience with cows. These ones began to worry me. They had to weigh at least a quarter ton each. The trace was only a few yards wide. If I wanted to go on, I'd have to squeeze right through their midst. Maybe they'd find that insulting. Maybe that's what those horns were for — all the big ones had squat little toothlike hooks over their ears.

I decided to skirt around them through the woods. I had only gone in a few yards, however, when I came up against a stout wire fence paralleling the trace — it bordered the old Nike base. It didn't leave me much room. I imagined sidling past the bulk of the herd when a few of its touchier members decided to stomp on my face. None of the trees looked large enough to dissuade them. It seemed to me I'd do better if I just sat quietly and let them go by. As I said, I know nothing about cows.

So I crouched down in the dead leaves and watched them shuffle past. They took about ten minutes. None of them paid me any notice. It occurred to me that if this were 20,000 B.C. and I were a hungry Ice Ager, I would probably starve before I could bring down one of these dreadnoughts.

When they were all past I stepped back out onto the trace. One of them turned for a last look before it vanished over the next rise. I went on in the other direction. I felt a little foolish, but of course it was just between me and the cows.

About twenty minutes later a dark-haired man in a blue pickup with a reedy teenage girl alongside drove all the way up the trace, turned around, and drove back again. Missing something?, I wondered.

I never found out under what arrangement these cows were allowed to graze inside the park. I did learn, however, that a working farm bordered the Randolph section on the south, so there was no need to have trucked them in from Vermont.

Until that day I would have said there were no more cattle in the Blue Hills than there are camels on Boston Common. The suburbs reach clear down to Providence; buildable land around the Reservation starts at $100,000 per acre. The biggest cash crop in Massachusetts is cranberries; if Boston had to feed itself on the yield from its own hinterland it would starve in a week. Farmers are regarded as an endangered species. The Massachuset Indians probably raised more corn in this part of the state than is grown here today.

This is the most recent stage of a decline that is already 250 years old. By about 1750 the farm towns of eastern Massachusetts had put nearly all their suitable land under cultivation and couldn't add many more inhabitants without either bringing in food or eating less heartily. And since large families remained typical, there was no lack of recruits for untilled lands in the interior — oftentimes dozens of people would decamp en masse, and name their new settlements in Maine or the Berkshires after the towns they had left.

By a century later, in 1850 or so, the railroads and the rich soils of the Midwest had made the stony Yankee farms almost superfluous, and many converted from grain crops to specialty produce for close-at-hand urban markets — apples, fresh milk, summer vegetables. Those farms occupying unproductive hillsides or sand plains were turned into sheep pasture or abandoned. By Thoreau's time countless empty cellarholes already speckled the back roads.

The retreat from the land peaked after the Civil War. Thousands of acres of former pasture and cropland began to grow up in trees. A town that had once boasted several hundred farms might be reduced to as few as a dozen. They were the last; everything else was returning to woods. Urbanization aside, this collapse and withdrawal was the central event in the New England countryside in the nineteenth century, and today a herd of cows along Route 128 nearly qualifies as an apparition.

This exodus might have been good news for *Crotalus* if he hadn't long since been reduced almost to nothing. His enemies were pulling up stakes; in the future not every bare ledge or outcrop would be regularly scrutinized from downslope by a horny-handed proprietor. If the land had been abandoned wholesale, if every farm boy between Boston and Springfield had moved downtown or out of state, he might have begun to recover. As it was, however, enough stayed behind — they knew where he lived, they knew how to get at him, and if the job needed finishing, they finished it. The Blue Hills aside, the nineteenth century was the end for *Crotalus* in eastern Massachusetts.

He left some legends behind. As the old way of life vanished, New Englanders marked its passing with a spate of local histories that began to appear about 1840. These books, customarily entitled *History of the Town of X,* were the work of local antiquarians and were most often funded and sold by subscription. Nostalgic in tone, they generally gave no account of the water-powered industries then transforming the social and economic landscape of Yankeedom, but instead concentrated on lists of early settlers, short biographies of the succession of town ministers, inscriptions from the local burying grounds, and items illustrative of the rural past gleaned from town-meeting records. Where earlier sources generally assert that *Crotalus* is still present, if rare, some of these go so far as to declare him exterminated and name the person local tradition honors for having completed the work.

In the *History of Oakham,* a chronicle of a hill town in Worcester County, the hero thus designated is James Mulholland, a Scots-Irish immigrant who arrived in 1755, barely a decade after the town's settlement. Having determined to rid Oakham of rattlesnakes, he proceeded to their main haunt at Deacon Allen's pasture, stripped down to his shorts, and began bashing reptiles in earnest. Although "treacherously assailed in the rear," he ignored a bite on his calf and killed the offender, along with every other rattler in sight. "No evil consequences being felt from the attack, he ever afterwards entertained the opinion that rattlesnakes were of little account anyway." Mulholland fathered ten children and later moved west to the Berkshires; three of his daughters migrated north to Vermont.

Mulholland's counterpart in Manchester, a rocky town on Cape Ann, was John D. Hildreth, who reputedly destroyed the last den sometime prior to 1844 by building a fire at its entrance in midwinter. The heat drew the snakes out, and the community was troubled no further. Hildreth apparently spoiled a good thing for himself, since he had formerly turned the rattles in for bounties and sold the oil from the carcasses as a home remedy.

Not all of these champions had no other claim to fame. George Catlin, the painter and historian of the Plains Indians, was celebrated for emptying a notorious *Crotalus* den on a mountain above his boyhood home in Wilkes-Barre, Pennsylvania. He had accompanied a party of local farmers on a springtime pilgrimage to the place and was shooting and clubbing snakes in the usual manner when one of the men pinned one down alive with a forked stick. Catlin suggested that they tie a powderhorn with a lighted fuse to its tail and set it down by the den entrance. They did so, and it immediately crawled back inside. "In a minute or two an explosion like a clap of thunder shook the ground. The result was extermination to the snakes."

It's unlikely, of course, that *Crotalus* vanished from town after town as the result of a single exploit by a homegrown Saint George. But once his absence was noticed, it's easy to see how stories like these could become part of local tradition. The snakes were gone; there had to be a reason; storytellers took the facts and conflated them into a memorable incident. Some of these histories also record the name of the hunter who shot the last deer or bear in town, but the event is usually left unembroidered.

*Crotalus*'s progressive withdrawals can also be traced in the specimen catalogues of Agassiz's Museum of Comparative Zoology and the Boston Society of Natural History. At the start of the nineteenth century, for instance, there were still rattlesnakes available for pickling in towns as widely dispersed as Lynn, Sutton, Ipswich, and Walpole. By the twentieth, these scattered sources had gone dry, and although collecting continued, no more examples arrived from anywhere in Massachusetts east of the Connecticut River, with the exception of the Blue Hills.

Perhaps the most interesting account of a nineteenth-century-style *Crotalus* hunt in this half of the state appears in Adin Ballou's *History of the Town of Milford* (1882). Milford, a former red-brick mill town thirty miles southwest of Boston, now lies in the suburban fringe along the outermost beltway, Route 495, and is not noted for rattlesnakes. When Ballou arrived there from Rhode Island in the 1820s, however, he was "somewhat astonished" to hear that *Crotalus* had not yet been ousted, and as he had never seen a rattler, he felt "a strong curiosity to find a specimen." It was late in May, still denning season, and a local man named Carmel Cheney promised that if Ballou "would go on a hunt with him, he was sure we might kill some."

They visited a spot in Rocky Woods and smashed an unlucky straggler, then went on to a ledgy, south-facing hill west of Deer Brook, "killed four or five more, and returned satisfied." Writing sixty years later, Ballou mentions that few snakes have been seen lately, and speculates that they are "almost extinct."

Ballou's reminiscence suggests that murder at the dens, once most vigorously pursued by local farmers determined to forestall accidents in the hayfields, was then becoming a desultory, almost touristic pastime. Ballou wasn't a farmer; he came to town as the new pastor of the Universalist church. He has a naturalist's vocabulary; when he heard about *Crotalus,* he wanted to "find a specimen," although when Cheney equated this with killing snakes, Ballou didn't demur. No other option, in fact, seems to have occurred to him. Nor does he make any connection between his own practice and *Crotalus*'s subsequent extinction. Perhaps he considered it too obvious for comment. It's as though he regarded snake clearance as an inevitable and unremarkable concomitant of progress; if he admits that rattlers are fascinating rarities, that is no argument for sparing them. In his view all of Milford's native wild animals face a similar fate, and should expect no other. Here is how he sums up his survey of the town's scant remaining fauna:

> It is obvious that the contrast must be great between the present meagre show of wild-animal life, on our nineteen square miles, and that which presented itself to the Nipmucks two centuries and more ago. Then the dense and towering forest teemed with ferocious bears, wolves, panthers, and venomous reptiles, as well as the more harmless multitude; and then fish and fowl abounded luxuriantly in their highest excellence. Let us indulge a momentary glance at the scenes of the aboriginal wilderness, only to rejoice the more gratefully that we live amid the innumerable blessings of a hard-earned civilization. The old savage grandeur and wealth of vegetable and animal life presents but a beggarly exhibition, compared with the fruits of cultivation and our manifold domestic animal wealth.

I might not make so much of Ballou's casual dustbin-of-history attitude toward *Crotalus* if there were not other reasons to suppose he might see things differently. Before he became a historian he was the preeminent pacifist of his generation, and lectured widely throughout New England on his doctrine of Christian Non-Resistance. In 1841 he and some thirty other like-minded persons founded a community in Milford based on his teachings. They pledged to abstain from "murder, hatred, unchastity, use of liquor as a beverage, and all participation in military or civic activities, including the vote." This community, which they called Hopedale, was much more successful than several other utopian experiments of the time, such as Brook Farm and Fruitlands. It lasted fifteen years, quadrupled in size, and included a successful manufacturing enterprise. The serpent returned, however, in the form of a "free love" scandal and a financial power play by two of the larger stockholders, George and Ebenezer Draper, who transformed Ballou's socialist commune into a family business. Despite these setbacks Ballou remained faithful to his pacifist ideals, and ended his career as the pastor of the local Unitarian church, corresponding with Tolstoy and speaking out against violence in all forms.

Clearly Ballou saw the war on *Crotalus* as a special case; it didn't come under his indictment of wars in general. Maybe it's a strictly modern conceit to suppose that smashing rattlesnakes could have anything to do with smashing Mexicans or Indians. It would be hard to deny, however, that pacifist or not, the old Puritan fervor still glowed in Ballou; he meant to assemble a few kindred spirits, carve out a space in the wilderness, and preserve it untainted from the corruptions so prevalent elsewhere. As we have seen, this cycle of withdrawal and purgation tends to make things hot for any persons or creatures of doubtful affiliation who happen to inhabit the site to be redeemed. Thoreau apparently sensed that he himself might not measure up. After going to hear Ballou lecture at Concord in 1841 he wrote, "As for these communities, I think I had rather keep bachelor's hall in hell than go to board in heaven."

But whatever the rationale, it's evident that the nineteenth century was the time when *Crotalus* was finally driven to extinction in eastern Massachusetts, the Blue Hills population excepted. His exit didn't go unnoticed. Many contemporary observers remarked on the fact. If such an event were to occur today — if a large, colorful species such as the black bear or the great blue heron were to disappear as a direct result of human activities — it would rouse a considerable furor, and the environmental press would lament it as a tragic and unnecessary result of our inveterate shortsightedness and perverted values. Did any such critique emerge on behalf of *Crotalus*? Was anyone sorry to see him go?

Even today it's a risky proposition to declare oneself in favor of rattlesnakes. In the late 1970s a four-and-a-half-foot female *Crotalus* was discovered under a parked car in a small Berkshire town. A snake expert from the Massachusetts Audubon Society retrieved it and brought it to a nearby facility. Politically sensitive town officials, aware of Audubon attitudes toward native wildlife, passed an ordinance prohibiting the animal's release within the town limits. And so, in addition to a considerable amount of bad press, the Audubon Society was saddled with a large, delicate, and not particularly attractive reptile. No matter that no one had ever been bitten by a rattlesnake in the area. No matter that the animal belonged to an endangered species. Snakes don't vote, people do.

One hundred and fifty years ago there was no Audubon Society and no endangered list. The snake would probably have been beheaded and tossed into the bushes. People were aware that wildlife was disappearing — it was probably disappearing even more rapidly than it is today — but for some reason no one got excited.

Why was this? Why, in a historical moment little different from our own, at least in regard to its position atop an ever-steepening curve of ecological mayhem, did so few recognize any cause for alarm? It's not as if New Englanders weren't familiar with the costs of uncontrolled exploitation. They had successively ruined, with enthusiasm, the fur trade, the coastal whale fisheries, the white-pine lumber business, and the fragile fertility of many of the shallow local soils, not to mention the herring and salmon runs strangled by dams and the game animals hunted to extinction. No latter-day environmentalists, whisked back to 1840, would have trouble identifying a host of despoilers. And yet the conservation movement, with its ideal of responsible stewardship and its nightmare of violated maidenhood, would not gather force for another half century. Why?

Times change. Maybe the world looked bigger then, and human successes less awesome. It still took five weeks to cross the Atlantic, and months to reach California.

It's clear, however, that before any fears could be expressed for *Crotalus,* two things had to be established: first, that his demise was imminent, and second, that the landscape would be poorer without him — in other words, that he had a value independent of any particular use, simply because he happened to exist.

All snakes, it's true, were beginning to benefit from the quasi-spiritual interest in unadulterated nature brought from Europe with romanticism, though their generally bad reputation put them far behind mountain scenery, Hudson valley sunsets, and wind-music in the treetops as possible regenerative influences. It comes as something of a shock, then, after two hundred years of Puritan anathemas, to encounter Berkshire poet William Cullen Bryant's "sliding reptiles of the ground, / Startlingly beautiful" in "The Prairies," written after a trip to the Illinois frontier in 1832. So far as I know, this is the first time any white person from New England thought to call a snake lovely. Some years later the Brahmin historian Francis Parkman, describing these same lush grasslands in his *Conspiracy of Pontiac* (1878), retreated somewhat: a water snake winds its "checkered length of loathsome beauty" across a swamp. Parkman was sympathetic to traditional views; a few sentences earlier, introducing his monster, he dredged up the old libel: "And yet this western paradise is not free from the primal curse."

Did Parkman really think snakes embody God's vengeance on mankind? Probably not. If the Brahmins of his generation were very serious about being Brahmins, they were not particularly so about the Old Testament. In this case I suspect he was merely juicing up his sometimes overheated prose. Compare, for instance, his lurid (and inaccurate) picture of *Crotalus* rampant: "His neck is arched; his white fangs gleam in his distended jaws; his small eyes dart rays of unutterable fierceness; and his rattles, invisible with their quick vibration, ring the sharp warning which no man will dare to contemn."

Parkman was apparently too conservative in outlook to find snakes anything but perversely seductive. He knew that the black legend was false, that snakes were not Satan's confidential agents, but unlike Bryant, he couldn't quite discard the idea. It's as if, though no Puritan, he was sentimental, even nostalgic, about the ancestral prejudices, and so could not present a snake without a little Victorian melodrama; otherwise it might not give off the necessary whiff of brimstone. The persistent habit of snake killing probably has similar roots — though no longer a religious duty, it can, like wood chopping or deer hunting, revive for a moment the fabulous American past, and make any rube a Natty Bumppo.

The next Yankee after Bryant to notice an aesthetic value in snakes was Henry Thoreau. In his 1842 review of Dr. Storer et al.'s *Reports on the Fishes, Reptiles, etc.,* he confessed that he was "particularly attracted by the motions of the serpent tribe." He often found harmless garter snakes and blacksnakes beaten to death in the woods, and it puzzled him: "I have the same objection to killing a snake that I have to killing any other animal, yet the most humane man that I know never omits to kill one." On October 10, 1851, Thoreau came upon a blacksnake sunning itself in a clearing. It lifted its head, hissed at him, and dashed off into the woods. This is, I believe, the first documented encounter in New England between a man and a snake that ended amicably on both sides.

Thoreau never saw a rattlesnake on his rambles through Concord because earlier settlers had killed them all off, if indeed they ever inhabited that low, alluvial town. In his review of the aforementioned *Reports* he lists some of the other natives long since exterminated: bear, wolves, lynxes, wildcats, beaver, deer, and marten. But unlike his modern descendants, he doesn't sigh after their ghosts, or suggest that the place is in any way impoverished by their absence. Throughout his work, in fact, he never sounds that panicky, apocalyptic note so typical of present-day writer-naturalists, many of whom crisscross the world and suffer innumerable hardships in order to hymn the twilit sublimities of one last dying Eden after another. When Thoreau does notice a near-at-hand piece of nastiness, as when a neighboring farmer chops down a favorite patch of woods, or his companions in Maine shoot a moose, skin it, and leave the carcass to rot in a streambed, he doesn't ache for the victims but ridicules the spoilers, whom he considers too dull and witless to enjoy life properly. Though he likes to brag about Concord's redeeming wildness — "There are square miles in my vicinity which have no inhabitant" — it was really no different from most Massachusetts towns of its time, a patchwork of small farms, small factories, and second growth, with the added convenience of daily trains to Boston. One can only conclude either that he did not foresee the wholesale scarring and wastage typical of modern development or that he counted on "Nature" to survive regardless, and was more concerned with the sad state of our own souls.

And so his love for the nonhuman never translates into intimations of doom or a call to the barricades. If he objects to snake bashing, he never raises the specter of a snakeless future. He seems to live outside history; his natural world is not a once-healthy growth already cut to the quick, but instead a mirror of eternity brimming with light.

Was he naïve? Provincial? Did he define wildness too broadly and neglect his alarm-sounding duties in order to fish for ecstasies in a suburban frog pond?

At any rate, one looks in vain in his work for any nostalgic or guilt-driven fear of tomorrow, the sort of paralyzing fear that can only find relief in crusades. His neighbors can't threaten his paradise; they wouldn't know where to find it. What he seeks in the woods is not a cause to fight for, a chance to range himself with the righteous and perhaps win a little respite for treasures that would otherwise vanish. No, he goes to locate his best self, a self that might most accurately be described as a certain quality of attentiveness. And he is confident, somehow, that he will indeed find it, regardless of how many tall pines crash down or how few rattlesnakes survive.

In this view, then, snake bashing is regrettable not so much for its effect on the landscape — fewer snakes, and eventually none at all — but for the state of mind it reveals in its practitioners, a sort of squinting, twitchy narcosis masquerading as common sense. Thoreau's contemporary Edward Tuckerman, the White Mountains botanist for whom Tuckerman's Ravine on Mount Washington is named, also noted the syndrome; in his 1865 edition of John Josselyn's *New England's Rarities* (first published in 1672), he adds this cryptic dissent to Josselyn's description of *Crotalus:* "There are perhaps no worse prejudices in common life than those which breed cruelty."

This is as far as nineteenth-century New Englanders would go in defense of rattlesnakes. They knew that *Crotalus* was vanishing;

they knew he was not the monster he was made out to be; they could even admit that snakes in general were wonderful creatures, and that habitual snake murder wasn't necessarily heroic, or even rational. What they could not imagine was that a day might come when there would be no more rattlesnakes, much less that there might exist reasons to delay it.

Today *Crotalus* is all but extinct in eastern Massachusetts. It is estimated that there are six or eight dozen left in the Blue Hills; their nearest relatives are far to the west. Three hundred years ago, when rattlesnakes were still commonplace, New Englanders had a good practical sense of how they behaved and what could be expected of them. Now that knowledge is lost, and their reputation for deviltry is perhaps stronger than ever, since so little firsthand experience exists to counteract it. Believe it or not, there are plenty of people in the towns around the Blue Hills who wish the *Crotalus* had been exterminated locally also, and who have no trouble imagining rattlers assembling, guerrilla-style, at the park boundaries and spreading death and destruction through the surrounding suburbs. The idea that they deserve the same protection as ospreys or striped bass seems to them absurd. And yet none of these people has ever seen the effects of a *Crotalus* bite, and many of them regularly douse their lawns and gardens with poisons that could kill a horse.

Clearly we have certain ideas about venomous snakes, ideas too solidly entrenched to be dislodged by the facts. Within five years of Boston's settlement William Wood was writing that rattlesnakes, contrary to popular report, were at most an annoyance. Today, almost four hundred years later, the snakes are long gone but the slanders persist. Why is a monster that never existed so precious to us, while the genuine article, the animal on which the monster is supposedly based, receives no consideration? A foreigner, noticing the grizzly bear on the California state flag (long since gone from that state) or the bald eagle on our twenty-five-cent piece (rarely seen elsewhere), might conclude that we like our wild animals large, fierce, and safely out of the way.

One nineteenth-century Yankee had the foresight to see, not only that *Crotalus* might soon disappear from Massachusetts, but that the event might become cause for regret. Curiously enough, he did nothing to debunk *Crotalus*'s hellish reputation, but instead labored to enlarge it. Maybe he thought we wouldn't want to lose such a glamorous villain.

The man was Oliver Wendell Holmes, professor of anatomy at Harvard Medical School, son of Abiel Holmes, minister of Cambridge's First Congregational Church, and father of Oliver Jr., chief justice of the U.S. Supreme Court. Holmes became interested in rattlesnakes when he began spending summers in the Berkshires — newly accessible by rail — and heard some of the local folklore concerning them. He arranged to have one sent to his office in Boston, where he kept it for several months. It refused to eat or drink, killed several rats, and was eventually bitten to death by another.

An urbane and good-humored man, Holmes became famous for a series of essays he wrote for James Russell Lowell's new Boston-based magazine, *The Atlantic Monthly,* essays later collected as *The Autocrat of the Breakfast-Table* (1858). In them he appears as an unassuming practical moralist, and often takes for his targets some of the surviving Puritan rigidities, such as the doctrine of infant damnation, which had been drummed into him as a boy from his father's pulpit. Holmes wanted no part of the old New England gloom, which he considered as formidable as it was ridiculous, and he suggested that there were other lights in the sky besides the glare of eternity. It was Holmes who rechristened Governor Winthrop's "City on a Hill" as the not-so-rigorous "Hub of the Solar System," and he also invented the half-ironic "Brahmin" to describe the successors to Cotton Mather's "Saints." He liked to spoof old verities by inflating them; perhaps this accounts for his picture of *Crotalus:* "The one feature of the Mountain which shed the brownest horror on its woods was the existence of the terrible region known as Rattlesnake Ledge, and still tenanted by these damnable reptiles, which distill a fiercer venom under our cold northern sky than the cobra himself in the land of tropical spices and poisons."

To anyone familiar with *Crotalus,* this can only be satire. Exaggeration, however, is also the stock-in-trade of the carnival barker and the teller of campfire horror stories, and it's not easy to say which role Holmes is playing here. His readers in Massachusetts couldn't be expected to know anything about *Crotalus;* when the passage was written, even aging country doctors had no experience with snakebite. Was he trying, in time-honored touristic fashion, to give a romantic whiff of terror to the Berkshire Hills?

The passage is from *Elsie Venner,* a best-selling novel published in 1861 and still occasionally reprinted. It is the only New England work that can be said to revolve around *Crotalus.* In it a young and handsome Harvard undergraduate in modest circumstances comes to a remote Berkshire town to teach school and inadvertently infatuates one of his students, a wild and dark-haired beauty named Elsie Venner. When he ignores her advances she sickens and dies, presumably of a broken heart. In the climactic episode the hero ascends Rattlesnake Ledge and freezes when a large *Crotalus* rises up barely inches from his face — he is only saved from certain death by the sudden appearance of Elsie, who in a mysterious, witchy fashion persuades the snake not to strike. Elsie, it turns out, has a quasi-genetic connection with *Crotalus.* Her mother, when pregnant with her, suffered a rattlesnake bite and died from its effects, but not before giving birth, and the villagers ever afterward attribute the girl's cold, violent streak to this event. It is not explained, however, why Elsie's hypnotic powers have so little effect on the hero, who spoils the story by not showing the least sensitivity to her ambiguous charms; he closes it by returning to Cambridge for his diploma.

*Elsie Venner* is not a success as drama. It is a gothic tale without gothic feeling and has a curious mixed effect, as if Ben Franklin had attempted to write *Wuthering Heights.* Here, for example, is how Holmes means to persuade us that his hero is helpless under the gaze of *Crotalus:* "His ears rung as in the overture to the swooning dream of chloroform. Nature was before man with her anaesthetics: the cat's first shake stupefies the mouse; the lion's first shake deadens the man's fear and feeling, and the *Crotalus* paralyzes before he strikes."

One senses that if Holmes had really believed in snake mesmerism, he would not have multiplied analogies but would have simply portrayed it in action. But having kept a live rattlesnake by his desk for some months, and having successfully resisted both paralysis and poisoning, he was presumably aware that the effect was nothing but an old libel, and perhaps was somewhat embarrassed to be exploiting it for literary purposes — he was, after all, a medical man.

At the end of the novel an earthquake destroys Rattlesnake Ledge, exterminating the last rattlers in town. It is *Crotalus*'s final appearance in the work of a prominent New England author; as he disappeared from the landscape, so he disappeared from the books. Holmes anticipates the dominant note of twentieth-century nature writing — what we might call the Lost Paradise school — in his description of the wistful, troubled, almost elegiac feeling present in those communities which have killed off all their rattlesnakes: "Yet, strangely enough, many persons missed the possibility of a fatal bite in other regions, where there were nothing but black and green and striped snakes, mean ophidians, having the spite of the nobler serpent without his venom." This sounds almost like regret.

Did Holmes feel a bit guilty for having revived *Crotalus*'s longsince-exploded black legend merely to give extra spice to a novel? He was aware that rattlesnakes were nearly gone from Massachusetts; did he paint them so darkly, and in colors he knew to be false, in order to justify a massacre after the fact? His contemporary John Gorham Palfrey, a Unitarian minister and the most eminent New England historian of his day, employed just such a strategy to banish any second thoughts concerning the near-total destruction of the local Native Americans. Here are a few of his pronouncements on the subject from his magnum opus, *The History of New England* (1865):

— These people held a low place on the scale of humanity.

— Both parental and filial affection were feeble and transient . . . there was no process of education to be carried on.

— It is surprising to observe how destitute he [the New England Indian] was of mental culture or capacity.

— Their therapeutics consisted of the grossest nonsense and imposture.

— Little of social order and organization that was definite and durable at any time existed.

— The puerile immaturity of the Indian's mind betrayed itself by the poverty of his language.

— All their history shows them to have been a race singularly unsusceptible to the influences of a humane civilization.

Perhaps this was some small excuse for having burned their towns and sold them as slaves.

History belongs to the winners. If we meant to make *Crotalus* into a monster, imagine ourselves threatened, and spend two hundred years scouring him out of his last hiding places, there was little he could do about it. The human capacity for self-delusion is not so unlimited that we can't stick to our ends, whatever they might be, and at length accomplish them, whether they make sense or not. The old-style *Crotalus,* the *Crotalus* that was finally evicted from eastern Massachusetts in the nineteenth century, was not really a native. In a very real sense he disembarked with the first Europeans, who were sure that this strange, bewildering land must contain deadly and terrible creatures, creatures that must be removed before civilized men could inhabit it — is it any surprise that such creatures were found? This *Crotalus* proved so durable that he nearly outlived the retiring reptile he was confused with, and would have done so if not for the geological accident that produced the Blue Hills. In other parts of the United States he is still a beast to be reckoned with, where enough rattlesnakes survive to maintain his legend.

But this is a new century, and we have a new rattlesnake. Not everyone kills him on sight. His presence is not always a threat, a piece of unfinished business — on the contrary, the rare spots where he hangs on gain something from his stubbornness, as if he testifies to their health.

This new-style *Crotalus* is mortal. He threatens to vanish. We don't like that, somehow — it's as though, having wiped out tens of thousands, we are troubled that the lone survivors look sickly. We can envision their funeral. It will take place in a trash-strewn parking lot beside a ditch full of poisons.

This new-style *Crotalus* isn't confined to Massachusetts. He has appeared in nearly every state where there were once many rattlesnakes and there now are few: Connecticut, New York, Indiana, even Florida and Arizona. Attempts are under way to export him to Costa Rica and Paraguay. He exists alongside the hellish, man-hating one. Each implies a vision of the world; each speaks to us about ourselves.

But before we look into the history of this latest and perhaps final *Crotalus*, we owe it to his predecessor to find out just how worthy he was of his unenviable reputation. Few would deny that rattlesnakes can, under certain circumstances, destroy human life. Did they ever do so in Massachusetts? Did they ever do so in the Blue Hills?

# An Abominable Mystery

If these snakes bite a man they kill him.

— Pedro de Cieza de León,
*La Crónica del Perú* (1554)

Most snakes are harmless. Some are not. A few, a very few, are so dangerous that even the best contemporary countermeasures cannot save all those who are bitten.

Most snakes bigger than a shoelace will bite if stepped on or otherwise provoked. And since a life-threatening bite looks much like a harmless one, at least to begin with — a tiny puncture or two, a scratch, a few beads of blood — it makes sense to assume that any bite could become trouble and to avoid getting bitten by snakes of all kinds. To say, as the experts do, that a bite from snake A, B, or C is nothing to worry about, while a bite from snake D could be another matter entirely, is too fine a distinction for anyone peeling a sock back on a fresh set of tooth marks.

Maybe this is why many kinds of snakes that have never hurt anyone are widely believed to be dangerous. It is, after all, no easy matter to find out whether any given species can or cannot kill with a bite — as long as bites are avoided, the question remains moot. Most early writers on *Crotalus* were content to repeat whatever stories they heard about the hazards of snakebite, stories not always inaccurate, but nonetheless secondhand. It isn't until the eighteenth century that evidence appears of more determined attempts to get at the truth — in this instance, a 1727 letter to England's Royal Society from a Captain Hall of South Carolina, who together with a surgeon named Kidwell and several other persons contrived to put *Crotalus*'s bad name to the test.

Having procured "a fine, healthful rattle-snake about 4 feet long" — either *C. horridus* or the more formidable *C. adamanteus,* the eastern diamondback — Captain Hall tied it to a stake in the ground and brought out three neighborhood mutts. He looped a rope around the first in such a way that he and a man at the other end could lead it over the snake. They did so, the dog jumped, and the snake struck at it. Although Hall immediately pulled the dog away, it was dead in fifteen seconds. As they could find no blood or wound on the corpse, they scalded its hair off and examined it again, discovering a single bluish-green puncture on the side of its chest.

The second dog, slightly smaller, was bitten on the ear. It "reeled and staggered about for some time; then fell down, and struggled as if convulsed, and for two or three times got up, each time wagging its tail, though slowly, and attempting to follow a negro boy, who used to make much of it." Hall told the boy to put the dog in a shed and keep an eye on it.

About an hour later they led the third dog over the snake and then found a bloody spot where it had been bitten under the ribs. Since it showed no ill effects they let it go.

Shortly thereafter the boy reappeared and said that the second dog was dead. It had survived two hours. Dr. Kidwell opened it up and found that although the heart looked normal, the brain appeared "more red and swoln than he had ever seen," and later reported that the blood "had turned very black."

The next day the third dog was dead, as they learned from the woman who owned it, who was understandably aggrieved. Though she didn't know when it had died, she said that at seven P.M. (three hours after it was bitten) it was so weak it could "scarcely wag its tail."

Hall and his associates reapproached the same snake four days later with two more dogs about "as large as common bull dogs." The first, bitten on the inner thigh, died in thirty seconds; the second, bitten an hour later on the outer thigh, died in four minutes. Having run out of test subjects, Hall scooped up a cat that had the ill luck to be on hand. Since the bite clearly made it uncomfortable, it was put in the shed. The cat later got out, and during the night it died in the garden, "much swoln, so that nobody cared to examine or search where it was bitten."

In the meantime Hall persuaded the snake to strike at a chicken twice. Though the bird "seemed very sick and drooping, and could not, or did not, fly up to its usual place of roost," it appeared healthy the next day. Hall killed it and plucked it that evening and found two punctures on its thigh and a livid scratch on its breast. It was the first animal to survive a bite.

Already minus five dogs and a cat, Captain Hall perhaps concluded it might not be wise to risk any more pets. During the following weeks he offered the snake a large bullfrog, which died in two minutes, and another chicken, which expired in three. A three-foot blacksnake lasted eight — though it bit the rattlesnake and drew blood, the rattler showed no ill effects.

Finally Hall hung the snake up by its middle and teased it with a stick until it bit itself, dying in ten minutes. A hog then ate it up greedily, head included. The hog appeared none the worse.

Although Hall described these results closely in his letter to the Royal Society, he didn't state the obvious conclusions: that rattlesnakes are dangerously venomous, that a large one has enough venom to kill several animals in succession, and that this venom is perhaps not inexhaustible, since the last bites in a series appear somewhat less lethal than the first. Anyone in London who read this account would perhaps be less likely to dismiss tales of killer snakes as typical colonial exaggerations.

Some of these tales might indeed have tested metropolitan credulity. Boston's indefatigable scribbler Cotton Mather, author of more than two hundred books, had repeated several in a letter to the society fifteen years earlier. In one story a rattlesnake bit a steel ax head, causing it to discolor and break into pieces. Mather speculated that rattler venom might be related to alkahest, the elusive universal solvent of the Renaissance alchemists. Another story recounted the sad end of a traveler who beat a rattler to death with a cut switch; in its struggles the snake bit the switch, poisoning its sap, and when the traveler later scratched a mosquito bite on his temple with the cut end he swelled up and died. Though Mather didn't vouch for these tales, he didn't question them either. Other versions are still current today.

At least one individual tried to cash in on the interest in *Crotalus* overseas, an interest responsible for many of these early accounts, some of which were written in response to direct queries — at the time no live rattlesnakes had been brought back to Europe. The following is an item from *Parkins' London News* for February 19, 1725:

> We have a surprising account from Maryland, that a Rattle-snake of prodigious size infested a part of that Country, and destroyed abundance of Men, Women, and Cattle, to the great prejudice and danger of the Inhabitants, till Mr. Bartlet an Englishman (who about two years ago lodged at the Elephant and Castle in Fleet Lane), going SuperCargo in the Service of Mr. Farlow a Merchant, undertook to engage the Rattle-snake, and killed it, and having the curiosity to bring it over to England, is now landed with it at Weymouth, where 'tis to be seen, and will in a few days be in London, being intended to be presented to the Royal Society.

People with little desire to gape at a six-week-old dead snake, much less pay for the privilege, might soften somewhat if it was also presented as a bona fide mass murderer; the staffer who wrote the advertisement, if he was skeptical at all, confined his doubts to his initial adjective. By this time ships had been sailing back and forth between England and the Chesapeake for over a century, and thousands of visitors had had opportunities to size up *Crotalus* for themselves. Even so, one could still apparently get a hearing for the most unlikely claims.

This particular type of story — Killer Rattler Scourges Mudville — is still occasionally presented as fact. Here's an example from a book of natural history, *Snakes & Their Ways,* published by a well-known herpetologist in 1937:

> There have been many records of snakes escaping from circuses and "zoos" and causing considerable excitement before their capture, but probably the most distressing incident of this kind occurred in Windsor, Ontario, during the month of May, 1906. At this time eight rattlesnakes and two pythons escaped from the Mount Clair clinic and within one week the rattlers caused the fatal poisoning of

eleven people, one of the victims, a man, being bitten while he slept. For some inexplicable reason these snakes showed a strange preference for houses and office buildings, possibly because they had been in captivity for a long period and felt more at home under a roof than in their natural habitat out of doors. Of the ten that escaped, two, both rattlers, were never recaptured or killed.

Maybe rattlesnakes are like movie stars; we are always ready to believe the worst. At any rate, when I went to confirm this disaster in the Detroit and Toronto papers of the time, I was strangely annoyed to find not a trace of it. There was indeed a circus in Windsor that month, but the biggest story to come out of it involved a tiger that got too frisky and scratched its trainer. Nothing at all about the mysterious "Mount Clair clinic," not to mention rampaging snakes.

The author, Carl Kauffeld, was for many years the director of New York City's Staten Island Zoo. Maybe he'd had too many nightmares about accidents involving his charges to dismiss stories like this — if you have, for instance, a king cobra in a glass-fronted box that can be opened only from above, you must hope it doesn't dart out at the first inch of daylight. Or maybe Kauffeld was part showman himself and didn't mind repeating a few questionable tales. Someone named C. H. Curran co-wrote the book; maybe he was less critical.

One finds, if one attempts to verify horror stories about man-killing rattlesnakes, that one often gets just so far and no farther. The clinching bit of evidence — a contemporary account, a physician's report — is almost always mysteriously absent. It's as though someone else has been there before and has artfully lifted the key documents. Kauffeld's colleague Raymond L. Ditmars, the curator of mammals and reptiles at the Bronx Zoo and undoubtedly the most accomplished and reliable popular authority on *Crotalus* of his day, spent many years studying the remaining snake dens of southern New England. He wrote that three bites had occurred in the Berkshire area in twenty years, one of them fatal, but he unaccountably left out names and dates. Similarly, George Herbert Lamson, in his state-financed *Reptiles of Connecticut* (Hartford, 1935), unequivocally finds that "less than one-half dozen cases of death due to poisonous snakes [have occurred] in Connecticut in the last 25–30 years." If he knew of any at all, he would have done well to give details. As it is, the claim can still be reasonably made that no one in the state's entire history has been killed by a native rattler.

What's going on here? Why, at the center of *Crotalus*'s aura of fatality, does one so often find an empty space and a typed label: "Exhibit Temporarily Removed"? One almost senses a conspiracy at work, a centuries-old campaign to shore up a fearsome reputation by the use of hint, half-truth, and baldfaced howlers. If a rattlesnake's bite is truly as dangerous as Captain Hall's experiments seem to indicate, where are the casualties? Or, if there were never any to begin with, why is the horror so durable?*

As we will see, a bite from a full-grown rattlesnake is no joke. Maybe this is the lone fact that has fathered so many lies. Maybe all the lies are a way of remembering the fact — a way of reminding ourselves, in a suitably fabulous manner, that *Crotalus* is no impossible monster — that he is real, that he exists, and that he is not to be toyed with. No such body of folklore has collected, for instance, around garter snakes or pond turtles.

The first complete account of a rattlesnake bite in that portion of North America now known as the United States comes, appropriately enough, from the Blue Hills. The victim was a hunting dog, breed unknown, belonging to Thomas Morton, Boston Harbor's rowdiest pioneer, who was later driven out by the Puritans. One day in the 1620s while Morton was out shooting, his dog came across a rattlesnake, annoyed it, and was bitten. The dog quickly swelled to such grotesque proportions that Morton feared for its life. He tried pouring a saucer of "salet oil" (probably olive oil) down its throat, and the dog recovered, the swelling gone by the next day. "The like experiment," Morton writes, "hath bin made upon a boy that hath by chance trod upon one of these [rattlesnakes], and the boy never the worse. Therefore it is simplicity in any one that shall tell a bugbeare tale of horrible, or terrible, serpents, that are in that land."

---

*Even Hall's account is somewhat suspicious. The late Laurence M. Klauber, author of the monumental 1,500-page *Rattlesnakes* (Berkeley, 1972), was unable to find any contemporary corroboration of Hall's existence. And what about that surgeon, Kidwell? Good name for a hoaxer.

Here is a theme that is constant in nearly all the lore about *Crotalus,* beginning with the Algonquin and extending into modern medical practice — namely, that although rattlesnake bites can be deadly, remedies exist, and if they are applied soon enough, few tragedies should result. This is perhaps less a reflection of the actual strength of these remedies than of the need to believe in at least the possibility of effective treatment. It may be doubted, however, that a few gulps of olive oil saved Morton's dog, or the unnamed boy either. Compare what one of Morton's enemies, Francis Higginson, the first minister of Salem, Massachusetts, has to say in his *New-England's Plantation: or a Short and True Description of the Commodities and Discommodities of That Country* (1630):

> There are some Serpents called Rattle Snakes that have Rattles in their Tayles, that will not flye from a man as others will, but will flye upon him and sting him so mortally that he will dye within a quarter of an houre after, except the partie stinged have about him some of the root of an Herbe called Snakeweed to bite on, and then he shall receive no harme.

This is probably the same weed that the commonwealth's first governor, John Winthrop, carried in his pocket, knowledge of its use coming from the best local authorities, the Massachuset.

Reverend Higginson also notes the earliest fatal New England snakebite we can still point to today, an Indian reportedly killed three years before his arrival, "but wee heard of none since that time."

Snakes or no snakes, the first Englishmen found Massachusetts an unhealthy country. Nearly half — forty-four out of one hundred — of the *Mayflower* emigrants didn't survive their first winter, succumbing to flu, tuberculosis, and other infections magnified by poor diet and wretched living conditions; the Bay Company Puritans suffered nearly comparable losses, including Higginson himself. But the chroniclers mention no surefire cures for these sorts of afflictions, perhaps because none existed. On the other hand, lethal snakebites were almost unknown; after Higginson's Indian, no particulars surface for over a century. The next victim to enter the record is Timothy Mirick, a twenty-two-year-old from the Wilbraham area of the Connecticut valley who, according to family tradition, died on August 7, 1761, of a bite he received while cutting hay.

It would be foolish to insist there were no other fatalities, given the vagaries of reportage in colonial Massachusetts. Even so, there is no denying that, as a correspondent for *Harper's New Monthly Magazine* wrote in 1855 (speaking of the United States as a whole), "it requires the industry of the naturalist and the historian to find authentic records of the species [*Crotalus*] doing injury to man."

Why is this surprising? Generally speaking, it takes some effort to make a name as a killer, and even after the evidence becomes incontrovertible, the neighbors can be counted on to say, "He seemed like an ordinary sort of person. This is a quiet, family-type area. We never suspected," et cetera. But in *Crotalus*'s case, everybody already knows the worst, and to hear that the damning testimonies are missing is akin to being told that Billy the Kid ran a day-care center, or that Hitler never meant to become a tyrant.

The belief that rattlesnakes can be deadly is not without foundation. Here in New England, however, they seem to have acquired that reputation without earning it. Are they more deadly than revolving doors, day-old bread, or retired postal workers? This is a riddle for statisticians.

Here we are entering, I believe, the realm of myth. We have, on the one hand, an animal that has been vilified and slaughtered for generations on the presumption that it represents a clear and perennial threat to life and limb. On the other hand, in the space where we should expect to find a long list of victims, we find only dust, cobwebs, and vacancy. People are not, by and large, insensitive to facts; in a situation where the facts are so stubbornly devalued and cannot penetrate to consciousness, the suspicion mounts that other forces are at work.

The Puritan invasion of New England produced some account of the symptoms of rattlesnake bite. Here are a few examples:

> Whosoever is bitten by these snakes his flesh becomes as spotted as a leper.
> Wood, *New England's Prospect* (1634)

> He that is stung with any of them, or bitten, he turns the color of the snake, all over his body — blue, white, and green-spotted — and swelling, dies, unless he timely get some snakeweed.
> Lechford, *Plain Dealing* (1642)

[The bite] turns all the body into a speckled hue in a few hours, with great pain, tongues and heads work with the poison.

> Reverend Samuel Lee of Bristol, Rhode Island (late seventeenth century)

Those that are bitten with him sometimes die miserably in 24 hours, their whole body cleaving into chops.

> Nehemiah Grew, London botanist, in the Royal Society's *Catalogue* (1681)

Since these remarks come from an era when there were more New England rattlesnakes (and presumably rattlesnake bites) than at any time afterward, and since they all (except the last) allude to the marked discoloration now recognized as one of the main diagnostic signs of *Crotalus* poisoning, they carry an air of authenticity — it seems probable that people *were* bitten by rattlesnakes in seventeenth-century New England, and that some of them developed alarming symptoms. But except for the far-off Mr. Grew, with his horrible picture of the "whole body cleaving into chops," these writers downplay any danger to life, mentioning it as a preventable hazard rather than as an observed result.

Dozens of timber rattlesnake bites have been treated in hospitals in this century, and the frightening swelling and discoloration, almost always confined to the arm or leg bitten, are well known. With or without treatment, however, these symptoms usually moderate abruptly sometime after the first twenty-four hours, giving the appearance of a miraculous recovery. Other typical accompaniments include nausea, dizziness, and excruciating pain near the bite.

Religious and cultural prejudices aside, these terrifying local symptoms are, I suspect, at the root of *Crotalus*'s lethal reputation. If, as the result of two tiny punctures at the base of one's thumb, one's arm quickly swells to the diameter of a six-pound shank ham and large portions of its surface turn red, then purple, then deep blue-black, one is unlikely to underestimate the power of the venom or to believe that one's life is not in the balance. Anyone witnessing the event would probably agree. The fact that rumors of death from such bites were largely that, rumors, might go unnoticed. In the meantime, the much greater number of people killed in more typical accidents — drownings, fires, and falls, even lightning strikes and ox gorings — would not help to build any such legend of horror. These risks are somehow less frightful.

At no time in New England history has there been any lack of authorities willing to declare that rattlesnakes represent a negligible danger:

> Seldom falls it out that any hurt is done by these.
> Higginson, *New-England's Plantation* (1630)

> This is the most poisonous and dangerous creature, yet nothing so bad as the report goes of him in England.
> Wood, *New England's Prospect* (1634)

> I never heard of any mischief that snakes did.
> Josselyn, *Two Voyages to New England* (1674)

> It is rare that one hears of anyone being attacked by it, despite the fact that people travel so much about the woods.
> Kalm, *Travels into North America* (1771)

> This animal has there [Europe] been commonly supposed, but erroneously, to be very dangerous to man. His bite is, indeed, a strong poison, but it is both certainly and easily cured. Besides, he is so clumsy as to be avoided without any difficulty.
> Dwight, *Travels in New England and New York* (1821)

> An accident is seldom known to occur.
> Storer, in *Reports on the Fishes, Reptiles, and Birds of Massachusetts* (1839)

> Such, however, are the habits of the reptile that there is little danger of an attack from it, even if met with.
> Teele, *History of Milton* (1888)

> Danger to humans is grossly exaggerated.
> DeGraaf and Rudis, *Amphibians and Reptiles of New England* (1983)

And yet this long tradition of clearsightedness has had little effect on a parallel and equally persistent set of attitudes that regard an open-air encounter with a rattlesnake, any rattlesnake, as mortally dire, since the animal is deeply malicious and its bite incurably fatal.

Certain prejudices, it seems, are so ingrown that their removal would require surgery. I don't pretend to know why a patch of woods with no rattlesnakes in it is widely regarded as safer, more healthful, more bucolic, and less worrisome than one containing them. If you asked someone of that opinion to explain, and he said, "Don't you know the damn things can kill you?," you might answer, "Yes, and so can any rock on the path, provided you trip and split your head on it. In fact the rock is more deadly, since it won't rattle a warning or crawl out of the way." But I doubt this would convince.

The entire question is almost academic in Massachusetts, since so few snakes remain. There are still places, a few places, where people and rattlesnakes mix, but bites are rare and fatalities — human fatalities — unheard-of. But two hundred years ago, when *Crotalus* was still present in force, a man who lived just south of the Blue Hills had convinced himself not only that rattlesnakes pose an outstanding threat to life and limb, but that he could bring back their victims from the edge of the grave. Let's move on to his story.

# 14

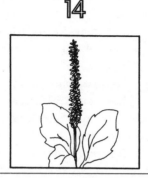

# The Country Doctor

Whoso breaketh an hedge, a serpent shall bite him.

— Ecclesiastes, 10:8

Charles Eliot Jr., the conservation-minded landscape architect who laid out the Blue Hills Reservation a century ago, was not the first Massachusetts Eliot to draw a line around these woods in order to define an oasis. Over two hundred years earlier, in 1657, Pastor John Eliot of Roxbury (no relation) had done the same for an overlapping six-thousand-acre parcel just to the south, which he called Ponkapoag Plantation. This prior effort culminated in a successful plea Eliot made before the Dorchester Town Meeting, which held title to the lands, on behalf of six or eight dozen Massachuset Indians then living at the site and absorbing his preaching. These Indians needed such a grant, Eliot argued, because they had been "much molested" in their attempts to settle elsewhere.

It may seem odd that less than thirty years after the Puritans stepped ashore they were doling out land to the original inhabitants. One might suppose that a war of conquest had intervened, a war that reduced the Americans to impotence. But there hadn't been any war; there had been, instead, one or more imported pathogens (perhaps the measles virus), which had killed approximately 90 percent of the local Americans forty years earlier. A subsequent smallpox epidemic reduced them further. And so by the time of Eliot's petition the Massachuset tribe was outnumbered in its original homeland, Boston Harbor and its environs, by more than fifty to one.

The Puritans thanked God for these disasters, and took them as a sign of divine favor. Little evidence survives of what the Massachuset thought.

Though primarily farmers, the Massachuset had been accustomed to a migratory existence. In the spring they went down to tidewater, planted their corn and beans, feasted on shellfish, and smoked the returning salmon and alewives they had caught in their weirs. In the fall the women gathered the harvest, and the men dispersed into the interior for the annual deer hunt. In the winter the clans reassembled at a sheltered spot in the uplands to sit out the cold months.

The Puritans quickly discovered that the old Massachuset cornfields contained the best local soils, and lost no time sharing out those ones freed up by the epidemics. They also drew up countless deeds giving themselves title to these fields and to whatever other lands they thought they could use — they persuaded the Massachuset to sign by handing out wampum, tools, clothing, and so forth. In no time all the lands once occupied by the tribe were consumed by this welter of conflicting instruments.

Here arose a misunderstanding. The Massachuset, perhaps not quite aware that they had bargained away their right to exist, continued to go down to the water every spring to plant and fish, using fields not yet cultivated by the Puritans. They discovered, however, that their new neighbors were in the habit of fencing their crops and letting their hogs and cattle roam free in the woods, and that these outlandish beasts not only ate up any young corn not so protected, but rooted up and ruined the best shellfish beds. They also found that many of their customary activities, such as fishing on the Sabbath, setting snares for game, or simply occupying space on their old campgrounds, were now illegal, since the land had become Puritan property, and Puritan law made no exceptions for non-Puritans. Often they were hauled into court and fined several beaver or otter skins; more often, I suspect, they were simply told to clear out immediately.

And so the Massachuset were left with two choices: either retreat to the interior and sue for asylum from their old and still-powerful enemies — the Wampanoag, the Narraganset, and the Nipmuck — or stay at home and try to adapt to Puritan methods, hoping to receive consideration from the magistrates. It was those who remained that Pastor Eliot was concerned with; besides Ponkapoag Plantation, he arranged for the creation of half a dozen other "praying towns" on the periphery of white settlement. In each of them a few dozen Massachuset attempted to settle down, still hunting the fast-vanishing game and planting their corn and beans with or without plows and ox teams. Since the grants rarely contained much good land, and since most offered no access to the shoreline bounty of fish and shellfish, their inhabitants quickly became impoverished. The Ponkapoag Indians mitigated the problem by cutting and splitting the cedars in the bog alongside Ponkapoag Pond and selling them as shingles and clapboards in Boston.

Ponkapoag Plantation might have lasted longer if the Puritans and their neighbors in Plymouth had been able to keep from antagonizing those tribes not crippled by disease. But the Wampanoag, in particular, who lived in the sandy lowlands between Boston, Plymouth, and Rhode Island, resented certain high-handed practices. Their leaders were chronically summoned to appear at the settlements to answer rumors about uprisings, and on several occasions the entire tribe was forced to surrender all firearms in its possession. In 1662 a son of Massasoit, the chief who befriended the Pilgrims, was seized and dragged into Plymouth for one of these interviews, and he died before returning, probably of a contagious illness, but foul play was suspected. Some years later John Sassamon, a Ponkapoag Indian, was found dead, probably murdered, on Wampanoag land; Plymouth Colony claimed jurisdiction and executed three Wampanoags for the crime. Insults like these were compounded by widespread encroachments on tribal lands prompted by Puritan land-hunger. By 1675 Massasoit's other son, Metacomet, had had enough, and he led the Wampanoag into war.

They fought a new-style war, not a typical low-intensity Algonquin campaign, which might have been satisfied with a few prisoners brought home for torture or a daring and particularly elegant raid. They fought the kind of war the Puritans had shown them forty years earlier, when they massacred Connecticut's Pequot tribe. The Wampanoags killed as many whites as they could as fast as they could, surprising farmers in the open, butchering families in dooryards, and catching rescue parties off guard in the woods. When they were finished a year later, they and their allies had cut down one of every sixteen Puritans of military age, burned or emptied all the outlying towns, and turned Boston into a tent city full of penniless refugees. They themselves were nearly exterminated; most of those who survived, women and children in particular, were sold into the West Indies as slaves.

At the war's outbreak Eliot's Ponkapoag Indians were at first considered reliable, and several were enrolled as soldiers. But as terrorized Puritans began to stream back toward Boston and the extent of the carnage became apparent, Ponkapoag Plantation began to look like a possible nest of guerrillas, and Dorchester prohibited Eliot's converts from straying more than a mile from their village without escort. Shortly thereafter the entire group was rounded up and interned on uninhabited Deer Island in Boston Harbor, where they joined evacuees from the other praying towns.

During the winter of 1675–76, when Puritan fortunes reached their nadir, plans surfaced in Boston for an expedition to the island to slaughter the Massachuset, not because they were hostile but because they were within reach. The authorities squashed the idea. But since the island was small and exposed and offered little food or shelter, many Indians starved or froze to death anyway, and barely half of the Ponkapoags returned to their village at the end of the war.

By then Indian power in eastern Massachusetts was decisively broken, and the pressure to maintain good relations had vanished. Over the next two decades dozens of white settlers moved onto the Ponkapoag grant and carved out farms for themselves on its more attractive portions. They quieted the Ponkapoags by purchasing leases with small gifts and offers of employment. By then Eliot was dead; when, in 1706, these encroachments on supposedly inalienable tribal lands finally came to the attention of the colony's legislature, the General Court, it declared them illegal and ordered the squatters to leave, though if they presented their leases to the General Court within sixty days they might be awarded compara-ble grants outside the plantation, the proceeds to go to the Ponka-poags.

The squatters ignored the order. Any attempt at enforcement would have been politically costly, if not suicidal, and shortly there-after the General Court backed down and turned the matter over to the town of Dorchester, which amounted to capitulation, since the squatters formed a sizable bloc at town meeting. Over the next century the rest of the plantation was gradually nibbled away, the Ponkapoags' state-appointed guardians periodically selling off pieces to support indigent Indians, and in 1834 the last scrap disappeared. By then the Ponkapoags had lost their language, their landscape, their economy, and most of their folkways, and the few residents remaining of primarily Indian blood were barely distinguishable from their poorer neighbors. The town of Canton (incorporated 1797) occupies what was once the heart of the plan-tation.

Pastor Eliot's Ponkapoag sanctuary lay entirely south of the Blue Hills proper, and did not include any of the hilltops. Its northern boundary ran across the middle of Ponkapoag Pond, a low-lying, spring-fed jewel of about two hundred acres a half mile distant from the range itself. The younger Eliot didn't include the pond in his 1893 plan for the Blue Hills Reservation — there were several hog farms nearby, and he generally opposed taking active farm-land — and it was added only later in a series of private bequests. But in Pastor Eliot's time this half-mile-wide corridor between the Indian grant and the Hills was equally attractive to farmers, and during the Wampanoag war it became a sort of refuge for whites.

The Blue Hills form a rocky bulwark guarding the southern rim of the Boston basin. When Metacomet's warriors began to ravage all the country down toward Rhode Island, the Hills were regarded as one of Boston's last lines of defense. Late in the war, when it became apparent that the Ponkapoags, despite much abuse, were still loyal to the Puritans, a party of them were dispatched from Deer Island under Puritan officers to build and man a fort under the southwest slope of Great Blue Hill; they were meant to keep the Wampanoags from slipping past into Boston. This outpost's exact location is unknown today, but it was apparently effective: although settlers were ambushed in Braintree and Weymouth, none were killed in Milton, Dorchester, Roxbury, or anywhere else inside the rampart of the Hills.

Some of the Puritan farmers driven out of the outlying settlements in the war's first months were none too eager to return and plant again at the edge of the wilderness. They must have sensed, however, that the narrow corridor between Ponkapoag and the Hills was relatively safe, since several took up land there and stayed. Houghton's Pond, for instance, which is today the premier swimming hole in the Hills, was named after an early settler of Lancaster, Massachusetts, who left that town when the Indians destroyed it in February 1676. Although Houghton returned to Lancaster after the war, he apparently never got comfortable again, because he departed for good in 1682 and moved to the shore of the pond now bearing his name, which was fifteen miles closer to Boston.

Another Puritan frontiersman, Matthias Puffer of Mendon, was widowed when the Nipmuck killed his wife and twelve-year-old son at their farmstead near the Rhode Island border in July 1675. Puffer and his two younger sons escaped to Braintree and started over on several dozen acres between Ponkapoag and the Hills. Five years after the war the General Court tried to persuade Puffer to return to Mendon, which was still struggling to rebuild itself. Puffer begged off in a petition to the court inventorying his losses, and his descendants remained on his land under the Hills for three generations.

Over the next century or so, as Ponkapoag Plantation and the narrow strip to the north were gradually converted to cropland and pasture, a new war replaced the war with the Indians — the war with the snakes. Apparently the Ponkapoags hadn't bothered to exterminate them, and by 1760 the Stoughton selectmen were paying area residents for as many rattles as they could deliver. Although there were still several dozen Ponkapoag Indians in town, no Ponkapoag names were prominent in the early *Crotalus* bounty books, and perhaps a reluctance to kill snakes was one of the last traditions they surrendered.

And so for the first time in their history the Blue Hills were completely surrounded by a sea of snake killers, perhaps 2,500 farmers, woodcutters, and herdsmen in Braintree, Milton, and Stoughton, with daughter-towns Canton, Randolph, and Quincy to follow. The Hills themselves remained largely uninhabited, being too steep and rocky for cultivation, although picnickers and berry pickers are reported on their slopes as early as 1681, when Reverend Peter Thacher of Milton dined with Quartermaster Thomas Swift atop Great Blue Hill at a spot where earlier visitors had already erected a pillar of stones.

Knowing that the Hills were then, as now, prime *Crotalus* habitat, and that the wooded lowlands underneath their bold, south-facing ledges were rapidly becoming checkered with Puritan farms, one might expect to see some evidence of conflict other than the hundreds of rattles turned in for bounties — this was, after all, virgin snake-killing country, and prospective snake-victims were moving in wholesale. Curiously enough, however, the first evidence of a Blue Hills envenomation following Thomas Morton's too inquisitive bird dog in the 1620s comes a full sixty years after Ponkapoag Plantation broke up under pressure, when the following item appeared in the *Massachusetts Gazette and Boston News-Letter* for August 16, 1764:

On Wednesday the first of August instant, about XI o'clock in the Morning, one Mary Littlefield, the daughter of Mr. Moses and Mrs. Mary Littlefield of the third parish in the town of Braintree, as she was picking Whirtleberries [blueberries], was bitten by a Rattle-Snake, in the foot of her left leg, inside, between the Ankle Bone and the great Cord of the Heel. The principal Medicines that were administered to the Patient for 16 hours after she was bitten were Sweet Oyl and Rhubarb; but these did not seem to expel the Virus in the least; the patient continued swelling more and more, and every time she respired made a clucking kind of a Noise, which prognosticated present Death. One Mr. Abel Puffer of Stoughton hearing of the girl's misfortune went of his own accord to see her, and made use of a certain Medicine both internally and externally; that in the space of about two Hours after the Administration of that, the Virus was driven from the various Parts of the Body into the Foot of that Leg which had been bitten, and it swelled to such a prodigious Degree, that he was obliged to lance it in three several Places, in order that the virulent Matter might be discharged, and it continued constantly running out of those orifices for thirty Hours, till the whole virulent Matter was discharged; and the Patient soon recovered to a good sound State of Health as ever she was favored with.

We the subscribers can safely attest to the above Relation, that it is true, and thought ourselves in Duty bound to inform the Public of it, for the good of Mankind in general, that there is a speedy Cure to be obtained for all those who happen to be bit by that venomous Serpent the Rattlesnake.

(signed)

| | |
|---|---|
| Braintree | Moses Littlefield |
| Aug. 14 | Mary Littlefield |
| 1764 | Mary Littlefield, jun. |
| | Delight Hunt |

This testimonial was probably written and planted in the *News-Letter* by Abel Puffer, possessor of the unnamed "certain Medicine." Puffer was a great-grandson of Matthias Puffer, the refugee and widower from Mendon, and he had a house and farm on Ponkapoag Pond. The girl who was bitten, Mary Littlefield, then ten years old, lived on another farm a mile or two east, near what is now North Main Street in Randolph, an area currently cut off from the Hills by Route 128, but then probably included in the home range of their resident rattlesnakes. Mary signed the document, as did her parents, Moses and Mary, and her mother's sister, Delight Hunt.

Clearly Puffer thought he had saved Mary's life by drawing the snake's venom back into her foot, where it ran out through his incisions. He seems to have convinced Mary's parents and her aunt as well. What isn't so clear is his purpose in publicizing the exploit without revealing his method. If a present-day doctor tried to promote a revolutionary life-saving technique while reserving its use to himself, he wouldn't get far, I hope.

But Puffer wasn't a doctor. He was a farmer, and happened to live in an area where doctors were scarce and rattlesnakes common. He dreamed up a bite remedy, found an opportunity to try it, and when his subject recovered he, like Morton, awarded himself the whole credit. Maybe he hoped to supplement his income with gifts from grateful patients; maybe he believed only he could administer the cure properly; maybe he merely meant to become important.

That attempts were made to cash in on *Crotalus*'s deadly reputation is evident from the following petition submitted to the General Court twenty years earlier by Palmer Goulding, a Worcester butcher and tanner (spelling corrected):

### Province of Massachusetts Bay

To his Excellency the Governor, the Honorable Council, and House of Representatives, in General Court assembled September 23, 1741

The memorial of Palmer Goulding of Worcester Humbly Showeth:

That your memorialist, in his travels, has with Considerable Cost attained to Such Skill and Knowledge in Curing the bite of a Rattlesnake, that were he present when a person was bit, he Could so soon Effectually cure it, that the person would never be Sensible of any hurt, and the Same medicine, if rightly applied, has no less operation on the Body of men to Cure any Inflammation of the blood, or to prevent or Cure any breeding Sore Whatsoever, a woman's Sore breast or fever Sore. It is also an infallible medicine to Cure or prevent the Coming of fistula or poll Evil in horses, which Knowledge he is Very willing to Communicate for the good of mankind.

But inasmuch as he was Really at Considerable Cost in gaining the Same, he most humbly prays your Excellency and Honors would, upon his so doing, be pleased to make him a grant of Some of the wild and uncultivated Lands of the Province, and your memorialist will Cheerfully Submit to such terms and Conditions Respecting the Settling as your Excellency and Honors in your Great Wisdom Shall think proper.

And as in Duty Bound Shall ever pray, &c.,

PALMER GOULDING

Here we have a small-town operator unabashedly attempting to trade a medical secret for a piece of publicly owned land. The offer would be even less likely to find favor today; *Crotalus* is apparently extinct in Worcester County.

Curiously enough, the General Court opted to negotiate, and awarded Goulding a grant of up to two hundred acres, provided he met the following conditions: (1) that he bring at least six acres of the grant into mowing and plowing condition within three years,

(2) that he share his remedy with his neighbors and provide a full description of it to the General Court, and (3) that he give "credible proof" that the remedy worked in the cases he cited, "whereof as yet there is no certain demonstration."

Apparently the General Court wasn't convinced by the testimonials Goulding submitted, which were perhaps much like those he included in an earlier petition — signed statements from Joseph Freson and Joseph Frost of Brimfield, each of whom alleged that he had been bitten by a rattlesnake and had recovered completely after a session with Goulding. Freson affirmed that he was well again "in an hour or two," and that the remedy itself was "a small root, the bigness of a walnut." Although Goulding claimed that his secret drug was also useful against breast cancer and certain equine infections, he seems to have included no testimonials to that effect, perhaps because he had had fewer successes. Here again we see how a stubborn faith in the mortal potential of all untreated snakebites could allow any backcountry horse doctor to pose as a medical wizard. If bad bites had been common, and people had routinely died from them, these supposedly infallible cures might have been rated at their true value.

The records don't show whether Goulding received any land.* Maybe the General Court was amused by his pretensions and merely strung him along; maybe he had friends in high places and hoped to get something for nothing under the guise of a reward for public service. Whatever his merits as a physician, he was no babe in the woods — he speculated extensively in real estate, held a variety of town offices, ran several large businesses, and commanded a company at the capture of Louisburg, the French citadel in Acadia.

Posterity hasn't suffered from the loss of Goulding's secret. Countless snakebite cures of this type were touted in colonial America; most are forgotten today. Abel Puffer found it necessary to cast doubt on two of them, "Sweet Oyl [Morton's choice] and Rhubarb," in order to promote his own. None of them permanently outdistanced the others, probably because they were all

---

*Another petitioner, a slave named Caesar from North Carolina, was more successful. That colony's legislature voted to buy him his freedom in return for the details of his snakebite remedy.

harmless at best. In contrast, quinine — also known as cinchona, or priest's bark, a product of a Peruvian tree — quickly became a staple of international commerce, and remained important well into this century, since it was genuinely effective against a major killer, malaria.

There were no medical schools in colonial Massachusetts. Doctors learned their trade by serving apprenticeships or from books printed in Europe; most were unlicensed. In this casual environment there was plenty of room for confidence men like Puffer and Goulding. If it seems today that they devoted too much attention to *Crotalus* — physicians were still largely helpless against infectious disease, and periodic viral epidemics carried off Yankees in droves — it is perhaps because they, like their modern descendants, preferred grateful survivors to ungrateful corpses. It took courage to face the true killers. Dr. Zabdiel Boylston, who along with Cotton Mather championed the revolutionary technique of inoculation against smallpox, had to weather vicious attacks from his peers and was widely regarded as a public menace.

Apparently Abel Puffer of Ponkapoag didn't get the results he hoped for from publicizing his success with Mary Littlefield, since he later surrendered his secret in an almanac published in 1771. Perhaps he concluded that "the Benefit of Mankind" required full disclosure. Here is his recipe:

> A sure and certain cure for the bite of a Rattle-Snake made Public by Abel Puffer, of Stoughton.
>
> As soon as may be after the Person is bit, cut a Gash or Split in the Place where the Bite is, as the Teeth went in, and fill it full of fine Salt. Take common Plantain and pound it, add a little Water to it, then squeeze out the Juice, and mix it with clean Water; then make a strong Brine with fine Salt and the Juice, till it will not dissolve the salt; then make a Swath or bandage with Linnen Cloth, and bind it around just above the swelling (but not too tight); then wet the Bandage with the afore-mentioned Brine, and keep it constantly wet with the Brine — for it will dry very fast — and keep stroking the Part with your Hands as hard as the Patient can bear, toward the Cut you made, and you will soon see the Poison and virulent Matter flow out of the Cut; and it will often flow so fast that it will swell below the Cut, and if it should, you must cut below the swelling to let out the virulent Matter, and it will not leave running till it is

discharged. You must keep the Bandage moving downwards as the Swelling abates. It is proper to give the Patient something to defend the Stomack, as Sweet Oil, Saffron, or Snake Root. It very often bleeds after the Poison is out; but be not surprised at that — it is Good for it. It will run some time after the Poison is out; there must be Care taken that none of the poison that runs out gets to any sore, or raw Flesh, for it will Poison the Person.

I expect that some will slight this Publication, for the Remedies being so simple a Thing; but I hope no one will so slight it, if he is bit, as to neglect trying the Experiment, and the Effect will prove what I have said to be true. I should not have published this had I not been certain of its performing the Cure by my own Experience; for I have cured two Persons dangerously bit, and a Horse and a Dog, with no other Thing but what is mentioned in the before Direction, and make this Public for the Benefit of Mankind, tho I have been offer'd a considerable Sum by some Persons to make it known to them, but then it must be kept as a secret.

ABEL PUFFER

Stoughton, Oct. 4th, 1770

This incision-and-tourniquet method is not unlike certain first-aid techniques still recommended today; the point is to remove whatever venom is still in the bite and slow the remainder's absorption into the bloodstream. The use of plantain, however, hasn't survived.* Plantain is a cosmopolitan weed (*Plantago major* or *P. lanceolata*) found in countless back yards and dirt driveways in Massachusetts — an annual with coarse basal leaves and erect, tightly packed seed stalks. The Indians knew it as "Englishman's foot," since it appeared nearly everywhere Puritan livestock trampled the soil, and one species (*P. lanceolata*) was probably brought from Europe with their fodder. Apparently Puffer believed that its juice, when applied to a tourniquet, had an important therapeutic effect, since his cure is otherwise not much different from typical New England practice of the day. A more prominent physician, Dr. Benjamin Gale of Connecticut, also recommended salt, incisions, and a tourniquet in a letter to the Royal Society published seven years earlier, and he reported two instances of their effective-

---

*Except as an aid to digestion: the active ingredient in Metamucil, Procter & Gamble's immensely popular dietary fiber, is derived from the seed husks of psyllium, a type of plantain.

ness — in one of these, the common herbs burdock and bloodroot were substituted for plantain; in the other no plant juices at all were employed.

So it appears that considerable progress had been made since the time, a century earlier, when Governor Winthrop carried snakeweed in his pocket. There was less reliance on orally administered cure-alls and a greater attention to the bite itself and its local effects. Tourniquets were used to slow the advance of the swelling (which was correctly interpreted as a gauge of the venom's spread), and incisions over the bite, guarded from infection with salt, supported a common-sense effort to remove or counteract the venom where it was most accessible. Until the 1920s, when specific antivenoms based on horse serum became available, primary treatment improved no further.

Therefore it would be less than fair to Puffer to portray him as no more than a wishful thinker, a meddlesome bumpkin peculiarly susceptible to self-delusion. If he worked no miracles, he at least made himself available and gave hope to people half frightened out of their wits. His treatment itself, if painful, was admirably logical and conservative, and much safer than some of the experiments that have been tried more recently. If he hadn't believed his cure was effective and could genuinely improve a bite victim's chances for survival, what good would he have been? What he seems to have overlooked is that no evidence existed that those chances had ever been less than 100 percent, at least locally — since Morton's time, so far as we know, all bite victims had been treated and all had recovered. The specific remedies used don't seem to have mattered in the slightest.

Puffer's ten-year-old patient, Mary Littlefield, was the oldest of nine children, and grew up to have seven of her own, all born underneath the Blue Hills. By the first decades of the nineteenth century, fifty years after she was bitten, *Crotalus* fades, like the Ponkapoags, from the local records — apparently snakes had become so scarce that it was no longer considered necessary to subsidize their extermination. Abel Puffer, a lifelong bachelor, died in Canton in 1813 at the age of seventy-six, and his farm on Ponkapoag Pond passed to his brother, also childless, and thence out of the family.

If we could end the story here we might consider ourselves satisfied. We have traced *Crotalus* from his heyday in Pastor Eliot's time to his near-extinction two centuries later, and we have found no sign that he delivered a single fatal bite over the interval, despite considerable provocation. Like the Ponkapoags, he was crowded against the Hills and gradually reduced to nothing — not in return for crimes, but on general principles. If we need a hero, we have Abel Puffer, who in his own estimation prevented a tragedy on at least two occasions, when ungrateful snakes struck back, albeit blindly, at their two-legged persecutors. By the time Puffer is gone, the snakes are nearly gone also, and raw Nature has had its teeth pulled. The stage is set for the younger Eliot, a champion in his own right, who will take this much-battered Nature and give it a little space to recover, now that it has been brought to heel.

But we can't end the story here. There exists a grain of evidence that *Crotalus* did not in fact go quietly, and made at least one individual pay dearly for all the snakes bludgeoned to death in and around the Hills. All we know of this person comes from an account first printed one hundred years after his death, and never since corroborated. Even so, if we were to leave him out we would be giving up on our purpose, and admitting that when the facts become inconvenient, we become surreptitious.

What we know about this person — or, more accurately, what was said about him years later — is that his name was Strowbridge, that he was under twenty-one years of age, that he lived in that part of Stoughton later incorporated as Canton, and that on July 27, 1791, he was bitten by a rattlesnake and died within hours. Someone went to get the local snake doctor, Abel Puffer, but the boy was gone before he arrived.

This is not an incredible story. People have died from the bites of timber rattlesnakes, although the only certain instance I know of occurred in Florida less than ten years ago, when a sixty-seven-year-old man who kept snakes decided to cut one up for dinner, and after chopping its head off made the mistake of picking the head up. It bit him at the base of his thumb and he expired in a hospital two days later. It is not, therefore, inconceivable that a boy named Strowbridge was living in Canton shortly after the Revolution, and that a bite from a Blue Hills *Crotalus* killed him, although he would have to be called unlucky — the doctors who treated the Florida man, for instance, had in the decade preceding handled two hundred other cases of pit-viper bite without a fatality.

What makes me uncomfortable about the story is that it was first documented, so far as I know, in Daniel Huntoon's *History of the Town of Canton,* published in Cambridge in 1893. Huntoon writes that he heard the story from his father, Benjamin Huntoon, long-time pastor of Canton's First Congregational Church, who grew up in New Hampshire and didn't arrive in town until 1821; hence the version he in turn heard must have been at least thirty years old. Huntoon's notes for his *History* belong to the Canton Historical Society. Ed Bolster, the society's current president, assures me they contain no references to a fatal snakebite.

Oral traditions are notoriously plastic. In a case like this we would like to see some notice of the facts closer in time to the event itself, and the most obvious source is a newspaper account. Unfortunately there were no Blue Hills–area papers until the Quincy *Patriot Ledger* began publication in 1837, and the Boston journals of the day — the *Argus,* the *Gazette,* the *Semi-Weekly Advertiser,* and the *Columbian Centinel* — printed no snakebite stories in the summer of 1791.*

What about a death notice, then? In eighteenth-century Massachusetts many towns elected a clerk, one of whose duties was to keep a record of births, marriages, and deaths occurring within the community. In the late 1700s the town of Stoughton (including present-day Canton) had such an official — he was George Crosman, a farmer, justice of the peace, and sometime physician, and he recorded hundreds of personal milestones in several ledgers he used for town business. These notes were later edited by Frederic Endicott and published in Canton in 1896, and they mention no one named Strowbridge who died for any reason in July 1791. But even this is not conclusive; according to Endicott, "The records of death are very poor for the whole time covered . . . probably half of the whole number were never registered."

---

*They did, however, report a fatal mill accident in Watertown, a grotesque and lethal brain tumor in Charlestown, several deaths by lightning in Connecticut, and a surprising item from Concord concerning a youth who voided several large, snake-like worms.

Stymied again. But lest anyone think that the entire incident was fabricated, let me include certain dates and events that did not escape Crosman's notice, diagrammed here as a family tree (see next page).

As is evident, there was no lack of Strowbridges, or Strobridges, in late-eighteenth-century Canton. The patriarch, Samuel Strobridge, was probably the son of John Strobridge, a Scots-Irish immigrant who arrived in Boston on the *Elizabeth* in January 1719 and was warned out of town shortly thereafter. "Warning out" was a tradition of Puritan hospitality allied to present-day vagrancy laws. Newcomers were informed that if they did not acquire a piece of land or join the church or hire out to an existing household within a specified period, usually a few weeks, they would be cordially escorted to the town limits. Most Scots-Irish immigrants were desperately poor, having spent everything they had for their passage, and most immediately decamped for the hazards of life on the frontier, where the authorities were less particular. John Strobridge, however, managed to stick, and three or four years later married Elizabeth Andrews in Dorchester. Perhaps it was her family that gave the newlyweds the means to stay on, and later helped set up their son Samuel (born 1723) in Canton.

Do any of Samuel's descendants fit Huntoon's description of the *Crotalus* victim? Apparently not. Samuel's sons, Seth and Samuel Jr., were too old (Samuel Jr., twenty-nine in 1791, could hardly be described as a boy), and his grandsons, though ranging in age from nine to seventeen, were all born to his daughters, and thus were named Crane or Jordin. Samuel's oldest son, Seth, married for the first time in 1775 (the year of Bunker Hill) and could easily have had a son of the right age, but appears to have had no children at all.

Was Town Clerk Crosman's attention to the Strobridge family as spotty as his record as a whole? Was the *Crotalus* victim a visiting relative (there were other Strobridges in Middleborough, near Taunton) and therefore ineligible for the books? Why did the event's exact date survive as hearsay, but not the victim's name? And why did Huntoon, normally so careful with his sources, fail to look into this one?

Like it or not, it is probably too late now to come to any firm

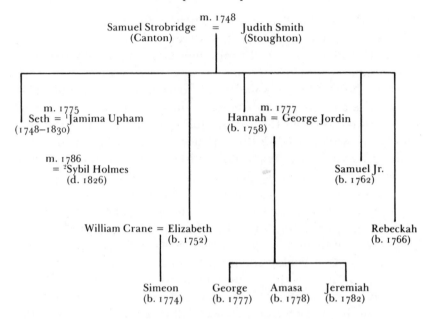

conclusion concerning whether a boy named Strobridge, or Strowbridge, was killed by a Blue Hills rattler in the summer of 1791.
The people who were there and knew the truth are long gone.
From the perspective of this inquiry, it was by no means a trivial
occurrence, and if it happened at all, it must have struck the
victim's neighbors and contemporaries, even as far away as Boston — less than fifteen miles to the north — as a very tragic and
singular event. Why, then, did it sink so securely out of sight?

Snake haters may be displeased to know that this incident, as
shaky as it is, is the best-authenticated instance of a fatal *Crotalus*
bite in Massachusetts history, or in New England history for that
matter. Its chief rivals are:

1. the early-twentieth-century Berkshire-area bite mentioned, but
   not documented, by Raymond Ditmars — quoted in Lamson,
   *Reptiles of Connecticut* (Hartford, 1935)
2. the fatal poisoning of Timothy Mirick, twenty-two, bitten while
   mowing his father's hayfield on August 7, 1761, in Wilbraham,
   Massachusetts — family tradition reported by Charles Merrick
   of Wilbraham in the *Valley Advocate*, vol. 4, no. 43 (1977)

3. an ancient, decaying tombstone in Putney, Vermont, bearing
   the legend "Killed by a Serpente" — reported by Ted Levin in
   *Backtracking: The Way of a Naturalist* (Chelsea, Vt., 1980).

All in all, a poor showing for a legendary assassin.

I am not about to argue that none of the above instances had any
basis in fact. On the other hand, not one of them would impress an
average insurance adjuster. If *Crotalus* is a killer, why is it so difficult to convict him on the evidence? New Englanders have had
almost four hundred years to do so; maybe they'll have more
success in the next millennium.*

Huntoon also mentions the last Blue Hills rattlesnake bite to
which we can attach a name — in 1808 Polly Billings was bitten in
the Randolph Woods, the same area where Mary Littlefield came
to grief a half century earlier. This incident may be one of two
anonymous nineteenth-century bites mentioned by Teele in his
*History of Milton*. So far as is known, there have been no poisonings
since.

And so we will have to leave the Blue Hills if we want to examine
the development of *Crotalus*-bite therapy subsequent to the colonial-era efforts of Abel Puffer; since then local medical men have
had no opportunity to try their skills on anything but a couple of
copperhead envenomations. The snakes are still here, and still
threaten, but have been so inactive, actuarially speaking, that anyone who hesitates to tramp through the Reservation on their account ought to consider never emerging from bed, since the world
bristles with greater hazards — one could drown in one's bathtub,
for instance, or become fatally entangled in a telephone cord.

Elsewhere, however, bites have been more frequent, particularly
in the warmer and less urbanized portions of the United States.
Some have had lethal results, particularly in the coastal pinewoods
of the Southeast, home to *Crotalus*'s larger relative, *C. adamanteus*,
the eastern diamondback, undoubtedly the most dangerous snake
in North America. *Crotalus atrox*, the western diamondback, is still
common in parts of west Texas and is similarly formidable — as

---

*A well-known local herpetologist, James D. Lazell Jr. of Ayer, has offered a $500
reward for information confirming a fatal *Crotalus* bite in Massachusetts. There have
been no takers to date.

much for its irritable temper as for the strength of its venom. Although bites from these animals have never been a major public health problem, as recently as 1930 they may have been responsible for as many as thirty deaths per year and a greater number of permanent injuries. Since then, effective antivenoms and improved rural access to hospitals have cut the toll to something like five to fifteen fatalities nationwide annually, a large proportion of them resulting from "illegitimate" bites, that is, bites suffered by people who went out of their way to expose themselves — members of fundamentalist snake-handling cults, snake collectors, careless snake bashers, and so forth.

This is not to say that the Blue Hills are not a dangerous place. Despite their relative emptiness, in the last half century many fatal injuries have occurred there, and in a later chapter I will show exactly what makes them hazardous. But as far as snake accidents go, the continued presence of *Crotalus* has not been a factor since long before the Civil War — he may as well have been absent, for all the trouble he has caused. And so there was no opportunity for a local M.D. to inherit Abel Puffer's office of snake doctor extraordinaire, no succession of poisonings over which to demonstrate one's mastery. This was perhaps just as well, because a time was coming when physicians would no longer be satisfied with modest Puffer-style treatments. Firm believers in *Crotalus*'s black legend, and convinced of the terrific toxicity of rattler bites, these men would not have the patience to let events take their course — not at all, they would consider themselves obliged to attempt heroic and radical measures. In many instances the truly dangerous stages of an envenomation didn't begin until the doctor arrived, and the best advice many bite sufferers could have received was to flee as far and as quickly as possible from medical attention. Incredibly, this tradition of do-it-yourself havoc continues right up to our times.

# 15

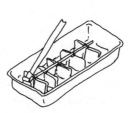

# First, Do No Harm

He drank, during the first four days, seven quarts of brandy
and whiskey, with very slight symptoms of inebriety.

— L. E. Whiting, in the *Boston Medical
and Surgical Journal* (1854)

Alcohol, like snake venom, is a poison. Unlike snake venom, it is
not broken down by gastric juices, and is readily absorbed from the
intestine, and so is just as dangerous taken internally as it would be
if injected.

The fatal dose of alcohol for an average adult is three to four
hundred milliliters, or a little less than a quart of whiskey. This
amount, if consumed in under an hour, will typically produce
stupor, coma, and death by respiratory collapse. Children are particularly susceptible.

During the nineteenth century the medical fraternity in America
almost unanimously recommended gigantic doses of alcohol for
the treatment of snakebite. It was believed that alcohol and snake
venom neutralize each other in the bloodstream, and that a badly
bitten patient could therefore absorb a much greater amount than
would otherwise be tolerable. The medical journals of the day are
peppered with letters from physicians describing cases in which
they persuaded snakebite victims to imbibe truly massive amounts

of liquor, and although the decorum is more strict than in Puffer's time, and the writers rarely claim a cause-and-effect relationship between medication and recovery, this is clearly the inference — in fact, the letters are so much alike that each might be subtitled "How I Cured Snakebite with an Eye-popping Bender."

Any M.D. today who attempted this treatment could expect to hear from a lawyer. Even in nontoxic doses alcohol is contraindicated in cases of snake-venom poisoning; its stimulant effect, which increases peripheral circulation, probably hastens the spread of the dangerous proteins.

*Crotalus* authority Laurence M. Klauber collected some examples of these fearsome nineteenth-century prescriptions, all taken from the doctors' own testimony:

— a quart of brandy in the first hour, and another quart within two
   hours
— a half pint of bourbon every five minutes, until a quart had been
   taken
— one and a half quarts of whiskey (given to a young girl)
— three quarts of apple brandy in four hours.

In these instances the patients survived. This is perhaps less an indication of an alcohol-buffering element in rattlesnake venom (there is none) than of a tendency among medical men to trumpet their successes and bury their failures — even today, accounts of lethal snakebites are rarely published by the attending physicians, for obvious reasons. But it may be doubted that all such treatments ended happily. Klauber mentions an instance where a man was bitten by a harmless, nonvenomous snake and died, after appropriate medication, of acute alcohol poisoning. In 1908 an investigator estimated that as many as 5 percent of all "snakebite" deaths in the United States were actually alcohol overdoses. But by then the treatment was already in decline.

Honest error? Criminal idiocy? The snakes, it seems, merely prepped these unfortunates; the doctors finished them off.

In 1895 Leonhard Stejneger of the Smithsonian Institution recommended, for *Crotalus* bite, repeated injections of strychnine "until slight tetanic spasms appear." Today it is generally admitted that strychnine, although an excellent rat poison, has no legitimate business inside a syringe.

During the First World War and for some years after, most snakebite kits sold in the United States contained a supply of potassium permanganate crystals. This chemical had been shown to destroy rattler venom, and bite victims were instructed to sprinkle it on the wound or make incisions and rub it inside. Unfortunately the same reactive qualities that broke down venom proteins also destroyed organic compounds of all kinds, and bite sufferers might with as much wisdom have been advised to rub dirt in their wounds — at least that would not have killed the surrounding tissues outright.

Not so long ago in Australia, snakebite fatalities were believed to be the result of fright-induced shock. The important thing, then, was to keep bite victims relaxed and alert, and to this end they were given plenty of whiskey to drink, forced to run or jog in place, and whipped until they collapsed. Nowadays, with the greater emphasis on antivenoms, this approach is no longer popular, and by 1971 one of its remaining adherents, a professor of medicine at the Royal Melbourne Hospital, had downgraded it to a first-aid measure: "It is probably wise to keep [the patient] awake with stimulants such as coffee, or by hurried walking or even slapping."

Treatments like these blur the distinction between illness and therapy. It's as if snake venoms were regarded as poisons so terrible, so horrific, that the only hope of combating them was with measures equally radical and abusive. According to this school of thought, patients who arrive at a hospital with a skull fracture should have their arms and legs broken.

Don't get me wrong — I'm not suggesting that victims of snakebite should avoid doctors at all costs. But it is nonetheless true that snakebite therapy has long been a treacherous backwater of medicine, plagued by outmoded theories, ambitious quacks, poor reporting, lack of standards, and monstrous miscalculation. Bite sufferers have paid a high price.

Snake venoms include some of the most complex organic substances known. When they kill, as they sometimes do, it is rarely possible to reconstruct the exact sequence of tissue reactions leading to death. While the doctor's report will say "renal failure" or "cerebral hemorrhage" or "respiratory collapse," there is still little understanding of precisely how these syndromes develop, or of why they appear in some people and not others, or of which venom components are most responsible — this despite all the lab rats, dogs, and cats that have been sacrificed over the years in pursuit of answers.

One thing is certain, however: snake venoms are dangerous not merely in the way any foreign substance injected under the skin can be dangerous. No, they are dangerous because evolutionary processes have refined them for millennia, concentrating and intensifying precisely those properties which make them strong poisons. In some instances this genetically based weapons-development program seems to have succeeded far beyond any imaginable utility. The venom glands of a large *Oxyuranus microlepidotus* (a rare, whiplike snake of the Australian outback), for example, have been estimated to contain enough poison to kill a quarter-million white mice.

Fortunately human beings have discovered a way to use snake venoms against snakebite, and effective antidotes, or antivenoms, now exist despite all the pharmacological riddles still surrounding the poisons themselves.

This recent and happy development can be said to have originated in 1887, when Henry Sewall, then a professor of physiology at the University of Michigan at Ann Arbor, managed to obtain a useful quantity of venom from the local variety of rattlesnake, *Sistrurus catenatus,* otherwise known as the massasauga — a small, swamp-dwelling species still present in the area. By injecting graduated amounts of this "cloudy yellow liquid" into common pigeons, he established just how large a dose was likely to be lethal. More important, he gave pigeons who withstood smaller doses increasingly greater ones — training them, so to speak, to survive — and eventually produced birds that could endure amounts many times larger than those which would kill an unprepared animal. This research demonstrated the existence of "venom immunity," an innate resistance to snake toxins which, although normally latent, could be stimulated to considerable strength.

Of course there was no question of giving every American who happened to live or work in snake country a course of graduated venom injections — besides the considerable health risk involved, it would be virtually impossible to collect and preserve the amounts of venom required. In addition, the immunity itself tended to wear off almost overnight. And so if Sewall's discovery was to become medically useful, a way would have to be found to package the venom-neutralizing agents present in immunized animals. Perhaps these agents, if introduced to a human snakebite victim, could mitigate the venom's toxic effects.

Only a few years earlier Louis Pasteur had worked out the concept of immunity in his experiments with infectious diseases. He discovered that people bitten by rabid dogs could be protected from the onset of rabies by injections made from the spinal cords of rabbits killed by the disease — a sort of quasi-curative vaccine. Snakebite, however, was not an infectious illness but rather a variety of poisoning — the symptoms couldn't be passed from person to person, and venoms remained toxic even when carefully filtered. But poisons were not generally associated with immunity. A quart of alcohol, for instance, remained powerfully toxic no matter who swallowed it, an alcoholic or a teetotaler. Why, then, did Sewall's birds develop resistance?

It had been known for some time that the dangerous elements in snake venom included an organic (protein) component — Charles-Lucien Bonaparte, Napoleon's writer-naturalist nephew, had recognized it in 1843. In this sense snake-venom poisoning resembled the microbial illnesses diphtheria and tetanus, in that the symptoms were produced not by the attacking organism itself but by its nonliving and toxic secretions.

At about the same time Sewall began working with pigeons and rattlesnakes in Michigan, several of Pasteur's students at his institute in Paris attempted to develop vaccines against diphtheria and tetanus by taking blood from infected animals, straining out the cell elements, and injecting it into others. They found that these blood sera could not only heighten resistance in unexposed animals, but improve the prognosis for those already infected but not yet symptomatic. And so they went a step beyond Sewall: they not only showed that immunity could be developed against certain organic toxins, but also that this immunity could be transferred, at least in part, from one animal to another.

They called their serum-based drugs antitetanus and anti-diphtheria, and advocated their use against suspected infections. Before long another student at the institute, bacteriologist Albert Calmette, recognized that serum drugs might also be helpful against another organic poison, snake venom. He obtained a quantity of cobra and viper venoms, and in 1894 began immunizing horses by giving them larger and larger doses, preparatory to drawing their blood. The result was a new drug he called *sérum antivenimeux*, and by 1897 it was being marketed worldwide.

Although it was subsequently discovered that the venoms of different snakes vary widely in their composition and effect, and that a serum, or antivenom, useful against one will often be no help against another, antivenoms based on horse serum are still the essential ingredient in snakebite therapy throughout the world. They contain antibodies that can combine with and neutralize the dangerous proteins. Laboratories for their production exist on every continent except Antarctica — all one needs to make anti-venoms are a supply of snakes (for venom), a string of horses (for immunization), and some blood-fractionation equipment (for serum). Nonetheless, these drugs remain expensive and somewhat difficult to manufacture — the horses, for instance, tend to develop long-term health problems — and it is hoped that recent gene-splicing techniques will make the process much cheaper, by transferring the antibody-producing chore to bacteria.

At first the United States lagged badly at this work. In 1899 a Philadelphia pathologist, Joseph McFarland, attempted to make a *Crotalus* antivenom, but with little success. Five years later another local man, pathologist Simon Flexner of the Penn Medical School, attempted the same feat; in collaboration with Hideyo Noguchi, a Japanese bacteriologist, he produced an effective *Crotalus* anti-venom from rabbit serum. Money was lacking, however, as were volunteers willing to undergo clinical trials — few persons are bitten by rattlesnakes in Pennsylvania — and so the drug was never tested on humans, nor licensed for manufacture and sale.

Things moved more rapidly in Brazil, home to *Crotalus durissus terrificus,* or the cascabel, most formidable of all rattlesnakes and the most dangerous snake in the New World. Native to the drier southern and eastern parts of Brazil, where they are sometimes found around farms and plantations, these large and heavily armed snakes possess a venom that sets them apart from all other rattlers, in that its most obvious early effects are neurological. A fatal *terrificus* bite typically produces almost none of the local swelling and hemorrhaging characteristic of *C. horridus* or *C. atrox* bites, but instead attacks the cranial nerves, so that within an hour the patient cannot raise his eyelids above halfway, or focus on distant objects, or move his pupils from side to side. Sometimes the neck muscles relax as well, producing the so-called breakneck syndrome. Death, which occurs in a few days, is usually the result of renal failure — the kidneys develop microscopic lesions in the tubules, lose their ability to excrete urine, and the patient dies of blood poisoning.

Perhaps it was the presence of this big, very lethal, and not uncommon rattler that gave the impetus to research in sub-Amazonian America. At any rate, by 1901 Dr. Vital Brazil was producing *Crotalus* antivenoms in a São Paulo cowshed. They proved lifesaving: they reduced the mortality rate in severe *C. d. terrificus* envenomations from four or five out of six to something less than one out of six, provided treatment began promptly. Before long Dr. Brazil was manufacturing antivenoms in quantity and making them available to the medical profession.

Bite sufferers north of Mexico did not benefit from this work for another quarter century. Dr. Brazil's drugs were not licensed for importation and sale in the United States, and since no comparable domestic product existed, any doctor wishing to use the anti-*Crotalus* serum had to do so in secret. Some did, apparently, and became convinced of its effectiveness against native rattler bites; certain persons began to speak out against the local situation; finally, in the mid-1920s a group of doctors, herpetologists, and public health officials organized the Antivenin Institute of America, its stated goal being to develop and make available in this country the sort of antitoxin serums long since put to good use elsewhere. This effort succeeded. In 1927 a new pharmaceutical called Crotalid Polyvalent Antivenin appeared on the American market. Currently manufactured by Wyeth Laboratories of Pennsylvania, it is basically unchanged, and remains the critical ingredient of the drug-based therapy recommended against all serious rattlesnake bites. Now, if a doctor detects symptoms of a moderate-to-severe *Crotalus* envenomation and does not immediately begin preparations to administer Wyeth antivenom, he is stepping onto thin ice, and his patient may be in deep trouble.

New England's rattlesnake, *Crotalus horridus,* doesn't contribute to the Wyeth product. It is prepared by immunizing horses with venoms from his most dangerous relatives: *C. adamanteus* (the eastern diamondback), *C. atrox* (the western diamondback), *C. durissus terrificus* (the cascabel), and *Bothrops atrox* (the barba amarilla, sometimes called fer-de-lance). These are the species responsible for the majority of life-threatening snakebites in the western hemisphere. Although the drug is useless against cobra venom, it is called polyvalent because it has been shown in the lab to be effective against toxins from all the American pit vipers tested.

The drug comes in a package of two small vials, one containing freeze-dried proteins derived from horse serum, the other sterile water treated with a preservative. The physician is directed to puncture the second vial with a hypodermic, draw out the water, and inject it into the first, then shake it gently. As soon as the crystalline proteins dissolve, the drug is ready for use. It is usually diluted further and administered by intravenous drip. In severe bites as many as fifteen or more vials may be indicated.

Wyeth antivenom hasn't put an end to snakebite mortality in the United States. Some bite victims do not seek or obtain prompt treatment; some who do don't receive sufficient antivenom; some of those who receive large amounts die anyway. It's also hard to say how much the antivenom has improved mortality rates, since although these are now under 1 percent for all pit-viper bites, and under 2.5 percent for bites from the most deadly species, *C. adamanteus,* no one knows exactly where these rates stood prior to the drug's introduction, so many cases having been complicated by such items as alcohol, strychnine, and clumsy backwoods surgery. Even today hospitals are not required to report admissions for snakebite, unlike those for gunshot wounds and certain contagious diseases.

What is certain, however, is that most physicians with any experience agree that Wyeth polyvalent antivenom can dramatically improve the condition of persons suffering from serious rattlesnake bites. As soon as they are convinced such a bite has occurred, they immediately make ready to provide it. One of these preparations is a skin test for sensitivity to the antivenom, since it contains alien proteins that can provoke a very serious allergic reaction known as anaphylactic shock. This reaction kills fifty to one hundred U.S. citizens per year who develop it in response to bee and wasp stings, and die within minutes. But since good countermeasures exist against this kind of shock — epinephrine (adrenaline), antihistamines, and resuscitation techniques — and since no effective alternatives to antivenom are known, most authorities agree that if confronted by a severe rattler bite from one of the more dangerous species, they would advise antivenom therapy despite a strong skin-test reaction, in the belief that a well-equipped intensive-care unit is better able to overcome allergic shock than it is all the complications resulting from a large and unchallenged dose of rattler venom.

Antivenom therapy is now the standard of treatment worldwide for dangerous snakebites. No venoms have yet been discovered that cannot be at least partially neutralized by serum drugs. In this country, where most people wear shoes outdoors and there are no masses of peasant farmers with little access to modern health care, fatal snakebites are almost unknown. There are now about ten per year, and since these generally include several "illegitimate" bites, the average person's chances of being killed by a snake are about one in forty million. In Massachusetts, home to only one dangerous species and that one nearly eliminated, these chances approach the vanishing point — perhaps one in four hundred million, or the practical equivalent of zero.

One might think, then, that despite a long history of false starts and cruel mistakes, the introduction of antivenom therapy has finally provided medicine with a reliable and effective answer to snakebite, and that henceforth no doctors will see a need to "save" bite sufferers with well-meaning and inexplicable tortures, sometimes killing them outright — through the late 1970s, for instance, the leading snakebite specialists in the Southwest, Dr. Findlay E. Russell and his collaborators at the University of Southern California Medical Center in Los Angeles, treated more than 650 cases of pit-viper bite without a fatality, many of them involving severe

*Crotalus* envenomations. But during the last forty years, despite widespread use of antivenoms, several dubious alternative or complementary treatments have emerged, and their advocates have succeeded in promoting them in the most prominent journals. Thanks to a string of stunning clinical disasters and some very contrary laboratory findings, the most damaging of these treatments is now discredited. Even so, one can't help but wonder what further bright ideas may pop up in the future, and at what cost. In order to make these cautionary instances clearer, I will have to say something about the effects of a serious rattlesnake bite.

When a rattler bites and envenomates its usual prey — small mammals weighing a few ounces on average — death follows quickly, and the snake swallows the corpse. When a rattler bites a human being, typically on an arm below the elbow or on a leg below the knee, the same toxins may be introduced in the same quantities, but quick death does not ensue. Instead the venom is diluted in a much larger system, and the qualities that would be rapidly lethal in a small animal produce something entirely different, a sort of local catastrophe.

Most students agree that snake venoms evolved from saliva, and that the venom is produced by modified salivary glands. In land animals saliva typically functions as an aid to swallowing and digestion, moistening the food and initiating the process of biochemical disassembly that will continue in the stomach and beyond — our own mouth juices contain an enzyme, ptyalin, that can convert starches to disaccharide sugars. Snakes, which are anatomically precluded from chewing their food, have to break it down by other means, and hence are structurally predisposed to develop powerful digestive secretions. And so the question of how their mouth juices became stronger and stronger over time, while still remaining short of the lethality necessary to make poisoning effective, is not the evolutionary riddle it might be. The presumption is that venoms did not begin as true poisons but merely as aids to digestion, and that it was only when a certain level of strength was reached that a corollary toxicity came into play, at which point natural selection could begin to refine the awesome killing powers some venoms now possess.

This digestive function is still notable, if not preeminent, in many viper venoms. It has been observed, for instance, that a rattlesnake that bites and swallows a dead rat takes considerably longer to digest it than one that bites and swallows a live one. This is probably because the venom remains localized in the dead rat and cannot produce its typical disintegrative effects, whereas in the live one it spreads quickly through the system, its action facilitated by the rat's own metabolic processes.

So far as I know, no rattlesnake has ever attempted to swallow a human being. In a bad bite, however, the bitten area often reacts *as if* it were shortly to become snake food: tissues deteriorate, proteins and fats break down in solution, blood vessels weaken, red blood cells leak out and burst, and the whole neighborhood becomes unhealthy, clogged as it is with moribund elements and racked with biochemical alarms. This phenomenon is known as necrosis, and is familiar as the gaudy colors in ordinary bruises. In a rattler bite it can become so generalized and extensive that repairs become impossible, inviting bacterial attack and resulting in tissue loss, amputation, or worse.

This is why it's a bad sign if a bite victim develops immediate swelling near the fang marks, or experiences severe pain, or shows rapid discoloration in the affected limb — all these indicate that venom has been injected (it is not in about one bite out of four), and the speed with which these symptoms progress is a rough gauge of the bite's seriousness. The swelling, in particular, indicates that capillary walls are failing and that escaped plasma is bloating the tissues; in severe bites this edema becomes so pronounced that the bitten arm or leg balloons into a grotesque, drum-tight, and sausagelike monstrosity, and the fluids thus lost dangerously lower blood volume and pressure, impairing heart function and threatening the circulation as a whole.

In most bites, treated or not, these symptoms stop expanding by the second or third day. Apparently the venom's effects reach a peak and start downward. At that point the body must attempt to overcome all the damage sustained — reabsorbing fluids, cleaning out dead material lodged in the tissues, restoring normal circulation, reestablishing proper blood chemistry and composition. In rare instances the task is too much, and further crises — a wave of microscopic hemorrhages, for example, or a kidney shutdown, or an irreversible collapse in blood pressure — result in death. Sometimes the system as a whole recovers well but an area of muscle near the bite cannot, having been choked by lack of oxygen, drowned in cell fragments, or simply dissolved in place, and the price is permanent impaired function. Most bites involve nothing so serious, and scar only the memory.

And so a rattler bite of any seriousness, and they are all potentially so, can present a very disturbing clinical picture: skin rapidly discolored over large areas, severe pain, bleeding from eyes, mouth, and rectum, incoagulable blood, shock, tachycardia, limbs so bloated the skin threatens to burst, inability to urinate, fever, vomiting, wildly volatile blood titers, labored breathing, and so forth. Although the extent and variety of these symptoms are not a reliable indicator of the danger to life — some fatal bites display few of them — it is easy to see how any M.D. who has observed them might shy at conservative treatment — antivenoms and supportive therapy — in favor of a more vigorous approach.

In 1957 Herbert L. Stahnke, a zoologist at Arizona State College, published an article in the *American Journal of Tropical Medicine and Hygiene* advocating a *Crotalus*-bite therapy he had personally developed and found effective. He called it ligature-cryotherapy. It is summarized here:

1. Immediately after the bite and before swelling begins, place a tight ligature or tourniquet around the affected member. Tie it close to the bite, and between the bite and the body.
2. Place a piece of ice on the bite.
3. As soon as is feasible, immerse the affected member in a tub of ice water.
4. Five minutes after immersion, remove the ligature.
5. Two hours or more after immersion, remove the affected member from the ice water and pack it in crushed ice. Leave it there for at least twenty-four hours, renewing the ice as necessary. It may have to remain iced for three days or more, depending on the bite's severity.
6. At twenty-four hours, and at subsequent intervals, remove the affected member from the ice and allow it to warm, to restore feeling. If there is no pain at the bite (the patient should be able

to distinguish this from warm-up pain), discontinue ice treatment by repacking the member and allowing the remaining ice to melt gradually. If pain persists at the bite, repack in ice and continue replenishing ice.

7. Make sure that the rest of the patient is kept warm at all times, perhaps even uncomfortably so.

Stahnke's rationale for his method of treatment is as follows:

A. Since the main hazard in rattler bites is not death but local tissue destruction, treatments should concentrate on the latter.

B. The venom components that cause most local tissue destruction are enzymes, and since cold restricts or impedes enzyme activity, cooling will delay destruction.

C. Since cooling does not halt circulation, long-term cooling will allow the destructive enzymes to disperse at low temperature, and with considerably less damage.

In short, Stahnke's treatment meant to keep the venom proteins temporarily confined to the bite area by ligature, and minimize their harmful effects by cooling.

Stahnke backed up his argument by describing two cases. In the first, a young snake fancier was bitten on the web of skin between his thumb and index finger by a four-foot eastern diamondback *(C. adamanteus)*. Although he received antivenom promptly, he became critically ill, was hospitalized for weeks, and lost his index finger and the first joint of his thumb. In the second case, a young lab assistant was struck on the thumb pad by a three-and-a-half-foot western diamondback *(C. atrox)*. This case, in contrast, took a nearly benign course. Ligature and cryotherapy were followed by timely improvement and complete recovery, a small skin graft excepted.

Stahnke admitted that evidence from two cases was hardly conclusive. Even so, he stated that "the use of cryotherapy is definitely indicated" in all venomous snakebites, and that it was "far superior to any therapeutic agent at present employed." Perhaps the most surprising aspect of his method was the small role allotted to antivenom.

Although Wyeth polyvalent had been in use for a quarter century by this time, and its effectiveness had been repeatedly confirmed by tests on lab animals, many doubts still existed. Doctors cited numerous cases where its use in the prescribed manner hadn't prevented significant long-term injury or even death, and some experienced practitioners declared that its introduction had made no important difference in the prognosis for *Crotalus*-bite sufferers. Many physicians, in addition, were leery of the drug's antigenic potential, and although very few anaphylactic reactions had been reported, a milder, delayed syndrome known as serum sickness wasn't uncommon.

Today it is generally acknowledged that the reason Wyeth antivenom wasn't more successful in the early part of its career was that it was still poorly understood. Too often persons suffering from severe bites received only one or two vials injected intramuscularly, sometimes many hours after their accidents. This had little therapeutic value — an adequate dosage required ten or more vials administered intravenously within three or four hours of the bite. Other problems derived from the drug itself, which was fragile and tended to deteriorate in storage; stricter potency standards have since been introduced.

Stahnke's method spoke to the doubters. Ice packs had long been a popular, almost intuitive first-aid measure for venomous bites and stings in Arizona and elsewhere; he elevated them to a basis of treatment. And although his argument was not impressive theoretically — he had performed no tests, and he was no biochemist — it originated in considerable personal experience with *Crotalus* bites, an experience hard to gainsay in an area of medicine characterized by a scarcity of cases and the merest trickle of domestic research interest. Perhaps the most attractive (and deceptive) aspect of ligature-cryotherapy was its ability to stave off the gruesome local effects of a severe rattler bite. After several days, for instance, a bitten limb that had not been iced might be black-purple, swollen enormously, and covered with blood-filled blisters, whereas an ice-treated one might appear virtually unchanged — an impressive contrast.

Ice was not without its detractors, however. In 1953 physician and herpetologist Frederick Shannon, answering an earlier publication by Stahnke, had questioned the value of cooling in an article for *Southwestern Medicine*. A year later *Crotalus* expert Laurence Klauber approached Dr. Findlay Russell, the leading Los Angeles snakebite specialist, at a conference and showed him three letters he had received from doctors who had treated rattler bites with "ice immersion." In each case the patient had suffered considerable tissue loss; Klauber wondered whether the treatment itself might be responsible.

These occasional doubts coincided with a spate of excited hosannas in the popular press: "Freeze Away the Horrors of Snakebite," "Revolutionary New Approach," "Only Known Single Therapeutic Method" — some of them the result of Stahnke's promotional efforts. Later, in the 1960s, sportsmen's magazines began to carry advertisements for quick-freezing ethyl chloride sprays, touted as effective first aid for snakebites. This publicity may have had some influence — at any rate, many physicians and lay people chose to treat *Crotalus* bites with lengthy regimens of ice packs and ice water baths.

The results were horrific. All went well until the affected hand or foot was finally removed from the ice. Then, as if making up for lost time, it deteriorated rapidly: it changed color, lost feeling, became unable to sustain any measurable pulse, and in short quickly transformed itself into a lump of inert, rotting meat. Attempts to cut away the dead matter went right down to the bone. Even the most sanguine doctors knew what this situation required — immediate amputation.

Cases like this were difficult to characterize as successful. Few of the responsible physicians cared to make the facts known. Some doubtless chalked it up to experience; some perhaps told themselves that they had lost a limb but saved a life; many probably never encountered another serious rattlesnake bite. Nevertheless, no standard procedure existed to document and collate these scattered disasters — at most a few hundred nationwide — and evaluate them for their bearing on the treatment itself. As in the heyday of the alcohol cure, a self-correcting mechanism was notably absent.

And so it was up to those physicians who had made inquiries of their own to raise a red flag and point out the facts. Fortunately some did, and in 1963 cryotherapy received its first major blow, a study by Florida snakebite specialists N. C. McCollough and J. F. Gennaro entitled "Evaluation of Venomous Snakebite in the Southern United States," and published in the *Journal of the Florida Medical Association.* In it they revealed the surprising fact that out of thirty-two Floridians who had undergone amputations following snakebite, twenty-seven had received cryotherapy, twenty-two of them for more than twelve hours. In other words, although ice treatment was by no means the dominant therapy for snakebite in Florida, the vast majority of amputees had received it.

One didn't have to be a genius to look at these figures and conclude that snakebite combined with ice therapy might be considerably more harmful than snakebite alone. But the treatment's advocates, of course, had a personal interest in resisting any such reading. And so although McCollough and Gennaro's bombshell was accompanied by several other exceptions and demurrals in the medical press — Ya and Perry's (1960) laboratory study, for instance, which showed that cooling had no effect on the tissue-destructive qualities of rattler venom, or the American Academy of Pediatrics' (1965) recommendations, which suspended judgment on ice treatment and insisted on the importance of prompt and sufficient administration of antivenom — the cryotherapists did not, as a result, immediately abandon their positions. Indeed, one in particular chose to stand up and shoot back. This was a southwestern M.D. named William E. Lockhart. For a while he made Alpine, Texas, one of the more unhealthy spots in America for people bitten by rattlesnakes.

Alpine (population 5,465) is the largest town in Brewster County, an enormous stretch of high, rugged desert running a hundred miles north from the Rio Grande and including all of Big Bend National Park. This area is one of the dustiest, emptiest corners of the West, and is inhabited by seven species of rattlesnake, four of them implicated in human fatalities: *Crotalus horridus* (the timber, or canebrake), *C. scutulaus* (the Mojave), *C. viridis* (the western), and *C. atrox* (the western diamondback).

In August 1965 Dr. Lockhart published a defense of cryotherapy in *JAMA,* the *Journal of the American Medical Association.* It included four accounts of rattler bites suffered by children, two ascribed to

*C. viridis* and two to *C. atrox*. Only one, the least serious, ended positively; the other three resulted in one death and two permanent injuries. All received lengthy ice treatment. Although the attending physician is not named — any personal note is frowned on in this type of reporting — internal evidence strongly suggests that in each case it was Lockhart himself.

Four bites — one death, one foot with toes permanently curled underneath ("shortening of flexor digitorum longus"), and one hand unstrung at its base ("wrist droop") — not an enviable record, one might think. But according to Lockhart, these failures are not evidence against cryotherapy. On the contrary, they merely show that this subtle and demanding treatment is still, a decade after Stahnke, in its formative stages, and not yet perfected. In the three less-than-optimal cases, he argues that the ice was either removed too soon (after four days, in two instances, in one of them at the repeated insistence of the patient's mother) or applied too late (after two hours, in the bite ending fatally). What strikes the reader most forcefully, however, is the short shrift given to antivenom. In no case did the bite sufferer receive more than one vial in the critical first hours, and none was administered intravenously. This was much less than the officially recommended dosage at the time, and was probably the functional equivalent of no antivenom at all. One wonders if, given his druthers, Lockhart would have avoided the drug entirely.

The fatal case involved a twelve-year-old girl bitten on the top of her foot by a large rattler, probably *C. atrox*. She had a tight tourniquet on her ankle for eight hours, and her leg was iced for four days, during which the swelling progressed as far as her hip. On the fifth day she became delirious, and on the eighth she died. Had she lived, she would have lost her foot, since it had become gangrenous.

Dr. Lockhart doesn't say what killed her, though he does mention an autopsy finding of fat embolism in the lungs. This suggests that the venom damaged them to a point where they became unable to transfer sufficient oxygen to her blood. One might guess that she simply stopped breathing, and that whatever respiratory assistance was employed proved ineffective.

Lockhart doesn't argue that this calamity represents any kind of vindication for ice treatment. He includes it, instead, to show how inexact use of the technique — a tourniquet left on too long, and ice applied too late — will not have the desired results. He excuses the inadequate dosage of antivenom with the argument that the Wyeth drug is too weak and that no variety of it is specifically designed for use against western diamondback (*C. atrox*) bites. These supposed drawbacks, combined with the threat of allergic reactions, make the existing drug a poor choice, in his view, as a primary or exclusive basis of treatment. In short, his opinion is that any physician faced with a severe rattler bite in *C. atrox* country should at least consider cryotherapy, since bites of this kind are likely to result in permanent disability or worse, and antivenom plus ice treatment can be more effective than antivenom alone in preventing a bad outcome.

Here at last was the sort of target those investigators convinced of cryotherapy's brutal effects were looking for — a defense of the technique published by a practicing physician in the preeminent medical journal. Four months later, in February 1966, two sharp and aggressive rebuttals appeared in the same organ, and they tore Lockhart to pieces.

One of them originated at Wyeth Laboratories in Philadelphia. This article pointed out that Lockhart had nowhere produced evidence that cooling reduces venom toxicity. It also suggested that, venom or no venom, the subjection of an arm or a leg to near-freezing temperatures for days at a time was at best a very risky procedure, as anyone with experience with frostbite would agree. And although it did not come right out and accuse him of murder, it emphasized that children, because of their small size, require proportionately larger dosages of antivenom, and that the amounts received in the cases described were totally inadequate.

This attack was accompanied, in the same issue, by a letter signed by, among others, Drs. Findlay Russell in Los Angeles and Frederick Shannon (Stahnke's old antagonist) in Arizona. They agreed with McCollough and Gennaro, authors of the Florida study, that cryotherapy was worthless, if not positively harmful, and noted that the treatment was involved in seven of the nine snakebite-related amputations that had come to their attention in the past decade. They were especially critical of Lockhart's admission that "some permanent disability" was more or less inevitable after severe bites. They announced that in the 112 cases they themselves had treated, there had been no deaths, only a single amputation (a finger, in a case that received no antivenom), and only five "permanent contractures or disabilities," despite the fact that many of the cases had been referred to them because they were especially severe, or because a positive skin test for antivenom sensitivity had made the referring physician reluctant to use it. In none of the cases had they resorted to cryotherapy.

Perhaps Russell, Shannon, and their colleagues angered the gods in citing this admirable clinical record. Only weeks after they composed their letter, and before it was published, Frederick Shannon was bitten and killed by a Mojave rattlesnake, a small, desert-dwelling species notorious for the extreme toxicity of its venom. The letter's target, Dr. Lockhart, couldn't pass up this opportunity to snipe at his tormentors, and in his reply to their attack, published alongside it in *JAMA,* he wrote, "Their 112 cases without a death are now, grimly, 113 and one death."*

Dr. Shannon's demise did not save cryotherapy from its critics. Although Lockhart argued, in his rebuttal, that amputation was not an unusual outcome of rattlesnake bites, and that cryotherapy could indeed reduce local tissue damage, he had no arsenal of studies and statistics to match that presented by his opponents, and no colleagues willing to support his ideas. The controversy forced him to appear as he was, an old-fashioned, rusticated, and somewhat ornery M.D. who valued his own judgment more than the pronouncements of big-city drug companies or university professors. And so his method, whatever its merits, would not be likely to appeal to any clinician aware of the professional hazards associated with a treatment widely condemned by the leading authorities. Dr. Lockhart, in fact, was a sort of throwback to the era of Abel Puffer and Palmer Goulding, for whom medicine was not a collective enterprise driven by large-scale research and the quest for improved standards, but instead a solitary art based on personal

---

*I have seen no clinical account of this bite, and don't know how it occurred, or where and how it was treated. Dr. Russell, however, was apparently not in attendance, since he doesn't include it in subsequent breakdowns of his cases.

experimentation and intuition. If he deluded himself, he at least had the courage of his convictions, and his willingness to stand behind his ideas made it possible for cryotherapy to undergo the sort of public ordeal necessary to expose it at its true worth. He took the heat for all the anonymous M.D.s who escorted bite sufferers down the lonely road from ice baths to gangrene to amputation. In contrast, the three physicians who wrote privately to Laurence Klauber in the 1950s about bad experiences with ice treatment managed to shield their own names, but did little to halt the carnage.

In 1970, four years after the flurry of *JAMA* articles, Dr. Lockhart published another in *Texas Medicine* entitled "Pitfalls in Rattlesnake Bite." In it he conclusively divorced himself from cryotherapy, writing that it "has been defined and tried, but experience has proved the method inadequate." He recommends cooling as a short-term first-aid treatment for pain, but makes no claims for its effects on venom activity. Once again he is remarkably outspoken; most physicians, I suspect, would rather be bitten by a dozen rattlesnakes than make this kind of admission of error in public.

Cryotherapy is a dead issue today; it didn't survive Dr. Lockhart. The last case-study in the literature appears to be that detailed by Charles Sparger, M.D., in *Archives of Surgery* for January 1969, which involved a thirteen-year-old Navaho boy who was bitten on the fingers by a large rattlesnake in August 1965 and taken to a local hospital in New Mexico, where he was given five vials of Wyeth polyvalent intramuscularly and had the affected arm packed in ice. Six days later the ice was removed, and three days after that he was transferred to Public Health Service Hospital in Gallup, where Sparger saw him. At that point his arm was swollen to the shoulder, blistered to mid-biceps, and blue-black, "very cold," and without feeling from the wrist down. No pulse was palpable anywhere below the armpit. The limb eventually had to be amputated at mid-forearm, and required skin grafts to heal. Sparger regarded this as a good result, considering the boy's condition on arrival, which seemed to him toxic and quite possibly terminal. He concluded that cryotherapy "can be dangerous and is *not* recommended."

But if ice, like alcohol or strychnine, is no longer a means by which doctors commonly brutalize *Crotalus*-bite victims, this is not because the golden age has arrived. There is still plenty of disagreement over the relative values of various therapies still in use, and their respective adherents are far from unwilling to try them out on whatever patients come their way, so that one wonders if the medical profession as a whole doesn't sympathize with Lockhart's carte blanche for free-lance investigators: "All forms of therapy should be explored — biologic, chemical, and physical." Apparently we can all contribute to the advancement of knowledge.*

Perhaps the chief division of opinion in rattlesnake-bite therapy today exists between two loosely organized groups we will call the Cutters and the Drippers. The Cutters, who are less numerous, and who are mostly surgeons, believe that antivenom often fails to mitigate a bite's local effects, especially when it isn't made available until hours afterward. They maintain that additional treatment is therefore sometimes necessary — in particular they recommend opening the area of the bite surgically and removing damaged tissue, or even slitting the tough membranes surrounding the muscle compartments underneath. This latter operation is known as a fasciotomy, and is intended to relieve internal pressure by allowing the muscles to bulge outward through the incisions. Without the procedure, the Cutters argue, this swelling-induced pressure may rise so high that it blocks the flow of arterial blood to the area and sometimes permanently cripples the muscles involved, even if the affected fibers are not suffocated outright. The same operation, they point out, is widely used to treat a similar problem known as crush syndrome, occasionally seen in accident injuries. Why, they ask, shouldn't bite sufferers benefit from it as well?

The Drippers, on the other hand, insist that prompt intravenous administration of antivenom is the best available treatment for snakebite, and that there is no evidence that cutting skin, removing tissue, or exposing muscle will reduce the venom's damaging local effects in the slightest. On the contrary, they argue, all this slitting

*In 1986, at Honolulu, a snakebite symposium was held at the forty-sixth annual session of the American Association for the Surgery of Trauma. During it, Dr. C. D. Haynes of Opelika, Alabama, said that he'd heard of a physician who had begun treating snakebites by attaching ignition wires to the affected area and giving it a good jolt. Haynes remarked that he was "looking for a snakebite in Alabama" in order to try the experiment himself.

and slicing only compounds the insult, extending hospital stays and often producing terrible scars. Dr. Findlay Russell, in his *Snake Venom Poisoning* (Scholium, 1983), the most authoritative study of *Crotalus* bites to date, includes several very unattractive photographs showing snakebitten hands and limbs treated by fasciotomy, his implication being that the treatment was at least partially responsible for their heavy scarring and skin loss. Some of the Cutters, in contrast, have gone so far as to abandon antivenom entirely, and since they seem to have no greater percentage of cases resulting in death or permanent injury, they have been able to argue that the drug is a fraud and benefits physicians more than patients — primarily as a shield against lawsuits!

This controversy might have been settled by now if a series of controlled clinical trials on humans had ever been performed using Wyeth polyvalent. This series would ideally include a large number of bite victims treated under identical conditions, except that half would receive antivenom and half would receive a look-alike placebo — even the doctors themselves would not be permitted to know which was which. But snakebite — unlike arthritis, say, or diabetes — is not a widespread, chronic illness that might allow researchers to assemble numerous volunteers with matching histories. It is instead a rare medical emergency that strikes unpredictably. In the only such study ever performed on an antivenom — Dr. H. A. Reid's 1963 Malaysian effort, which confined itself to bites inflicted by the Malayan pit viper, *Agkistrodon rhodostoma* — patients with severe poisonings were excluded, and all of these patients were given antivenom, since the physicians involved were already so convinced of the drug's indispensable benefits that they couldn't permit themselves to withhold it. What the study showed, however, was that while the drug appeared to reduce bleeding somewhat, it had no effect on local tissue destruction. In 1985 Dr. Douglas Lindsey, of the University of Arizona College of Medicine in Tucson, called for a similar trial to test Wyeth polyvalent, and announced that "a first-class university hospital in Mexico" (probably the San Luis Potosí, which treats about ninety pit viper bites a year) had granted authorization, but declared that Wyeth had blocked the project by refusing to quote him a price for the antivenom and a matching control serum, and that the U.S. Food and Drug

Administration had not even acknowledged receipt of his letter requesting funding. Dr. Lindsey appears to have a case; one might ask why he has received so little response. (Wyeth polyvalent currently sells for about $100 per vial.)

Even the most accomplished Drippers are not without doubts; if they condemn wholesale cutting, they do not consider dripping a cure-all. In 1988 Drs. Willis Wingert and Linda Chan, successors to Dripper-in-Chief Findlay Russell at the USC Medical Center in Los Angeles, conceded, "Physicians should not be deluded that this [Wyeth polyvalent] is a highly potent antidote, especially for bites of Crotalidae species other than those species used in its production." Russell himself, now at the University of Arizona's medical school in Tucson (I hope not next door to Dr. Lindsey), has developed an improved sheep-based serum that takes advantage of the sophisticated protein-separation techniques afforded by gel chromatography. However, as he has admitted, snakebite is not the sort of health problem that attracts major resources — it kills about ten persons per year in the United States, out of more than five thousand bitten by venomous species — and the big drug companies are not likely to see a profit advantage in devoting large sums to creating more effective antivenoms.

And so the matter rests. Drippers argue that tests on animals, not to mention years of clinical experience, make it overwhelmingly evident that Wyeth polyvalent has saved lives in the past and will save more in the future. Cutters retort that surgical techniques are equally appropriate and avoid the small but significant risk of serum reactions. Who's right? In other parts of the world, where the snakes are sometimes more deadly, evidence is stronger that antivenoms can rescue bite victims who might otherwise be doomed. In this country, however, where even the most dangerous species rarely inflict fatal bites, and teams of well-equipped specialists stand ready to tide compromised lungs or kidneys over a crisis, antivenoms occupy a sort of limbo: those who use them swear by them, but those who do not don't appear to obtain significantly poorer results. Now that physicians no longer commonly employ rattlesnake bites as an excuse to kill patients by other means, one might say that getting bitten by a rattler is a small but essential step toward being killed by a rattler — one's chances of reaching old age are still remarkably good, but all the resources of modern medicine can't guarantee recovery, and it may not matter in the slightest whether one is pumped full of antivenoms or expertly dissected. In fact, the type of treatment received seems much less important than certain other factors: size and species of snake, amount of venom injected, the patient's overall state of health, and so forth.

This lack of agreement — I hesitate to say confusion — over appropriate therapy was highlighted recently when a Connecticut man suffered what is perhaps the most frightening New England *Crotalus* accident on record. What made it alarming was that all the circumstances seemed to indicate that the bite would result in a mild poisoning at worst. Instead, it became a monster.

The man, Robert Fritsch of Wethersfield, a suburb just south of Hartford, is a police officer and an ardent conservationist who has done more than anyone to draw attention to the dim future faced by Connecticut's few remaining rattlers, and it is largely thanks to his efforts that *Crotalus* is now on the state's endangered species list and can no longer be eradicated with impunity. Fritsch is also a healthy, vigorous individual in his middle years, and the snake that bit him, a thirty-three-inch adult, had probably expended most of its venom just a few moments earlier. Fritsch had the additional advantage of quick arrival at a hospital, not to mention timely and expert medical care. None of this, however, seemed to make any difference.

Just across the river from Hartford, in suburban Glastonbury, lies a forested hill of no great height known as Kongscut Mountain. In the early 1980s a developer bought up some wooded land on its western side, put a road in, and erected forty-odd pricey hillside homes, which he quickly marketed and sold under the name of Mountain View Estates. As it happened, the slope above the development sheltered one of the few surviving *Crotalus* dens in Hartford County, and the new householders soon noticed that twice a year, in spring and fall, several very large snakes with rattles on their tails appeared unexpectedly on their lawns and driveways, being in mid-crawl to and from their summer hunting grounds farther downslope.

The new residents, some of whom had small children, were

understandably upset, and killed the trespassers, nine in all. The state retroactively absolved them by passing legislation permitting the people living on Goodale Hill Road to destroy any rattlers they discovered within five hundred feet of the road. Bob Fritsch visited the development, talked to the residents, and convinced most of them that they could safely let the snakes be, provided they kept their lawns cut short, offered no attractive hideouts such as wood-piles or blackberry thickets, and took care to educate and supervise their children. He also promised to come immediately and remove any reptiles that proved troublesome. A few families were not persuaded, and vowed to continue killing snakes at every oppor-tunity, but most were remarkably sympathetic, choosing to accept a small but genuine risk in return for the chance to live alongside one of the region's most rare and dramatic inhabitants.

Fritsch was one of the few persons aware of the den's location — its elusiveness probably accounting for its survival into this cen-tury — and he periodically visited it in the following years to check up on its occupants. It was in the course of one of these visits, in the fall of 1986, that he came to grief.

He and a friend, Doug Fraser, were collecting a few of the snakes in order to weigh and measure them. Fritsch had noticed a small one sunning itself in a low tree, and he walked past it several times before deciding to bag it. This involved lifting it out with a snake stick — a long, hooked instrument much like a golf putter — and lowering it into a cloth sack. Although heavy, bite-resistant gloves are sometimes worn during this operation, Fritsch prefers a lighter touch and didn't have his on.

Once lifted out of the tree, the sun-warmed snake took exception to its treatment, and instead of dropping obligingly into the bag, it clung to the stick and struck several times at the opening, spotting the fabric with venom. Annoyed, Fritsch turned and twisted the stick, trying to steer the snake's head inside. It was at this point that he momentarily lost his balance and swung his bare hand within range of the snake. It hit him with one fang on the side of his middle finger, piercing the skin. Fritsch dropped the stick, stepped back, and examined the tiny wound. Damn, he thought. Bitten.

He told Fraser to go on with his business. Fritsch had been bitten by pit vipers before, twice by copperheads, most recently only thirty days earlier by an injured one he had been keeping in his basement. These bites hadn't amounted to much, and he expected he could shake this one off also, if in fact he had been envenomated. Within minutes, however, his thigh muscles started to quiver, a loud buzz rose in his ears, and he fell flat on his face. Startled, he remained there until he felt Fraser slapping his cheeks.

Fritsch's arm over his shoulder, Fraser tried to walk him up the hill through the dense laurel thicket. It was hopeless; Fritsch kept slipping off. Fraser stood him against a tree, said "Don't move," and ran off. The noise of his crashing quickly receded.

Fritsch waited. It occurred to him that if he slipped down into the laurel, he would become invisible and no one would be able to find him. Even so, it had become impossible to remain standing. He slid to the ground.

A little later he discovered that there wasn't room in his chest for all the air he wanted to breathe. He rolled onto his elbows and knees, trying to free up more space. Here was a grown man doubled up in fallen leaves in the October woods, scratching and snuffling like a skunk grubbing up earthworms. His gasps and wheezes probably attracted a few songbirds. They received no attention — Fritsch was deep in himself, curling and uncurling around a question proffered to God: *Is this it?*

In about a half hour several men with a stretcher appeared out of nowhere and lifted Fritsch onto it. They carried him out of the woods and loaded him into a helicopter. Ten minutes later the machine floated down at Hartford Hospital. Fritsch's blood pressure was one-third normal. His body was covered with hives. His left arm had the bluish tinge associated with shock and had swollen enormously. He had had, it was clear, an allergic reaction, not uncommon among persons bitten more than once by pit vipers. But his vital signs were recovering; it appeared he would live.

Ninety minutes postbite Fritsch began receiving Wyeth polyvalent by intravenous drip. The doctors were worried about his balloonish left arm. Its internal pressure measured eight times that of his right, and certain of its muscles were hard to the touch. Unless this pressure was reduced, Fritsch's heart could not keep his arm supplied with blood, and it would begin to deteriorate. The Wyeth brochure advised vial after vial of antivenom until the symptoms showed signs of improvement. Fritsch eventually received twenty vials. Neither the first nor the twentieth seemed to improve his arm's condition in the slightest.

The physician in charge, Dr. Lynch, told Fritsch that he wasn't convinced further antivenom would help matters. He also said that the compartment pressures inside his arm had been so high for so long that permanent disability was almost a certainty without appropriate action — his fingers, for instance, might curl into his palm, and certain muscles might be replaced by fibrotic scar tissue. Appropriate action, in his view, would consist of a multiple fasciotomy, several deep incisions running from middle finger to elbow. They would relieve pressure and maintain vascularity until the venom's effects moderated.

Fritsch's livelihood as a police officer depended on use of both arms, and he consented to the surgery. His left arm was indeed suffering from dangerous internal pressures. When, in the operating room, the first cut was made, some of the watery fluids trapped inside burst out and spattered the ceiling.

He remained in intensive care for five days, and in the hospital for ten. Several operations were required to close his wounds. The strategy was a success; Fritsch's arm is now fully functional, though heavily scarred. He is still as committed as ever to *Crotalus*'s survival in Connecticut, and big rattlers still cross Goodale Hill Road twice a year.

This incident reminded interested parties throughout New England that neither Wyeth polyvalent nor quick hospital access have made *Crotalus* bites equivalent to a sprained ankle or a head cold. Here was a small snake low on venom that had connected with only one fang, but it had knocked out a grown man for ten days and convinced him he was lucky to be alive. The snake was also responsible for Dr. Lynch's rapid conversion from a typical Dripper to an all-out Cutter. A less flexible M.D. might have stayed with the drug, and gotten less happy results.

Most snakebites, more than 90 percent of them, are not nearly so dire as this. When any symptoms appear at all, they are usually confined to local pain and swelling. In New England, where bites are rare — only a handful per year — few doctors can accumulate experience with them. In some other regions, where they are more common, an internist may see a few every summer and easily suppose he knows all about them, when in fact he has never encountered a truly dangerous one. The result, unfortunately, is that he may be caught off guard and not recognize the exceptional case. There have been instances where patients sent home with an antibiotic and a painkiller have returned, critically ill, to an emergency room twenty hours later. Most of the malpractice settlements recently awarded to bite sufferers have involved similar incidents — severe poisonings initially mistaken for typical localized bites. An opposite situation obtains in Massachusetts, where accidents are so scarce that even copperhead poisonings can cause a sensation, and a bite victim's charts may be scrutinized by half a hospital's staff, even though many hundreds of such bites occur annually nationwide and fatalities are virtually unknown.

It is fair to say that *Crotalus* bites are just as dangerous today as they ever were, despite the astonishing progress medicine has made in the last two hundred years. Nobody knows why the vast majority of bite victims recover, or why a handful do not. Nobody knows whether the chief drug used in snakebite treatment, Wyeth polyvalent, is a genuine antidote or merely the next best thing. Nobody knows whether routine surgery on snakebites most often solves problems or creates them. And yet we all, I suspect, would prefer the sort of attention Bob Fritsch received to that Abel Puffer gave ten-year-old Mary Littlefield two centuries ago. Because if we are suffering, we want concern and quick action, and not just any variety either. We want brainy wizards in white coats, and spotless cabinets full of drugs, not to mention microscopes, computers, and nurses who hurt when we hurt. We want these things because we need to believe they can help us, and nowadays they are the commonly recognized objects of faith. But if we give them this faith, does that mean they deserve it? Not at all — what we give them is a chance to take chances with us. Doctors battle disease; we give them our bodies so that they may come to grips with the enemy. But if the history of *Crotalus*-bite treatment is any guide, they have too often turned this gift into a license to take too many long chances. Like us, they have too easily swallowed *Crotalus*'s reputation for murder, and as a result have occasionally become murderous themselves.

This is not to say that nothing has been gained. If medical science is still largely unable to reverse the effects of that tiny percentage of rattlesnake bites which are indeed life-threatening, it has at least learned to question itself and root out those treatments which are definitely harmful. In this sense Wyeth polyvalent may be a blessing in disguise. If its critics are correct and it offers little positive benefit, it has at least shown itself reasonably safe, and its widespread acceptance as a primary basis of treatment has given physicians sufficient confidence to resist shots in the dark like whiskey and ice baths. Maybe the serum is not unlike Governor Winthrop's long-vanished snakeweed, or Abel Puffer's plantain — harmless herbs that, by posing as good medicines, dissuaded their users from other, more dangerous recourses and thus allowed a truer picture of the actual hazards of snakebite to emerge. These hazards are real — there is no doubt about it — but we are perhaps just now learning how uncommon they are. Some recent epidemiological studies have concluded that the mortality rate in all copperhead, cottonmouth, and rattlesnake bites in the United States is now on the order of one in a thousand. One in a thousand — not a figure calculated to inspire terror.

But, as Bob Fritsch's experience shows, a particle of truth remains behind when all the smoke and hot air associated with *Crotalus*'s nimbus of horror is fanned away. Not every snakebite adds itself to the 999 recoveries; now and then one falls on the other side of the divide. Considering that there have been no rattler envenomations in the Blue Hills in this century, and perhaps a total of three since the year 1800, few would argue that such a bite should be expected here; even so, I can't leave the subject without at least attempting to draw a picture of the circumstances, medical and otherwise, that might surround a like incident. Failures are often more interesting than successes; in this case we will rule out success from the outset.

# 16

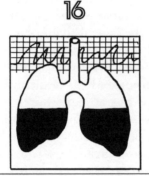

# A Worst-Case Scenario

A narrow Fellow in the Grass
Occasionally rides —

— Emily Dickinson,
"The Snake" (1860)

It's the third week in September. Sunny and bright after three cold nights in a row. Asters and goldenrod glow against the roadside shadows; flocks of blackbirds spill through the woods. In the low places swamp maples already flare scarlet and orange. Last week it was summer — long, lush, steamy, bug-ridden, interminable summer. Today summer is mortal.

Halfway up the side of a knobby hill a large female *Crotalus* lies buried in dead leaves. She hasn't eaten in over a year. Neither have the other two females concealed nearby. They occupy a quarter-acre thicket of scrub oak atop one low cliff and beneath another. Around them, hidden in patches of huckleberry and heaps of lichen-spotted rubble, are the twenty-nine eleven-inch newborns they gave birth to a week earlier. This brushy pocket looks no different from dozens of others scattered across the side of the hill. None of those others, however, contains any snakes.

In a week or two the adult females will leave the pocket and cross a narrow valley to the next hill over, where their den is. They will leave scent trails that most of the newborns will follow. Maybe a few will catch their first meal on the way — a fat cricket, a young mouse. They will all be underground by mid-October. The females will spend the entire next summer restoring their weight and won't return to the pocket for at least twenty months, and then only if they are pregnant.

The local chipmunks, squirrels, and mice know about the pocket and avoid it. A dog fox who lives under a boulder in the woods downslope knows that it smells funny, but doesn't know why. A woodcutter killed a five-foot rattler here during the Rutherford B. Hayes administration, but there have been no such incidents since.

A few charred cedar stumps indicate that the pocket has burned; the height of the oaks suggests that it hasn't done so in years.

At about one P.M. a gray squirrel races out of the brush above the pocket, crosses it in a few leaps, and dives off the far side. Heavy footsteps approach from the same direction. A young man scrapes through the knee-high oaks at the lip of the pocket and looks down. He is wearing ankle boots, a long-sleeve shirt, and a backpack.

He's not aware that there are thirty-two snakes scattered across the rock-strewn platform beneath him. Even one would surprise; he has spent all morning clambering over this hill and the next, and his expectations are considerably dulled. What interests him now is the bit of hard-packed trail visible in the shade of the tall trees farther down. It promises an easy walk to the car.

He examines, out of habit, the clutter of dry leaves, huckleberry brush, and sweet fern just below, with its patches of stunted oak and scattered rocks. The glossy oak leaves weave a patchwork of light and shadow on the parched undergrowth. He pays particular attention to the brushy section he will have to cross immediately underneath. Even so, he doesn't see the large female *Crotalus* all but buried in dead leaves in a small opening two steps away.

The snake has lain there nearly motionless for several hours, having come out from under a favorite boulder nearby to warm herself in the late-season sun. She has nine rattles and weighs five pounds. She has not bitten anything all summer and her venom glands are full, each containing about seventy milligrams of straw-colored fluid.

She didn't see the young man emerge up above, thanks to a leaf that half covers her face. Her first warning is the heavy thud of his boot as he steps down two feet away. She flinches, tensing, and her tail flicks up, ready to buzz. In the next moment his other foot swings forward and lands squarely on her back.

Her jaws flash up and her half-inch fangs pin his jeans to his calf just above his boot top. The shock and pain of a crushed spine make her hang on, squeezing. About eighty milligrams of venom, more than half her reserve, pass into his leg. The young man barely notices; what startles him is the look and feel of a large, angry worm squirming under his foot.

A moment later he is stretched out on a patch of bare bedrock. Three steps away the injured snake is lashing back and forth, buzzing. The young man crooks his leg in toward his hip and hurriedly pushes the cuff up toward his knee, revealing a smear of blood and two oozing punctures. They are accompanied by a sharp, burning pain. He forgets the snake; he is seized by a feeling of unbelief, or rather of fear mixed with helplessness.

Thirty-five minutes later an alarmed-looking woman with a sweater over her shoulders hurries into the emergency room of a local hospital. She tells the nurse at the desk that she has a man in her car who has been bitten by a rattlesnake. She goes out again and watches several white-suited aides help him out of her car and onto a gurney. They roll him down a hall and around a corner. She is back at the desk when a doctor comes out and asks her if the young man has any history of allergies. She doesn't know; she has never seen him before in her life.

The young man watches as a nurse cuts off his boot and his bloody sock with a pair of heavy stainless steel shears. It seems to him that his entire leg is on fire. His throat tastes of vomit and his face is prickly and damp. She puts the cut-up boot aside and begins work on his pant leg. A few moments later she scissors into his hip pocket; a shower of pennies and nickels jingles over the floor.

Down the hall the man in charge at the ER is on the phone to Boston talking to another doctor, a toxicologist. He scribbles rapidly on a notepad and says, "Yeah . . . uh-huh . . . I see." He doesn't like what he's hearing. It's messy — transfusions, heart catheters, serum drugs. "Look," he says, "first things first. I'll call you back, O.K.?" As he hangs up he sees the pharmacy aide at the door with a plastic tray. "How many?" he asks.

"Twenty."

"I want twenty more. Call Poison Control. I want them here in an hour."

When he returns to room B the young man, now shirtless, is coughing ropey driblets of blood into a bedpan the nurse holds under his chin. He has IVs taped to both arms. The saline and plasma expanders are hooked up and ready to go.

The doctor steps up to the bedside. "Mr. D——," he says.

The young man drops back onto the pillow. He seems to have trouble focusing. His bleeding gums have tinged his teeth pink.

"I think you have indeed been poisoned by a snake. How do you feel?"

He squints up at the doctor, frowning. It's as if he's reminded of something but can't quite recall what.

"I'm your doctor, Mr. D——. "I'm going to start helping you now. I'm going to give you Demerol for your pain, I'm going to give you fluids to bring up your blood pressure, and I'm going to give you antivenom. I think you need all of them. Is that all right?"

Once again the words barely seem to penetrate. Suddenly the young man's face clears. "Doctor," he says, "am I going to die?"

"Of course not." The doctor starts the plasma IV and hands a bottle of Demerol to the nurse, pointing at a syringe on the table. "Now as far as this antivenom goes, it's not uncommon to have a reaction. So I'm going to start you off on a small amount and increase it gradually. If you develop a rash, or begin to wheeze a little, don't be upset — all that means is that we'll have to slow down a bit. But whatever happens, I'm going to make sure you get as much as you need. O.K.?"

The young man looks merely dazed. He nods.

"Good. You can help us best by just sitting back and letting us get to work. Keep us up to date now and then on how you're feeling. All right?"

No answer. He has turned away and is gazing up at the fluid-filled bag draining into his arm.

In the fifty minutes since the bite, the venom proteins have raced through the young man's system like a pack of kids at an amusement park. Some are attracted to his red blood cells and make them puff up and roughen; some open tiny holes in his capillary walls; some snag certain blood-clotting agents and pull them out of solution, prompting other agents to dissolve them again. Perhaps half of the proteins are still within a few inches of the bite and are busy gnawing away at the local cell structures, so that bits and pieces float free and clump up. Wave after wave of white cells rush in to attack this debris, swelling the tissues further, and the concentration of large molecules in solution creates an osmotic gradient that the capillary walls, in their damaged condition, cannot mediate, so more and more water leaves the circulation and accumulates. The resultant swelling is not unlike a rush-hour traffic jam; it spreads by absorption, and the exits are too narrow to let the captured elements disperse.

At two-thirty, ninety minutes after the bite, the doctor takes a tailor's tape measure out of his pocket and measures the circumference of the young man's left leg at several places between ankle and mid-thigh, noting the results on a clipboard. It is just as the man in Boston had predicted: though the leg does not look particularly swollen, its diameter is more than a half inch greater than that of his right over most of its length. This increase in volume could easily account for a liter or more of fluids lost from the bloodstream, and the doctor believes that this deficit in turn produced the shocklike symptoms the patient arrived with — rapid heartbeat, sweating, lowered blood pressure, pallor, confusion. Now his pulse has come down and his pressure has stabilized at about 80 percent of normal. Maybe it's not just the extra fluids, the doctor thinks. Maybe the serum is working.

He uncaps a green felt-tip pen and makes a hash mark on the young man's leg about three inches above the knee, locating the leading edge of the swelling. The leg is dusky in color and shows some local bleeding under the skin behind the knee and between the toes. The hash marks, made at fifteen-minute intervals, are marching up toward the hip three inches at a time. If they reach mid-thigh, he thinks, I'll start the next ten units of antivenom.

By five o'clock a total of fourteen news organizations have called the hospital. Yes, they are told, the staff is treating a case of rattle-snake bite. The patient is a college boy whose name is being with-held until relatives are notified. He appears to have been bitten around one P.M. in the Blue Hills Reservation. He flagged down a car and a Milton woman took him to the hospital. No, no one else saw the snake — the diagnosis is based on the symptoms and his own account. He is listed in guarded condition. No details of treatment are being released.

At five-thirty the hematology technician wipes down his counter and logs out on the time chart. His relief, Mrs. Castillo, is down the hall with the supervisor. Once again he picks up the slide he saved for her, the slide whose shallow well contains a single drop of blood he placed on it forty minutes earlier. It is still bright red. He blows on it; it trembles. It's not good, this blood, he thinks. It simply won't harden. It might as well be cranberry juice.

The last sunlight fades from the hillside pocket where the young man was bitten. The snake that bit him is still in place, killed by internal injuries suffered when he leaped off her body. Now she is lying partly on her back, her pale chin exposed. Tiny ants blacken her open mouth.

A crow swoops into the crown of a nearby pitch pine and folds its wings, croaking softly. After a few minutes it drops to the ground and hops over to the dead snake. A few exploratory pecks produce no reaction. It begins to eat, looking up every few seconds.

The young man would like to get up, walk around, make a few phone calls. It's doubtful, however, whether his leg would stand it. They've put the heel in a sling and raised it a few inches. It still hurts, but not as bad. It is swollen, almost spongy under his fingers and is decorated here and there with red-purple splotches — around the ankle, behind the knee.

At any rate, he's got too much baggage to go anywhere fast. A tube now runs up his urethra, draining his bladder into a clear plastic bag. Thin wires taped to his chest are connected to an EKG monitor. Both IVs are still patched into needles in his arms. He feels like a fish hooked by several anglers at once.

This whole thing, he knows, is going to turn into a major embarrassment. People will say he went looking for trouble. Why didn't the damn snake rattle sooner? Now his mother will drive up from Connecticut and his girlfriend will come in from school, and everyone will get upset and excited over nothing. As if he had nothing better to do than lie in bed and grin bravely. Meanwhile his seat will remain empty in organic chem. It'll take all week to catch up. No wonder he's sick to his stomach.

He drags himself up a little higher in the bed, wincing as his leg throbs. He can barely feel the pillow wedged under it. The room is dim except for the bright light directly above. Several more ragged and pea-size spots, almost like blood blisters, have appeared on his stomach.

To the doctor's surprise, the man in Boston is not interested in all the signs of recovery — the stabilized blood pressure, pulse, and swelling. All he cares about is the one abnormal test, the blood fibrinogen level. He won't get off of it.

It's just after seven. The doctor and his relief, an intern, are standing in the resident's office at the ER with the printouts from the latest blood work spread on the counter. They have the man from Boston on the speaker phone.

"Look," Boston says, "I agree. At this moment you don't have a problem. Unless you are pre-op, low fibrinogen is not a problem. And even then it's easily controlled. But in snakebite, as I said, low fibrinogen is the most reliable indicator of a bite's severity. Now your patient has already had thirty units of antivenom, and you've given him fibrinogen also. But in your latest test, he is still defibrinated. Why?"

The doctor answers, "Apparently we didn't give him enough."

"No — you gave him plenty. None would have been plenty. As you said, his bleeding problems are minor. My only point is this — this case began as a severe bite, and so far as we know it is still a severe bite. If it isn't, what happened to all that fibrinogen? After thirty units of polyvalent, he still had enough venom in him to wash it all out."

What the man from Boston wants is to have the young man transferred to a downtown hospital with a good intensive-care unit, a place with dozens of night nurses expert in assisted breathing and dialysis. Not necessarily for admission — just to have it close by. He has already mentioned someone at Mass. General who will take the case.

The doctor doesn't want to give up his patient. He has already decided to stay late with him. Small hospitals like his are too often, he believes, undercut by the big warehouses downtown.

"We already graded it a severe bite," he says. "But we took him off the antivenom two hours ago. He's feeling better, he's alert, and he's breathing well. The pain and swelling have moderated. And you said yourself that this fibrinogen washout is typical not only of severe cases but of a lot of moderate and even mild ones also. So aren't we in better shape now? And if he does need assistance, I'm not worried about it. We do some geriatric surgery here — we know how to keep people ventilated."

"Well . . ." Boston doesn't sound convinced. "It's your patient, of course. I'd say it's maybe a five percent risk, at most, that he won't keep improving. But this friend of mine regularly treats adult respiratory distress. That's the wild card in *Crotalus* bites — pulmonary edema. You get hypotension too, but if you treat the hypotension with fluids, you risk flooding the lungs. Once you get into that, you're looking at fifty, sixty percent mortality. Very rare, but it happens. I'd say this case still has two days to go before it can be ruled out."

The doctor is quiet for a moment. He crosses his arms, cups his chin in his hand, glances at the intern. At last he says, "All right. I'll go have another look at him now. I'll call you back."

The young man's lungs contain approximately 750 million tiny and elastic gas-filled sacs known as alveoli. Each time he inhales, a large proportion of them swell up with inspired air. Their combined interior surfaces measure almost one hundred square yards.

Their walls are thin and enclosed in a similarly elastic layer of tiny blood vessels, or capillaries. Bluish, oxygen-poor venous blood is pumped through these capillaries by his heart's right ventricle. It reddens as it passes, absorbing oxygen through the alveolar walls and releasing $CO_2$ from solution. Rejuvenated, the blood returns to his heart, ready to be driven through the rest of his body.

Both the alveolar and the capillary walls are only a single cell wide. These walls are delicate; nowhere else do the young man's inner tides stream so close to the outer world. If these membranes are damaged, fluids will seep through, filling his alveoli like water swelling a sponge. If enough of them fill, his lungs will become stiff, sodden, and largely airless.

The same factors in rattlesnake venom that degrade capillary walls and cause swelling and hemorrhaging near the bite can have similar effects elsewhere. The young man's alveoli may or may not be particularly sensitive to these factors; nonetheless, their respiratory function makes any damage they sustain critical. If his circulation carries these factors to his lungs in sufficient quantity, and if the leakage, or edema, they cause outruns his local capacity for repairs and reabsorption, he may drown in his own blood.

*Crotalus horridus* bites are unlikely to become fatal unless forty or more milligrams of venom are injected. Snakes ration their venom; timber rattlers very rarely expend this amount in a defensive strike. However, if they are badly frightened or injured they may hang on and pump in much larger quantities. The snake that the young man inadvertently crushed under his heel squeezed eighty milligrams of venom into his leg. This was over half her reserve, and twice the estimated lethality threshold.

The young man is not having any trouble breathing. He is in good health, at rest, and partly sedated. Even so, in the thirty-five minutes it took him to get off the hillside and into the hospital, his blood absorbed venom proteins and his active heart pumped some of them into his lungs. More have arrived there in the meantime, though not at the same rate, since many have been neutralized by antivenom. But his tissues are already reacting, and his alveoli are filling with blood-derived fluids. He hasn't noticed because his lungs' latent capacity has thus far covered the loss. If, however, he were to try to do six or eight push-ups, or bench-press a bowling ball for a minute or two, he would collapse.

•

The young man's girlfriend is standing by his bed when the nurse wheels in a small, flat machine with a length of stringy black wire piled on top. The nurse straightens up, nods to the girl, and turns to the young man. "How's it going?"

"Pretty good."

She touches his bare chest, stroking some of the small purple blotches. "More of these, huh?"

"What are they?"

"Petechiae. Minor hemorrhages." She unwraps a blood-pressure cuff and nods at the machine. "That's a pulse oximeter. We're going to put that little clip on your finger for a bit. Then we'll roll you down the hall for a chest x-ray."

"How come?"

"The doctor wants to get a close look at your lungs. He thinks they might be affected."

"Are they?"

"I don't know. But you can ask him in a minute." She puffs up the cuff with the squeeze bulb and holds the stethoscope to his arm, listening, then unwraps the cuff again. Crossing to the foot of the bed, she picks up his chart and begins writing. "After these tests you should be able to get a nicer room upstairs — a TV, a big window, the works. I'm going home now. I'll be back in the morning. No hanky-panky in the meantime." She smiles, replacing the chart. "Oh, I got the name of that woman who brought you in." She slips a folded paper on the night table and leaves.

The young man turns to his girlfriend. "Do it now. Before they chase you out."

She makes a face. "Oh, all right." She takes a camera out of her leather handbag and begins snapping pictures of his swollen, blotchy leg.

An hour later, at eight-thirty, the doctor and the intern are back in the resident's office. The heavily marked-up hematology readout sprawls across the counter; above it, clipped to an illuminated panel, are several cloudy x-rays.

Arms crossed, the intern is staring down at the linoleum. After a long moment he glances up at the doctor. "If you ask me, I don't think there's any question about it."

The doctor curses under his breath. Suddenly he turns to the phone and stabs out a number. The man in Boston answers immediately. "O.K.," the doctor says, "you win. He's all yours."

After a twenty-minute ambulance ride downtown the young man is wheeled deep into a hospital and placed on a foam-cushioned bed with long straps dangling from its sides. His private room is pale blue, brightly lit, and cluttered with enigmatic machinery. Nurses cluster around the raised, U-shaped counter visible through the glass wall fronting the corridor. Though he can see no other patients, he can hear numerous half-muffled hummings, pumpings, gurglings, and sighs.

He seems to have been forgotten for the moment. This move would not have been made, he knows, unless a suspicion existed that he had big-league health problems. Even so, he would prefer to be elsewhere. There's no telling what they might do to him here.

It's not his leg anymore, it's this heaviness in his chest. Every time he inhales, he's pushing against it. He pushes, it pushes, he pushes, it pushes — it's work. It's worse when he has to answer questions as well. What he would really like is for everyone to turn the lights out and leave him alone.

The nurse comes in again. She wants to crank up the bed. "You'll breathe better, I promise," she says. She reaches down by his hip and starts turning. A broad hand lifts his shoulders; the far wall tilts into view.

He notices a pale tendril of hair that has come loose from her cap and wonders how much better he might feel if she undid her blouse and nuzzled him. It would have to be a whole lot better.

She stops cranking just as his weight starts to sag. She's right; there seems to be a little more room in his chest.

Down the hall is a small waiting room furnished with two short couches and a low table. At ten P.M. the young man's girlfriend and his mother are the only occupants. They both stand up when the doctor comes in.

"I don't want to alarm you," he says, "but we are walking a fine line. The young man is having serious breathing difficulties. We've decided to put him on a respirator. He will probably remain on it until the situation is resolved — that could take as long as forty-eight hours."

Neither woman answers. The surprise is plain on their faces.

"The problem is that he has fluid in his lungs, fluid that makes it difficult for him to obtain sufficient air. This is a problem that we see every day, but it's not easy to deal with. The respirator reduces the work of breathing, allowing him to rest, and it also permits us to give him an enriched oxygen mixture at optimum pressures."

The two women continue to stare. Sometimes he imagines saying other things: Congratulations. Merry Christmas. You may now kiss the bride.

"For the next hour or so our main job will be to see that the respirator is working as efficiently as possible. At this point I believe his lungs are in good enough shape to carry him through. But if they deteriorate further, the outlook may worsen. In that case you should be prepared for bad news."

There, he's said it. The effect is immediately evident. Like warm rain on a snowman.

"I don't think we'll be able to say that the danger has passed until this time tomorrow, at the earliest. This isn't to suggest he won't start improving before then — we just don't know. But if he can get through the crisis, there's no reason to expect he won't recover completely."

He waits, motionless. The two women have moved together, the girlfriend hanging on the mother's arm. At last the mother says, "When can we see him?"

"Very soon. Once he's on the respirator, we'll insert a pulmonary catheter to monitor his blood pressure — I'll ask you to wait until that's in. It shouldn't take more than twenty minutes. The respirator will prevent him from speaking, and he'll be sedated, but he may be able to write on a board — there's no reason you can't stay as long as you want. Someone will let you know as soon as it's time."

After a moment the doctor turns and goes out. They always look that way, he thinks, hating it.

For the first time in his life a hole appears in the young man's subclavian vein. A long, thin plastic tube enters from outside and slides easily along it, searching for his heart. Blood rushes past it for a split second, then stops, then rushes on again. The vein widens as other veins join it. Before long it expands into a sort of muscular antechamber; at its far end an O-shaped mouth opens, gulps deeply, and puckers shut. The tube dives through this aperture also.

A moment later the head of the tube swims out of the right side of the young man's heart and stops a few inches beyond. The blood-filled tunnel it occupies — the pulmonary artery — is here at its widest point; a little farther on it begins dividing and redividing almost *ad infinitum,* its smallest branchlets becoming the tiny capillaries that surround the alveoli. Many of these alveoli are now flooded with a deadly protein-rich soup that leaked in through their membranes. The blood that squeezes past them encounters no oxygen and returns to his heart unreddened. This is the problem that is responsible for the other tube that now occupies the young man's throat — a large one, lodged in place by an inflatable cuff, so that the machine at its far end can regularly pump a given volume of gases in and out of the still-elastic portions of his lungs.

A tiny balloon emerges from a hole near the head of the tube and swells to pea size. The rush of blood guides this balloon and the attached tube down the pulmonary artery and into one of its branches, where it becomes wedged in place. The balloon quickly deflates; the tube is now positioned to measure blood pressure in the pulmonary capillaries. Every now and then the balloon will swell again briefly as a nurse squeezes a syringe; when it does, a transducer in the tube's head will begin to take readings, and a tiny wire attached to it will carry the readings back down the tube's length and out to a machine. The machine will convert the readings to light energy and display them as a wavelike trace on a screen. The doctor will watch this trace closely; his task will be to maintain the blood pressure in the young man's lungs at a figure high enough to keep his veins filled and his heart pumping efficiently, but not so high that it drives more fluid into the lungs. Unfortunately there is nothing he can do about the damaged alveoli themselves.

A sort of squat plastic clothespin clipped to the young man's left index finger monitors how well his lungs are keeping his blood oxygenated. A diode on the inside of one of its flat pincers shines a beam of reddish light through his fingertip at a photoreceptor mounted on the other. If his lungs are functioning well, much of this light will not get across, since it will be scattered by oxygen-rich hemoglobin in his arterial blood. If, however, a significant portion of his hemoglobin carries no oxygen, and is bluish in color, more red light will reach the receptor.

The clothespin is wired to a machine — a pulse oximeter — which continuously displays a two-digit number representing the percentage oxygen saturation of the young man's arterial blood. Normally stable at a high level (95 to 98 percent), it can dip to as low as 75 before major organs begin to suffer. But if it drops to 50, the prognosis worsens. At this level the heart, kidneys, liver, and brain cannot process enough oxygen to maintain their functions, and if there is no improvement they will fail.

The jittery number is now hovering between 78 and 83 — not a promising figure, considering that the respirator is giving the young man an $O_2$ concentration three times that of normal air. But if the doctor sets the machine to provide an even richer mix at higher pressures, he will risk permanent damage to the lungs.

The young man has no idea what the various numbers visible on the readouts mean. A hard plastic tube fills his throat; every five seconds his chest laboriously shudders and heaves as large amounts of air are forced in and out. He would prefer to breathe faster; the doctor told him, however, that if he fights the machine he may have to be put under. The doctor meant "put under general anesthesia"; the young man thought he meant "put underground." He is confused. He thinks the doctor wants to kill him but has not yet found the right combination of tortures. Not fighting the machine is one way to keep the doctor at bay. The young man would probably be more alarmed than he is if he had not received a large dose of intravenous lorazepam (Ativan). His brain is not getting as much oxygen as it is used to; he is only vaguely aware that the scene around him represents anything out of the ordinary. But without the fluids, antivenom, and oxygen he has already been given, he would have been dead hours ago.

There are two new faces in the room, his mother and his girlfriend. His bed is still tilted up and his eyes meet theirs on a level. He is glad they are here, even if they don't seem aware of the situation's ludicrous quality. It's not easy to smile with a plastic pipe in one's throat, but he attempts it.

The packed red cells intended to maintain his fluid volume begin to drain into his arm. A nurse stoops by his hip and unclips his catheter tube from a bag containing several teaspoons of bloody urine, then attaches it to a fresh one. Two more doctors are standing just outside the door.

Shortly before midnight the young man loses consciousness, and at around two A.M. he dies. The cause of death is multiple organ failure secondary to arterial hypoxia. An autopsy report later describes his lungs as "beefy, edematous, and congested in appearance." His kidneys, micrographs show, are clogged with the casts of broken red cells.

The headline in the morning papers is "College Student Killed by Rattlesnake." The stories briefly excite thousands over coffee and oatmeal. The location of his abandoned Subaru is described; a small-scale search for the offending reptile begins at that point. No rattlers are found, and the killer is never identified.

Local snake enthusiasts privately curse the young man — every accident of this kind, they believe, is the result of carelessness. No campaign of extermination develops, however. During the next few weeks the Trailside Museum in Milton prudently keeps its lone *Crotalus* off public display.

The young man's medical bills come to $14,200. His college's health plan remits promptly. His girlfriend keeps up with his family for several years, then moves out west and never sees them again. The doctor at the suburban hospital will remain on staff until retirement, but will treat no other snakebites. In his opinion, shared only with colleagues, Wyeth polyvalent is not a particularly useful drug. He later takes his wife and two sons on a horseback safari in Africa, encounters a puff adder at a campsite, and kills it.

Of the twenty-nine newborn snakes present in the hillside pocket when the young man stepped down into it, three survive to adulthood. None of them ventures more than a mile from the site. The next person to enter it is another unaccompanied snake hunter, who arrives in May of 1998. He sees nothing, and is gone in less than a minute.

•

The events described above represent an extreme case — a set of ordinary circumstances combined with the worst possible luck. I

had to resort to invention because the history of encounters between people and rattlesnakes in New England provides no solid
evidence of an equivalent disaster. Perhaps in fairness to *Crotalus* I
should point out the spots where I had to lean hardest against the
weight of probability.

Timber rattlesnakes rarely grow more than five feet long. The
record is six feet two inches, reported a half century ago by Raymond Ditmars for an example from the Berkshire town of Shef-
field, Massachusetts. Large snakes carry more venom than small
ones, and the length of their fangs enables them to strike more
deeply. The average adult size of the Blue Hills population is
probably no more than two and a half or three feet; the snake that
bit the young man was twice as big, and larger than any ever
recorded from the area.

Rattlers are thick-bodied snakes, much more so than their harmless relatives. As adults, any increase in length is accompanied by
an impressive increase in bulk, so that a five-foot specimen is a
conspicuous monster, and considerably bigger than any snake normally encountered in this part of the world. Coiled on a level
surface, it might stand as much as four or five inches high, making
it unlikely to be stepped on in daylight.

The snake that bit the young man, however, was buried in a
concealing blanket of huckleberry and dry leaves. What's more,
she hadn't fed in over a year (pregnant females usually fast), so
that her glands contained a much greater volume of venom, and
with a higher concentration of toxins, than is typical of all but a
few rattlesnakes. He came upon her suddenly, giving her no time
to buzz. And the weight of his heel, carrying his entire bulk directly
onto her spine, killed her in mid-bite, so that in her agony she
squeezed most of her juices into his leg.

At that point he was a quarter mile from the road and nearly
four miles from the hospital. Perhaps if he had received twenty or
more units of polyvalent right away, the result might have been
different. Lab tests have shown that a delay of as little as ten
minutes can have significant effects. As it happened, he was without help and unwilling to wait for it; he staggered up and began
walking, exercising his leg and hastening the spread of the toxic
proteins. By the time he emerged on the road, he was probably
already doomed.

The local doctor immediately recognized the bite's severity, sought expert consultation, and by starting the antivenom at once, without waiting for the results of a skin test, showed that he wasn't afraid to take risks in response to what he correctly considered an emergency. His impression, after thirty units of antivenom, that he had successfully blunted the threat to the young man's life wasn't strictly erroneous; the polyvalent and the plasma expanders probably did halt a collapse in blood pressure that would have been fatal otherwise. Given the delay in administering the antivenom, it's unlikely that any amount would have reversed the more insidious problem developing in the small structures of the lungs.

These structures are largely beyond the reach of contemporary medicine. When circulating toxins degrade them, allowing fluids to flood the alveoli — as in septicemia, certain drug overdoses, and dangerous *Crotalus* bites — current treatments attempt to maximize the lungs' blood-oxygenating potential, buying time for treatment of the underlying insult, with the hope that the damaged membranes will recuperate on their own. Textbooks call this disastrous form of leakage ARDS, or adult respiratory distress syndrome, and emphasize that it is a medical emergency and can be rapidly fatal. Strictly speaking, it cannot be reversed but only temporarily alleviated. Recently medical scientists hoped that a remarkable new machine known as a membrane oxygenator could make a difference in ARDS cases — it takes oxygen-poor venous blood through a tube, passes it across membranes through which it soaks up oxygen, and returns it to the patient, thus duplicating lung function and making it unnecessary for the weakened alveoli to carry the entire blood-oxygenating load. They soon discovered, however, that ARDS-type lung damage often reaches a point of no return, beyond which the alveoli do not reabsorb fluids and permit restored gas exchange, but instead remain sodden and skin over inside with fibrous scar tissue, rendering them permanently impotent. A membrane oxygenator cannot stand in for the alveoli forever — for all its sophistication, it is a crude device compared to a healthy human lung, and the mechanical damage it inflicts on the blood proves at length insurmountable. Studies soon showed that these machines had no positive effect on survival rates for ARDS patients; this is why the young man was not offered one. Perhaps in one or two hundred years hospitals will maintain vats full of fresh, ready-to-install lungs grown from embryonic cell cultures, and emergency transplants will routinely save lives. For now, however, ARDS is a killer.

Lung damage is a consistent autopsy finding in *Crotalus* fatalities. Of the nine postmortems Dr. Findlay Russell detailed in his *Snake Venom Poisoning*, eight involved rattler bites and eight showed pulmonary congestion, edema, or hemorrhage. What makes the imaginary young man's case exceptional is not the way he died but the way he was bitten and the amount of venom he received. If more bites were like this, many more would be fatal.

Here is the paradox: it is estimated that a full-grown timber rattlesnake possesses enough venom to kill two or three human beings, and yet deaths from bites are remarkably scarce. This is probably because snakes rarely waste their venom on a defensive strike, but instead save it for their prey. In other words, these rattlers appear to require considerable persuasion before they will deliver a killing bite — they must be stepped on or grabbed and squeezed. In New England, where they have been written about for nearly four hundred years, no solid evidence of such a bite has emerged. This looks like remarkable restraint. If, for instance, every Massachusetts citizen habitually left for work in the morning carrying a .38 automatic, we would probably not have to wait centuries to record the first murder. One can only conclude that it is a lot easier to convince a man to kill a snake than it is to provoke a snake to kill a man.

But enough of doctors, medicines, hospitals, and snakebites, hypothetical and otherwise. I have made the case against *Crotalus*, such as it is. Have I been wasting my breath? Do New Englanders already know all they care to know about rattlesnakes? Certain recent incidents suggest that the answer is yes.

# Four Bullets and an Ignoramus

> I ride around the town
> I use a rattlesnake whip
> Take it easy Arlene
> Don't give me no lip.
>
> — Bo Diddley, "Who Do You
> Love" (1956)

Not every Blue Hills rattler resides in the Blue Hills. Anyone eager to see one, in fact, might do well to avoid the Reservation entirely, where they are famously elusive, and make a visit to nearby Harvard University in Cambridge. There, in the basement of the north wing of Agassiz's Museum of Comparative Zoology, are forty-four pickled examples of *Crotalus horridus,* nineteen of them from Massachusetts and ten of them from the Blue Hills. The oldest local specimen was purchased before the Civil War from a Mr. Blaine Grover; the most recent was donated in September 1980 by S. J. Tuma Jr., who found it dead on a roadside near Route 128.

Granted, these snakes are not at their best. They are unresponsive, they reek of preservative, and they have the pale, clammy look of drowned sailors. Coiled in gallon jars and squirreled away like vintage wines, they can't rattle and hiss — they serve, instead, as a permanent reservoir of anatomical detail. Even so, there are probably more of them here than can now be seen alive in any one spot in the Hills.

One of these yellowing sociopaths, catalogue number 153966, is of particular interest. Like his shelfmates, he lies at the bottom of a jar full of 70 percent ethanol, where his four-foot length spirals through several soggy coils. He's a male, as is evident from the swollen, two-headed penis protruding from his vent. His eyes are blind and clouded, his jaws shriveled and slack. Pick up the jar and turn it; he merely swivels in place.

Unlike his companions, however, he doesn't look as if he died quietly — several large, ragged wounds spoil his nakedness. One goes clear through his neck; two more tatter his midsection. This isn't the sort of damage a stout stick might do. It's as if he swallowed explosives.

The wounds are bullet holes. They came from a .38 service revolver issued to Officer Arnold LeMoine of the Metropolitan Police. According to LeMoine's report, on August 31, 1976, he came upon the snake while patrolling a bridle path in the Blue Hills Reservation and fired four of six cylinders into it — three in quick succession, the fourth a careful, two-handed squeeze.

LeMoine didn't think twice about shooting the snake. It was lying in the middle of the trail; the sight of it spooked his horse, Chico, so badly that he was nearly thrown off. The snake then coiled up and buzzed, striking several times in Chico's direction. Here was a heavily armed suspect making a distinctly hostile demonstration. Policemen take such threats seriously. LeMoine's marksmanship quickly restored order.

Imagine his surprise, then, when a representative of the Trailside Museum arrived at police headquarters to pick up the carcass and told LeMoine that he had not only broken the Reservation ordinance prohibiting harassment of wildlife, but had shot and killed an animal officially regarded by the commonwealth as an endangered species. In this view his exploit was not a commendable action in support of public safety, but a rash gesture quite possibly liable to prosecution. Needless to say, LeMoine didn't agree.

Word of the difference of opinion soon reached the newspapers. Several stories recounted the incident. Subsequent letters and phone calls supported LeMoine by an overwhelming majority, many of them marked by real outrage. How, it was asked, could anyone question a police officer's judgment in removing a deadly reptile from a public and widely used park, especially when that reptile was directly threatening both him and his mount?

Trailside personnel hastened to point out that LeMoine had been in no danger once his horse stopped short, and that the rattler may even have forestalled an accident by advertising its presence. If the officer had simply waited a few moments the snake would most likely have crawled off the trail; if it hadn't, he could have hurried it along with a stick. He had never come near being bitten.

LeMoine half validated these criticisms by emphasizing that the danger lay not so much in the snake itself as in his mount's violent reaction: "The attitude of the Trailside Museum seems to be they'd rather have a rider with a broken neck than a dead snake." In his view, apparently, any animal that might frighten a horse had no business in an MDC park. "The Trailside Museum doesn't bother me at all," he added. "We are out here to protect the public — hikers and horsemen. This snake was dangerous to both."

No one had the effrontery to suggest that LeMoine ought to be disciplined. He had felt threatened; he had perhaps overreacted; the victim was not a house pet. The community was of two minds on the matter. Though it no longer actively encouraged *Crotalus*-smashing by offering bounties, it was not yet ready to back up the promise of legal protection implicit in the Reservation ordinances; some kinds of wildlife, it appeared, were less equal than others. Perhaps the appropriate statute (General Laws chapter 92, section 37) should have been amended to read, "Injuring or otherwise disturbing animals or birds is prohibited *except in self-defense, or when authorized persons deem such animals or birds to present a hazard to visitors.*"

Four years later, in the summer of 1980, a similarly armed patrolman came across another big, buzzing rattler on a Blue Hills path. Thanks in part to the furor attendant on the earlier incident, he did not immediately draw his revolver. He instead picked up a forked stick, pinned the snake's head down, grasped it behind the neck, and brought it unharmed to the Trailside Museum, where he turned it over to the animal care director, Norman Smith. Though Smith perhaps wished the officer had left the snake where he found it and had not risked a bite, he nonetheless thanked him for his efforts and commended his restraint. Smith later announced that he wouldn't keep the animal on display indefinitely, but would release it before winter.

Here was a blow to the orthodox! For the first time in memory an officer entrusted with the public safety had not only declined to kill a free-roaming rattler but had willingly delivered it to the enemy, the same enemy who was openly planning to return it to the woods, once it had been exploited for propaganda!

Sure enough, a champion emerged to set matters straight. This was a local resident, George V. Higgins, novelist, attorney-at-law, and columnist for the *Boston Globe*. Writing in the *Globe*'s Sunday magazine for August 17, Higgins opened in classic style by constructing a monster:

> If you have never seen a rattlesnake, you may be assured that it is a very menacing creature fully equipped to do considerable damage in very short order. If you see one, or hear one, with its dander up, and you do not happen to be a policeman equipped with a service revolver, you stand an excellent chance of having an extremely unpleasant experience that will probably require some convalescence.

Let's look at this a little more closely:

> If you have never seen a rattlesnake, you may be assured

Higgins knows very well that most of his readers have never seen a rattlesnake in the woods. Few Bostonians have, and I suspect he hasn't either. Nonetheless, with the phrase "you may be assured" he acquires a flavor of authority without emerging from the passive voice, and so enjoys the pretense of expertise without actually claiming it.

> If you see one, or hear one, with its dander up, and you do not happen to be a policeman equipped with a service revolver, you stand an excellent chance of having an extremely unpleasant experience that will probably require some convalescence.

This is the crux of his argument. Trimmed of verbiage, it goes as follows: If you see or hear an aroused *Crotalus*, you are likely to be poisoned. This snake resurrects the legendary medieval basilisk, which could fell strong men with a glance. But Higgins cannot avoid making this claim, because if his reptilian stooge is not shown to be patently injurious, then there is no rationale for a lynching.

He is apparently unaware, however, that it is precisely the rattlesnake that does *not* coil up and buzz that is dangerous, because a snake that has been noticed is a snake that can be left to itself, like a snarling dog or a spitting, hunchbacked cat. Higgins likewise implies that Officer LeMoine escaped harm only because of his trained reflexes and expert gunplay. He doesn't explain how the other patrolman, who was similarly armed, managed to pick up an angry snake and bring it safely to the museum without so much as fingering his nightstick.

But having established that the mere sight of an aroused rattler puts the observer's health in dire jeopardy (by the same logic, anyone who so much as glimpses a school bus is lucky to escape a flattening), he can go on to argue that Officer LeMoine "acted as any common-sensical human would who spots a rattlesnake and has ready at hand the means of doing something fatal to the snake before the snake does something fatal to him." Here Higgins converts a simple man-*Crotalus* encounter into an all-out gladiatorial showdown, omitting to note that it is certainly more hazardous to attempt to kill a venomous snake than it is to leave it alone — most animals, human beings included, tending to react unpredictably to sudden, murderous attacks. Higgins calls LeMoine's hail of bullets (which were fired from a nervous horse, and in a boulder-strewn area) "common-sensical." Perhaps, as Voltaire once remarked, common sense is not so common.

Having vindicated his hero, Higgins finishes by describing the law that protects all Blue Hills wildlife, rattlers included, as "wrong, badly drafted, and stupidly enforced," and concludes that if *Crotalus* "is open to extinction by human means, it would seem appropriate to set about it with high spirits and get it done with."

This was written ten years ago. Despite his bold stand, there is no evidence that Higgins ever heeded his own advice and set off into the Hills in order to smash a few snakes. There have been no *Crotalus* poisonings in the interval, either — in fact, not a single such poisoning has occurred in the park's entire hundred-year history.

He did find time, however, to answer a couple of criticisms that appeared in the Sunday magazine's letters column five weeks after his performance. To one writer, who complained of his use of the term "eastern diamondbacks" to describe rattlers from the Blue Hills (the nearest eastern diamondbacks, or *Crotalus adamanteus,* live somewhere south of Virginia), Higgins replied that he was merely repeating what the cops had told him. To the other, who like the first wondered if the Blue Hills rattlers were really so threatening as to require a change in park policy and an active campaign of extermination, he submitted this valentine: "As for the rest of the above prose, I do not wish to seem venomous, but it does appear to be the sort of foolishness I would expect from anyone who prefers rattlers to people." Whether his target, Marilynne K. Roach of Watertown, prefers rattlers to people, or people to ice cream, or ice cream to newspapers, we do not know. What we do know is that Higgins is ducking her question.

It is reasonable to conclude that Higgins the columnist never had much interest in park rangers, rattlesnakes, or the wisdom of current environmental regulations. If he had, he might have made some effort to unearth the facts. But that effort would have proved ruinous; what attracted him, it seems, was precisely the opportunity to dispense with the facts. If snakebite were a real threat to life around Boston and had claimed numerous victims, like drunk drivers or school kids with handguns, would he have approached it in this sneering, know-nothing manner?

Probably not. It's safe to say that Higgins already knows all he cares to know about rattlesnakes, and that the only reason he focused on them at all was his itch to tweak the persons he glimpsed behind them — environmental purists, ecological bureaucrats, and conservation advocates. Indeed, there is a significant current of opinion that is bone-weary of the endless dos and don'ts publicized and promulgated by these individuals, and that fondly remembers a time when it was still perfectly acceptable to burn leaf piles on roadsides, pour motor oil down storm drains, and heave conked-out air conditioners into the nearest swamp. Back then no one imagined that road salt was a poison or that the waters of Boston Harbor might be anything else but black and disgusting. This army of grumblers thinks that the protectionists have gone overboard, and is so tired of hearing about acid rain, toxic diapers, invisible radon gas, and so forth, that it supposes we shall all soon be required by law to crap into our hands and stick our turds behind our ears — what, after all, have things come to when you can't even kill a goddamn *snake?* (What stings this current most cruelly, of course, is its sense that in spite of its rich past, it has lost the initiative and may be retreating forever.)

But let's suppose, just for fun, that Higgins really was concerned about potential dangers to park goers, and his argument that the needs of wild animals should not necessarily take precedence over public safety represents something more than a screen for potshots at environmentalists. In 1980, the same year in which he attempted to tell us the ugly truth about rattlesnakes, another indigenous form of Massachusetts wildlife was responsible for the deaths of 146 citizens — 146 more in twelve months than *Crotalus* has been successfully charged with in the commonwealth's entire 350-year history. According to the Registry of Motor Vehicles, these vicious remnants of the original New England wild can be summed up in a single word — trees.

Collisions with fixed objects are responsible for a large proportion of Massachusetts highway fatalities, and among these objects trees perennially lead the list. Trees, admittedly, are more numerous than rattlers, and are thought by many to add charm to our scene. Nonetheless, if the facts are any guide, they genuinely harbor the murderous impulses Higgins ascribes to *Crotalus,* and should pay dearly for the least sign of belligerence. But just as Higgins provides no evidence of ever having seen a Blue Hills rattler, much less having dueled one in mortal combat, he gives no indication that he has ever answered a challenge from a woody plant.

But enough. It is doubtful, as I said, that Higgins ever had any compelling interest in killing rattlesnakes, or even in persuading others to do so. When he says "Let's wipe out the rattlers," I believe he means something else — namely, that the presence or absence of *Crotalus* in the Blue Hills is essentially a matter of no consequence, but since efforts are being made by environmentalists to protect them, here's a chance to make a little noise and perhaps get oneself paddled by the opposite side — which is what he likes best, I suspect.

The fact is that the old New England tradition of snake clearance, though still alive and well in Texas and elsewhere, has been moribund in eastern Massachusetts for quite a while, and dilettantes like Higgins are unlikely to revive it. It depended on a rugged population of small farmers who knew the land and knew their quarry. Today both farmers and snakes are all but gone, and snake haters, though still numerous, are not aggressive; they prefer writing letters to the editor to the more arduous work of seeking out the remaining dens and emptying them. Just last summer a Milton man came across a small rattler on a golf course near Route 128, and instead of instantly clubbing it to death, as Higgins might have recommended, he picked it up and zipped it into his golf bag, planning to take it home to show to his kids — a risky maneuver, but indicative of the distance local attitudes have traveled.

Strictly speaking, of course, it isn't necessary to make *Crotalus* into a fantastic harpy in order to argue that he doesn't belong in the Hills. Rattlesnakes are venomous; their venom is a strong poison; just because no one has been poisoned in six or seven generations doesn't mean that a bite will not happen, nor that this bite won't fall into the small category of those with lasting consequences. As long as the park remains public, the only way to rule out such a bite would be to get rid of the snakes, which would make Massachusetts virtually *Crotalus*-free east of Springfield. In terms of effort required, this is hardly an unfeasible proposition, and if we can reduce the chances of bad bites to zero, why should we tolerate even the remotest possibility?

The only defense against this argument is the claim that *Crotalus* somehow adds something valuable to the Hills, or that if he does not, we would nonetheless injure ourselves by hunting him to extinction. What, in these circumstances, constitutes an acceptable risk? If our laws put a stop to snake killing and a small child steps on a large rattler and dies, who'll be responsible?

From an absolute standpoint, any such risk, no matter how small, is intolerable, and I don't mean to belittle it. As it happens, however, the Hills have developed a very lethal reputation over the last fifty years, and it has nothing to do with rattlesnakes. Readers with little stomach for disasters should perhaps skip the next chapter.

# 18

# Death Made Easy

This is where the serpent lives. This is his nest,
These fields, these hills, these tinted distances,
And the pines above and along and beside the sea.

— Wallace Stevens, "The Auroras of Autumn" (1948)

After skirting their southern outworks for six miles, Route 128 makes an end run around the eastern, or seaward, edge of the Blue Hills, picks up Route 3 from Cape Cod, and spills onto the floor of the Boston basin, ready for the final dash north to the city itself, which has sailed into view eight miles away. Drivers admiring the sky-colored towers in the distance may not notice the patch of high ground pivoting past their left shoulders — an unremarkable forested slope topped with a water tank on stilts and a few radio masts puckered with microwave dishes. This slope is the last gasp of the Hills, and the road carves it into a cliff before leaving it behind.

The cliff deserves some attention. A steep, rocky wall, it is made higher and steeper by an enormous jumble of loose boulders stacked precariously on top. These boulders are mostly long and flat-sided — some as small as refrigerators, some as large as Cadillacs. Even glaciers do not grub out ten-thousand-pound bricks like these and align them in windrows on precipices. Someone has been making improvements.

A ledge overlooking a highway may seem like a poor place to stack rocks eight or ten high, especially rocks big enough to squash tractor-trailers. They give the cliff a brutal, forbidding appearance, as if a race of misanthropic titans lived behind it. The cliff is not what it seems, however. It doesn't front a broad, fortresslike eminence, but instead is merely the back side of another cliff, a cliff so sheer, steep, and plunging that it makes the one over the highway look puny.

This second cliff plummets straight to the floor of a boxy, rectangular pit chopped out of the high ground. The pit is about the size of a football field and, if flooded, might easily be mistaken for an extra-large swimming pool. With the water out, it would become evident that the pit is a little on the deep side for swimming — 345 feet deep, to be exact. If a twenty-five-story office tower were built inside, one could step from the rim onto its roof.

This pit, also known as Swingle's quarry, is an accomplished man-killer. Year after year people stray near its rocky lip, slip, and fall in. Its latest victim was a twenty-two-year-old Quincy man, a jogger, whose coat and gloves were discovered on its edge by a hiker in January 1989.

There are other pits nearby, so many that the cliff over the highway and the area behind it, which form the northeasternmost bulge of the Hills, might be compared to a set of molars that have been drilled completely hollow but never filled in. None of the pits are quarried today. Interestingly enough, one of the last to shut down, Swingles's, was forced to do so in 1954 by the construction of Route 128, since the road cut away that part of the cliff which had anchored the cables supporting the main hoist. One reason the boulders are piled so high over the expressway is that there was no expressway when they were stacked up.

Swingle's now belongs to the city of Quincy, which acquired it by default after it was abandoned by its last owner in 1963. Technically, then, Quincy is responsible for policing the pit and keeping people away from its edges. To this end, the city has built a sturdy chain-link fence topped with barbed wire around the perimeter and put up numerous signs marked DANGER and warning of heavy fines for trespassers. Unfortunately the pit has traditionally served as a gathering point for thrill-seeking adolescents from all over greater Boston, and some of them apparently never come without wire cutters, and so the fence has been repeatedly snipped and peeled back in several places, and no matter how many times it is patched, it never remains intact for long. Probably the only way to secure the pit would be to staff it with round-the-clock guards. Quincy is not a wealthy city, however, and since the pit occupies a high, lonely, and out-of-the-way spot, a spot nonetheless easily accessible by car, there is no reason to expect that it won't claim further victims.

The pit wasn't dug in order to attract and kill teenagers. It was once the center of a thriving industry that employed many hundreds of workers and was largely responsible for the conversion of Quincy from a typical New England farming and fishing village to a populous, many-tongued hive. The object of this commotion was the material that once filled the pit — a tough, coarse-grained igneous stone famous nationwide a century ago as Quincy granite.

Granite is by no means a scarce commodity. Much of New England is made of it, not to mention New York's Adirondacks and California's Sierra Nevada. The local stuff, however, had the advantage of being only a mile or two from tidewater, with Boston just a short float up the harbor.

The first few generations of Bay colonists discovered that the granite's extreme hardness made it an excellent material for stoops and foundation stones, and they appropriated most of the stray boulders the glaciers had left lying around, splitting them by building fires underneath them and then dousing them with water or dropping cannonballs on top. They later learned that if one drilled holes in the rock, stuffed them with hardwood plugs, and then wetted the plugs, the swelling wood fibers could split the rock by themselves — with luck, a neat row of such holes could fracture a boulder to order. But these methods made little impression on rock still in the ground, and as the supply of loose boulders dwindled, the settlers began to wonder if they would run out of workable stone. In 1753, shortly after King's Chapel — a squat, dour, and truncated roost built for Boston's Anglican merchant-princes — was constructed of blocks cut from Quincy boulders, Quincy's parent town, Braintree, voted to prohibit any more removals of stone from the town's common lands without an express order. Similar restrictions had been passed as early as 1715.

It wasn't until 1803, following independence, that Quincyites found a way to prize chunks out of the bedrock itself, which lay exposed in huge masses in the ledgy hills dominating the western half of their town. Instead of hardwood plugs, they placed pairs of iron shims in the holes they drilled in the rock, then inserted stout iron wedges between the shims. Pounding these wedges with sledgehammers forced blocks to split free. Suddenly granite was common again.

This breakthrough permitted the growth of an industry that converted Quincy's barren and scrubby uplands into the stuff of its future. Strong, durable, and impervious, Quincy granite became the premier building material for an age that aspired to something more than wood and brick but hadn't yet imagined concrete and steel, and a complete technology grew up around the difficulties inherent in freeing, shaping, and moving large blocks of stone. Gridley Bryant's Granite Railway, often cited as the first commercial railroad in the United States, was built in 1826 to carry stone down from the quarries to barges on the Neponset, and a flock of massive projects began to take shape around Boston Harbor: the Bunker Hill Monument, the Charlestown Navy Yard, Fort Warren, Quincy Market. As often happens, a sort of can-you-top-this dynamic set in, culminating in the completion, in 1847, of the Boston Custom House, each of whose thirty-two fluted columns is thirty-two feet high, weighs forty-two tons, and was cut, shaped, and transported in one piece — they are still the largest monolithic columns in the country.

Most of this rock hadn't been disturbed since it crystallized from hot magma approximately 440 million years earlier, when life on land was limited to algae and proto-insects, and the rocks that would make up New England hadn't yet crossed the equator on their way northward. It is thought that all of the Blue Hills have cores of Quincy granite, and that the range as a whole is the remnant of a single pluton, or batholith — a mass of molten rock that pushed up from deep in the crust and cooled and hardened before reaching the surface. Plutons often resist erosion better than their covering rocks, and it is probably this power of resistance (concentrated in the granite's outer shell, the granite porphyry) that has allowed the Hills to stand up well above their surroundings despite their great age. Twice in the last 100 million years most of

New England has been worn down to a gently sloping plain, only to be dissected again following a period of uplift, and in each instance a few isolated eminences survived the general leveling, thanks to their extreme hardness — eminences like Mount Monadnock, Mount Wachusett, and the Blue Hills.

The granite industry never exhausted its mammoth cache of ancient stone. Even after the Metropolitan Park Commission bought up much of Quincy's uplands in the late nineteenth century for the Blue Hills Reservation, there remained many millions of tons of rock still available for blasting and cutting. What killed the granite business was technological advance; architects discovered that it was more economical to frame large buildings with an iron or steel skeleton and employ stone only as a thin cladding, with the result that demand dried up for the huge, pharaonic blocks that the Quincy pits specialized in. The stone's very hardness and toughness made it less suitable for the remaining markets, such as ornaments, veneers, and grave monuments, since its coarse grain, though capable of an excellent polish, doesn't lend itself to fine carving.

And so the pits and workshops shut down one by one, and the hundreds of Finns, Swedes, Irishmen, Italians, and Yankee farm boys who had gathered near the quarries, and made West Quincy considerably more populous than the original town, had to seek work elsewhere. The landscape itself, if not a complete ruin, had been scraped bare in many places and gnawed and pocked into a dizzying labyrinth full of mountains of rubble, winding cliffs, and sudden drop-offs hundreds of feet deep.

Quincy continued to grow regardless, aided by its proximity to Boston; the first rail link opened in 1845. Shipbuilding, primarily warships, replaced quarrying as the main pursuit; the Fore River yard launched thirty-six destroyers during World War I, following them between wars with the cruisers *Quincy* and *Vincennes* (both sunk by Japanese shell-fire off Guadalcanal), and the 35,000-ton battleship *Massachusetts* (currently docked as a museum in Fall River). During World War II Fore River delivered ninety-two boats in all, or about one every fifteen days. This business is now defunct also, and the yard is being converted into a plant for baking greater Boston's sewage sludge into fertilizer pellets, a product that may or may not find a market. Just recently Quincy succeeded in fending off another dubious honor: a massive toxic-waste incinerator that would have sat just up the estuary from the sludge plant.

Quincy, it is clear, is a classic hard-luck town — it always goes the extra mile to succeed, but its successes prove as costly as failures. Its first white settler, Captain Wollaston, landed with a small fortune in indentured servants, planning to enrich himself on their labor; he lost his shirt when they deserted him to team up with freebooter Thomas Morton in the fur trade. Morton in turn did so well with furs that the Bay Colony Puritans locked him in irons until his legs were "much decay'd." His lands fell to Bay colonists Anne Hutchinson and John Wheelright, whose campaign to bring their neighbors nearer to God through prayer proved such a hit that they were both exiled to the wilderness — Wheelright going north to New Hampshire, Mrs. Hutchinson south to Manhattan, where she was killed by Indians. Kitchamakin, the Massachuset sachem whose clan summered just up the beach from Morton, saw himself named titular owner of the entire region on the day he leased all but forty acres of it to the Puritans. He regarded this deal as a great coup, in that it ratified his sovereignty, but the Puritans saw it as a license to evict him, and soon prodded him twenty miles inland to Natick.

But even those residents not waylaid by their own triumphs tended, over time, to find Quincy uncomfortable and to begin looking for ways to get out — chief among these is the Adams family, once America's foremost political dynasty. Henry Adams had this to say about his hometown, cradle of two presidents, in 1869: "Nothing but sheer poverty shall ever reduce me to passing a whole season here again." Twenty years later, when he returned to close up the old homestead, he wrote: "Apparently I am to be the last of the family to occupy this house . . . none of us want it, or will take it. We have too many houses already, and no love for this."

Henry's elder brother, the wealthy railroad man Charles Francis Adams, held out somewhat longer, but at length concluded that Quincy had been ruined by the influx of quarrymen and their "fierce democracy"; he retreated to the plush western suburb of Lincoln, where he found an atmosphere more to his liking.

John Cheever, the town's most well-known recent product,

stayed barely past eighteen but perhaps should have left even sooner, since it could be argued that his entire literary career represents a not wholly successful effort to get out of Quincy. As his journals make clear, he sweated every trip back.

What's going on here? Where is the pride, the attachment that even the most difficult landscapes can be counted on to inspire in their natives?

Of course not everyone who can get out of Quincy hurries to do so; some even fight to defend it. A few years ago a local state legislator, William Golden, then serving as Quincy's city solicitor, was jogging along Wollaston Beach at low tide when he noticed that the flats were littered with small brownish lumps that seemed to him suspiciously fecal. His suspicions confirmed, he filed a lawsuit on Quincy's behalf against the metropolitan sewer authority, a suit that culminated in a historic federal court order requiring the cleanup of Boston Harbor. In appreciation for this effort, the commonwealth forced Quincy to accept the aforementioned sludge-baking plant. But the state showed no such eagerness to actually implement the order, an omission that proved damaging to then-Governor Michael Dukakis. In the midst of Dukakis's 1988 presidential campaign, the Republican nominee, George Bush (a Milton native), took a cruise in the harbor and invited reporters to inspect the filthy water and compare it against his opponent's environmentalist pretensions. Dukakis later carried Quincy in the election; according to some, Quincy had already carried out Dukakis feet-first.

The latest exemplar of Quincy's tradition of political ill-luck is resident and former state attorney general Francis X. Bellotti. He hoped to succeed Dukakis as governor, and in a primary campaign that demonstrated his incomparable fund-raising ability, he confessed that the main purpose of government, as he saw it, was to "help people." Unfortunately he ran at a time in which the voters believed that the government had done entirely too much helping of late, as evidenced by ballooning taxes and deficits, and so an attractive candidate who in most years would have been regarded as a clear front-runner, even a shoo-in, was helped to a stunning defeat. In the same election local water-quality champion William Golden, now wearing the sludge plant like an albatross, lost his senate seat in an unsuccessful run for lieutenant governor.

Quincy, it seems, is no ordinary town. It remains risky to love, and can be prodigal with disappointments. In the late 1940s its business and political leaders, aware that new highway construction and the rise of suburban shopping centers would soon endanger its downtown's position as the retailing mecca of Boston's South Shore, decided to take vigorous countermeasures — the problem, as they saw it, was that traffic congestion prevented shoppers from getting into town quickly enough, and that when these shoppers arrived, they had nowhere to park. Their solution was to buy up, raze, and pave over nearly every other block in the surrounding streets, making room for thousands of cars, and they also built an enormous concrete ditch/expressway from Route 3 all the way to the city center. For whatever reason, these efforts did not have the results intended, and the hemorrhaging continued. Today the mainstays of downtown Quincy's slightly ratty luncheonettes, shoe stores, and five-and-dimes are the residents of the immediate area, plus the commuters drawn in by the remaining banks and municipal offices. The program's side effects, however, were major and lasting: it turned a dense and coherent nucleus adjusted to foot traffic into a thinned-out jumble of buildings with no obvious relation to one another. A stroll down Hancock Street today is something like crossing a plank bridge, half of whose floorboards have been rudely torn out.

Perhaps this was inevitable, given the deep tidal forces involved — 1960 was the first year most Americans were classified as suburbanites — but the results, as usual, seem particularly unfortunate in Quincy, as if the city's own strength drove it to bite deeper into itself than was typical elsewhere. The epitome of this story is a large, modern structure recently placed at the rear of a broad plaza only yards away from the city's most venerable monuments: the antebellum Town Hall, the President's Church, and the Masonic Temple. This new construction is framed on both sides by smaller commercial blocks, giving it an even greater centrality and prominence. But whereas in another town one might expect to find this site reserved for a major civic monument — a post office, a main library, a courthouse — here it has been awarded to . . . a parking garage. Close inspection reveals that this squashed stack of cement waffles has a rail station and a bus terminal tucked underneath. This strikes me as similar to leveling Washington's Capitol Hill in order to put in an airfield — as if the chief merit of the place is the speed with which one can get out!

Stunts like these have made Quincy's eighty-five thousand remaining inhabitants (down from a peak of eighty-eight thousand in 1970) into a scrappy, prideful, and stiff-necked bunch not afraid to give each other a good once-over on its far from crowded streets. They know that their city is not beautiful, and has seen better days, but in their minds this only throws their personal outlines into greater relief. It was Quincy, for instance, that agreed to stage O'Neill's *Strange Interlude* in order to outflank Boston's censors in 1929, and more recently the city has found ways to absorb a large population of Southeast Asians. It's as if Quincy knows it can't afford the dodges by which other towns seek to resist change, but chooses to regard this as a point in its favor, in that it makes for a more knotty and independent brand of citizen.

But I'm getting away from my story. On a map Quincy looks something like a dustpan — a broad, scooplike apron dipping northeast into Boston Harbor, heavily crosshatched near its edge with a thick deposit of streets, with a long, narrow tailpiece tapering inland like a handle. The handle is nearly all high, rocky ground, much of it contained within the Blue Hills Reservation. Since the demise of the quarrying business, and more especially since the construction of Route 128 (which cut it off at its base), the handle has become a place apart in Quincy — uninhabited, troublesome, and unpopular. Only one road traverses it, Eliot's carriage road along the ridgeline to Milton, and the city confirmed its low estimate of the area's value by bulldozing a flat spot on its flank and converting it to a dump. Though this dump occupied some of the highest land in town, it remained invisible; to reach it trucks had to go under the expressway, over the cliff (which looks, with its crowning jumble of boulders, not unlike the ramparts of Mordor), and about a mile past the quarries, where the noise and stink excited no one except a few thousand sea gulls.

With only the dump, the defunct quarries, and the inviolable lands of the Reservation to recommend it, it's not surprising that the handle received little attention from Quincy officials. There were other, smaller quarries down below — these, being surrounded by dense neighborhoods full of voters, were better equipped to become nuisances. For years these smaller quarries had been used as dumps on a casual, at-need basis, and most of them were at least half full of tree stumps, junked cars, and demolition debris. On occasion local kids would fall in and get hurt; more often anonymous pranksters set the refuse on fire, and these deep-burning fires would smolder for weeks, defying the fire department's efforts to extinguish them. The taxpayers demanded a solution, and eventually money was made available to fill and cap nearly all of these quarries. Today the rocky hummocks they occupy, sometimes known as the North and South Commons, are still overgrown and littered with rubble, but they are no longer particularly troublesome.

It was different across the highway and atop the cliff. Here the rock-busting had been pursued on a truly cyclopean scale, and any efforts at repairs would have to be equally ambitious. Swingle's quarry alone bottoms out at two hundred feet below sea level, and could easily consume, according to a recent contractor's estimate, at least one million tons of fill. There are more than a dozen other pits, some of comparable size; most are full of water and their actual depths are unknown. No homes abutted these quarries, however, and no office seekers promised to make them disappear.

And so these abandoned and extremely hazardous workings, far from remote but effectively shielded from sight, were primed to become a sort of no-man's-land, a place where school-age kids were constantly warned not to go, but where, if they went, they rarely found anyone on hand to chase them away. Resorts suitable for free and unfettered swimming, drinking, hallooing, and deviltry are rare in our cramped and closely held landscape. The results were not too hard to predict; almost before the quarrymen's hammers stopped ringing, a black legend was born.

The boulders heaped atop the spine of rock separating Swingle's quarry from Route 128 are sometimes known as the Grout Pile, "grout" being a stonecutter's term derived from the same root as "groats," and referring to large blocks quarried from their matrix but not, for whatever reason, wanted further. On a Saturday night in early August 1960, a group of youths from Cambridge, Somerville, and Everett were swimming at the Granite Railway quarry and decided to take the short way back to their car, across the top of the Grout Pile. In the lead was an eighteen-year-old from Everett. His weight caused a large stone on the Pile's highway side to come loose. As it began to slide, one of its neighbors upslope dislodged and struck him from behind. He fell seventy-five feet down the cliff and died almost immediately. Before he was moved, a priest from St. Mary's Church in West Quincy gave him the last rites.

In June of 1962, two more boys — one from Quincy, one from Milton — were killed in the same way: a Grout Pile rock slide carried them down the cliff above the highway. A writer for the Quincy *Patriot Ledger* assigned the Massachusetts Department of Public Works at least partial responsibility, since construction of the expressway had greatly increased the slope of the Pile.

In July 1965, a sixteen-year-old boy from Whitman fell seventy feet down the Pile and broke his back. He had been swimming with friends at the quarries. In December 1973, Quincy police received a call after dark from the parents of two experienced high-school rock climbers, both seventeen, a boy from Randolph and a girl from Belmont. They had gone to the quarries together and hadn't returned. The police arrived at the area with flashlights and found a dog belonging to the girl wandering alongside the highway. They later found the bodies of the boy and girl in a mass of fallen rock underneath the Grout Pile.

All of these kids presumably thought that the crest of the Pile, which is not particularly narrow, was stable enough to cross on foot, since the boulders comprising it weigh, on average, several tons apiece. Their great mass is deceptive, however, since the blocks were piled up haphazardly when there was no cliff underneath them, and have no more inherent stability than a heap of bottle caps piled atop a book stood on edge — even the weight of one or two persons is enough to set the top layer in motion. The result was five deaths in fifteen years.

One would think that a toll like this might have been enough to prompt a serious effort to disassemble the Pile, so that it would carry no more kids over the cliff, a very costly mode of demolition. I don't know if any such effort was made, but it would not have been easy. Blasting the Pile, for instance, would risk tumbling it down on a road that carries a large portion of Boston's commuters to work. The more elegant and dangerous option — dangerous, that is, to those performing it — would be to bring in a crane, strap up the boulders, and lift them away one by one. But since the Pile lies atop a wall that has a pit 350 feet deep on one side and the delicate raised bed of an expressway on the other, it would be no simple matter to find a good base for the crane.

While blood and grief repeatedly pooled underneath the cliff by the highway, the pits on the reverse side of the Grout Pile were doing their own thriving business in corpses. Late in August 1963, three stonecutters from Lowell who held regular jobs at a Chelmsford quarry were at work at the bottom of Swingle's, having been hired for the day by a new owner who had begun some small-scale weekend quarrying. For reasons not clear in newspaper accounts, a charge was detonated near the pit's rim, and it apparently loosened a large mass of rock. This rock plunged down and crushed two of the men instantly; the third, who saw it coming, escaped by diving into a crevice. The owner called the event "a work of nature."

These deaths ended Swingle's career as a quarry. Records on the number of cutters killed inside it are scarce, although in 1939 the *Patriot Ledger* reported that Swingle's and its neighbors had taken eighteen lives in the ten years preceding. In 1983 a member of the Swingle family, which operated the pit from 1902 to 1954, told an interviewer that it had become unprofitable toward midcentury and may have had to shut down even if Route 128's engineers hadn't paved over its cable moorings, since by then the flow of immigrants willing to do the dangerous and low-paying work inside had dried up. Swingle's quarry killed one of these immigrants, a fifty-three-year-old native of Finland, in 1944 when a stone on its rim gave way under his boot, and he fell 250 feet to the bottom.

As the pits were abandoned they began to fill with water, and the water attracted swimmers. On summer weekends in the 1960s dozens of kids gathered at the smaller quarries behind Swingle's. They were notoriously unsafe, however; even those which had filled to the brim, and thus required no long plunges, concealed huge tangles of rusted cable and other debris, sometimes just under the surface, and in many of them rafts of old booms floated like toothpicks at various depths. Quincy authorities attempted to make the pits unattractive to swimmers by dyeing their contents a deep, lurid red, so that they resembled clogged drains in a slaughterhouse. Not everyone got the message.

In August 1965, barely a week after the Whitman youth broke his back on the Grout Pile, two amateur scuba divers, an eighteen-year-old from East Bridgewater and a fifteen-year-old from Brockton, decided to visit Blue Hills quarry. The following morning the body of the older boy was discovered by a Pembroke fireman and underwater specialist at a depth of 126 feet.

According to the Brockton youth, who survived, the two had completed a pair of shallow dives and were starting up from a third, having taken pictures of each other, when the trouble began. The flashbulbs had dazzled them, and a dark layer near the surface — the red dye — made it difficult to tell which way was up. They may have headed in the wrong direction; at any rate, they hadn't gone far when the older boy got the other's attention and began pointing vigorously at his own mouthpiece, as if it were failing. He then grabbed at his partner's.

Both boys were wearing air vests that could be inflated by yanking a cord. The fifteen-year-old pulled the one on his friend's vest, but nothing happened. The older boy didn't seem able to trigger it either; he had bought it only a day earlier. They began kicking toward what they believed was the surface, sharing the fifteen-year-old's mouthpiece as they went.

Before long the older boy fell behind. On the earlier dives he had seemed to lack buoyancy. Now he panicked and began clawing at his friend. In the confusion the younger boy's weight belt came off and his vest inflated. He began to shoot upward, away from his partner. In an instant they had become separated. Helpless, he looked back and saw the older boy fade into the murk — a paleness dissolving in shadows. It was the last time anyone saw him alive.

Earlier that day the boys, who had five years of scuba experience between them, had stopped at the West Quincy firehouse to ask directions. The firemen told them to stay out of the quarries.

Nobody did much swimming at Swingle's in those years. It had just started to fill; the water was still hundreds of feet below the rim. It was possible, however, to descend to the bottom by climbing down the skidway, an absurdly steep and rough ramp about a dozen feet wide that slopes diagonally across the eastern wall of the pit. Ever since Swingle's became city property, the Quincy Police and Fire departments have found regular and very unenviable employment creeping into the pit to rescue kids who have crawled down the skidway and have been unable — because of injury, fright, or exhaustion — to climb back. In the late fifties and early sixties, when cutting hadn't quite ended and at least one boom was still operable, some of these prisoners were lifted out in a bucket lowered straight down from the rim.

By the early 1970s, rain and an underground spring had brought the water level in Swingle's to a considerable height — higher, certainly, than the ground level just outside, at the foot of the cliff. Early in March 1972, a work crew was doing some blasting for fill nearby. Following one of the explosions, some of the residents of Willard Street, which cuts under Route 128, looked up and saw a wall of water rushing toward them from the direction of the cliff. The blast had cracked Swingle's like a tall glass, and a large portion of its contents was making its exit. Fortunately no one was drowned.

The pit gradually began to refill again. By 1980 the water was high enough to coax swimmers down to some of the steplike ledges on the north side. It lapped the base of these ledges, permitting bathers to clamber out with little difficulty, although it was still sixty or eighty feet below the rim elsewhere. In June of that year a sixteen-year-old boy from Charlestown dived from one of these ledges, cracked his head on a floating timber, and drowned before his friends could retrieve him.

Three years later, in June of 1983, a similar incident set off a year-long string of events that must stand as the most characteristic episode in the troubled afterlife of the quarries. On the twentieth of that month, a warm Monday, some two hundred youths from throughout the Boston area were swimming at Swingle's. One, a seventeen-year-old from Brockton, was dared by his friends to leap off a ledge sixty feet above the water. He did so, and he tipped forward just before he hit, so that his head and chest took much of the impact. He resurfaced, glanced around, swam a couple of strokes, and went down.

Some of his friends were in the water nearby. They reached the spot within seconds, but could find no trace of him. Neither could the Quincy firefighters who searched the quarry from a raft, nor the divers from the underwater rescue team who explored it till sundown. They concluded that the boy had drowned and had most likely gone to the bottom, which was as much as three hundred feet below, and well out of reach.

Quincy officials, perhaps embarrassed that Swingle's, a notorious killer, had been swarming on that afternoon with two hundred adolescents but not a single police officer, decided to make a serious effort to recover the body and destroy the pit's appeal to swimmers. To this end they assembled several heavy-duty pumps, set them up on the rim, and attached them to portable generators. The pumps had a combined capacity of six hundred gallons per minute. The draining began on August 3; the water began dropping at about eight inches per day. Once it was down one hundred feet, much of the quarry's bottom would come within effective range of the divers.

A much larger pump, rated at 2,200 gallons per minute, arrived later in the month. Senator Edward Kennedy arranged for the loan of several more high-powered generators, these coming from the Army's Fort Devens in Ayer. A raft was lowered into the quarry, the pump was hoisted down onto it, and the workmen who made the last adjustments returned to the rim in a cage suspended from a crane. The new pump lived up to its billing, and by early September, three months after the Brockton youth vanished, the water was down 120 feet, more than a third of the total.

Then, at approximately 4 A.M. on the night of the ninth, a huge lens of rock fell away from the wall of the pit, perhaps loosened by the drop in pressure consequent to the draining. This lens, or flake, was later estimated to have measured 70 by 140 feet. It smashed down on the pump, snapped the raft's cables, and sent both pump and raft to the bottom, which was still about two hundred feet under water.

Quincy drew back to reconsider. It had already spent $35,000 of its limited discretionary funds; the pump itself had a value of $27,000. The seventeen-year-old from Brockton was presumably still in the pit. How much more would it take to get him out?

Finances aside, the risks were considerable — another rockfall, for instance, this one smashing men as well as machines, or perhaps a volunteer diver trapped by debris at the bottom.

The winter passed without a decision. Then, in March 1984, Quincy signed a lease agreement with J. F. White Contracting of Newton, a large construction firm. White agreed to drain the quarry, search for the body, and secure the site against trespassers for the next fifteen years. In return it received the right to use the quarry, following the draining, as a dump for clean fill from its excavation sites elsewhere, paying the city $1 to $1.50 per ton. It was anticipated that this dumping would continue until the pit was filled to the brim.

White had the skills and resources to get the water out of Swingle's. In early June, just short of a year after the accident, the Brockton youth's father came to the quarry, signed a liability waiver, and was lowered to the bottom, which was dry except for a puddle four feet in depth. Though he saw more than a dozen smashed cars and trucks scattered inside, he could find no sign of his son. The body was never recovered. It's believed it was buried by the rockfall that demolished the pump. Two weeks later the quarries' next victim was located by divers in a nearby pit: a senior from Hyde Park High in Boston who had walked there from Mattapan with a friend for a swim.

Today Swingle's is as hungry for victims as ever. Though J. F. White Contracting has paid out more than a quarter-million dollars in drainage costs, legal fees, and fence repairs, it has never received all the permits necessary to begin filling the pit, and has yet to deposit a single truckload. In 1985 the commonwealth, in a fit of apparent lunacy, declared that the pit's bottom constituted a wetland, and thus could not be tampered with unless a whole new cadre of officialdom received satisfaction. Quincy's mayor recently remarked that the dumping fee set by the original contract would be reviewed, and that tripling it might result in a handsome return.

While jockeying of this sort continued, J. F. White dispatched its trucks elsewhere, and Swingle's slowly refilled with water. By July 1989, the level had risen to 150 feet below the rim. One morning late in the month, four young men from South Boston visited the quarry to do some recreational drinking. One of them, honoring tradition, took a running leap off the rim. He landed with a re-sounding smack; when he resurfaced he couldn't move his legs, and yelled for help. A companion found the courage to dive in after him. This man was not injured, and he pulled his friend to a ledge.

Before long the rim swarmed once again with firefighters and police officers, some from Quincy, some from the MDC. A few attached grapples, roped themselves around the waist, and started down the skidway with a basket stretcher. Moving cautiously, they alternately hoisted and muscled the injured man up the ramp. It was the first bad accident since a twenty-two-year-old jogger blood-ied the ice in January.

So far as I know, there have been no deaths since, although the water is once again approaching the ledges that will make it attrac-tive to swimmers. In January 1990, police received a report that a child had fallen in; when they got to the scene, close inspection with binoculars revealed that the small, battered figure lying on the ice was in fact a doll strapped to a tricycle. Later that month another prankster enlarged a hole in the fence by pointing a car at it and wedging the throttle open. This car leaped off the rim, smashed through the ice, and has not been seen since.

In those parts of the world floored by limestone rather than granite, pits not unlike Swingle's, though not nearly so large, form naturally as groundwater eats out subsurface caverns and their roofs erode or collapse. Much of our knowledge of prehistory has come out of such pits, since fossil hunters have long recognized that they collect large numbers of passersby, animal or human, who stray too close and fall in; sometimes their bottoms are literally paved with lithified bones. Swingle's acid waters don't favor this kind of preservation, but even so, in the last fifty years the quarry has repeatedly shown that it can catch, kill, and tuck away surface dwellers indefinitely, and it will doubtless continue to do so, be-cause it will be quite a while before remains of this type fill it up.

Thousands of people around Boston know this, and agree that it is regrettable. But since so few feel personally threatened, and since so many whose voices are listened to prefer no solution to a problem rather than any that doesn't strain to accommodate them, there is little sign that the pit will go hungry in the future. It currently takes only a handful of lives per decade, which is apparently well below the threshold of tolerability.

I haven't lost any sleep over this — I'm as blithe as the next guy, and know that few landscapes can be made foolproof. My interest, in addition, is purely casual; no friend or relative of mine has died in the quarries. And yet I can't drive past them on 128 without feeling uncomfortable. It's as though all the curses, howls, and tears they have sponged up over the years have coalesced into a shadow, a persistent smudge. I resent this shadow. It crowds me — it squats atop the Grout Pile like a toad. Why, I want to know, was this piece of earth allowed to become hateful?

You don't have to know the history of the quarries to become aware of this shadow. It is evident almost as soon as you step out of your car. The paths leading to the pits go through woods that are not in fact woods but merely trees that have grown up over a thick impasto of rubble. Frayed and rusty cable ends stick up through their roots. Where the dirt is scuffed away, tiny cracks and rifts open into darkness. You sense immediately that you are on shaky ground, that the surface is not yet finished settling, and may come apart like rotten ice. Maybe this is why the hikers, birdwatchers, and berry pickers so much in evidence in other parts of the Hills are rarely seen near the quarries — it's as if they turn aside before their motives become conscious.

Farther in, more deterrents appear. Rags of torn fencing. Heaps of scarred, out-of-place boulders. Spray paint on exposed rock: BOMB IRAQ NOW. NIGGER HEAVEN.

Since the pits lie, for the most part, on level ground, you don't see them until you are upon them. Then, suddenly, a curious gap in the middle distance becomes a dizzying gulf at your feet. Far below, at the bottom, a lake of cold, green water stares upward, motionless. A whitish scurf of graffiti marks the farthest descents reached by daredevils. Below these, nothing but sheer, naked rock.

Abandoned quarries are not rare in Massachusetts; nearly every town has a few. They are often favorite spots for beer parties and midsummer plunges. In Quincy, however, they seem to have been designed expressly for darker purposes. As if it weren't enough merely to get at the rock, as if the fury for possession entailed, as a matter of course, a deep contempt for the landscape and a secret animus against the future. No one today remembers who originally opened the pits, or where the money went, or even what names they were known by a century ago. But anyone can tell you that they are a good place to avoid. This is advice worth heeding. Most of the kids who vanished into them weren't planning to die.

In the last decade attempts have been made to domesticate the quarries, not by rendering them harmless but by turning them into a park. In 1985 the MDC acquired a twenty-two-acre parcel from Quincy that included several, and subsequently added it to the Blue Hills Reservation, and now official parking areas have been designated, and interpretive signboards put up, and footpaths laid out with painted blazes (these paths wisely give Swingle's and the Grout Pile a wide berth; both are still fenced off, and were not included in the purchase). The area is advertised as an outdoor museum of the granite industry, and is patrolled by the Metropolitan Police. Somehow, though, the ghosts linger. Even the rock climbers at Little Granite Railway quarry (less dangerous than most, since it is not a pit but a cliff carved from a hillside) have not been able to lighten the atmosphere much, despite their easy camaraderie, their brand-name chatter, and their Day-Glo outfits; their favorite ascents are regularly defaced with spray paint, and broken glass still accumulates in every crevice. Inside the decrepit fence around Swingle's is a large boulder with an inset bronze plaque in memory of the Brockton youth who drowned in 1983, and is still presumably at the bottom. The plaque has been repeatedly beaten with stones and fogged with paint. It was not the ghosts who did this, of course. It was their perennial allies, the kids who regard this place as their own and resent attempts to make it any less ugly and terrifying.

On my last visit to the quarries I saw this conservative tendency in action. As usual, it was a dim, wet, leafless, and leached-out day somewhere between summer and winter — the weather is always bad at the quarries — and, true to form, I couldn't leave without stopping at the fence around Swingle's, looking both ways, and ducking through a convenient hole.

I pushed past the oak and birch scrub and emerged on the high western rim of the pit. If one slides a foot within six inches of the edge, it's possible to peer over and see most of the bottom. I had done so, and was examining the slate-colored water, which seemed to me much like an ocean viewed from a jetliner, when a distant and protracted clatter — the gravelly noise of falling stones — echoed up in my face. I looked across at the east wall and saw two tiny figures picking their way down the skidway. They were more than halfway to the bottom. The ramp was full of loose rocks, and despite their extreme care, some were skittering over the edge and, after a long, soundless fall, banging around far below.

*Kids,* I thought, straightening up. While I watched, they separated, one continuing downward and the other, badly spooked, inching up the ramp on his rear. The gap between them increased. They would have had to shout at each other for the noise to reach me. Fortunately most of the stones the retreating one set in motion kicked off the ramp before they laid open his companion's head.

I didn't watch for long. It was of no great interest to me whether one or both of them fell, and merely to wait for it seemed a bit morbid, and an invasion of privacy. I had never seen anyone in the pit before, and I didn't like it much. I turned and slipped out the way I came. Since no item appeared in the papers, I assumed both kids got out safely.

If I were to tear down my house, dig a pit in the basement, then extend this pit to my property lines, and at length sink it several hundred feet into bedrock, no doubt it wouldn't be long before a few neighborhood kids fell down the hole. Holes are interesting places, the deeper the better, and do not make victims by chance; people will flock to them just to peer in. This is essentially what happened at the Quincy end of the Hills — a patch of woods that was once perfectly safe to negotiate on foot was transformed, through a combination of furious industry and woeful neglect, into a deadly playland full of one-way rides. Swingle's, for instance, is sometimes jokingly called "the Grand Canyon of the East," but while the Grand Canyon is celebrated as a magnificent spectacle, and has become a national icon, Swingle's is chained up behind a tattered curtain of wire, rarely emerges except to gulp down adolescents, and is hardly mentioned in polite company. One senses a certain embarrassment — the pit should have been muzzled years ago, of course, but since it was not, and since there is still little political incentive to do so, it has been left to its sole inhabitants, its ghosts — the ones already inside and the ones waiting to enter.

I am not opposed to ghosts. At a place like Swingle's, however, the site of at least a dozen senseless deaths in the last thirty years, they are particularly red-eyed and pathetic, and the surrounding squalor seems merely appropriate. These youthful phantoms, who rise to greet every visitor, need something more than memorial plaques. They will not lie down, I suspect, until the hole is filled and the rockpile disassembled, or they are in some other way quieted. Until that time Swingle's will belong to its victims, and will not succeed as a park, a museum, or whatever.

Perhaps it is no accident that the last potentially dangerous Blue Hills snakebite occurred in the quarries, as if in sympathy with the environs. Early in May 1968, a thirty-four-year-old Quincy woman in sandals was enjoying a stroll through the area with her husband when she felt a sharp prick on her little toe and glimpsed a rusty-looking snake disappearing into the underbrush. The toe subsequently became very painful, and showed the twin punctures typical of pit-viper bites. She was treated with Wyeth polyvalent at Boston City Hospital and experienced no further ill effects. Her husband, incensed at her suffering, called the manager of the Trailside Museum and demanded that they go together to the scene of the crime in order to do justice to the guilty reptile. The manager, though normally averse to snake bashing, agreed to the project, since he hoped to blunt the man's anger and was confident no snake would be in evidence. When they reached the spot, however, they discovered a copperhead lying in plain sight, and the Quincy man, who was an appliance repairman and handy with tools, rapidly tattooed it to a pulp.

Even snakes, it seems, tend to run out of luck at the quarries.

But I see that once again I have left *Crotalus* hanging. My subject, after all, is not so much the changes we have worked on the Hills, but rather what those changes have meant for our hero. Let's welcome him to the twentieth century.

# 19

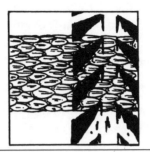

# The Snake Fence

If the whole world were like Bayonne, New Jersey, it wouldn't
bother me.

> — Congressman Barney Frank, then an aide to Boston
> Mayor Kevin White, qualifying his opposition to
> the Southwest Expressway Project (1969)

Every child born in Massachusetts comes from wealth. This is not a
matter of faith but of law, and derives from the ancient juridical
principle that the world and all its creatures belong to mankind. A
local statute currently declares, for instance, that every wild bird,
mammal, reptile, amphibian, and fish living in Massachusetts is the
property of the commonwealth, and since the commonwealth is
nothing else but its people in their political aspect, we see that one
of the privileges of citizenship is a proprietary interest in whatever
swims, creeps, or flies.

The Puritans would have located authority for this claim in
Genesis 1:26, where it is plainly stated; more recently it has become
less clear precisely where the assumption's support resides. As a
practical matter, however, it has gone almost uncontested. And so
every time another rattlesnake is born in the Blue Hills, it crawls
into our pockets.

As any lawyer knows, once a thing is defined as property, it becomes fair game for litigants. Hence the state of Massachusetts, as owner of every free-living *Crotalus* resident within its borders, has long had the standing to defend its interest in rattlers, and in the last few years has begun to do so, annoying many of those who regard venomous snakes as the black sheep of the peaceable kingdom.

This flurry of official activity is the result of a discovery made fairly recently, and now perceived to be rapidly gaining in significance — namely, that if you make a point of killing an animal at every opportunity, or even if you merely squash it inadvertently while going about other business, you may succeed to the extent that it vanishes entirely, not only from your own back yard but from the face of the earth. Once this happens, it doesn't reappear. So be it, one might say, and in *Crotalus*'s case, good riddance. Even so, there is a growing perception that successes of this type have been too prominent lately, and that far from improving the landscapes we regard as our patrimony, they impoverish them.

In the late 1980s two developers, the Ricciardi Company of Quincy and F. D. Rich Incorporated of Boston, proposed to build a $300 million office-hotel-condominium complex called Yankee Heights on a patch of woods on the north side of the Blue Hills. Scheduled to be completed in ten years, it was to have included two hotels, more than three hundred residential units, and 1.3 million square feet of office space. The state's Department of Environmental Affairs allowed construction to begin before the obligatory environmental impact statements had been filed and approved, on condition that certain protective measures already agreed upon in private would be faithfully carried out. One of these measures was a pledge to build a fence separating the project from the abutting Blue Hills Reservation and specifically intended to keep *Crotalus* and *Agkistrodon* (rattlesnakes and copperheads) from crawling out of the woods and into the parking lots, where it was suspected they would run into trouble.

In April 1989, a few months before construction of the first office building was to begin, the commonwealth withdrew its approval and brought Yankee Heights to a halt. In the press release announcing his decision, Environmental Affairs Secretary John

DeVillars cited the developers' failure to "adequately protect endangered species." They had indeed built a fence of the kind envisioned — a chain-link model six hundred yards in length, and shielded along its base with a yard-high strip of snakeproof "filter fabric" (a sort of plastic burlap). They had not, however, extended the fence to cover the entire tract they had cleared. What's more, they had erected it clumsily. In many places the filter fabric did not reach the ground, leaving room for snakes to scoot underneath, and in others the support posts had been set in loose fill, some of which had already washed away, creating additional bottom-edge gaps. Perhaps most important, the developers had not invited the state's snake experts onto the site for consultation while the fence was under construction, and so its defects went unremarked and unchallenged. The result was a structure that superficially resembled the one agreed on, but which was plainly incapable of fulfilling its purpose. According to Secretary DeVillars, Yankee Heights had "charged full speed ahead with little, if any, concern for the environmental agreement we negotiated. That was a mistake, and it's a mistake we plan to correct." He revoked the waiver awarded earlier and prohibited work from resuming until the developers submitted a full environmental impact report. This action had the potential to delay construction for many months. If not reversed, it could easily have derailed the entire project.

Within hours *Crotalus* made headlines for the first time in his history: *$300M Quincy Project Halted to Save Snakes. State Halts $300M Quincy Project, Saying Environmental Vows Broken. Snake Rattles Quincy Office Park Plans. Builder Strikes Back.* The project manager described himself as "shocked" and "seriously aggrieved," and threatened to file suit. An aide to Secretary DeVillars retorted that the commonwealth expected developers to honor their commitments: "You'd better follow the rules and procedures" or "your feet are going to be held to the fire." The snakes themselves withheld comment, and remained out of sight.

Two centuries earlier Vice President John Adams, enjoying his last summer as a farmer before journeying south to succeed Washington as President, had kept tabs on *Crotalus* in Quincy. On July 18, 1796, he informed his diary that his neighbors on Penn's Hill had encountered two rattlers: "One kill'd. The other escaped."

Now these same snakes, having squeaked through the interim, were being wielded like clubs by officials appointed to protect them, and had raised large welts on a pair of major developers. One can't avoid concluding that an epoch had passed and that the local phase of the age-old war with the snakes had closed with a bang. Whatever their future, these rattlers had come in from the cold, and wouldn't be caught friendless again.

What happened? How did a public enemy become a darling child without altering his *modus* in the slightest?

There's a story here, a story I don't have space to tell, about a revolution in attitudes brought on by a wildly successful effort to remake the world. Beginning in about 1875, this revolution began to darken the American myth of abundance with Old World specters of scarcity. It was thanks to its effects that "varmints" became "wildlife," and "progress" became "exploitation" — it's as if we woke from a dream and discovered ourselves surrounded by corpses. The national park system, the Audubon societies, and the U.S. Fish and Wildlife Service were among the results.

By all accounts, *Crotalus* was already a basket case in eastern Massachusetts by the time anyone thought twice about killing him. Several colonial-era writers remarked that he had vanished from most areas. In 1850 he existed in a few scattered pockets; by 1900 these had nearly all vanished, with the exception of the Blue Hills. North of Boston, specimens were collected in Groton in 1870, in Lynn in 1878, and in Ipswich in 1896; the Lynn colony may have persisted into this century but was gone by 1940. It appears to have been the last. In 1933 Dr. Harold Babcock of the Boston Society of Natural History, writing in its *Bulletin*, noted this contemporary scarcity and contrasted it with the prior abundance evident in early town records. He ended his survey with the hope — the first time, so far as I know, that anyone expressed it for *Crotalus* — that "this unique member of our fauna will not eventually go the way of the passenger pigeon."

And so it was up to the Blue Hills population to carry *Crotalus* through the twentieth century in the eastern end of the commonwealth. There were still rattlers to be found in its rugged and comparatively empty western third, but they were becoming rare also, and were too far off to be any help.

Eliot's Blue Hills Reservation (established 1893) could have been expressly designed as a hideout for rattlesnakes. Pine Hill in Quincy excepted, it included nearly the entire six-mile length of the range, and subsequent bequests added more than a thousand acres along its southern rim. These additions ensured that snakes could leave their upland haunts in hot weather and move down to foraging grounds along the Blue Hill River without invading developed areas — a seasonal movement the Puritan farmers had noticed and cursed centuries earlier, when it brought rattlers into their hayfields in July. Only two roads of any consequence crossed the new Reservation, the Randolph Turnpike (now known as Route 28) and Hillside Street, and since both ran north-south and thus paralleled rather than intercepted the likely axis of snake travel, they had the potential to divide the *Crotalus* population but were unlikely to eliminate it.

Although the surrounding towns hadn't paid bounties to snake hunters for half a century at the time of the park's creation, local people were aware that the Hills still concealed a few rattlers. According to Huntoon's *History of Canton* (1893), "The Blue Hills have always been noted as an especial haunt of the snakes, which to this day are sometimes killed in the vicinity." The Reverend Albert K. Teele, reporting from the other side of the ridgeline in 1888 (*History of Milton*), asserted that *Crotalus* "is found at the base of the Hills in stone walls, and about cultivated grounds. In these localities some are killed every year." Substitute "seen" for "killed" in the above sentences, and you get a glimpse of modernity. But these writers don't seem to have anticipated it. They imply that there was still no space for decision between noticing a rattler and killing one.

Huntoon and Teele each devoted several pages to *Crotalus*, unlike most town historians of their day, including dozens of others whose communities had once supported sizable numbers of snakes. The reason, perhaps, is that both men realized that these old-timers had vanished nearly everywhere else, and that their persistence in Canton and Milton had made them hometown celebrities, and worthy of extended treatment. (My godmother remembers driving out of Boston in the thirties with her family and hearing her father say, as they passed the Hills, "There are still rattlesnakes up there," as if this made their heights a little steeper and shaggier.) Edwin M. Bacon, a travel writer who got around mostly on streetcars, explored the Reservation in the 1890s and likewise reflected *Crotalus*'s eleventh-hour turn toward the picturesque. In his *Walks & Rides in the Country Round About Boston* (1898) he adds this note to one of his charming itineraries:

> A shallow cave in the cliff which comes quite near the stream on the northern side, goes by the name of *Rattlesnake Den;* and it is here that the rattlesnake collectors who valued the creatures for their oil used to gather them by the basketful — at least, so runs the legend. But now these serpents are rarely met with, and the lover of nature should not be deterred from seeking this haunt by fear of a disagreeable encounter.

"Disagreeable," he says — not "fatal," "desperate," or "loathsome." Here *Crotalus* can be observed edging a bit closer to legitimacy.

The Blue Hills Reservation wasn't created to give rattlesnakes or any other wildlife a little breathing room around Boston. The Board of Metropolitan Park Commissioners intended, instead, to provide our own species with a large patch of close-at-hand woods wherein we might unkink our cramped souls. But this gesture, though a mere courtesy to us, was a stay of execution for *Crotalus*. It meant that his last and best stronghold in eastern Massachusetts would not be carved up for house lots or shipped away as building stone or smothered under municipal refuse. He had shown that the campaign of extermination so effective elsewhere had been unable to dislodge him from the Hills, and now that it had died down and he was marooned in the suburbs, it looked as though he'd stumbled on his first piece of luck.

The Park Commission appointed landscape architect Charles Eliot Jr., the moving force behind the Reservation, as its initial manager. Two hundred years of fires and indiscriminate cutting had turned the Hills into a desolate thicket of stubs, stumps, and sticks; he got busy re-creating the sort of open, grand, and fully domesticated forest he had admired on a park-hopping tour of England and the Continent. These forests weren't managed for game, timber, or watershed protection but for their appeal to the spirit. And so he set to work suppressing fires, nurturing seedlings, removing deadwood, and laying out the carriage roads and bridle paths he hoped would lure stressed-out Bostonians off their mean streets and into the calming bosom of Nature.

For the next fifty years or so his successors followed his lead. The Hills greened up again. Wealthy abutters enlarged the park through bequests. Thousands of day-trippers climbed Great Blue Hill, swam at Houghton's Pond, skated on the dammed brook at St. Moritz, and swatted golf balls across the course opened at Ponkapoag in 1932. There is no evidence that these activities had much impact on *Crotalus:* at seven thousand acres, the Reservation was apparently roomy enough to accommodate both them and himself. No visitors or park workers were bitten by rattlers, and no program of snake clearance developed.

This is somewhat surprising, considering the level of effort the park's managers put into the landscape in this period, not to mention their no-prisoners approach to undesirables. In 1893, for instance, they hired hunters with dogs to track and kill foxes. In 1907 they opened their half-century war with the gypsy moth, which began with creosote and tanglefoot, and later escalated to lead arsenate and DDT. They thinned the woods aggressively, dragging away and burning snags, deadfalls, and underbrush — activities now recognized as very unfriendly to wildlife. In the meantime they planted two million white pines.

Any rattlesnakes casually encountered during these years were probably killed. In June 1933, a Civilian Conservation Corps camp opened on the back side of Chickatawbut Hill, and several hundred jobless young men moved in and went to work under officers on loan from the Army. They built culverts, bridges, and fieldstone buildings throughout the park, and some of the elegant mortarless stone staircases they added to trails ascending the steeper ledges are still in excellent shape today. That they didn't mind taking time off for snake bashing is apparent in several sepia-tinged photos in the MDC archives that show groups of grinning hunters standing in knee-high scrub oak and holding up what look like scraps of old rubber — none thicker than a fan belt, but all tipped with rattles. If these men had put aside a few weeks every spring for a serious effort to find and empty the remaining *Crotalus* dens, they might easily have succeeded. (The camp closed four years later, in September 1937.)

The first sign that the Park Commission* managers had begun to consider themselves responsible to their nonhuman users came in 1921 when they started varying their plantings with berry shrubs and nut trees, hoping to attract birds and mammals. Two years later they announced that "valuable assistance is being received in feeding the birds in the Blue Hills from members of the Audubon Society." An increasing sophistication became evident in 1935 when a new management plan developed by Arthur A. Shurcliff, the MDC's landscape consultant, overturned many of Eliot's strong-arm tactics. His plan recommended that one quarter of the park's acreage be set aside as "hands-off" areas where no planting or cutting of any kind would occur, and that the strictures against underbrush be relaxed in the remainder, with no clearing to take place within one hundred feet of pond margins, and a greater tolerance to be allowed for thickets of greenbrier, blackberry, and wild grape. Shurcliff also expected the cutters to recognize sixteen different species of native shrubs and low trees, and to leave them alone wherever encountered. Eliot would probably have characterized this plan as an elaborate formula for doing nothing.

This noninterventionist philosophy still has many advocates among ecologists and park managers. It argues that if you want to bring a landscape into a "natural" condition, often the best solution is simply to leave it alone. It is currently the reigning doctrine in the Blue Hills — virtually the only cutting done now involves clearing deadfalls off the trails and maintaining sight lines at road intersections. Eliot's dramatic values have suffered: many of his carriage paths, which he designed to lead viewers from one pleasing prospect or "scene" to the next, are now shut up and roofed over in trees, and most of the high, beetling ledges he liked to expose for effect have sunk into patches of brush.

This trend toward restraint, if it affected *Crotalus* at all, probably helped him — at any rate, it meant fewer men with shovels and peaveys tramping around in the woods. If this was all he had had

---

*merged with the Metropolitan Water and Sewer Board in 1919, and renamed the Metropolitan District Commission, or MDC.

to contend with, he might have recaptured the Hills and returned in the sorts of numbers evident in the early bounty books, when some den sites appear to have sheltered as many as a hundred individuals. Of course this kind of success wouldn't have gone unnoticed, and would probably have been nipped in the bud by assorted snake baggers and vigilantes. Even so, it would at least have remained a possibility. In our time, when *Crotalus* enjoys legal protection and snake massacres have to be furtive affairs, the Blue Hills rattlers might have had an even better opportunity to prosper.

But these are fairy tales. *Crotalus*'s second honeymoon in the Hills was over almost before it began, thanks to a creature Eliot had taken little notice of, but which within ten years of his death was well on its way to becoming one of the dominant facts of American life, the automobile.

Eliot's scheme for getting crowds of beauty-starved urbanites into his forested paradise on weekends and holidays took advantage of a time-tested mode of travel around Boston, the streetcar. Lines already ran south from the city past either end of the Hills: one through West Quincy and another through Readville. At their turn-of-the-century peak, trolley lines were so numerous in eastern Massachusetts that one could ride all the way from Newburyport to Fall River at speeds rarely in excess of 20 mph. Eliot liked streetcars; a line ended at Mattapan, the most direct approach to the Hills; he wanted to extend this line down the grassy median of a broad boulevard that would serve as the main gateway to the Reservation.

By 1906, a decade after his death, his program was complete. The Blue Hills Parkway, a broad and tree-lined promenade, ran across Milton from Mattapan to the park border, and streetcars shuttled up and down tracks laid in its median. At its terminus a gravel drive curved up into the Reservation, where it connected with his network of bridle paths and carriage roads. Other cars ran down Canton Avenue to the base of Great Blue Hill; in good weather dozens of horse carts and buckboards loaded with sightseers creaked sedately through the woods. For a moment it looked as if Eliot's vision was sound, and much of wage-earning Boston appeared willing to divert itself by touring his oasis.

Almost immediately, however, the streetcars withered and died. In 1920 the Blue Hills Parkway line closed for lack of riders; the Canton Avenue branch had already met the same fate. Eliot's successor, writing in the MDC's 1920 *Report,* complained that "very few people as compared with previous years have used the reservation during the past season." He blamed the lack of cheap access. But I wonder if what kept visitors away wasn't the increased cost of the trip, but instead the reduced appeal of the destination.

Eliot's scenic drives had undoubtedly seemed perfectly adequate for their purpose until horseless carriages began tearing them up in clouds of dust. But once this sort of commotion became established, they could hardly offer the quiet, tree-shaded bliss they had been designed for. How many Bostonians packed lunch baskets, put on their best clothes, and rode the cars to the Hills, only to be repeatedly forced onto shoulders and spattered with mud by huge, chattering stinkbugs?

These invaders first appear in the records in 1905, when the park managers discussed banning automobiles from the carriage roads. They decided against it, and three years later they found that the roads, as a result, were deteriorating rapidly. Someone suggested prohibiting the use of tire-mounted chains. This idea also seems to have gone by the boards, and before long the managers capitulated completely: in 1913 they rebuilt the gravel drive leading up from the parkway to accommodate private cars, and in 1921 they asphalted the parkway itself. In the next few years they paved all the main routes in the Hills — Unquity Road, Hillside Street, Randolph Avenue, Wompatuck Road, Chickatawbut Road, and the summit road on Great Blue Hill. In 1928 they cleared and graded a spot at the Chickatawbut overlook in order to install their first specimen of what is perhaps the most characteristic feature of the twentieth-century American landscape, the parking lot.

By these actions the managers confirmed their view that the Hills were not, as Eliot supposed, a tranquil outdoor picture gallery Boston's laboring masses owed to the generosity of Boston's Brahmin elite, but instead an all-purpose playground that Boston's burgeoning middle class had bestowed on itself, and Boston's middle class drove automobiles. If you had one of these machines — and thanks to Henry Ford nearly everyone could hope to get one — an outing to the Hills didn't require a long ride in a streetcar and a dull jog through the woods in an oversize horse cart alongside people you didn't know, and perhaps didn't want to know. No, a trip to the Hills meant only going out to the curb and getting into a glassed-in box that, wherever it went, remained a private extension of one's front parlor. The view from this box was at once privileged, independent, and free-ranging, and Americans soon came to believe that it should be able to go wherever they wanted to go, and if it could not, something ought to be done about it. Today the interstate highway system alone covers a surface area equivalent in size to the state of West Virginia.

If Eliot had known that his winding and picturesque carriage paths would, within thirty years of their construction, become asphalt raceways along which drivers would whiz from Milton to Quincy, or from Quincy to Canton, would he have troubled to build them? They demolished his vision. They chopped his upland temple of Art and Nature into eight or ten irregularly shaped woodlots, and in many instances reduced his carefully framed "scenes" to nothing more than blurs in a windshield. In recent years the park managers, recognizing that heavy through traffic destroys those values the roads were built to showcase, have taken to closing them to cars and motorcycles on nights and weekends. So far as I know, no one has suggested letting them rot in place.

Paved roads, especially roads that receive moderate to heavy use, are hell on rattlesnakes. California *Crotalus* expert Laurence Klauber noted that whenever such a road was put through a canyon or flat in the hills around San Diego, the local rattler population dropped precipitously. *Crotalus* can't fly over a road like a warbler, or dash across it like a blacksnake, or avoid it entirely like a tadpole. He succeeded, as a genetic phenomenon, in a world whose dry surfaces were for the most part hospitable to his deliberate and heavily armed mode of travel. Not that hazards didn't exist — rivers, snow lines, cliffs, seacoasts — but these were major features, and many areas hundreds of square miles in extent were virtually free of them.

Asphalt and concrete heat up and cool off at different rates than soil or humus or the air above them. If a rattler happens onto a sun-warmed pavement after dark, it may purposely linger in order to adjust its temperature upward. A friend of mine who took her high school class on a cross-country bike trip from Oregon to New

Hampshire told me that as they were crossing Wyoming's high plains in early summer, they saw hundreds of small rattlers stretched out like sunbathers along the edge of the road in the first hour or two after daybreak. Behaviors like these make the neighborhood of any paved road dangerous for rattlesnakes, and wherever such roads are particularly common, as in and around greater Boston, snakes that wander can't expect to get far.

There is no solid evidence that the paving of Eliot's carriage roads, and the subsequent increased auto traffic, had any major downsizing effect on the local *Crotalus* population — not because such an effect was unlikely, but because no one was counting. All that can be said now is that as soon as these roads were improved, dead snakes began to turn up on them. In 1928 a new two-lane route, Blue Hill River Road, was built along the steep southern base of the Hills; it connected West Street in Braintree with Hillside Street in Milton. Signs that this road had interrupted a significant snake migration route appeared immediately, in the form of donations to the Boston Society of Natural History (recorded in the society's *Bulletin* for January 1930): "One interesting acquisition was a group of Banded Rattlesnakes and two Copperheads, all killed by automobiles within two days on the new 'River Road' in Milton." It is perhaps notable that New England's chief repository for such gifts, Harvard's Museum of Comparative Zoology, has in the last forty years received no Blue Hills rattlers that were not either shot by policemen or squashed by cars.

But this conversion of Eliot's park into a base for vehicular shortcuts was only a foretaste of what *Crotalus* would have to confront after World War II, when Boston's construction and real estate interests laid claim to the Arabian bonanzas recoverable from an entirely new species of snake hurdle — the limited-access expressway.

Between 1950 and 1970 the Blue Hills Reservation lost approximately one sixth of its total area to expressways, or about one thousand acres in all. These roads did not merely clip off a corner here and there, but headed straight for the wide open spaces in the center of the park, where they spun themselves into two major interchanges.

One would think that highway planners might try to avoid carving up public parkland, especially in the neighborhood of large cities. But this is a recent idea and did not become powerful until the mid-sixties. Up until that time, as a glance at a map of Route 128 will show, planners purposely sought out parks — which they referred to as "vacant land" — as sites for cloverleafs and T-merges, because it was cheaper to seize parks than it was to condemn private property.

The expressways were good business. Setting aside the thousands of construction jobs they provided, they had the ability to jack up real estate values in their vicinity by as much as a factor of twenty, so that if one were privy to the design process and happened to know where the various on-ramps and off-ramps would go, one could quietly string together a few options on the appropriate parcels — a legitimate end in itself, if one meant to get rich.

What's more, the expressways cost almost nothing to build. Thanks to the efforts in Congress of lobbyists for the automotive and highway-construction industries — a highly organized group sometimes known as "the Road Gang" — the federal Highway Act of 1956 ensured that revenues from federal gasoline taxes would not become available for general expenditures, but would be reserved for an account called the Highway Trust Fund. States would be permitted to draw from the fund provided they used the money to build expressways. Once their plans were approved, they would receive ninety cents from the fund for every ten cents they committed themselves. This generous arrangement permitted the states, which had control of the design process, to pump millions into their economies without voting a penny in new taxes. And so the ostensible purpose of road making, to serve transportation needs, became largely irrelevant; the message the Highway Act sent to the states was "Build, build, build."

In 1956, the year the act was passed, Boston's first beltway — also known as Route 128, the Golden Semi-Circle, and later, America's Technology Highway — had already been completed from Beverly on the North Shore through Weston in the western suburbs to Route 138 in Canton on the south. Here it had halted at the edge of the Blue Hills Reservation. To complete its arc and link up with the Southeast Expressway in Quincy, it would have to drive its six lanes approximately five miles east along the southern base of the Hills. The most logical path followed the low-lying bed of the Blue Hill River, where space for subsequent linkups with Route 28 and Interstate 24 was at a maximum. This route would flay a sizable strip from the park and permanently amputate most of its acreage in Canton and Randolph.

Up to this point Route 128 had been largely financed by the state in collaboration with the Boston investment firm of Cabot, Cabot, and Forbes, and the wave of development that had accompanied its construction had made it a huge success. Now that Washington was ready to pick up the tab, the incentive to finish was even greater. All that stood in its way was the sanctity of Eliot's Reservation.

This never became an issue. The dismemberment of the park went forward without the least ripple of opposition or debate. A few squawks surfaced here and there from nearby property owners unhappy with their compensation, but the courts made short work of them. It's as if the inhabitants of the towns around the Blue Hills regarded Route 128 as a force of nature, and the Department of Public Works as destiny itself. At the time, of course, superhighways were a recent invention, and had the advantage of surprise. No fund of painful experience existed to counterbalance the gleaming Tomorrowland visions of their promoters. No one guessed, for instance, that in twenty years many millions of Americans would be spending much of their lives creeping along these epitomes of speed, freedom, and mobility at 10 mph (today highway planners generally admit that expressways do not reduce commuting time, but only lengthen the average distance between home and workplace).

But whatever Route 128 meant for us, it was worse news for *Crotalus*. It was headed right underneath the heart of his domain, the south-facing ledges of the Hills. And unlike the old Blue Hill River Road — which was negotiable, if dangerous — it would wall him off permanently from the gentler terrain to the south. He would have nothing left but the hilltops.

As it happened, *Crotalus* succeeded in holding up Route 128 longer than any human opponents did. The architects had placed one of their on-ramps across a ledge that sheltered the largest remaining snake den in the park (the same mentioned by Edwin Bacon earlier in this chapter), and when the crews began blasting it, and learned what was lurking underneath, they refused to continue unless they were provided with knee-high leather boots. The state brought in Larry White, a snake man from the Boston Museum of Science, and with the aid of several live specimens he persuaded them that *Crotalus* neither flies through the air nor springs out of treetops nor is even easily moved to take offense. The men reconsidered, and blew up the ledge without incident. (This was the last time, I believe, that rattlers were killed en masse in the Hills.)

By 1967, a decade later, the freeways had completed their triumph. Boston's beltway cradled the Hills at the bottom of its curve. Interstates 95 and 93, not to mention state routes 138, 28, 24, and 37, had all been spliced into it either within the park or on its borders. The valley of the once-remote Blue Hill River displayed a curious layered effect — at its bottom the stream itself, choked with silt and streaked with half-rotted hanks of gently undulating litter, switched back and forth through culverts under the expressway. On its north bank the roughening macadam of the forty-year-old Blue Hill River Road lay chopped into snippets and was slowly yielding to weeds. High above both, behind guard rails and atop twin embankments, the beast that had squashed them thundered by, tossing off Styrofoam, dead possums, stinking breezes, and an occasional wreck.

Surprisingly, Route 128 didn't remove *Crotalus* from the Hills, though it greatly reduced his home turf. Maybe the expressway was too noisy to attract and kill many snakes, once the ones that normally migrated across its path had vanished. Its chief victim appears to have been the park's herd of white-tailed deer, which numbered about twenty in the early sixties. Walled inside the beltway, and perhaps panicked by a feeling of encirclement, it disintegrated — those animals which didn't escape to the south were probably killed by cars.

In the meantime the state Department of Public Works, anxious to engorge itself further on federal gas-tax millions, announced plans for three additional beltways. Route 128 swept out an arc about ten miles from downtown; the new roads would occupy similar curves with radii of five, fifteen, and twenty miles respectively, and would be connected by a half-dozen spokelike arterials. Considering that urban freeways often form impassable barricades at least fifty yards across, and that a simple cloverleaf interchange can be as much as a mile in diameter, it is evident that the highway planners intended to transform metropolitan Boston into a sort of detritus occupying the interstices between expressways.

Most of these roads were never built. They were brought to bay and eventually overwhelmed by a wave of popular disgust. Congressman Thomas P. O'Neill was the first prominent Boston-area official to join this groundswell. In May 1967 he accompanied several busloads of protestors to the offices of Washington's Bureau of Public Roads, where he described the proposed Inner Beltway as "a China Wall dislocating 7,000 people just to save someone in New Hampshire twenty minutes on his way to the South Shore."*

For the next two years "Tip" O'Neill's point of view gathered strength, adding Senator Edward Kennedy and Boston Mayor Kevin White to its supporters. But the road builders kept their grip on the governor's office, the state legislature, and the *Boston Globe,* and were able to continue seizing land and bulldozing it until early 1970, when a special task force headed by MIT political scientist Alan Altshuler and appointed by Governor Frank Sargent released the results of its investigation of the freeway design process. This report minced no words. It called the state DPW's highway-approval methods rigid, insensitive, and politically and environmentally irresponsible, and declared that they were driven not by public needs, nor even by a rational approach to cement pouring, but solely by a rapidly worsening addiction to "ten-cent dollars" from Washington. "To be blunt," the report stated, "we perceive a great mindless system charging ahead."

This was the coup de grâce for the Inner Beltway, and the last leeches soon began dropping off its corpse. The *Globe,* which eight weeks earlier had blasted Mayor White for his support of a moratorium on highway construction inside 128, publicly confessed its errors and reversed its stance. Governor Sargent, who in a former incarnation as highway commissioner had convinced the legislature to kill local vetoes against interstates, now ordered a freeze on property taking by the DPW. Of the three beltways in the works,

---

*The Inner Beltway, an eight-lane racetrack barely five miles in diameter, was scheduled to displace 1,300 households and demolish 300 homes on its circuit through Cambridge, Brookline, Boston, Charlestown, and Somerville.

only the outermost one, Route 495, was eventually allowed to go forward. The reprieve came too late for Roxbury, however, which lay in the path of the proposed Southwest Expressway (meant to extend Interstate 95 from 128 to the Inner Beltway) — here 326 families had already been moved out, and their homes turned to rubble.

There is a monument to this struggle, a monument that, unlike the swath bulldozed through Roxbury, has never been obscured by new construction. It lies just north of the junction of Interstate 95 and Route 128, and consists of a pair of abandoned three-lane roadbeds extending several hundred yards toward Boston, together with their associated ramps. These lanes, which were built when the Southwest Expressway was still gathering momentum, were never opened to traffic and today peter out in the maple swamps alongside the Neponset River. Bittersweet and grapevines are creeping out from their edges, and the open fields on their shoulders are growing up in red cedar and sumac. Now traveled mostly by feral cats, cottontails, garter snakes, and caterpillars, they have become a neighborhood magnet for casual strollers, none of whom — in contrast to the sightseers on 128 — are eager to be anywhere else.

I won't argue that 128 should never have been built. But it's worth noting that the highway planners prophesied widespread misery and stagnation unless all three additional beltways were completed as designed. And yet after two of the three were defeated, Massachusetts enjoyed one of the greatest economic booms in its history.

The massive insult dealt to the Blue Hills Reservation (and *Crotalus*) by Route 128 would have been strictly illegal today. During the 1960s and 1970s state and federal laws were passed to protect the integrity of public parklands, and these statutes have stood up in court. Nowadays would-be freeway builders are expected to steer clear of such areas and to push their roads through private property — property that tends to receive real-world compensation. The good old days appear to be over, the days when road builders sweet-talked legislatures into parting with public treasures for next to nothing.

Interestingly enough, although the 1956 Highway Act was lavish in its support of new expressways, it provided no funds whatsoever for their upkeep, and now the states are scrambling to find money to maintain the roads they already have. The biggest highway scheme currently on tap in Massachusetts is the multibillion-dollar Central Artery Project, which is intended to repair the damage wreaked by Interstate 93 when it slithered along Boston's waterfront at treetop level. This road, it is hoped, can be sunk underground, so that the city can become reacquainted with its famous harbor.

*Crotalus* emerged from the road-building spree in worse shape than ever. The only place where he was vulnerable in eastern Massachusetts was the Blue Hills; here 128 went straight for his throat. Today, thirty-five years later, perhaps the most surprising aspect of this trauma is that he survived it at all, since it carved his domain into four distinct pieces, only one of which, so far as I know, still supports rattlers.

But if he had never seen superhighways before, he had several thousand years' experience with the trend they represented — namely, the wholesale reworking of landscapes by human agency. For the last three hundred he had been actively persecuted as an enemy of peace and good order, and only his fugitive nature, abetted by the stubborn crust of the Hills, saved him from extermination. Now, however, he was about to become a sort of totem or guardian spirit, and would be granted a dignity and afforded a degree of respect he hadn't enjoyed since the heyday of the Massachuset Indians. His crimes, such as they were, would seem less important, and attention would turn toward his rarity. Anxious well-wishers would gather at his bedside, some of them with considerable power to affect his fortunes. The novelty of this development wouldn't make it any less pivotal. The war with the snakes lasted fifteen generations; today it is all over but the shouting.

On December 27, 1990, Governor Dukakis signed into law an act making anyone found guilty of killing a rattlesnake subject to a fine of not less than $500, or a term in jail not longer than ninety days, or both. For the second or subsequent conviction the fine is not less than $5,000, and the jail term not more than six months. This act, entered as Chapter 131A of the General Laws, doesn't mention *Crotalus* by name. It is entitled "An Act to Provide Protection for Endangered and Threatened Species." It recognizes both plants and animals, defining the latter as "any member of the animal kingdom including, but not limited to, any mammal, bird, reptile, amphibian, fish, mollusk, crustacean, arthropod, or other invertebrate or any part, product, egg, or offspring or the dead body or any part thereof."

As is evident, this language abandons the old distinction between "good" creatures and "bad" ones, and substitutes a concern for "common" versus "scarce." It associates scarcity with value, and seeks to take control of that value. It surrounds a kernel of guilty knowledge: Species are mortal, and we have proved it too often.

What distinguishes this law from countless others going back to the first white settlement of Massachusetts — laws intended to preserve specific resources in fish, game, or timber — is its quality of ambition, or universality. It marries the ancient idea of conservation to the twentieth-century science of ecology, by recognizing that every species plays a role in the economy of nature and mandating the presumption that each of them benefits us, whether we can show it or not. Hence it works against the idea that some species are more desirable than others; the law says, "Not A or B, but A *and* B." It declares — not as an argument but as a first principle — that all forms of life naturally occurring in Massachusetts embody value, and it arms itself to defend each and every one of them.

It's doubtful that anyone could have passed a law expressly prohibiting rattlesnake killing. And it remains to be seen if state officials will risk the inevitable backlash that must follow any attempted prosecutions for exploits like Officer LeMoine's. *Crotalus* is a special case, even his friends admit that. But the votes were recorded and the language stands: any creature recognized to be in danger of extinction in Massachusetts occupies a special atmosphere, and is shielded by a presumption of inviolability. More important, Chapter 131A allows the commonwealth to designate pieces of land where such creatures occur as "significant habitat," so that any improvements planned for them will be subject to special review, and may even be disallowed. This is the kind of law that makes development and real estate interests sit up and take notice, and can give environmental officials a sting like a rattler's.

Ideally, Chapter 131A will operate like the governor mechanism on an elevator. Once a species, any species, begins to plummet toward oblivion, a switch will be thrown and the brakes will engage. It cannot outlaw extinction — a biological impossibility — but it can perhaps dampen its momentum. Approximately seventy species of animals and plants are known to have disappeared from the commonwealth since the *Mayflower* threw out its anchor, many as a result of our efforts. These losses, whether casual or deliberate, are what Chapter 131A means to stem. Similar laws now exist in many other states; if they succeed, they may reduce wear and tear on the federal Endangered Species Act of 1973, since fewer animals and plants will become so scarce that they trigger its provisions.

There may be, and probably are, certain natives of Massachusetts that are in even worse shape than *Crotalus* and yet don't enjoy the same protections. This is because nobody knows about them; they are rare burrowing beetles, or microscopic snails, or parasites of parasites. In order to add an animal to the endangered list, you have to know not only where it is found but where it is not found — it may be commoner than you think. It is just short of impossible, for instance, to prove that a three-acre marsh harbors no examples of an obscure variety of mosquito, whereas it is easy to determine that the same marsh contains no bald eagles. The result is that the list is tilted toward large, conspicuous beasts like *Crotalus,* and he had already been on it for some years when Chapter 131A became law.

The agency responsible for keeping tabs on the commonwealth's nonhuman inhabitants is its Department of Fisheries, Wildlife, and Environmental Law Enforcement. This office was not always friendly to rattlesnakes. In late 1961, when it was simply known as the Division of Fish and Wildlife, and when its main business was to ensure that the state's sportsmen had enough deer, ducks, and trout to chase after, it published an article in its magazine, *Massachusetts Wildlife,* entitled "Hunting the Mountain Eel." It describes a vintage springtime expedition to a snake den in Berkshire County, the same sort of hunt that put *Crotalus* on the endangered list and which the department is now enjoined to prevent.

Five men went along on the trip, including two local guides and the director of a nearby Audubon sanctuary. In its course they found and captured five rattlers; the Audubon man, Alva Sanborn, planned to display two at his museum and give the rest away. Although the usual stories were exchanged about the good old days when snakes could be collected by the dozen, no one expressed any concern about their current scarcity, and the writer (a Fish and Wildlife man) noticed nothing exceptionable in the guides' stated intent to beat to death any snakes that started to escape into crevices.

Here the contemporary gulf between snake killers and snake champions is still only a hairline crack — the writer, for instance, carries a camera instead of a cherry stick, but holds no brief against snake bashing. He seems to have no inkling that in thirty years he will be required to arrest anyone doing what his companions are doing. By then mountaineers who like to seek out and kill rattlers will know better than to invite the Audubon Society along.

What makes a species endangered? According to Chapter 131A, it is any naturally occurring plant or animal that is at risk of vanishing from Massachusetts in the near future. Thanks to his strongholds in the Alleghenies and the southern Appalachians, *Crotalus*, though declining, is not on the brink of extinction nationwide. But if he is not close to death as a species, he is nonetheless near to it in Massachusetts, since there are only a half-dozen restricted sites where he is still holding out. And so Chapter 131A narrows its view to the commonwealth itself, and rates species solely in regard to their status within its borders — a status that may, as in *Crotalus*'s case, be considerably more tenuous than elsewhere. This limitation is especially likely to come into play for animals and plants for whom Massachusetts lies at the edge of their range. Copperheads (*Agkistrodon*), for instance, are even rarer than *Crotalus* here, and are thus listed as endangered, but they are common enough in the northern suburbs of New York City. Hence one state's endangered species can be another state's picture of health.

And so the Massachusetts endangered list is not a purely biological document, and reflects political boundaries. It legitimates local pride, and says, "We do not so much care what's going on elsewhere. We mean to cherish what we have, and keep it." If, for example, all of New England were included in a single state (a monster that would be less than half the size of Texas or California), it might be hard to argue that *Agkistrodon* belongs on the list, given his numbers in Connecticut. But as it is, the Massachusetts boundary gathers in his northernmost outposts, and entitles him to special consideration as a rarity.

No genuine preservationist sees this tunnel-vision aspect of Chapter 131A as a drawback, since any law that gives a community the means to protect its inhabitants must, from this perspective, be regarded as a plus. Rattlesnakes were once as common as dirt in Massachusetts; they are now only slightly more abundant than dinosaurs; what difference does it make how they're doing in Tennessee or Kentucky? Chapter 131A codifies the admirable principle that the state of the world is a local responsibility.

For the last fifteen years the Massachusetts Department of Fisheries, Wildlife, and Environmental Law Enforcement has been making lists of scarce species, as if in anticipation of a milestone like Chapter 131A. During the 1970s, when it began, much of the impetus for this work came from the Nature Conservancy, a non-profit foundation that subsidized similar inventories in many states. In 1977 the Conservancy's lobbyists helped Colorado to become the first state to put a checkoff on its individual income tax forms, a means by which taxpayers could elect to steer a dollar of their money toward their state's wildlife preservation efforts. Other states followed suit, and today all fifty fund and maintain Natural Heritage programs, agencies that inventory plant and animal populations and make it their business to identify rare species and do whatever is feasible to keep them from vanishing.

In Massachusetts *Crotalus* popped up on these lists as soon as they appeared, since it had long been evident that he was absent from most areas where he was formerly common. In 1978 he was classified as "state rare," meaning he belonged among those unfortunates "quantitatively documented to be declining," "facing extirpation from the commonwealth," and "considered likely to disappear without special action." In 1980, after further study, the department declared that although *Crotalus*'s precise numbers were unknown, he was being reclassified as "endangered," not because his condition had changed, but in order to underline his vulnerability. Today, a decade later, he shares this distinction with three other native reptiles (out of twenty-four in the state, sea turtles excluded): the bog turtle, the Plymouth redbelly turtle, and the copperhead. If by some unforeseen circumstance he begins to recover, he may move to the less critical category of "threatened," and from thence to "special concern," the mildest degree of alert.

*Crotalus* is in similar straits throughout the Northeast. Believed extinct in Maine, Canada, and Rhode Island, he is listed as threatened or endangered in New Hampshire, Vermont, Connecticut, New York, and New Jersey. Pennsylvania is now the only eastern state north of the Mason-Dixon line where he is still fairly widespread, although in recent years hunters have brought in only a hundred or so snakes, on average, to Tioga County's annual rattler roundup — a figure that would be laughed at in Oklahoma. In the Midwest he is almost gone in Nebraska, and rare or marginal in Ohio, Indiana, Minnesota, and Kansas. The range of the swamp-dwelling subspecies, *Crotalus horridus atricaudatus,* also seems to have frayed at its edges; *atricaudatus* is considered endangered in Virginia, threatened in Texas, and scarce enough to merit close watching in Florida. Only in the heart of the South, and in the Ozarks and central Appalachians, does *Crotalus* still lay claim to large contiguous areas.

Perhaps this should be no surprise — after all, a lot has changed in the last two or three hundred years. Some animals have vanished, others have prospered, and a remarkable number have staged comebacks after perilous declines — the beaver, the coyote, the white-tailed deer, and some of the hawks and owls have all successfully invaded suburban and exurban landscapes in areas where they hadn't been seen for generations (the coyote may be a complete newcomer in this respect). In contrast, *Crotalus* seems less able to rebound from setbacks. There is no sign that he has ever reclaimed terrain from which we have ousted him. He appears to be the most chthonian or troglodytic of the large predators. He spreads slowly, likes to stick to his home turf, and doesn't move on when pressured, but instead merely dwindles to nothing. As a result, his range in New England resembles a jigsaw puzzle with all but a handful of pieces missing.

Thanks to information garnered from snake enthusiasts, newspaper files, and local experts, the Massachusetts Natural Heritage

Program now has a fairly detailed and accurate picture of where the state's surviving rattlers can be found. This locality data, which in some instances extends to the feet-and-inches level of den sites, is jealously guarded, since any commercial collector who got hold of it could personally decimate and perhaps even wipe out one or more populations — today it is no easy matter to obtain in any quantity the striking color variants typical of northeastern rattlers, and illicit snake keepers pay healthy prices for them. Recently an official of the program obtained a special exemption from Freedom of Information laws in order to protect this intelligence. Even so, some knowledgeable individuals will not contribute to the inventories, on the theory that *Crotalus*'s best hopes lie with silence and obscurity.

Until the passage of Chapter 131A, the Natural Heritage Program had no custom-made legal instrument to back up its species-protection agenda, and as a result was not always taken seriously. It concentrated on fact gathering, education, and free advice. If the program learned, for instance, that a landowner planned to build a road across a limestone ridge, it might tell him that limestone is scarce in the acid soils of Massachusetts, that his particular chunk of it supported several uncommon wildflowers, and that if he could see fit to reroute the road a hundred yards to one side, he could preserve his property's special character instead of degrading it. If the owner had no particular attachment to his original design, he might consent to the change. It was this advisory role, coupled with its placement of *Crotalus* on the endangered list, that drew the program into the Yankee Heights project.

Like the Codex headquarters, Yankee Heights underscored the long-term impact of Route 128 on the Blue Hills Reservation. By making open land on the park's borders easily accessible to large volumes of traffic, 128 made such areas especially enticing to major employers, and today dozens of six- and eight-story office buildings occupy these formerly out-of-the-way sites — sites rendered doubly tempting by the adjacent "pristine" hillsides (premium window-dressing for perimeter offices). In these areas the Reservation boundaries had a weird polarizing effect: though they preserved an unbroken sweep of greenery on one side, they stimulated an equally heavy growth of structural steel on the other, a growth significantly denser than was typical a mile or two farther out. It was as if the park attracted cement mixers like honeybees.

Yankee Heights was to have occupied one of the last and largest of these marginal tracts, one that had long been ignored because it lay next to Quincy's vast and noisome landfill, and because it was riddled with engineering problems — defunct granite quarries. But in 1987 a judge ordered Quincy to close and cap the landfill because it was polluting streams inside the park (it was also creeping, like a glacier, across the border). At the same time Boston was enjoying what Governor Dukakis, in his bid for the presidency, called the Massachusetts Miracle, a yeasty business expansion fueled by Reagan's high-tech defense budgets. As a result the creators of Yankee Heights, encouraged by their bankers at Chase Manhattan, were able to put together a ten-year, $300 million plan to turn these rubbly, overgrown woods into a 128-acre showpiece of mixed-use development. This was the scheme that hit the front pages when *Crotalus* sank his teeth into it.

At the time Chapter 131A was still being regularly shot down in the legislature, and the new-wave environmentalists at the Natural Heritage Program, though aware that Yankee Heights would further cramp endangered-list veterans *Crotalus* and *Agkistrodon*, did not imagine that they could do much about it. The project would be built as planned, and the role of the program would be restricted to proposing and monitoring "mitigation measures" — design adjustments intended to minimize the impact the project would have on snakes living in the park alongside it. The program had the right to suggest such adjustments because Yankee Heights fell under the provisions of the Massachusetts Environmental Policy Act of 1969. This law required developers whose projects, when completed, would be large enough to exceed certain thresholds — in traffic volume, water and sewer use, and so forth — to submit in advance detailed estimates of the increased burdens that would be imposed on local infrastructures, and to develop a plan for managing these burdens in such a way that they would not unduly strain or degrade local resources. These plans and estimates had to be collected and published by the developers in a final environmental impact report. By law, construction could not begin until the report was approved by appropriate state and local agencies.

In practice, this cumbersome design-and-approval process was almost never completed beforehand, since the state's Environmental Affairs secretary customarily exercised his power to waive the requirement for an early impact report, with the understanding that the developers would submit up-to-date drafts of their plans at every stage, remain within original guidelines, and negotiate suggested adjustments in good faith. In this way the report could go through a number of drafts, and there would be only one final edition, which might not appear until the project was well under way.

As noted before, the waiver of Yankee Heights' environmental impact report was contingent — as they were all contingent — on the fulfillment of certain undertakings agreed to by the developers. One of these undertakings was suggested by the Natural Heritage Program: the building of a stout fence intended to keep snakes and people on their respective sides of the park-development boundary. When this fence was put up in a slipshod, perfunctory manner Jay Copeland, a program staffer, wrote a formal letter to his superiors, pointing out its deficiencies, which were glaring enough to persuade him that the Yankee Heights developers, at least insofar as the Natural Heritage Program's recommendations were concerned, didn't intend to go beyond the most superficial and cosmetic compliance. To Copeland's surprise, the head of his department, Environmental Affairs Secretary John DeVillars, not only shared his misgivings but backed him to the hilt, and chose to raise the developers' snake-consciousness to a shocking new level by revoking their impact-report waiver, thus bringing their entire $300 million snowball to a halt. It was the first time a waiver of this type had been withdrawn.

The page-one treatment this event received in Boston spared the developers the nasty chore of breaking the news to their bankers at Chase Manhattan. At any rate, they knew what the response would be: Fix this now or find another sugar daddy. And so they were forced into the sorts of unseemly postures the Codex Corporation had had to adopt a decade earlier: loud protestations of innocence, assertions of the warmest regard for *Crotalus* and his protectors, and a behind-the-scenes scramble to reassure prospective tenants. Though the developers didn't care to admit there was anything substandard about their ill-fated fence, they offered to rebuild it to order, insisted that some of their best friends were rattlesnakes, and in every respect played the true-blue (though much-abused) Sancho to *Crotalus*'s imperious Quixote. Their performance was so lively and convincing that Secretary DeVillars reinstated their all-important waiver in a matter of weeks. They planned to break ground for their first office building in late 1989, four months away.

They never did. It was at about this time that the Massachusetts Miracle ran out of steam, initiating a fall in real estate values that has not yet hit bottom, though it has reached 30 percent in some markets. Many office and condominium projects finished late in the boom never found tenants, and now stand empty. If *Crotalus* did indeed delay work on Yankee Heights, he probably did its lenders a favor. One of the developers, deep in hock on several schemes much nearer to completion, has since filed for bankruptcy.

All that remains of Yankee Heights is the much-disputed snake fence, the blue-green plastic burlap along its base considerably more decrepit than when it was first deemed inadequate, and a few nearby commercial buildings erected piecemeal on parcels pinched off in the project's early stages: a lumberyard, a produce wholesaler, and an oblong, largely windowless, and somewhat mysterious red-brick bunker belonging to the Motorola Corporation. All three sit on land that until recently served as a functional annex of *Crotalus*'s Blue Hills domain; perhaps Chapter 131A will ensure that they remain isolated. A few bulldozed patches, a few bleaching mountains of grubbed-out stumps, several knee-high and inconspicuous inch-and-a-half-thick steel pipes protruding from low spots and capping test wells — no, there is not much evidence that these ragged woodlands were about to disappear.

Perhaps the most impressive relic of Yankee Heights is its *Final Environmental Impact Report,* released by the developers in early 1990. This massive document, which is about the size and weight of the largest one-volume dictionaries, incorporates the results of extensive surveys of the site conducted by archeologists, hydrologists, traffic engineers, wetlands ecologists, hazardous-waste specialists, and shadow and noise analysts. It probably cost several hundred thousand dollars to produce, and its countless charts, maps, photos, and diagrams constitute a remarkably complete picture of the area — a picture, ironically enough, whose sole purpose was to expedite a massive retouching of its subject. The report wasn't completed until well after Yankee Heights was dead in the water, but most of the research had already been paid for, and perhaps the developers published it in the hope that good times were just around the corner. Maybe it will come in handy if and when they get another crack at empire building.

*Crotalus* and *Agkistrodon*, the beasts over whom this furious rhubarb erupted, never took a direct part in it. Although dozens of consultants, salesmen, inspectors, loan officers, environmentalists, and construction workers tramped back and forth across the site over a period of two years, not one of them, so far as I know, ever encountered a pit viper. Perhaps the developers suspected at times that they were being victimized by a fiction.

Not so long ago, the idea that a major project ought to be delayed in order to pose the least possible inconvenience to rattlesnakes would have been regarded as eccentric, if not bizarre. But in this instance few questioned it. The *Boston Globe* perhaps expressed the majority view by remarking in an editorial that the issue was not so much whether rattlers deserve help but whether environmental rules should be taken seriously by developers — they most certainly should, it declared.

The obvious counterargument, that the state ought to be killing rattlesnakes and not protecting them, found few supporters. The usually outspoken *Boston Herald* (a Rupert Murdoch tabloid) barely hinted at this attitude in an editorial entitled "Snake in the Grass." Instead of finding the Environmental Affairs secretary's action outrageous and decrying grandstanding bureaucrats, it merely rehearsed the facts and asked coyly, "Is there something wrong with this picture?" The only glimmer of outright disgust surfaced in a *Globe* story on wetlands that appeared several months later and quoted a state representative from South Boston, Michael Flaherty. Flaherty, who was fined for partially filling a swamp at his summer place in Plymouth, thought the fine abused his rights, and tried to highlight its unfairness with a comparison to the Yankee Heights decision: "You can see a massive job held up because someone supposedly wants to protect a snake. That's the absurdity of it."

Apparently Flaherty found it incredible that the state could weigh a developer's prerogatives against the needs of a reptile and rule for the latter. But this critters-come-last point of view, which was merely common sense a few years ago, is now so rarely expressed by officeholders that it is almost revolutionary. (Representative Flaherty later voted for Chapter 131A, as did all of his colleagues; it passed 141–0.)

The new-model *Crotalus* — rare, fugitive, isolated, genetically impoverished, and clinging to life in a few rocky, tree-guarded fastnesses — is not easy to hate. Any large, dramatic animal that makes it onto the endangered list quickly becomes an epitome of pathos, and is increasingly difficult to portray without a decorative border of wet hankies (those who live in close contact with it, and who might not like having it around, are necessarily scarce). One might suppose, then, that the time is not far away in Massachusetts when *Crotalus*'s friends will outnumber his enemies, and the ebb of hostilities will allow him to stage a limited comeback.

As the Yankee Heights episode shows, however, the war with the snakes has always had two components: deliberate persecution (very effective, though now on the wane) and incidental destruction, typified in our time by road building, second homes, and suburban sprawl. Whatever relief *Crotalus* has gained from the first, the second is as active as ever. For example, when the Blue Hills became parkland in the late nineteenth century, they were surrounded by hog farms, country estates, old woodlots, maple swamps, and a few compact villages, and these environs made a large contribution to the space available to rattlesnakes. Today most of these areas have been buried under crowded subdivisions, industrial parks, and expressways — features toxic to rattlers. And so the Reservation boundaries have become genuine dividing lines, and *Crotalus* is as effectively walled in behind them as a guppy in a fish tank.

This trial by bulldozer has placed a cap on *Crotalus*'s numbers in the Blue Hills. He has become an islander, and the park is his Elba. It is a commonplace of ecology that a species cannot increase beyond the resources of its environment. And so the pressing question for *Crotalus* in the Hills is whether they are roomy enough, at six thousand–plus acres, to support a viable population.

According to the most knowledgeable observers, there are now about fifty adult rattlers in the park (twice as many as I would have guessed, and a lot more than I've seen in five years of looking). Nobody knows whether it contains enough good habitat to support a larger number, though it's likely that the total has been kept down by den robbers, MDC cops, and other two-legged interlopers. Fifty happens to be a rule-of-thumb figure accepted by wildlife biologists as the minimum number necessary to maintain genetic health in an isolated population of animals, although this is a test-model estimate that assumes random pairing, complete participation in mating, and other ideal conditions that do not often obtain in nature.

All natural populations fluctuate, and their cramped quarters make the Blue Hills rattlers particularly vulnerable to such changes. In the past, any large reduction in numbers and genetic diversity they suffered, because of bad weather, disease, or whatever, might have been at least partially made up by migrations from outside, since the snakes existed as a continuous film over most of eastern Massachusetts. Today that film no longer exists, and any bottlenecks the population has to squeeze through will have permanent straitening effects on its gene pool, effects that may make it less able to respond successfully to further challenges. Rattlesnakes also reproduce slowly. In the North, *Crotalus* females give birth only every third or fourth year, have only eight or ten young, and first-year mortality is high. The result is that the species can't make up losses with any rapidity, and two or three 50 percent reductions in succession could easily bring the Blue Hills population to the point of collapse. Perhaps it was this low reproductive potential, together with their tendency to gather at den sites, that made New England's rattlers vulnerable in the past — water snakes, blacksnakes, and milk snakes were probably slaughtered with equal avidity, but were never routed from large areas, and can be found nearly everywhere today.

Although Massachusetts is the third most densely populated state in the Union, it possesses several sizable forested reserves that might offer *Crotalus* better prospects than the Hills — Douglas State Forest and the Quabbin Reservoir, to name two. But these areas were cleared of rattlers long ago, and even if the will existed to reintroduce them, the know-how does not. A few years ago, in the only attempt of this kind I am aware of, researchers released thirty-odd adult rattlers at a remote den site in Pennsylvania. Most were never seen again, and only three were found the next year — an unimpressive record of adjustment.

It would make more sense, then, to concentrate resources on protecting existing colonies, and Chapter 131A appears to provide a powerful tool for that purpose. But similar legislative tokens of good will did not prevent John Eliot's Ponkapoag Plantation from being overrun by Puritan farmers, or keep Charles Eliot's Blue Hills Reservation out of the path of Route 128. It seems as if laws of this kind invariably go to pieces when they are matched against powerful political or economic forces — Yankee Heights, for instance, was not turned away from the Hills by the Environmental Policy Act, but only obliged to make a few largely symbolic obeisances. In those rare instances in which major outdoor renovations have been blocked, the laws appear to have had little part in it. In the case of the Inner Beltway, for instance, it was the people of metropolitan Boston, operating well ahead of the laws, who ambushed the scheme and killed it.

Staffers at the Natural Heritage Program will admit that *Crotalus*, with or without the help of Chapter 131A, is unlikely to spare the Hills from the next wave of the future, whatever it may be. When an environmental regulation gets in the way of a powerful interest, they recognize that the victory will almost always go to the latter. What they hope for is to become just pesky enough — in the courts, the media, and behind the scenes — to make the interest look for easier prey elsewhere, prey that won't complicate things with a noisy death-of-a-thousand-cuts defense. There is no bread-and-butter constituency for preserving rattlesnakes, and there probably never will be.

It is my hope, of course, that *Crotalus* doesn't disappear from the Hills, or from Massachusetts for that matter. Somehow his continued presence has become important to me — a curiously selective response, considering that the Hills once harbored bears, bobcats, and Algonquins, and yet I can't say that I miss them. But if, as appears likely, the Hills remain green, bushy, and uninhabited, it seems to me that if *Crotalus* belongs anywhere, this is the place. They gain something from him — not wildness, not authenticity, but a flavor of possibility, of fruitful encounter. A snake in the woods is not the same thing as a snake in a laundromat — why pretend otherwise? *Crotalus* gives the Hills a density of texture peculiar to himself. He is not indispensable — very little, it seems, is indispensable — but the argument that the Hills will be better off without him requires clarification. Why is nothing better than something? What use have we got for the space he occupies? In the hundred years of the park's existence, the threat to life and limb he represents has shown itself to be just short of nonexistent. This in itself is something we would never have found out had we had our way with him.

But no one is seriously advocating a renewal of the war with the snakes. Even in those parts of the country where rattlers are still common, primarily rural Texas and the Southwest, snake hating is acquiring the reactionary tone characteristic of old prejudices under siege. The practice of gassing snakes in their dens, for instance, is coming under attack for its environmental side effects. In recent years the festivities at rattler roundups have been somewhat dampened by wildlife activists who set up tables and hand out brochures suggesting that rattlers are not disgusting vermin but valuable neighbors who provide a legitimate source of local pride — their implication being that killing snakes by the thousand may not be the most farsighted way of celebrating this pride. Developments like these cast doubt on the theory that snake-attitudes are always a direct function of snake-numbers, a theory that locks many present-day prairie and desert communities into outlooks typical of New England towns in the seventeenth century, when rattlers were abundant and rattler killing was at once a popular pastime and a civic duty. The conflict now emerging between pro-wildlife viewpoints, strongest in the suburbs of Phoenix and Dallas, and anti-snake folkways based in the thinly populated hinterlands may have a large influence on how many of the dozen-and-a-half southwestern species of *Crotalus* go belly-up on endangered lists.

The snake fence at Yankee Heights was to have sent a message: This far, and no farther. Like the crumbling colonial-era stone walls running through the woods nearby, the fence would have expressed the belief that there is room in the Hills for more than one set of priorities, provided boundaries are respected. It could be argued, however, that if the history of life on earth teaches anything, it is that walls always fail and that future generations will, in each and every instance, couple furiously on their ruins. This argument has implications for our effort, here in Massachusetts, to protect *Crotalus* by sequestering him in a few hilltop retreats. I don't think we've learned all his secrets; I hope to show what I mean.

# Mother of Heroes

you egg
you eyeball
greasy turquoise
flashing SEX . . . SEX . . . SEX . . .
all night long

— Jason Sissick, "Note Found in a
Spacecraft" (1989)

I have a confession to make. Up to now I've pretended that *Crotalus* is the nearest reptilian equivalent to a romantic hero. See his allies fade, I have said; see his enemies surround him; see him battle for his life as his ancient world erupts and shatters. Watch his chief tormentors tie a hood over his face, paint it with their own worst features, and reach for their clubs. See his last retreats crumble underneath him. Join his mourners as they sift through his ashes.

The trouble with this story is not so much that it misrepresents the facts — it does not — but that it makes a dramatic entity, or character, out of a pattern of chromosomes. These patterns, which we call species, are genuine enough, but they are only one level of organization in a hierarchy that stretches from the individual cell to the sum of earthly life. To abstract such a pattern and call it *Crotalus* is one thing; to award that pattern a collective persona, and pretend that it suffers and struggles as a unit, is another. The

Blue Hills rattlers go about their business much as they did during the most recent interglacial, when humans had not yet penetrated America. None is born with a tag reading "Last of My Kind." That the pattern they represent — *Crotalus* — is in deep trouble locally, and has vanished everywhere else for a hundred miles around, doesn't seem to discompose them in the slightest.

No hero can be romantic if he can't feel sorry for himself. This is what *Crotalus* appears unable to do. He is equipped for a certain kind of life; that life, until recently, was a going proposition in Massachusetts; now the scene has changed and he is quietly making his exit.

There is an argument, a human argument, that maintains we ought to be concerned about this. It goes approximately as follows: You lesser beasts had better watch your step — *we'll* decide when you can leave. It recognizes that once patterns combine at the *Crotalus* level, they become unique and irreplaceable — you cannot make a rattlesnake, for instance, out of anything but more rattlesnakes. It looks at the speed at which such patterns are disappearing and shudders to think how empty our grandchildren's world might become, patternwise.

It is this argument, of course, that colors my picture of *Crotalus* and gives him a melancholy cast that is not, strictly speaking, part of his inheritance. In the last twenty years the argument has conquered much of the world, and may soon become part of the equipment of nearly every child fortunate enough to own schoolbooks, or who has access to a TV. I don't say that the argument is *responsible* for my picture — I happen to like rattlesnakes, especially ones living outdoors, and didn't need much excuse to investigate them — but it certainly dampened any wish I might have had (as if I had been born two hundred years earlier) to smash any I came across.

Biologists usually present the ascending order of patterns in a sequence like this:

cell $\rightarrow$ tissue $\rightarrow$ organ $\rightarrow$ organism $\rightarrow$ population $\rightarrow$
species $\rightarrow$ community $\rightarrow$ ecosystem $\rightarrow$ biome $\rightarrow$ biosphere

Each pattern represents an increase in size and complexity over the one preceding it, and this increase buffers each pattern against losses occurring below it. Death, for instance, is very typical and commonplace near the beginning of the sequence, but it becomes rarer and more final toward the end, and it has never succeeded in overtaking the last term. If it did, it would be the second most notable event in our planet's 4.6 billion–year history.

Perhaps it is because we ourselves are a species that we regard the species level as that at which deaths become truly irreversible. Populations, for instance, can and do fade in and out, like the white-tailed deer in the Hills; when a species dies, however, we call it extinct and retire its name forever, being reasonably certain that it will not reappear in its old form.

Students of evolution have shown that species death, or extinction, is going on all the time, and that it is an essential feature of life history. Species are adapted to their environments; as environments change, some species find themselves in the unenviable position of islanders whose islands are washing away, and go under. By the same token new islands (or environments) are appearing all the time, and they almost invariably produce new species.

What alarms so many life historians is not that extinctions are occurring, but that they appear to be occurring at a greater rate than at all but a few times in the past, raising the specter of the sort of wholesale die-offs that ended the reign of the dinosaurs. Do we want, they ask, to exile most of our neighbors to posterity? Exactly how much of our planet's annual increase do we mean to funnel into people making? It isn't necessary to conjure up ecological armageddons in order to show that such questions are serious. They involve choosing among futures, and some of these futures are already with us in the form of collapsing international fisheries, rich grasslands gnawed and trampled into deserts, forests skeletonized by wind-borne acids, and so forth. And so high rates of extinction are seen as a symptom of major problems in the way our species operates — problems that may, if we're not careful, be solved for us. A new word has appeared to define the value most threatened by these overheated rates: biodiversity. As species disappear, biodiversity declines and our planet's not-quite-limitless fund of native complexities, so it is argued, declines with it.

There's no denying that the process described above is indeed occurring. Human beings tend to change environments, and when they do, species vanish. It's somewhat ironic, for instance, that the

Puritans became famous for their efforts to discipline sexuality, since they indulged Massachusetts in an orgy of ecological licentiousness. They introduced dozens of microbes, weeds, and pests foreign to the region, some of which played havoc with the natives. Human beings tend to travel everywhere and to bring their cats, rats, and fleas with them, so that hardly any environment is truly isolated today, and creatures that evolved in such environments have paid a high price: of the 117 species of birds that have become extinct in the last three hundred years, for example, 106 were residents of remote islands.

Since extinction is a particularly final and comprehensive form of death, species preservation and its corollary, habitat protection, are now seen as the most important means available to stem the erosion of biodiversity. So far so good, but I wonder if these ideas, by concentrating attention on diversity at the species level, fail to give an adequate picture of recent biological history. If biodiversity is regarded as the chief measure of a landscape's richness, then the American continents reached their peak of splendor on the day after the first Siberian spearmen arrived, and have been deteriorating ever since. More recent developments, such as the domestication of maize, the rise of civilizations in Mexico and Peru, and the passage of the U.S. Bill of Rights, are neutral at best, and are essentially invisible, because they are the work of a single species, a species no more or less weighty than any other, and which was already present at the start of the interval. But what kind of yardstick matches a handful of skin-clad hunters against Chicago, Los Angeles, and Caracas, and finds one group no more "diverse" than the other?

There is, I think, a considerable amount of pessimism, if not misanthropy, built into this species-based notion of diversity. Nearly all change, on its scale, is change for the worse, especially human-mediated change. Change involves stress, and stress causes extinctions — each extinction is another pock in the skin of an Edenic original. This original is frozen in time; more often than not, it is defined as the blissful instant just prior to the arrival of the first human being. In fact, the only way to re-create this instant and restore biodiversity to its greatest possible richness would be to arrange for every human being on earth to drop dead tomorrow.

This is not to say that cities are better than coral reefs, nor that binary codes are an improvement on genetic ones, but only that "biodiversity" cannot adequately account for the phenomenon of *Homo sapiens*. And if it cannot do that, how much can it tell us about the last ten thousand years?

Maybe it's time to give up the notion of human beings as all-but-inevitable intruders, tramplers, and destroyers. We are all of these, there's no doubt about it, but they are not all we are. And yet the same mindset that interprets human history as little more than a string of increasingly lurid ecological crimes also insists that our species, and our species alone, represents the last, best hope of "saving" the planet. Is it any wonder that the future looks bleak?

Here we have the essential Puritan outlook disguised as science: man, the sinner, occupies center stage and cannot move a muscle without risking the direst consequences in a cosmic drama. At stake is the fate of the world; thousands of innocents (other species) rely on his shaky powers of foresight. One false step — and his fathers, as he knows, have taken almost nothing but false steps — and his dwelling place may be mutilated beyond redemption.

Where this outlook is realistic is in its recognition that our species is different in kind from all others, as any visitor from outer space would admit; where it is obnoxious is in the limits it places on the organic experiment. Human consciousness — in the form of Bach chorales, three-masted schooners, and microwave communications — cannot, in this view, contribute to biodiversity except by staying as far out of the picture as possible, so as to avoid tainting still-intact landscapes with unnatural influences. The possibility that items like those listed above might represent positive contributions to biotic richness — that they might, just as much as any rain-forest orchid, embody the special genius of this planet — is never admitted. Somehow an agreement has been reached to exclude whatever is human from the sum of "biodiversity," as if the *Apollo* moon landings, for example, do not represent an astonishing breakthrough *in strictly biological terms*.

This view has a certain legitimacy as long as its definition of diversity is narrowly chromosomal, or species-based. Those environments richest in species, the tropical forests and the shallow warm-water seas, are from its perspective the most diverse and complex. But I would argue that this definition, though accurate enough for most of the history of life, became obsolete about a half million years ago, when *H. sapiens* entered the scene. This creature released organic change from its age-old dependence on genetic recombination and harnessed it to new energies: culture, symbolic language, and imagination. As is becoming more and more evident, nothing has been the same since.

It is the reluctance to acknowledge this fact that has given ecologists, biologists, and environmentalists such fits trying to introduce our species into their models of the natural world. These models are based on the idea of balance, or equilibrium, wherein each variety of plant or animal plays a limited, genetically prescribed role in the cycling of materials and energy. The roles are not absolutely fixed — natural selection, by sorting and re-sorting chromosomes, can adapt lines of descent to new ones — but change, by and large, is assumed to be gradual, and millions of years can pass without any notable restructuring of communities.

Human beings, unlike rattlesnakes, cannot be worked into such models. You cannot look at a human being and predict what he will eat or where he will live or how many of his children a given landscape will support. If he inhabits a forest, he may burn it down and raise vegetables, flood it and plant rice, or sell it to a pulp-and-paper manufacturer. There's no telling what he might think of; the life his parents led is not a reliable blueprint, but merely a box with a thousand exits. Moralists in search of instructive contrasts will sometimes idealize primitive societies, claiming that they deliberately live "in balance" with their environments, but these examples don't stand up to scrutiny. The Massachuset, for instance, though sometimes presented as sterling conservationists, were the descendants of hunters who appear to have pursued a whole constellation of Ice Age mammals to extinction (including several species of horses). When, in historical times, they were offered metal fishhooks, knives, and firearms, they didn't say, "Thanks, but we prefer rock chipping."

The revelation that we are not like other creatures in certain crucial respects is an ancient one, and may be nearly as old as mankind. It probably contributed to the idea, central to several major religions, that we inhabit a sort of permanent exile. Until recently, however, it was still possible to imagine ourselves as encompassed, if not entirely contained, in landscapes dominated by nonhuman forces — weather, infectious illness, growing seasons, light and darkness, and so forth. This is no longer so. Today most human beings live in artificial wildernesses called cities, and don't raise the food they eat or know where the water they drink fell as rain. A sort of vertigo has set in, a feeling that a rhythm has been upset, and that there soon will be nothing left of the worlds that made us. The nineteenth-century conservation movement, which sought to preserve landscapes largely for aesthetic reasons, has become absorbed in the twentieth-century environmental movement, which insists that more is at stake than postcard views. We are, it argues, near to overstressing the carrying capacity of our planet's natural systems, systems whose importance to us will become very obvious when they begin to wobble and fail.

These are not empty warnings. There is no question but that human communities can and occasionally do self-destruct by outstripping their resource bases. Historical examples include the Easter Islanders, the lowland Mayans, and some of the classical-era cities of Syria and North Africa. But if we set aside the equilibrium-based models of the ecologists and do not limit ourselves to species-bound notions of diversity — in other words, if we seek to include mankind in the landscape of nature rather than make him an outcast — what sort of picture do we get of the phenomenon of life?

The difference between life and nonlife, according to the biologists, is a matter of degree. A glass of sea water, for instance, contains many of the same materials as a rattlesnake does. What makes one alive and the other not are the varying chemical pathways those materials follow. In the glass of water there are few internal boundaries, and gases diffuse freely across its surface. In the rattlesnake, by contrast, a much more complex array of reactions is in progress, reactions that maintain certain molecular energy potentials in an oddly elevated state, even though the snake as a whole shows a net loss. In other words, both the snake and the glass of water cycle energy, but in the snake the energy goes to support a level of complexity not present in the water.

Perhaps the snake is more like a candle flame — both burn energy, and that burning keeps certain patterns intact. The snake, like the candle, can burn out. But although you can relight the candle, you cannot relight the snake. It is too delicately tuned, too dependent on various internal continuities.

As useful as these distinctions are, they tend to blur under increased magnification. A virus, for instance, is more snakelike than flamelike, since the energy and materials it draws from its surroundings reappear, not primarily as heat, light, and simple oxides, but as viral protein and DNA, complex substances that the flame cannot construct but only disassemble. And yet most students agree that viruses are not alive, since they cannot build these substances without the aid of the machineries inside a living cell. A certain level of independence is necessary, for living things, according to this definition, not only must transform simple compounds into more varied and characteristic ones, but must be able to do so in an atmosphere of nonlife.

I won't belabor these niceties further. My point is that life, for the biologists, is an uphill or retrograde process. It adds order and complexity to environments whose overall tendency is toward diffusion and disorder. It captures energies released by decay and exploits them for growth and rebirth. It is startlingly anomalous in this respect: so far as we know, it occurs nowhere but on the surface of this planet, and even here its appearance seems to have been a one-time-only event; though many lifelike substances have been produced inside sterile glassware, none has ever quickened into veritable beasthood.

*Crotalus* and *Homo sapiens* are among the most recent products of this incessant tumult, with its paradoxical ability to swim upstream against time and produce sharper patterns from celestial silts. Despite his complex organic toxins, *Crotalus* was not so different from his predecessors. If, however, we believe that all life — in contrast to rocks and gases — shares a certain quality of sensitivity, or self-awareness, then *Homo sapiens* was an astonishing and wholly unpredictable leap forward in this respect, since he manifested an idea of personhood never before achieved. The exact moment of this discovery is of course problematic, as are most events in evolution, but I would date it from an early summer about sixty thousand years ago, when a group of Neanderthals living in a cave near Shanidar in present-day Iraq lost one of their members, dug a grave for him, placed his body inside, and covered it with yarrow blossoms, cornflowers, hyacinths, and mallows. Here, in the first instance known to history, a group of living creatures betrayed an awareness that creatureliness is a pose, a pose that can't be held forever.

The poignancy of this moment would not impress *Crotalus*. Though it is startling to consider, all the evidence suggests that most of life history unfolded unobserved, so to speak. I would bet that the dinosaurs, for instance, did not know that they were reptiles, or that they had faces like their neighbors, or that they once hatched from eggs like their offspring.

Consciousness. Mind. Insight. Here are qualities that, if not exclusively human, seem appallingly rudimentary elsewhere. Primitive peoples distributed them throughout their worlds; we moderns hold to stricter standards of evidence. Does a cloud yearn to drop rain? Is a seed eager to sprout?

The irruption of thoughtfulness our species represents is not inexplicable in Darwinian terms. Once our apelike and erect ancestors began using weapons, hunting large animals, and sharing the spoils, the ability to develop plans and communicate them acquired considerable survival value, and was genetically enhanced. This ability, and the tripling in brain weight that accompanied it, turned out to be one of the most revolutionary experiments in the history of gene sorting. It was as if Nature, after wearing out several billion years tossing off new creatures like nutshells, looked up to see that one had come back, and was eyeing her strangely.

The distance between that moment and today is barely a hiccup, geologically speaking. We are genetically almost indistinguishable from these bear roasters and mammoth stickers. But the world is a different place now. It's hardly recognizable. Grad students in ecology, for instance, are expected to do a certain amount of "field-work"; nowadays many of them have to travel hundreds and even thousands of miles before they consider themselves far enough from classrooms to be in the "field."

It is plain that our planet contained vast opportunities for a creature willing to consciously shape it toward his ends. The way was clear; there is still no indication that any other species has divined what we've been up to, or has a mind to object. What seems simple to us is far beyond them. It's almost as if we move so fast that we are invisible, and they are still trying to pretend, without much success, that the world is the same as it was before we arrived.

This speed on the uptake appears to be the chief advantage cultural adaptation possesses over the genetic variety. When human beings encounter new circumstances, it is rarely a question of which individuals are genetically best suited to adjust to them, so that these individuals may pass on their abilities more successfully and produce subsequent generations better adapted to the new order. No, human beings tend to cut the loop short by noticing the new, puzzling over it, telling their friends, and attempting to find out immediately whether it is edible, combustible, domesticable, or whatever. In this way we develop traditions that are immaterial, so to speak, in that they evolve on a track largely disengaged from the double helix.

This talent for endless jabber and experiment, and the pooling of useful knowledge it makes possible, means that human beings, unlike orangutans or rattlesnakes, do not operate primarily as individuals scattered over a landscape, but as shareholders in a common fund of acquired skills, many of them the work of previous generations. These funds are extraordinarily deep and sophisticated even among the most isolated bands of hunter-gatherers. When, as in recent times, they have included experience accumulated by thousands or even millions of forebears, they have enabled our species to become the most quick-acting agent of change in life history. In fact, it might make sense to think of the human species not as five billion distinct selves, but as five billion nodes in a single matrix, just as the human body is more commonly considered as a unit than as an accumulation of cells.

If life, as noted before, is a paradoxical chemical process by which order arises from disorder, and a movement toward uniformity produces more complex local conditions, then it must be admitted that the human enterprise, though full of disasters for other species, is not outside the main line of development. Equatorial rain forests are probably the most diverse and multifaceted communities of species on earth, but are they more densely stuffed with highly refined codes and labels than, say, the Library of Congress? Long ago certain moths learned to communicate over miles of thick woods by releasing subtle chemicals that prospective mates could detect at levels measured in parts per million. Today a currency broker in Tokyo can pick up a phone and hear accurate copies of sounds vocalized a split-second earlier by a counterpart on the other side of the world. Which system of signals is more sensitive and flexible?

I am concerned, as is obvious, with an image — the image of our species as a vast, featureless mob of yahoos mindlessly trampling this planet's most ancient and delicate harmonies. This image, which is on its way to becoming an article of faith, is not a completely inaccurate description of present conditions in some parts of the world, but it portrays the human presence as a blank, a sort of monolithic disaster, when in fact *Homo sapiens* is the crown of creation, if by creation we mean the explosion of earthly vitality and particularity long ago ignited by a weak solution of amino acids mixing in sunlit waters. Change — dramatic, wholesale change — has always been one of the most reliable constants of this story. To say that the changes we have brought, and will continue to bring, are somehow alien to it and are within a half inch of making its "natural" continuance impossible, displays some contempt, I think, for the forces at work, along with a large dose of inverted pride: who are we to say what's possible and what isn't? Have we already glimpsed the end? Where exactly did things go awry? It's useful to remember that just yesterday our main concern was finding something to eat.

I prefer to look at it differently. I prefer to suppose that we will be here a while, and that such abilities as we have, though unprecedented in certain respects, are not regrettable. The human mind, for instance, could never have set itself the task of relieving snakebite if earlier minds had not learned how to distinguish light from darkness, or coordinate limbs, or identify mates.

Perhaps it is because we have become so expert at interrogating our surroundings that we tremble a little at our own shadows. God has become almost a fugitive. We have disassembled the atom; we have paced off the galaxies; He doesn't figure in our equations. He has dissolved, it seems, into the mysterious order that pervades the universe, an order for which we can hardly conceive an alternative. And so it's easy to see how we might turn away from the cold, dark spaces we've uncovered and toward the terrestrial paradise, a place full of birdsong, clear waters, and sweet odors where we are always, like Columbus, just about to step ashore. Even *Crotalus,* from this perspective, looks like a pleasant traveling companion.

Maybe it would be useful at this point to compare our common birthplace to a fertile hen's egg. Nearly everyone has seen the delicate tracery of blood vessels that begin to spread across the yolk of such an egg within a few hours of laying. Before long a tiny pump starts to twitch rhythmically, and it drives a bright scarlet fluid through these vessels. The egg doesn't know that it's on its way to becoming a chicken. Chickens, for the egg, lie somewhere on the far side of the beginning of time. And yet the egg couldn't be better equipped to make a chicken out of itself.

I would argue that our planet, like an egg, is on a mission of sorts. We don't know what it is, any more than the nascent nerve cells in the egg know why they are forming a network. All we know is that things are changing rapidly and dramatically.

Today a widespread impression exists that many of these changes are for the worse, and represent a fever or virus from which the body of life will emerge crippled and scarred. We look back with longing on a time, only a moment ago, when the human presence barely dimpled the landscape — when the yolk, so to speak, was at its creamiest, and no angry little eye spots signaled an intent to devour everything.

I'm not convinced by this picture. I think it conceals a wish to clip our own wings, out of a mistaken belief that the outlines of earthly perfection are already evident. It has inspired a small army of doomsayers: if we burn the Amazon, we are told, our planet's lungs will give out and we will slowly asphyxiate. Surely we have better, more practical reasons for not burning the Amazon than to stave off universal catastrophe. The more convinced we are that our species is a plague, the more we are obliged to yearn for disasters.

Students of historical psychology have noticed that the end of the world is always at hand. For the Puritan preachers it was to take the form of divine wrath, and they warned that the Wampanoag war was only a foretaste. The Yankees saw it coming in the flood of nineteenth-century immigrants, who meant to drown true

Americanism. Today we are more likely to glimpse it in canned aerosols, poisoned winds, and melting ice caps.

The funny thing is that the end of the world always *is* at hand — the world dies and is reborn on a daily basis. A fertile hen's egg is never today what it was yesterday, or will be tomorrow. Here, it seems to me, is where *Crotalus* earns his claim on our sympathies. It is change that made him, and it is change that will unmake him. He is caught, like us, in a fleshy parenthesis.

At the moment he seems cruelly diminished. We rolled him back like a carpet, then settled in en masse, greatly reducing the space available to him. In Massachusetts, those few islets where he survives may, if time allows, transform him into a different creature, one whose tendency to wander is almost bred out and whose physical isolation might be compounded by reproductive barriers, so that even if other snakes filter back, they may not recognize him as a brother. But this would require hundreds or thousands of generations — lately things have moved a lot quicker.

Maybe, if current trends continue, we'll take responsibility for his bloodlines and make him an artifact. Many scarce species are now more common in zoos than elsewhere, and are being carefully crossed for maximum vigor. How long before most "wild" animals have been similarly manipulated? Here again we see how the natural world is beginning to look less like a Darwinian free-for-all and more like a multinational corporation, with ourselves as the chief planners, enforcers, and profit takers.

It would be foolish to decry this process. Nearly everyone in the environmental debate, from the flintiest champions of growth to the fieriest eco-radicals, agrees that choices should be made and that human beings should make them. Let's acknowledge, they say, that we have arrived. Even if not everything human is admirable, there appear to be no other applicants for the office.

I would say that this coming to terms is the sense in which the confrontation between *Crotalus* and *Homo sapiens* in New England has been most fertile and resonant. Once we knew nothing of each other; today, for better or worse, we have a history. For *Crotalus* that history is written in his pitiful remnants. He took a considerable pounding, and the surviving snakes are perhaps as shy and clandestine as any rattlers in the world. For us the results are more ambiguous. We won the war we shipped in from Europe, but we lost our hunger for victory — in fact, we began to wonder if we should have called off hostilities sooner. *Crotalus,* it became evident, was not quite the thing we had taken him for. He wasn't playing our game. All the names we threw at him didn't distract him in the slightest. He was here and then he wasn't, that was about all we could say. We had merely used him, it seemed, to define ourselves.

And so we have shaped one another, to some extent. This is the usual result of intimate encounters. We began as strangers; we are now comparing our wounds. In the meantime we have made a new world.

# 21

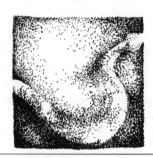

# Midsummer

Summer nights are darker than other nights in the Hills. Sometime around Memorial Day the shadows that have been deepening since late in March pause and become wakeful. For the next four months, until the first frosts tatter the maple swamps, they will shut in the woods like a black ceiling.

This ceiling has a few breaks in it. The largest, which follows Route 128, is strung with twin rows of vapor lamps. A few parking lots, ponds, and ball fields occupy others. Lights cluster at these openings; from the hilltops, which are also bared here and there, the lights look like fireflies half buried in thick grass.

The shadows lean out from the roadsides. Speeding headlights briefly splinter their margins. Up above, where the roads cut canals through the treetops, bats flutter and wheel along narrow lanes hazy with stars.

There's no point in carrying a flashlight into these shadows. The beam lights up a ragged green tube and leaves the rest of the woods twice as black. It's like trying to read a book one letter at a time.

Hardly anyone goes into the Hills at night. The only traffic is along the roads. In the lulls between cars the pavements hold a little light from the sky. They wind their way between the darkened porches of the woods.

If one walks into the woods for any distance after nightfall, one has to leave the light behind, and some nervousness results. Sometimes the nervousness won't go away, and the hushed and fully leafed shadows never lose their resistance, so that the path becomes a tightrope connecting pockets of fear. Sometimes, however, the shadows relax and turn spacious. Then a sort of reversal takes place — one becomes suspicious of light. One hesitates to cross open areas. The night is friendly, and one looks out from its center.

It is a curious feeling to come back to the road at a late hour and find that it, and not the wooded darkness, now seems threatening. It's empty; only an occasional set of lights whizzes by. But one's car, huddled dimly on the shoulder, is a dead giveaway. It says, *Here's where I went in, and here's where, if you're patient, I'll come out.* One tends to hang back, and look the scene over carefully.

It's uncommon to run into anyone after dark in the Hills. The park officially closes at eight; the turnouts are empty and the parking lots gated shut. With the trees in leaf, the trails through the woods are as black as sewers. Maybe this is the attraction. Walking along a path that floats like a phantom, one listens for noises of uncertain provenance — a dry rustle near the ground, water gurgling under rocks. Here, somehow, one's restlessness is held in check. One finds oneself paying attention.

Human beings, as a rule, don't wander around alone in the dark. We tend to gather where there are lights, and where we can make out a strange face. And so the Hills are never emptier than after nightfall. They swell up with secrets; they breathe an odor of intimacy. And one senses, perhaps without much justification, that they are never more alive, and that they contain plenty to see if one only had eyes. This is especially so in midsummer, when their shades are at their lushest.

Much of what we don't know is trivial, of course, and not the less so for not knowing it, but there is another category of the obscure that glows with significance, and that we tremble to explore. These mysteries are personal. They linger as unfinished business. Some of them we inherit, some we merely happen upon, and some we wear ourselves out trying to avoid solving.

I think my fascination with the Hills belongs to the last category. The questions they can answer quickly are the questions I am least concerned with. It is in my interest to suppose that this landscape is richly marbled with secrets. If not, then why do I keep coming back?

The odd thing is that my assessment, though deeply subjective, cannot be described as inaccurate. No satisfactory relief map, for instance, has been made of the Hills. Their geology remains controversial. Their wildlife hasn't been inventoried. The observatory atop Great Blue boasts the longest continuous series of atmospheric readings extant in the United States, but the operators of the snow-making machines just downslope still gamble regularly on cold weather and lose. Nobody knows who lived above most of their numerous cellarholes, or when they were abandoned, or if anyone is buried nearby. Nobody even knows how many squatters hide out there today.

Of course questions do not exist until someone becomes curious. And these ones could hardly be described as pressing. But maybe they are sufficient to show that there is no need to invest in air fares, tour guides, and foreign currencies in order to reach the edge of civilization.

*Crotalus* seems to me to embody the Hills' remarkable ability to conceal and reveal. They are not a Madonna painted on wood, a yellowing document encased in glass, or a pile of moon rocks in a bank vault — they are a landscape, a landscape anyone may look at, walk across, touch, taste, piss on, or scuff up. And so they cannot easily support a mystique; they lie too open to all comers. And yet this missing shield of the ineffable — this exile, so to speak, to ordinary daylight — has not prevented them from sheltering items like *Crotalus*. Thanks to them, he has found a way to hide in plain sight. Hundreds of books have been written about Cape Cod, not a few of them detailing pilgrimages attempted in pursuit of transcendance, but with the exception of Eliot's *Vegetation and Scenery*, no such efforts have centered on the Blue Hills. Somehow, in spite of their considerable mass, they have remained beneath notice.

*Crotalus* is nocturnal in hot weather. This is not so much an observed fact as an inference based on his catlike pupils, his heat-sensing pits, and his taste for furry gnawers. In June, July, and August rattlers are less often seen than in May and September; it is assumed that they hole up underground and go out prowling, if at all, after dark. That's when their prey is most active; that's when they're least likely to be noticed, and when sun-baked rock won't burn their tender bellies. Maybe they poke their way along stone walls, or lie in wait beside springs and seeps. Very little is known about their meal-locating routines.

But if they are rarely seen during the day in these months, they are almost never observed at night. I suspect that this is primarily because there is not enough light to see them by, and so few persons abroad to look. Our species is visually oriented; after dark in a fully leafed forest, when we have little more than our hearing and our all-but-useless noses to keep us informed, we are significantly impaired and apt to become uncomfortable even if there's nothing in particular to be worried about. On sunny summer weekends the Hills welcome thousands of visitors, many of whom can be found wandering through the woods; after dark they are virtually empty.

My own eyes, I have noticed, are optimistic — if there is any light at all, they like to give the impression that they are better than they are. Above treeline in the Hills, where a soft, city-bred glow always fills the night sky, the ledges and boulders remain visible after dark and take on a rounded, puffy appearance not unlike giant marshmallows. It's easy to suppose that these grayish, pillowy forms are indeed what they appear, and not the fractured, angular blocks evident after sunrise.

Down below in the woods, the wider trails look like winding cart paths in fine sand, with perhaps a strip of moss down the middle. This sand and moss are in fact large pebbles and hard-packed dirt, as is evident by the scratching and thudding underfoot. Maybe the trail is not really visible. Maybe what looks like the trail is only a hovering pallor brought out by the duskier tones on each side. The narrower paths, easy to follow in daylight, vanish totally on summer nights. So does most of the knee-high herb layer — sarsaparilla, huckleberry, Solomon's seal. The forest floor often looks as bare as a bedsheet; if you couldn't feel these plants brushing against your legs, you wouldn't suspect their existence.

If a Blue Hills rattler were to crawl out on one of these murky paths after dark, no one approaching on foot would be likely to see it. To be safe this person would have to carry a lantern or flashlight, and keep both it and his eyes on the ground. If no such precautions were taken, and the snake didn't rattle or move, it would probably escape notice unless it was stepped on.

I've never encountered *Crotalus* after dark in the Hills. So far as I know, no one else has either. The only animal frequently seen on the trails is a smaller one, a grayish, bottom-heavy lump first glimpsed as it abandons its exposed position and scrambles frantically for the undergrowth. If you grab one of these lumps, it will fill your hand with a moist, nubbly squirming, and will usually wet it as well with about a teaspoon of cold water — why, I don't know. This creature is, of course, a toad.

Any camping or backpacking guide to the American West or Southwest will warn you not to gather wood after dark or to wander off from your fire without a light. These precautions are prompted by rattlesnakes. Even so, it is extremely rare for a bite to take place under these circumstances. It seems that the snakes avoid accidents too.

The same dangers exist in the Hills. Hilltop beer parties aren't uncommon there at night in the summer months, and one of the fears of snake enthusiasts around Boston is that a lightly shod kid will stumble over a big rattler, and suffer for it. The Massachuset might have blamed such an event on bad karma; we would be more likely to accuse the snake, and respond accordingly.

To my knowledge, no incident of this kind has occurred. But the Hills still belong to *Crotalus,* and if you visit them after dark in the warm months, you must accept his companionship. And if one of the spots where you choose to plant a foot happens to have been chosen earlier by him, then you both may be unlucky.

I don't go to the Hills much after dark anymore. In the summer, when they're at their most fragrant and seductive, it's almost impossible to see anything. And I don't like running into two-legged shadows on the trails — suddenly I'm in a night-patrol sequence from a Vietnam movie, and I don't need the excitement. But my main bugaboo is the rattler who lies in the grayness a step or two up the path, and who declines to become visible. I'm spooked, I suppose. I feel as if I've had my luck, and it won't stand crowding.

On the other hand, bringing a flashlight and using it seems to me not much better than staying home.

Do I begrudge leaving the nighttime Hills to *Crotalus?* Not at all. I'm glad they're still his. Let him go about his business, and I'll go about mine. I doubt I would have gone looking for him if I wasn't convinced he lives in a world not identical to our own — a world we can seek to enter, albeit somewhat blindly. I like it that he has never been particularly eager to show it to me. That's his privilege; it wouldn't be there without him.

# Appendix

(*Crotalus* unless otherwise indicated)

1. *August 1764*   Mary Littlefield   Randolph (then Braintree)

   Mary, age ten, lived just west of present North Main Street, Randolph, on "the hill near the Blue Hill River." The oldest child of Moses and Mary Littlefield, she was bitten while picking blueberries at about eleven A.M. on August 1, "in the foot of her left leg, inside, between the Ankle Bone and the great Cord of the Heel." She was treated by Abel Puffer of Stoughton and recovered quickly.
   — *Massachusetts Gazette and Boston News-Letter,* August 16, 1764
   — Genealogical Card File, Quincy Historical Society ("Littlefield")

2. *July 1791*   Strowbridge (a boy, first name unknown)   Canton

   Strowbridge was bitten on July 27, 1791. Abel Puffer was sent for but the boy died before he arrived.
   — Daniel Huntoon, *History of Canton* (Cambridge, 1893), page 255.

3. *1807*   Polly Billings   Randolph

   Billings was bitten in the Randolph Woods and walked ¾ mile to widow Jerusha Wentworth's house.
   — Huntoon, *History of Canton,* page 255.

4. *Nineteenth century*   Milton

   Two bites remembered by older residents, one of them suffered by an imbecile. Both persons survived.
   — Albert Teele, *History of Milton* (Boston, 1888), page 80.

5. *Circa 1900*  Blue Hills Reservation

Dog killed by a copperhead bite on muzzle.
   — Robert Stanhope, *The Timber Rattlesnake in New England: A Symposium* (Springfield: Western Massachusetts Herpetological Society, 1978), page 29.

6. *May 7, 1968*  Carol Seltzer  West Quincy section, Blue Hills Reservation

Mrs. Seltzer of Quincy, thirty-four, was bitten by what was believed to be a rattlesnake or copperhead on the little toe of her sandaled left foot while walking with her family. She was taken to Quincy City Hospital and later transferred to Boston City Hospital. Her husband subsequently returned to the Reservation and killed a copperhead near the spot.
   — Quincy *Patriot Ledger,* May 8, 1968
   — personal communication, Bob Abrams, Milton

7. *Mid-1970s*  Don Adams  Blue Hills Reservation

Adams, a young naturalist, was bitten on one finger by a copperhead while collecting moths at night in the Reservation. He caught the snake in his butterfly net and brought it to the Boston Museum of Science, where staffer Ralph Lutts saw it and spoke with him.
   — personal communication, Ralph Lutts

8. *1966–1978*  Blue Hills Reservation

A total of three persons suffered copperhead bites in the Reservation during this period. All three were treated and were at home the next day (probably includes numbers 6 and 7, above).
   — Stanhope, *The Timber Rattlesnake* (1978), page 29.

9. *Summer 1981*  a Boy Scout  Blue Hills Reservation

A scoutmaster and his troop arrived at the Trailside Museum after a hike and showed director Ralph Lutts a paper bag with a small snake inside. Lutts told them it was a baby rattler and asked if anyone had been bitten. The scoutmaster said that the snake had struck and missed several times while being caught, and had indeed scratched one of the boys on his finger, but that the boy had hiked for several more hours without feeling any ill effects.
   — personal communication, Ralph Lutts

# Notes

## INTRODUCTION

### pages xi–xii

Herpetologists disagree over whether *Crotalus* ought to be divided into two subspecies, *Crotalus horridus horridus* (the "timber rattlesnake" of the Appalachian uplands) and *Crotalus horridus atricaudatus* (the "canebrake rattlesnake" of the Atlantic and Gulf coastal swamps). For the affirmative, see Christopher H. Brown and Carl H. Ernst, "A Study of Variation in Eastern Timber Rattlesnakes, *Crotalus horridus* Linnae (Serpentes: Viperidae)," *Brimleyana* (September 1986), vol. 12, p. 57. For the negative, see George R. Pisani, Joseph T. Collins, and Stephen R. Edwards, "A Reevaluation of the Subspecies of *Crotalus horridus*," *Transactions of the Kansas Academy of Science* (1973), vol. 75, p. 255.

## 1. YANKEE FROM ATLANTIS

### pages 1–3

For the geology of the Blue Hills, see Newton E. Chute, *Preliminary Report on the Geology of the Blue Hills Quadrangle* (Boston, 1940); and Richard Naylor and Susan Sayer, "The Blue Hills Igneous Complex," in Barry Cameron, ed., *Geology of Southeastern New England* (Princeton, 1976). Chet and Maureen Raymo's *Written in Stone: A Geological History of the Northeastern United States* (Chester, Conn.: Globe Pequot, 1989) is an excellent general account.

## 2. A PROSPECT

### pages 4–6

The epigraph is from L. H. Butterfield, ed., *The Adams Family Correspondence* (Cambridge, 1963), vol. 4, p. 301.

### 3. SNAKE HEAVEN

pages 7–11

The epigraph is from Oliver Wendell Holmes, *Elsie Venner* (Boston, 1861), p. 268.

The details on the town of Stoughton's eighteenth-century bounties are in Daniel T. V. Huntoon, *History of the Town of Canton* (Cambridge: John Wilson, 1893), p. 251.

Infants killed by pet pythons were reported in the *New York Times* on November 10, 1980 (p. 17), August 7, 1984 (sec. 1, p. 14), and August 19, 1984 (sec. 1, p. 34).

Readers interested in *Crotalus*'s diet should consult Howard K. Reinert, David Cundall, and Lauretta M. Bushar, "Foraging Behavior of the Timber Rattlesnake, *Crotalus horridus*," *Copeia* (1984), vol. 4, p. 976.

### 4. AN EXEMPLARY VICTIM

pages 12–17

All Thomas Morton's quotes are from his *New English Canaan* (Amsterdam: Jacob Frederick Stam, 1637). A subsequent edition, edited by Charles Francis Adams (Boston: Prince Society, 1883), has been reprinted as number 2 in the series *American Classics in History and Social Science* (New York: Burt Franklin, 1967).

The best account of Morton's adventures in the New World appears in Charles Francis Adams's *Three Episodes of Massachusetts History* (Boston, 1892).

Henry Adams's description of Quincy on p. 13 comes from *The Education of Henry Adams* (Boston, 1918), p. 14.

### 5. HABEAS CORPUS

pages 18–24

The epigraph is from Robert Lowell's play "Endecott and the Red Cross," in *The Old Glory* (New York: Farrar, 1965), p. 6.

The Quincy *Patriot Ledger* published photos of *Crotalus* on April 20 and 22, 1989.

Charles Breck, Milton treasurer, is quoted in Albert K. Teele's pamphlet "The Blue Hills," privately printed in 1884.

The Palmer, Massachusetts, *Crotalus* bite was reported in *Forest and Stream* (June 1900), vol. 54, p. 463.

The *Crotalus* sighting in Jamestown, Rhode Island, was reported by the Associated Press on May 14, 1955.

## 6. BLACK ARTS

### pages 25–30

The epigraph appears on p. 270 of A. B. Benson's edition of Peter Kalm's *Travels into North America* (New York, 1937), which is based on a translation from the Swedish by John Reinhold Forster (Warrington, England, 1771).

The Francis Parkman quote is from his 1851 history, *The Conspiracy of Pontiac* (Boston, 1878), p. 225.

The Henry Wadsworth Longfellow quote is from his poem "The Courtship of Miles Standish," in *The Courtship of Miles Standish and Other Poems* (Boston, 1858).

The James Fenimore Cooper quote is from his 1851 novel, *The Prairie* (New York, 1954), p. 51.

The Oliver Wendell Holmes quote is from *Elsie Venner* (Boston, 1861), p. 63.

Fur trader Alexander Henry's tale appears in a recent edition of his *Travels and Adventures in Canada and the Indian Territories* (1807), edited by James Bain (Rutland, Vt.: Charles E. Tuttle, 1969), pp. 166–67.

Naturalist William Bartram's *Crotalus* story appears in his *Travels Through North and South Carolina, Georgia, East and West Florida, etc.* (Philadelphia, 1791), and in an abridged version edited by Mark Van Doren (New York, 1928), p. 218.

The Amerindian folkways mentioned on p. 29 are from Laurence Klauber, *Rattlesnakes* (Berkeley, 1956), p. 1118 passim.

## 7. TREE HOUSE

### pages 31–44

The epigraph poem by Henry Lisle comes from Albert K. Teele, *The History of Milton, Massachusetts, 1640–1887* (Boston, 1888), p. 146.

The Codex building sale was reported by the *Boston Globe* on September 2, 1990.

The Charles Eliot quote on p. 34 appears in Charles W. Eliot, *Charles Eliot: Landscape Architect* (Boston: Houghton Mifflin, 1902), p. 341. His forestry plan for the Blue Hills appears in p. 498 passim of the same work.

The details of the gypsy moth and white pine campaigns are from the annual reports published by the Metropolitan Park Commissioners (Boston, 1893–1919) and from the more occasional reports published by the Metropolitan District Commission (Boston, 1920–39, 1947). These reports, especially the ones produced prior to World War I, were meticulously written and edited, and include many maps, photographs, and special supplements. They are by far the best sources for the early history of the Blue Hills Reservation.

For the cumulative effects of lead arsenate, see Robert L. Rudd, *Pesticides and the Living Landscape* (Wisconsin, 1964), pp. 163–64.

The Eliot quotes on p. 42 are from the 1902 biography cited above, p. 657.

## 8. PRIMITIVE WAR

### pages 45–52

The epigraphs are from Jimmy Carter, *An Outdoor Journal* (Toronto, 1988). Elsewhere in the book Carter mentions hearing of several fatal *Crotalus* bites in the Plains, Georgia, area during his lifetime.

The William Bradford quote is from Samuel Eliot Morison, ed., *Of Plymouth Plantation* (New York, 1952), p. 62.

The J. Frank Dobie quote is from his *Rattlesnakes* (Boston, 1952), p. 60.

The Ben Franklin quote is from a letter signed "Americanus" in the *Pennsylvania Gazette* for May 9, 1751. The letter objected to the British practice of dumping English felons in the American colonies, and suggested that the colonists ship back rattlesnakes in return. It was recognized as Franklin's work as early as 1790, when Condorcet did so in an elegy of Franklin delivered to the French Academy of Sciences. A. H. Smyth, ed., *The Writings of Benjamin Franklin* (New York, 1907), vol. 3, p. 46.

The Thomas Jefferson quote is from his June 28, 1793, letter to Governor Henry Lee of Virginia, in which he criticized William Thornton's design for a ceremonial mace to be used in opening and closing sessions of Congress. The design incorporated a rattlesnake. P. L. Ford, ed., *The Writings of Thomas Jefferson* (New York, 1904), vol. 7, p. 413.

The Teddy Roosevelt quote is from his article "Across the Navaho Desert," in *Outlook* (1913), vol. 105, p. 309.

Henry Adams's remark is from a November 26, 1914, letter to his longtime friend Elizabeth Cameron. Worthington Ford, ed., *The Letters of Henry Adams* (Boston: Houghton Mifflin, 1930), vol. 2, p. 628.

James Dickey reported on snake killing in his article "Blowjob on a Rattlesnake," *Esquire* (October 1977), p. 177.

Marjorie Kinnan Rawlings's account of her ophidian experiences appears in Brandt Aylmar, ed., *The Treasury of Snake Lore* (New York, 1956), p. 245ff. John Burroughs's confession is on p. 255 of the same work.

Governor Winthrop, by his own testimony, always carried a match, a compass, and, in the summer months, snakeweed: entry dated October 11, 1631, in John Winthrop, *History of New England (Journal 1630–49)*, edited by J. K. Hosmer (New York: Scribners, 1908), p. 68. The following year, on August 14, 1632, he wrote, "This summer was very wet and cold (except now and then a hot day or two), which caused great store of musketoes and rattle-snakes" (p. 89).

The precolonial Boston Harbor population estimate on p. 51 is based on Francis Jennings, *The Invasion of America: Indians, Colonialism, and the Cant of Conquest* (New York, 1975), pp. 26–30.

For the rapid decline of wildlife around the Blue Hills following coloni-
zation, see Edward Pierce, *A History of Milton* (Milton, 1957), pp. 14, 78.

## 9. JOE BLOW AND JAKE THE SNAKE
### pages 53–60

The epigraph is from Teele's *History of Milton* (1888), p. 625.

The Governor Winthrop quote is from p. 83 of the edition of his *Journal*
cited above.

The *New York Times* piece by Warren Sloat appeared on p. 60 of *The New
York Times Magazine,* January 25, 1987.

Thomas Walduck's 1714 report to the Royal Society on *Crotalus* is included in James R. Masterson, "Colonial Rattlesnake Lore," *Zoologica*
(1938), vol. 23, p. 213.

Cotton Mather's letter to the Royal Society, dated November 27, 1712, is
quoted in Albert Matthews, "Rattlesnake Colonel," *New England Quarterly*
(June 1937), vol. 10, p. 343.

The New York snake-tagging study mentioned on p. 56 is from William
S. Brown and Francis M. MacLean, "Conspecific Scent-trailing by Newborn Timber Rattlesnakes, *Crotalus horridus,*" *Herpetologica* (1983), vol. 39,
no. 4, p. 430. Brown, a professor of biology at Skidmore College, has been
studying wild populations of *Crotalus* in the foothills of the Adirondacks
since 1978. His publications constitute an essential starting point for anyone interested in the current understanding of the natural history of the
species. A partial list follows:

(1982)   William S. Brown, "Overwintering Body Temperatures of Timber Rattlesnakes (*Crotalus horridus*) in Northeastern New York," *Journal
of Herpetology,* vol. 16, no. 2, p. 145.

(1982)   William S. Brown, Donald W. Pyle, Kimberly R. Greene et al.,
"Movements and Temperature Relationships of Timber Rattlesnakes
(*Crotalus horridus*) in Northeastern New York," *Journal of Herpetology,*
vol. 16, no. 2, p. 161.

(1987)   William S. Brown, "Hidden Life of the Timber Rattler,"
*National Geographic* (July 1987), p. 129.

(1991)   William S. Brown, "Female Reproductive Ecology in a Northern
Population of the Timber Rattlesnake, *Crotalus horridus,*" *Herpetologica,*
vol. 47, no. 1, p. 101.

On the 1988 rattler roundup in Sweetwater, Texas, see Marion Bar-
thelme, "Local Spring Rite," *Time,* May 23, 1988.

The best source for colonial-era *Crotalus* bounties in Massachusetts is
H. L. Babcock, "Rattlesnakes in Massachusetts," *Bulletin of the Boston Society
of Natural History* (1925), vol. 35, p. 5. Other sources used here are Samuel
Barrows, "Dorchester in the Provincial Period," in Justin Winsor, *Memorial
History of Boston* (Boston: Ticknor, 1881), vol. 2, p. 362; Huntoon, *History of*

*Canton,* pp. 214, 251–55; and Arthur H. Cole, *Wholesale Commodity Prices in the United States: 1700–1861* (Cambridge, 1938). For the Micmac bounty, see Frank Johnson, "Mending a Broken Tribe," *Boston Globe,* May 30, 1989 (p. 13). For the Tioga County bounties, see John H. Galligan and William A. Dunson, "Biology and Status of Timber Rattlesnake (*Crotalus horridus*) Populations in Pennsylvania," *Biological Conservation* (1979), vol. 15, p. 52. For Vermont bounties, see Ted Levin, *Backtracking: The Way of a Naturalist* (Chelsea, Vt., 1980), pp. 89–90.

## 10. WHY CALVIN GRITH DOESN'T LIVE IN THE WOODS

### pages 61–75

The story of the Frenchman and his wife is told by Edwin M. Bacon, *Walks & Rides in the Country Round About Boston* (Boston: Houghton Mifflin, 1898), p. 353.

For the Center for Juvenile Offenders, see the 1973 *Report* of the Metropolitan District Commission, Boston.

## 11. FAMILY MATTERS

### *The Journey into the Underworld*

### pages 76–85

The epigraph appears in the first edition of Charles Darwin, *The Descent of Man* (London, 1871), vol. 2, p. 29. Since Darwin later expanded his remarks, he dropped it from subsequent editions.

Lamarck's theory of snake origins is quoted in A. Raynaud, "Development of Limbs and Embryonic Limb Reduction," in Carl Gans and Frank Billett, eds., *Biology of the Reptilia* (New York: John Wiley, 1985), vol. 15, p. 127. A discussion, illustrated with micrographs, of the author's studies of embryonic pythons begins on p. 117 of the same work.

For the relation between elongation and limb loss in skinks and other reptiles, see Carl Gans, "Tetrapod Limblessness: Evolution and Functional Corollaries," *American Zoologist* (1975), vol. 15, p. 455.

For the earliest snakes, see Jean-Claude Rage, "Fossil History," in R. A. Seigel et al., eds., *Snakes: Ecology and Evolutionary Biology* (New York: Macmillan, 1987), p. 51.

For the singularity of the serpentine eye, see Gordon Lynn Walls, *The Vertebrate Eye and Its Adaptive Radiation* (New York: Hafner, 1963), p. 627.

### *Eating One's Betters*

### pages 86–91

Good color photographs of the mysterious primitives *Loxocemus* (the Mexican dwarf boa) and *Xenopeltis* (the sunbeam snake) can be found in Chris Mattison, *Snakes of the World* (New York: Facts on File, 1986).

For the possible connection between the advent of flowering plants and the success of warm-blooded vertebrates, see Loren Eiseley, *The Immense Journey* (New York: Random House, 1957), p. 64.

## Becoming an American

### pages 91–98

The pit-organ studies mentioned on p. 96 are from G. K. Noble and A. Schmidt, "The Structure and Function of the Labial Pits of Snakes," *Proceedings of the American Philosophical Society* (1937), vol. 77, p. 263, and T. H. Bullock and R. B. Cowles, "Physiology of an Infrared Receptor: The Facial Pit of Pit Vipers," *Science* (1952), vol. 115, p. 541.

For the putative cold-adapted past of the New World vipers, see Wilfred T. Neill, "Viviparity in Snakes: Some Ecological and Zoogeographical Considerations," *American Zoologist* (1964), vol. 98, p. 35.

## The Belled Viper

### pages 99–109

John Adams's snake-boosting letter to Abigail (May 10, 1777) is in L. H. Butterfield, ed., *The Adams Family Correspondence* (Cambridge, 1963), vol. 2, p. 236.

For the similarities between *Bothrops* and *Trimeresurus*, see Bayard H. Brattstrom, "Evolution of the Pit Vipers," *Transactions of the San Diego Society of Natural History* (1964), vol. 13, p. 187. For prehistoric crotalines, see Brattstrom, "The Fossil Pit Vipers of North America," in the same journal: (1954), vol. 12, p. 31.

Paleontologist J. Alan Holman's detective work is drawn from three of his publications: "A Small Miocene Herpetofauna from Texas," *Quarterly Journal of the Florida Academy of Sciences* (1966), vol. 29, no. 4, p. 272; "Upper Miocene Snakes (Reptilia, Serpentes) from Southeastern Nebraska," *Journal of Herpetology* (1977), vol. 11, no. 3, p. 323; and "A Herpetofauna from an Eastern Extension of the Harrison Formation (Early Miocene: Arikareean), Cherry County, Nebraska," *Journal of Vertebrate Paleontology* (1981), vol. 1, no. 1, p. 49. For an overview of his conclusions, see his "Review of North American Tertiary Snakes," *Publications of the Museum — Michigan State University: Paleontological Series* (1979), vol. 1, no. 6, p. 200.

Charles Darwin describes his antics at the London Zoo's monkey house in *The Descent of Man* (2nd ed., revised and augmented, London, 1877), p. 71.

## 12. A CHANGE OF HEART

### *Incognito*

### pages 110–121

The epigraph is from a collection of Edwards's manuscript sermons edited by John Erskine: Jonathan Edwards, *A History of the Work of Redemption* (New York: American Tract Society, n.d.), p. 416.

The critique on pp. 114–115 is by Samuel H. Scudder and appears in Percy Creed, ed., *Milestones: The Boston Society of Natural History, 1830–1930* (Boston, 1930).

The quote from Thoreau on p. 115 is from his review of Storer's "Reports on the Ichthyology and Herpetology of Massachusetts" in H. D. Thoreau, *Excursions* (Boston, 1893), p. 161.

The main source for Louis Agassiz is Edward Lurie's scrupulous and sophisticated *Louis Agassiz: A Life in Science* (Chicago, 1960) — a wonderful book in every respect.

Allen's "Catalogue" is in the *Proceedings of the Boston Society of Natural History* (1868), vol. 12, p. 171.

Smith's 1835 list of native reptiles is in Edward Hitchcock, *Report on the Geology, Mineralogy, Botany, and Zoology of Massachusetts* (Amherst, 1835).

Storer's 1839 list elaborates on Smith's: D. Humphreys Storer, "Reports on the Ichthyology and Herpetology of Massachusetts," in Storer et al., *Reports on the Fishes, Reptiles, and Birds of Massachusetts* (Boston: Dutton and Wentworth, 1839).

John Josselyn's seventeenth-century list of snakes appears in an edition of his *An Account of Two Voyages to New-England* (London, 1674), edited by Paul J. Lindholdt (Hanover, N.H.: University Press of New England, 1988), pp. 82–83.

For William Forbes, see the Massachusetts Historical Society, *Guide to the Microfilm Edition of the Forbes Papers* (Boston, 1969); and A. S. Pier, *Forbes: Telephone Pioneer* (New York, 1953).

### *Transmutation*

### pages 121–134

Thoreau's complaint on p. 122 is from Dudley Lunt, ed., *The Maine Woods* (New York, 1950), p. 320.

Jeffries Wyman's views on snake swallowing are in the *Proceedings of the Boston Society of Natural History* (1851), vol. 4, p. 69. John Cotton's rebuke can be found on p. 521 of Charles Francis Adams, *Three Episodes of Massachusetts History* (Boston, 1892). For Thomas Hooker's remark, see David Hawke, *The Colonial Experience* (New York: Bobbs-Merrill, 1966), p. 136. Daniel R. Barnes examines other instances of the delusion in "The Bosom Serpent: A Legend in American Literature and Culture," *Journal of American Folklore* (1975), vol. 85, p. 113.

Emerson's pro-*Crotalus* comment on p. 128 is from R. W. Emerson, *Representative Men* (Cambridge, 1903), p. 235.

Agassiz's epithet for *The Origin of Species* — "an ingenious and fanciful theory" — is in the *Proceedings of the Boston Society of Natural History* (1860), vol. 7, p. 231.

Dr. Storer's inaugural specimens (p. 133) are listed in the *Boston Journal of Natural History* (1837), vol. 1, p. 515.

## Elegy

### pages 134–152

The epigraph is from Laurence Klauber, "Classification, Distribution, and Biology of the Venomous Snakes of Northern Mexico, the United States, and Canada," in W. Bucherl and E. Buckley, *Venomous Animals and Their Venoms* (New York, 1971), vol. 2, p. 150.

For James Mulholland's exploit, see Wright and Harvey, *The History of Oakham* (New Haven, 1947), p. 299. For John Hildreth's midwinter snake hunt, see H. L. Babcock, "Rattlesnakes in Massachusetts," *Bulletin of the Boston Society of Natural History* (1925), vol. 35, p. 8. The George Catlin story appears in "Rattlesnakes," *Harper's Weekly,* August 14, 1886 (p. 523).

For the Hopedale experiment, see Ernest S. Wooster, *Communities of the Past and Present* (Wilmington, Del., 1973). Thoreau's comment appears on p. 277 of Witherell, ed., *Thoreau's Journals* (1987).

The tar-baby Berkshire *Crotalus* is described by Wayne Hanley on p. 45 of *The Timber Rattlesnake in New England: A Symposium* (Springfield: Western Massachusetts Herpetological Society, 1978).

Francis Parkman's portrait of *Crotalus* is on p. 248 of his *Conspiracy of Pontiac* (Boston, 1878).

Thoreau's remark on snake killing comes from his *Journals* (entry of April 28, 1857), edited by Torrey and Allen (New York: Dover, 1962). His peaceable encounter with the blacksnake is dated October 10, 1851, in the same edition. The boast on p. 145 is from his essay "Walking." Thoreau, *Excursions* (Boston, 1893), p. 260.

## 13. AN ABOMINABLE MYSTERY

### pages 153–163

Captain Hall's 1727 letter to the Royal Society, "Experiments on the Effects of the Poison of the Rattle Snake," appears in an abridgment of the society's journal, *Philosophical Transactions,* edited by Hutton, Shaw, and Pearson (London, 1809), vol. 7, p. 196.

Cotton Mather's *Crotalus* yarns are summarized in G. L. Kittredge, "Letters of Samuel Lee and Samuel Sewall Relating to New England and the Indians," *Publications of the Colonial Society of Massachusetts* (1913), vol.

14, p. 175. Mather recounted them in a November 27, 1712, letter to the Royal Society, a letter the society did not publish.

For the Berkshire-area bites reported by Ditmars, see Raymond L. Ditmars, *Snakes of the World* (New York: Macmillan, 1937), p. 115. For the eighteenth-century bite in Wilbraham, Massachusetts, see the *Valley Advocate,* June 15, 1977 (p. 32). For the 1855 *Harper's* quote, see T. B. Thorpe, "The Rattlesnake and its Congeners," *Harper's New Monthly Magazine* (1855), vol. 10, no. 58, p. 483.

Samuel Lee's and Nehemiah Grew's seventeenth-century descriptions of *Crotalus* bites (p. 161) are from the G. L. Kittredge article cited above.

## 14. THE COUNTRY DOCTOR

### pages 164–182

For the Ponkapoag Indians, see Daniel Gookin, "Historical Collections of the Indians in New England," *Collections of the Massachusetts Historical Society,* First Series (1792), vol. 1, p. 141. See also Edward Pierce, *History of Milton* (Milton, 1957); and Daniel Huntoon, *History of Canton* (Cambridge, 1893). For the Wampanoag war, see Alden Vaughan, *New England Frontier: Puritans and Indians 1620–1675* (Boston: Little, Brown, 1965).

For the Houghton family, see Albert Teele, *History of Milton* (Boston, 1888), p. 566. For the Puffer family, see Charles Nutt, *Descendants of George Puffer of Braintree, Massachusetts* (Worcester, 1915), which includes Matthias Puffer's petition on p. 17. For the Littlefield family, see the Genealogical Card File on microfiche at the Quincy Historical Society, Quincy, Massachusetts ("Littlefield").

For Palmer Goulding's petition, see John Trask, "Petition of Palmer Goulding," *New England Historical and Genealogical Record* (1892), vol. 46, p. 215.

Abel Puffer's "sure and certain cure" is reprinted in Huntoon, *History of Canton,* p. 256. Dr. Benjamin Gale's salt cure is from a letter dated August 20, 1764, at Killingworth, Connecticut, and partially reprinted in Hutton, Shaw, and Pearson, *Philosophical Transactions* (London, 1809), vol. 12, p. 244.

For the recent Florida *Crotalus*-bite fatality on p. 177, see C. S. Kitchens, S. Hunter, and L. H. S. Van Mierop, "Severe Myonecrosis in a Fatal Case of Envenomation by the Canebrake Rattlesnake," *Toxicon* (1987), vol. 25, no. 24, p. 455.

For the Strobridge family, see Frederic Endicott, ed., *Record of Births, Marriages, and Deaths, etc.* (Canton, 1896); and Mary Guild, *Genealogy: Strobridge Morrison or Morison Strawbridge* (Lowell, Mass.: S. W. Huse, 1891).

## 15. FIRST, DO NO HARM

pages 183–211

The epigraph is from a letter to the editor, "Bite of a Rattlesnake: Recovery," by L. E. Whiting, detailing his treatment of a Mr. Belcher, a snake exhibitor at the New York State Fair at Saratoga Springs. *Boston Medical and Surgical Journal* (1854), vol. 50, no. 13, p. 258.

Laurence Klauber's instances of nineteenth-century alcohol cures are in his *Rattlesnakes* (abridged ed., Berkeley, Cal., 1982), p. 206. Leonhard Stejneger's questionable recommendation comes from Leonhard Stejneger, "The Poisonous Snakes of North America," in *Report of the U.S. National Museum for 1893* (Washington, D.C., 1895), p. 476. For the Australian advice on p. 185, see E. R. Trethewie, "Pathology, Symptomatology, and Treatment of Snakebite in Australia," in W. Bucherl and E. Buckley, *Venomous Animals and Their Venoms* (New York, 1971), vol. 2, p. 103.

For *Oxyuranus microlepidotus* (and for the history of antivenoms), see David Underhill, *Australia's Dangerous Creatures* (Surry Hills, New South Wales, 1987). For *Crotalus durissus terrificus*, see G. Rosenfeld, "Pathology, Symptomatology, and Treatment of Snakebite in South America," in W. Bucherl and E. Buckley, *Venomous Animals and Their Venoms* (New York, 1971), vol. 2, p. 346.

A description of Wyeth polyvalent appears on p. 2256 of E. R. Barnhart et al., *Physician's Desk Reference* (42nd ed., Oradell, N.J., 1988). For the U.S. snakebite mortality rates on p. 190, see Findlay Russell, *Snake Venom Poisoning* (Great Neck, N.Y.: Scholium, 1983), p. 257. For the 650 Los Angeles cases mentioned on p. 191, see Russell, p. 258.

The full title of Stahnke's article advocating ice treatment is Herbert L. Stahnke, Frederick M. Allen, Robert V. Horan et al., "The Treatment of Snake Bite," *American Journal of Tropical Medicine and Hygiene* (1957), vol. 6, p. 323. It stoked a fiery controversy highlighted as follows: F. A. Shannon, "Comments on the Treatment of Reptile Poisoning in the Southwest," *Southwestern Medicine* (1953), vol. 34, p. 367; N. C. McCollough and J. F. Gennaro, "Evaluation of Venomous Snake Bite in the Southern United States," *Journal of the Florida Medical Association* (1963), vol. 49, p. 959; P. M. Ya and J. F. Perry, "Experimental Evaluation of Methods for the Early Treatment of Snake Bite," *Surgery* (1960), vol. 47, p. 975; Subcommittee on Accidental Poisoning, American Academy of Pediatrics, *News Letter* (1965), vol. 16; W. E. Lockhart, "Treatment of Snakebite," *Journal of the American Medical Association* (1965), vol. 193, no. 5, p. 336; Mahlon Bierly and Eleanor Buckley, "Treatment of Crotalid Envenomation," *Journal of the American Medical Association* (1966), vol. 195, no. 7, p. 167; Findlay Russell, Frederick Shannon et al., "Snakebite" (letter), *Journal of the American Medical Association* (1966), vol. 195, no. 7, p. 189; W. E. Lockhart (letter in rebuttal), *Journal of the American Medical Association* (1966), vol. 195, no. 7, p. 189; Charles Sparger, "Problems in the Management of Rattlesnake

Bites," *Archives of Surgery* (1969), vol. 98, p. 13; W. E. Lockhart, "Pitfalls in Rattlesnake Bite," *Texas Medicine* (1970), vol. 66, p. 42.

The quote from W. E. Lockhart on p. 203 appears in his 1966 letter cited above. The quote from D. C. Haynes in the footnote on the same page appears in Jon M. Burch et al., "The Treatment of Crotalid Envenomation Without Antivenin," *Journal of Trauma* (1988), vol. 28, no. 1, p. 42.

For clinical and laboratory evidence in support of the "Cutter" point of view, see T. G. Glass, "Early Debridement in Pit Viper Bites," *Journal of the American Medical Association* (1976), vol. 235, no. 23, p. 2513; and T. G. Grace and G. E. Omer, "The Management of Upper Extremity Pit Viper Wounds," *Journal of Hand Surgery* (1980), vol. 5, p. 168.

H. A. Reid's 1963 study is H. A. Reid et al., "Specific Antivenene and Prednisone in Viper-Bite Poisoning: Controlled Trial," *British Medical Journal* (1963), vol. 2, p. 1378. For Dr. Lindsey's appeal, see Douglas Lindsey, "Controversy in Snake Bite: Time for a Controlled Appraisal," *Journal of Trauma* (1985), vol. 25, no. 5, p. 168. For the quote in the next paragraph, see Willis Wingert and Linda Chan, "Rattlesnake Bites in Southern California and Rationale for Recommended Treatment," *Western Journal of Medicine* (1988), vol. 148, no. 1, p. 37.

The chief sources for the 1986 Glastonbury, Connecticut, *Crotalus* bite are Joyce Winslow, "Who Should Live on Kongscut Mountain?," *Yankee* (August 1987), p. 76; and a September 2, 1990, phone interview with Robert Fritsch.

For the most complete of the "recent epidemiological studies" cited on p. 211, see World Health Organization, *Progress in the Characterization of Venoms and the Standardization of Antivenoms* (Geneva, 1981), p. 5.

## 16. A WORST-CASE SCENARIO

### pages 212–229

The epigraph quotes the first two lines of Emily Dickinson's lyric "The Snake," first published in the *Springfield Republican* on February 14, 1866. "The Snake" is one of only seven of her poems, all unsigned, that appeared during her lifetime. Willis Buckingham, *Emily Dickinson: An Annotated Bibliography* (Bloomington, Ind., 1970), p. 13.

The effects of rattler venoms on blood-clotting factors are described in C. S. Kitchens and L.H.S. Van Mierop, "Mechanism of Defibrination in Humans after Envenomation by the Eastern Diamondback Rattlesnake," *American Journal of Hematology* (1983), vol. 14, p. 345.

An estimate of the lethality of *Crotalus horridus* venom (p. 220) appears in S. R. Minton and M. R. Minton, *Venomous Reptiles* (New York: Scribners, 1980), p. 252–53.

For ARDS and pulmonary edema, see M. A. Matthay and Philip C. Hopewell, "Critical Care for Acute Respiratory Failure," in G. L. Baum and E. Wolinsky, *Textbook of Pulmonary Diseases* (Boston: Little, Brown,

1989), vol. 2, p. 1055; and Sattar Farzan, *A Concise Handbook of Respiratory Diseases* (Reston, 1985), chapter 25, "Respiratory Failure," p. 233.

For Dr. Russell's series of postmortem findings, see Findlay Russell, *Snake Venom Poisoning* (Great Neck, N.Y.: Scholium, 1983), p. 334.

Raymond Ditmars reports his record *C. horridus* on p. 114 of his *Snakes of the World* (New York, 1937).

## 17. FOUR BULLETS AND AN IGNORAMUS

### pages 230–237

Bo Diddley's song "Who Do You Love" appears on the 1972 LP *Got My Own Bag of Tricks* (Chess 2CH 60005). Lyrics published by Goodman Group Publishers (BMI).

For Officer LeMoine's exploit, see Andrea Rotondo, "He Shot a Rattler; Critic Strikes Back," Quincy *Patriot Ledger*, September 1, 1976 (p. 1). Letters in response to the story were published on September 7 and 9. See also the remarks of Robert Stanhope in *The Timber Rattlesnake in New England: A Symposium* (Springfield: Western Massachusetts Herpetological Society, 1978), p. 30.

George V. Higgins's column "Endangering the Dangerous" appeared in *The Boston Globe Magazine* on August 17, 1980. Letters in response appeared in the magazine on September 21.

For the highway casualty figures on p. 236, see statistics section, Massachusetts Registry of Motor Vehicles, *1980 Motor Vehicle Accident Experience* (Boston, 1981).

The snake-in-golf-bag story was reported in the *Boston Globe*'s South Weekly section on September 23, 1990.

## 18. DEATH MADE EASY

### pages 238–258

The epigraph, courtesy of John Herman, is from Wallace Stevens, *Collected Poems* (New York: Knopf, 1987), p. 416.

For the granite industry in Quincy, see William Churchill Edwards, *Historic Quincy, Massachusetts* (Quincy, 1954), and R. G. Goodby, R. Fitts, and D. Ritchie, "Intensive Archaeological Survey of the Yankee Heights Project Area," in H. W. Moore Associates et al., *Technical Appendix to the Final Environmental Impact Report: EOEA #6995* (Quincy: Yankee Heights, 1990).

The Henry Adams quotes on p. 243 are from Worthington Ford, ed., *Letters of Henry Adams* (Boston: Houghton Mifflin, 1930), pp. 167, 399. For Charles Francis Adams's thoughts on his hometown, see his January 7, 1899, letter to E. W. Marsh, on display at the Quincy Historical Society.

All details on deaths, injuries, and mishaps at the quarries come from articles published in the Quincy *Patriot Ledger* and the *Boston Globe*. The

*Patriot Ledger* articles are more accessible, since they have been indexed by the staff at the Thomas Crane Memorial Library in Quincy. In the text I left out the names of the dead in order to condense the narrative. A partial list follows:

| | |
|---|---|
| Steven Jablonkas | October 1930 |
| Richard Golden | October 1939 |
| Peter Soini | January 1943 |
| Albert Moscatel | August 1960 |
| Arthur O'Neil and Joel Ryan | June 1962 |
| Howard Trombly and Robert Lavoie | August 1963 |
| Lawrence Foster | August 1965 |
| Caroline Eckhardt and Robert Hanson | December 1973 |
| Thomas Feldon | June 1980 |
| Paul Gooch | June 1983 |
| Vincent Alcide | June 1984 |
| Gerard Arroyo, Jr. | January 1989 |

For the quarries-area snakebite, see "Woman Hospitalized After Snake's Bite," Quincy *Patriot Ledger*, May 8, 1968. Further details were supplied by Bob Abrams of Milton.

### 19. THE SNAKE FENCE

#### pages 259—291

The epigraph is from Alan Lupo, Frank Colcord, and Edmund P. Fowler, *Rites of Way: The Politics of Transportation in Boston and the U.S. City* (Boston: Little, Brown, 1971), p. 75.

The John Adams quote on p. 261 is from L. H. Butterfield, ed., *Diary and Autobiography of John Adams* (Cambridge, 1961), vol. 3, p. 230.

For details of park management in the Blue Hills, see the annual reports of the Metropolitan Park Commissioners (Boston, 1893–1919) and of the Metropolitan District Commission (Boston, 1920–present).

Laurence Klauber's views concerning the effects of highways on *Crotalus* populations can be found on p. 238 of his *Rattlesnakes* (abridged ed., Berkeley, Cal., 1982). The "interesting acquisition" quote on p. 270 comes from the *Bulletin of the Boston Society of Natural History* (1930), no. 54, p. 16.

For the interstate highway system, see Helen Leavitt, *Superhighway: Superhoax* (New York: Ballantine, 1971); and Phil Patton, *Open Road: A Celebration of the American Highway* (New York: Simon and Schuster, 1986). For Route 128, see Massachusetts Department of Commerce, *Survey of Route 128* (Boston, 1973).

The demolition of the Blue Hill River snake den is described in John Mitchell, "Rattlesnakes in Massachusetts," *Massachusetts Audubon Newsletter* (1978), vol. 17, p. 3.

The "Tip" O'Neill and MIT task force quotes are from the above-mentioned Lupo et al., *Rites of Way* (1971), pp. 55, 95. For state and federal legislative hurdles erected by the anti-expressway movement, see Massachusetts Department of Public Works, *Draft Environmental Impact Statement: Southwest Corridor Project* (Boston, 1972).

The tally of extinct species on p. 278 is from Dianne Dumanowski, "Sweeping MA Law on Endangered Species is Signed," *Boston Globe*, December 28, 1990 (pp. 1, 14).

The early-sixties Berkshire *Crotalus* hunt is described in "Hunting the Mountain Eel," *Massachusetts Wildlife* (November-December 1961), p. 7.

For the evolution of the Massachusetts Endangered List, see Massachusetts Division of Fisheries and Wildlife, "Massachusetts Species for Special Consideration," number 5 in the series *Fauna of Massachusetts* (1978); Paul Mugford, "Fish and Wildlife Existing in Limited Numbers in Massachusetts" (Massachusetts Division of Fisheries and Wildlife, 1980); and Massachusetts Natural Heritage Program, "List of Endangered, Threatened, and Special Concern Vertebrate Animals of Massachusetts" (Massachusetts Division of Fisheries and Wildlife, 1985).

The state-by-state *Crotalus* status reports on p. 281 were provided by Larry Master of the eastern regional office of the Nature Conservancy, February 1991.

Stories, editorials, and letters on the Yankee Heights–*Crotalus* imbroglio appeared in the Quincy *Patriot Ledger* on April 19, 20, 21, and 22, 1989; in the *Boston Globe* on April 20 and 22, May 6, 16, and 24, 1989; and in the *Boston Herald* on April 20 and 21, 1989. The quote from State Representative Flaherty appeared in the *Boston Globe* on August 14, 1989.

The Yankee Heights *Final Environmental Impact Report*, released January 1990, is registered as #6995 at the Massachusetts Executive Office of Environmental Affairs.

For the snake-release experiment mentioned on p. 289, see J. H. Galligan and W. A. Dunson, "Biology and Status of Timber Rattlesnake Populations in Pennsylvania," *Biological Conservation* (1979), vol. 15, p. 13.

### 20. MOTHER OF HEROES

pages 292–305

The bird extinction figures on p. 295 are from a lecture by David Quammen sponsored by the MIT Writing Program, March 8, 1990.

For the Neanderthal burial at Shanidar, see Richard Leakey and Roger Lewin, *Origins* (New York: Dutton, 1977), p. 125.

### 21. MIDSUMMER

pages 306–311

The epigraph is from Donald Jackson, ed., *The Diaries of George Washington* (Charlottesville, Va., 1976), vol. 1, p. 23.

# Index